RICH
MEDIA,
POOR
DEMOCRACY

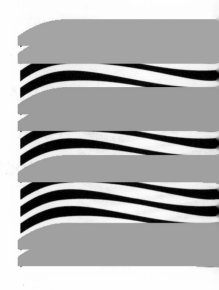

The History of
Communication

Robert W. McChesney &
John C. Nerone, editors
A list of books in the series
appears at the end of this
book.

Rich Media, Poor Democracy

Communication Politics in Dubious Times

Robert W. McChesney

University of Illinois Press

Urbana and Chicago

© 1999 by the Board of Trustees

of the University of Illinois

Manufactured in the United States of America

∞ This book is printed on acid-free paper.

Library of Congress Cataloging-in-Publication Data

McChesney, Robert Waterman, 1952–

Rich media, poor democracy : communication politics in
dubious times / Robert W. McChesney.

   p. cm. — (The history of communication)

Includes bibliographical references and index.

ISBN 0-252-02448-6 (cloth : alk. paper)

1. Mass media—Political aspects—United States.

2. Mass media—United States—Ownership.

3. Democracy—United States. I. Title. II. Series.

P95.82.U6M38   1999

302.23'0973—ddc21 98–58055

          CIP

C 5 4 3 2 1

For Inger, Amy, and Lucy

O let America be America again

The land that never has been yet

And yet must be

Langston Hughes

CONTENTS

PREFACE

This book is about the media crisis in the United States (and world) today and what we should do about it. The main point underlying the book is the contradiction between a for-profit, highly concentrated, advertising-saturated, corporate media system and the communication requirements of a democratic society. I elaborate upon this theme in a number of ways. I discuss, for example: the decline of journalism and the hypercommercialization of culture; the antidemocratic manner by which communication policy making has been and is being conducted in the United States; the close relationship of the media system to the broader (globalizing and neoliberal) capitalist economy with its dilapidated political culture; and the way that the Internet is being incorporated into the heart of the corporate communication system, decidedly undermining the democratic potential envisioned by its founders. I also develop two related themes: the use of mythology, particularly the myth of the free market, to defend this unaccountable private control over communication, and the spurious use of history by proponents of the corporate media status quo, particularly with regard to the origins of commercial broadcasting and the nature of the First Amendment to the U.S. Constitution.

I argue in this book that if we are serious about democracy, we will need to reform the media system structurally. The evidence points inexorably to this conclusion. In my view this reform will have to be part of a broader movement to democratize all the core institutions of society. Indeed, for the past several years I have been involved with a number of media reform efforts as well as broader political campaigns in the United States, and these experiences inform my analysis, particularly in the conclusion. This is a book, then, written both for citizens and for scholars. While the focus of this book is on organizing politically for media reform, there also is an implicit message to academic communication scholars: what we do is important and can be of crucial value to efforts to democratize communication. Sadly, I believe too much of U.S. communication research and education has dropped the ball in this regard. This is a point I have written about in several essays in the 1990s and that I intend to return to in the future.

The University of Illinois Press was my first and only choice to publish this book. I have co-edited a history of communication series for the Press since 1994 and have been pleased beyond words with the open-mindedness, professionalism, and commitment to quality of the entire operation. Karen Hewitt has overseen the editing and handling of the book since we first talked about it in 1997, and she has been absolutely terrific in her role as editor. I would also like to thank Patricia Hollahan for copyediting, Christina Dengate for proofreading, and Margie Towery for indexing.

Several people have read and commented upon sections of the book or have assisted me with my research otherwise. I am fortunate to have so many (very, very good) friends and acquaintances willing to assist me with my work. They include: Michael Albert, W. H. Locke Anderson, Patricia Aufderheide, C. Edwin Baker, Nick Baran, Patrick Barrett, David Barsamian, Greg Bates, Dennis Berman, Nolan Bowie, Harry Brighouse, Sandy Carter, Jeff Chester, Noam Chomsky, Alan Cocker, Jeff Cohen, Joshua Cohen, Susan G. Davis, Kate Duncan, Marc Eisen, Dianne Feeley, George Gerbner, Peter Golding, Peter Hart, Ronda Hauben, Ed Herman, Jill Hills, Allen Hunter, Janine Jackson, Jim Jaffe, Janine Jaquet, Sut Jhally, Jerry Landay, Tom Lane, Chris Lehmann, Mark Lloyd, Diedre Macfadyen, Ted Magder, Toby Miller, Vincent Mosco, Jim Naureckas, John Nerone, John Nichols, Joy Pierce, Marc Raboy, Adolph Reed, Joel Rogers, E. Joshua Rosenkranz, Matthew Rothschild, Allen Ruff, Greg Ruggiero, Danny Schechter, Dan Schiller, Sid Shniad, Doobo Shim, Gigi Sohn, Norman Solomon, John Stauber, Inger L. Stole, Victor Wallis, Jim Weinstein, Jack Willis, Ellen Meiksins Wood.

During the course of writing this book I got to know Mark Crispin Miller, whose research and political interests match my own almost identically. His constant feedback on the ideas expressed in it were instrumental in helping me formulate my arguments. His intelligence, passion, generosity, and good humor kept me on track when the weight of our demoralized times threatened to pull me down.

I thank John Nichols for letting me use material he researched for a collaborative project we are working on regarding global media activism. John, like Mark, has become a dear friend over the past few years. As one of the leading political reporters in the nation, John's conviction that media control is an absolutely central political issue in our times has been most heartening.

Rick Maxwell and Eric Rothenbuhler read the entire manuscript and gave me several outstanding suggestions, many of which are reflected in the book. I owe Rick a special thanks for coming up with the title. Eric's comments led to a thorough reorganization of the book.

Some readers will notice the clear imprint of three people in particular upon my thinking and the book's arguments. Paul Sweezy's analysis of capitalism, along with that of his *Monthly Review* colleagues Paul Baran and Harry Magdoff, has been the foundation of my education in political economy. Sweezy's commitment to writing clearly, too, has been a model I have tried to emulate. Noam Chomsky's work on media and, especially, democracy, has been central to my education in politics. Ed Herman's rich and detailed understanding of market economics as well as the politics of media behavior has been instrumental in helping me develop my media critique. I owe these three men an intellectual and political debt I will never be able to repay.

Two other individuals have been every bit as important in helping me develop my thinking on the issues covered in this book. John Bellamy "Duke" Foster and I became friends as college classmates in Olympia, Washington, in 1973; we have remained best of friends ever since. Vivek Chibber and I became fast friends in the late 1980s when we both moved to Madison. Duke and Vivek read and commented on much of what is written in this book. They also gave me numerous leads for sources and literature that is pertinent to my topic. But, most important, they each constantly educate me in political economy, history, philosophy, and politics. I have enjoyed spectacular good fortune to have each of them come into my life. This book, like all of my work, not to mention my life, would suffer materially without their presence.

My greatest acknowledgment goes to my wife, Inger L. Stole. Many scholars know the joys of having a spouse who is in their field and who can therefore give high quality criticism of their work. Inger not only provides that, she also has a critical edge that invariably challenges received wisdom on a subject. During the dog days of 1998, when I scrambled to get this book completed, Inger did the lion's share of parenting for our two daughters, Amy and Lucy. To do so she took valuable and much-deserved time away from her own career. I am forever in her debt.

THE
MEDIA/
DEMOCRACY
PARADOX

Our era rests upon a massive paradox. On the one hand, it is an age of dazzling breakthroughs in communication and information technologies. Communication is so intertwined with the economy and culture that our times have been dubbed the Information Age. Sitting high atop this golden web are a handful of enormous media firms — exceeding by a factor of 10 the size of the largest media firms of just fifteen years earlier — that have established global empires and generated massive riches providing news and entertainment to the peoples of the world.[1] Independent of government control, this commercial media juggernaut provides a bounty of choices unimaginable a generation or two ago. And it is finding a welcoming audience. According to one study, the average American consumed a whopping 11.8 hours of media per day in 1998, up over 13 percent in just three years. As the survey director noted, "the sheer amount of media products and messages consumed by the average American adult is staggering and growing."[2] The rise of the Internet has only accentuated the trend. Although some research suggests that the Internet is replacing some of the time people have spent with other media, other research suggests its more important effect is simply to expand the role of media in people's lives.[3] "People are simply spending more time with media," one media executive stated. "They don't appear to have dropped one medium to have picked up another."[4]

On the other hand, our era is increasingly depoliticized; traditional notions of civic and political involvement have shriveled. Elementary understanding of social and political affairs has declined. Turnout for U.S. elections — admittedly not a perfect barometer — has plummeted over the past thirty years. The 1998 congressional elections had one of the lowest turnouts of eligible voters in national elections in U.S. history, as just over one-third of the eligible voters turned out on election day.[5] It is, to employ a phrase coined by Robert Entman, "democracy without citizens."[6]

By conventional reasoning, this is nonsensical. A flowering commercial marketplace of ideas, unencumbered by government censorship or regulation, should generate the most stimulating democratic political culture possible. The response comes that the problem lies elsewhere, that "the people" obviously are not interested in politics or civic issues, because, if they were, it would be in the interests of the wealthy media giants to provide them with such fare. There is an element of truth to that reply, but it is hardly a satisfactory response. Virtually all defenses of the commercial media system for the privileges they receive — typically made by the media owners themselves — are based on the notion that the media play an important, perhaps a central, role in providing the institutional basis for having an informed and participating citizenry. If this is, indeed, a democracy without citizens, the media system has much to answer for.

I argue in this book that the media have become a significant *antidemocratic* force in the United States and, to varying degrees, worldwide. The wealthier and more powerful the corporate media giants have become, the poorer the prospects for participatory democracy. I am not arguing that *all* media are getting wealthier, of course. Some media firms and sectors are faltering and will falter during this turbulent era. But, on balance, the dominant media firms are larger and more influential than ever before, and the media *writ large* are more important in our social life than ever before. Nor do I believe the media are the sole or primary cause of the decline of democracy, but they are a part of the problem and closely linked to many of the other factors. Behind the lustrous glow of new technologies and electronic jargon, the media system has become increasingly concentrated and conglomerated into a relative handful of corporate hands. This concentration accentuates the core tendencies of a profit-driven, advertising-supported media system: hypercommercialism and denigration of journalism and public service. It is a poison pill for democracy.

Nor is the decline of democracy in the face of this boom in media wealth a contradiction. The media system is linked ever more closely to the capitalist system, both through ownership and through its reliance upon advertising, a function dominated by the largest firms in the economy. Capitalism benefits from having a formally democratic system, but capitalism works best when elites make most fundamental decisions and the bulk of the population is depoliticized. For a variety of reasons, the media have come to be expert at generating the type of fare that suits, and perpetuates, the status quo. I argue that if we value democracy, it is imperative that we restructure the media system so that it reconnects with the mass of citizens who in fact comprise "democracy." The media reform I envision, and write about here, can take place only if it is part of a broader political movement to shift power from the few to the many. Conversely, any meaningful attempt to do this, to democratize the United States, or any other society, must make media reform a part (though by no means all) of its agenda. Such has not been the case heretofore.

This book, then, is about the corporate media explosion and the corresponding implosion of public life, the rich media/poor democracy paradox. Its purpose is to analyze the existing situation by drawing upon history and pointing toward democratic change in the future. As such, this book goes directly counter to the prevailing wisdom of our times. The ultimate trump card of conservatism and reaction, after all their other arguments have been discredited, is that there is no possibility of social change for the better, so it is a notion not even worth pondering, let alone pursuing. This card has been played by ruling elites since the dawn of civilization, but never has it been waved more ferociously than at the close of the twentieth century. It has deadened social thought and has demoralized social movements and public life. And it is a lie, the biggest lie of them all. The world is changing rapidly and is doing so because of decisions made by actors working within a specific social system. If anything, humans now possess greater ability to alter their destiny than ever before. Those who benefit by the status quo know this well. They want to ensure that they are the ones holding the reins; they want everyone else to accept their privileges as "natural" and immutable. In my view, the duty of the democrat, and especially of the democratic intellectual, is to rip the veil off this power, and to work so that social decision making and power may be made as enlightened and as egalitarian as possible.

Because this book deals directly with the relationship of media to democracy, it might be wise to address what exactly I mean by the term *democracy*. One of the heartening features of our age is that the term is embraced by nearly all but a handful of bigots, fanatics, and xenophobes. This is a relatively recent development, and its new-found popularity is a reminder of how far humanity has traveled over the past few centuries. But the term is employed so widely that it has lost much of its specificity and meaning. Hence a product that is consumed widely is termed a "democratic" product, as opposed to a product consumed by the few. Indeed, the term "democratic" is seemingly applied to describe anything or any behavior that is good, while words like "fascist" or "Hitler-like" are used to describe negative behavior, regardless of any actual relationship to the Third Reich or fascist politics, or politics at all.

So it is that when the United States is characterized as a democratic society, what is meant varies considerably with the assumptions and values of the person making the claim. If we may generalize, however, when the United States is characterized as a democracy, this is meant to suggest that in the United States the citizens enjoy individual rights and freedoms, including the right to vote in elections, and that arbitrary government power is held in check by a constitution and laws and a legal system that enforces them. What is conspicuously absent from notions of the United States as a democracy is anything that has much to do with democracy, the idea that the many should and do make the core political decisions. In fact, very few people would argue that the United States is remotely close to a democratic society in that sense of the term. Many key decisions are the province of the corporate sector and most decisions made by the government are influenced by powerful special interests with little public awareness or input.

As Ellen Meiksins Wood has pointed out in brilliant fashion, what is called democracy in the United States and, increasingly, around the world is better thought of as *liberalism*. As Wood notes, liberalism developed in Europe in the movement to protect the rights of feudal lords from monarchs. Later, with the rise of capitalism, liberalism became an important set of principles to protect, among other things, private property from the state, especially a state that might be controlled by the propertyless majority.[7] In the United States today, therefore, some go so far as to present democracy as being defined first and foremost by individual freedoms to buy and sell property and the right to invest for profit. That there is any distinction between these liberties and the democratic rights to free speech, free press, and free assembly is dismissed categorically. The absurdity of this equation of market rights with political freedom, of capitalism with democracy, should be self-evident; in this century scores of nations have protected market rights while being political dictatorships and having little respect for any other civil liberties for that matter.

There is very much that is commendable in liberalism — and it is impossible to imagine a democratic society without core liberal freedoms — but the fact remains that it is different from democracy. When democracy is defined as liberalism, the notion of popular rule, rather than being the heart and soul of democracy, drifts to the margins. In contemporary U.S. society, citizens have precious little control over political decisions. In strict terms, what distinguishes the United States from a political oligarchy is that citizens do retain the right to vote in elections and thereby remove politicians from office, even if they have little control over what politicians actually do while in office. Since the elections are rather dubious enterprises — they are more like auctions favoring those with great sums of money, the campaign debate almost always avoids wide-ranging debate on the core issues, and the choices on the ballot are mostly inconsequential to the important decisions to be made after the election — even this democratic right to vote seems trivial. Yet in dominant thinking the existence of this right to vote is what qualifies the United States as a democracy. It is an awfully, awfully thin reed.

When I invoke the term *democracy,* then, I mean it in the classical sense, as the rule of the many. The democratic aspects of the liberal tradition are to be preserved and expanded — such as individual civil liberties and checks on state power — but the needs of the minuscule investor class can never be equated with the needs of the citizenry or with the foundations of a democracy. A society like the United States which has rampant inequality, minimal popular involvement in decision making, and widespread depoliticization can never be regarded as democratic in an honest use of the term. When I talk about "democratizing" our society, I mean that we should create mechanisms that make the rule of the many possible. This means among other things, as I will spell out in what follows, reducing social inequality and establishing a media system that serves the entire population and that promotes democratic rule. In structural terms, that means a media system that has a significant nonprofit and noncommercial component.

A major theme of the book is that the rise of *neoliberalism* is a main factor that accounts for the corporate media boom, on the one hand, and the collapse of democratic political life on the other hand. Neoliberalism refers to the policies that maximize the role of markets and profit-making and minimize the role of nonmarket institutions. It is the deregulation provided by neoliberalism that has been instrumental in allowing the wealthy media corporations to grow and prosper as they have. Likewise, neoliberalism is a political theory; it posits that society works best when business runs things and there is as little possibility of government "interference" with business as possible. In short, neoliberal democracy is one where the political sector controls little and debates even less. In such a world political apathy and indifference are a quite rational choice for the bulk of the citizenry, especially for those who reside below the upper and upper-middle classes.

Neoliberalism is associated with the rise of Reagan and Thatcher in the early 1980s, and it has boomed as a global phenomenon throughout the past two decades. But it would be misleading to present neoliberalism as an entirely new phenomenon. In fact the desire by the wealthy few to limit democracy predates capitalism, and has been present throughout U.S. history. At the time of the American Revolution, Tom Paine and Benjamin Franklin advocated universal adult male suffrage. Their opponents, John Adams, John Jay, and Alexander Hamilton, fought to see suffrage limited to property holders and the government structured in such a manner as to reduce the possibility of popular rule. Jay and Adams counted as one of their favorite expressions "those who own this country ought to govern it."[8] During the constitutional debates James Madison argued that the goal of government must be "to protect the minority of the opulent against the majority."[9] In short, the nature and quality of democracy is always the result of conflict and struggle between contending groups in unequal societies. Neoliberalism mostly reflects that the few are dominant politically and ideologically and able therefore to inflict their will on the subdued and unorganized population.

The media/democracy paradox I attend to in this book has two components. First, it is a political crisis. I mean this in two senses. On the one hand, the nature of our corporate commercial media system has dire implications for our politics and broader culture. On the other hand, the very issue of *who* controls the media system and for what purposes is not a part of contemporary political debate. Instead, there is the presupposition that a profit-seeking, commercial media system is fundamentally sound, and that most problems can be resolved for the most part through less state interference or regulation, which (theoretically) will produce the magic elixir of competition. In view of the extraordinary importance of media and communication in our society, I believe that the subject of how the media are controlled, structured, and subsidized should be at the center of democratic debate. Instead, this subject is nowhere to be found. This is not an accident; it reflects above all the economic, political, and ideological power of the media corporations and their allies. And it has made the prospect of challenging corporate media power, and of democratizing communication, all the more daunting.

The second component of the media/democracy paradox concerns media ideology, in particular the flawed and self-serving manner in which corporate media officers and their supporters use history. The nature of our corporate media system and the lack of democratic debate over the nature of our media system are often defended on the following grounds: that communication markets force media firms to "give the people what they want"; that commercial media are the innate democratic and "American" system; that professionalism in journalism is democratic and protects the public from nefarious influences on the news; that new communication technologies are inherently democratic since they undermine the existing power of commercial media; and, perhaps most important, that the First Amendment to the U.S. Constitution authorizes that corporations and advertisers rule U.S. media without public interference. These are generally presented as truisms, and nearly always history is invoked to provide evidence for each of these claims. In combination these claims have considerable sway in the United States, even among those who are critical of the social order otherwise. It is because of the overall capacity of these myths, which are either lies or half-truths, to strip citizens of their ability to comprehend their own situation and govern their own lives that I characterize these as "dubious" times in the book's subtitle.

I have broken the book into two sections for each of these components. The first section of the book consists of three chapters. Chapter 1 provides an overview of the main trends in U.S. media at the dawn of the twenty-first century. I chronicle the structure of the media industry and its main attributes; I also examine the decline of public service as a principle and the overall deterioration of public debate over media issues. In chapter 2 I extend the analysis from the United States to the world. Although this book is primarily concerned with the United States, a main trend over the past decade has been the emergence of a global commercial media market dominated by less than a dozen transnational firms. It is a process that must be understood if one is to appreciate both the nature of the existing media system and the tight relationship between media and capitalism. In chapter 3 I examine the Internet and the digital revolution and address how these may or may not upset the corporate media's applecart. In my view, most analysis of the future of the Internet has been imprisoned by its tendency to view the Internet as a unique and unprecedented new thing, rather than as part of a historical process and as a logical extension of the corporate media and communications system. When viewed in the latter light, I argue that the future of "cyberspace" seems decidedly less mysterious, romantic, democratic, or revolutionary.

The first section of the book relies almost entirely on literature from trade and business publications from 1997 and 1998. At present that is the only place where the changes taking place in the U.S. and global media and communication systems are being written about in any detail. These reports are very good in some respects, because as they are aimed at investors there is a premium on reliable information and reasoned speculation. But these accounts are entirely bereft of any concern, aside from a public relations angle, for the social implications or significance of these trends. I have used my own background as a historian and political economist to frame the current events, regarding, in the memorable expression of Georg Lukacs, "the present as history." And I have also made clear the political values that drive this research and analysis. Moreover, one cannot merely yank quotations out of context from a trade publication and consider that satisfactory evidence to establish a point. An author must be immersed in trade and business literature to use it as the foundation for a scholarly argument. I used trade publications extensively for my first book, a history of the development of U.S. commercial broadcasting in the 1930s, and have read over one dozen main trade and business publications consistently since 1994, when I embarked upon the research that led to my second and third books.[10] With this experience I believe I have developed the ability to assess when trade publication accounts are worth taking seriously and when their validity should be discounted.

The tone of the first three chapters is also unconventional by academic standards. It is difficult at any time for a scholar to write with certainty about current events; the degree of difficulty increases measurably when one is analyzing such a turbulent realm as media, where in some respects the entire system is being radically transformed before our eyes. Unlike a traditional history, where the author can take all the time needed to conduct research and craft an argument, what I attempt in the first three chapters is like shooting at a moving target with a strict time limit. The prudent course, then, would be to shy away from any normative assessment, adopt a neutral tone, and merely point to concerns that scholars will be better able to understand and comment upon after years and years of research, and after the current system crystallizes. In my view, this approach is inappropriate to the nature of the problems I address in this book. While the exact contours of the emerging digital media order can scarcely be predicted, some of the media system's tendencies are quite clear, and unless they receive prompt attention, they will only get worse. It may turn out, for example, a generation down the road, that my concerns about the deterioration of journalism (and what this means for democracy) and the commercial carpet-bombing of our children (and what this means for our culture) will prove to be much ado about nothing. But I see no evidence at present to suggest that my arguments are wrong and I therefore have an obligation to state that truth frankly in this book. And when I have seen convincing countervailing evidence to my themes, I have included it in the text and incorporated it into my arguments. In the final analysis, I have attempted to follow the admonition of Bruce Cumings, who wrote that "The historian should be a skeptic, a doubter, a detective, and an honest person."[11]

One thing we can be certain of is that the narrative presented in the first three chapters can be updated and revised every few months. Within a few years much of the factual data will need to be replaced. The test of these chapters is not how well they capture a moment at the end of the twentieth century but how well the overall framework, analysis, argument, conclusions, and recommendations hold up as the narrative needs to be updated.

The second section includes three chapters, taking up the use of history to provide ideological cover for contemporary corporate media interests. In chapter 4 I address one of the myths that buttresses corporate media power: the notion that a corporate commercial media system is the "natural" American system. I examine the movement to establish public service broadcasting in the 1930s. In particular, I look at the key role played by educators, who regarded broadcasting as no more "naturally" a commercial enterprise than was education. In chapter 5 I look specifically at the historical fall from grace of public service broadcasting. This chapter, like chapter 2, has a strong international component, as it is outside of the United States that the collapse of public service broadcasting is most severe. Both chapters 4 and 5 include new archival sources that expand the research I have already published in this area. I debunk the notion that public broadcasting is the result of spectrum scarcity, and that with the end of scarcity it is logical to turn all broadcasting over to private interests. I chronicle the political movement that, unlike that of its faltering comrades south of the border, successfully forced the establishment of public broadcasting in Canada in the 1930s. I argue that this broadly democratic vision of public broadcasting was the foundation of public broadcasting in Canada, and that such a vision is required if there is any hope for the survival of public broadcasting in the United States and globally.

Chapter 6 examines one of main developments in U.S. media policy over the past generation: the gradual but inexorable adaptation of the First Amendment ("freedom of the press") as a means of shielding corporate media power and the wealthy and limiting the possibility of the development of democracy in the United States. This is not merely a campaign by the rich and powerful; it has received vocal and aggressive support from many liberals and civil libertarians. So it is that Nat Hentoff spends much of his time chastising those who would wish to regulate political campaign spending or commercial broadcasting as being "Brothers and sisters under the skin" of the most reprehensible bigots, fanatics, and book burners.[12] I argue that putative "progressives" and "democrats," like Hentoff, who accept this new corporate-friendly, commercialized interpretation of the First Amendment are making a dreadful error. I believe it is imperative that groups like the American Civil Liberties Union (ACLU), which at one time battled first and foremost for political democracy, be urged to return to their roots and understand that the First Amendment cannot simultaneously protect the privileges of corporations and the wealthy and protect and promote the democratic rights of the many.

I conclude the book by taking up the point that is explicit throughout: the need to organize politically to enact structural media reform. I argue that if the United States is to change its media system for the better, it will require the emergence of a broad-based democratic left that makes media reform one of the core elements of its platform. The conclusion therefore concentrates upon why a left is necessary for extending democracy, and why any prospective American left needs to understand the critical importance of media reform better than any of its predecessors have. I also provide a brief history of left media activism as well as a description of core structural media reforms that deserve attention. I conclude by chronicling the impressive rise of media activism by anti-neoliberal democratic left political parties around the world in the late 1990s. The purpose of this book, ultimately, is to contribute to these movements everywhere and especially in the United States.

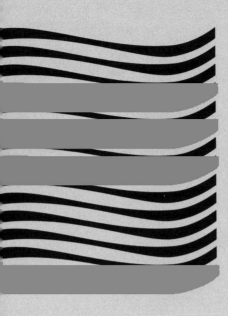

part one

POLITICS

CHAPTER 1

U.S. MEDIA
AT THE DAWN
OF THE
TWENTY-FIRST
CENTURY

The United States is in the midst of an almost dizzying transformation of its media system. In this chapter I address the main trends, the real trends, in U.S. media at the dawn of the twenty-first century. These are corporate concentration, conglomeration, and hypercommercialism. I argue that the U.S. media system is an integral part of the capitalist political economy, and that this relationship has important and troubling implications for democracy. I then discuss the flip side of hypercommercialism, which is the decline, if not elimination, of notions of public service in our media culture. In particular, I concentrate upon the corruption and degradation of journalism, to the point where it is scarcely a democratic force. Moreover, I analyze the undemocratic and corrupt manner in which the core laws and codes regulating communication, most notably the Telecommunications Act of 1996, have been enacted. The system I describe does not exist as a result of popular will, nor is it by any means a "natural" occurrence. The media system exists as it does because powerful interests have constructed it so that citizens will not be involved in the key policy decisions that have shaped it. In chapters 2 and 3 I extend the discussion to the globalization of the commercial media market in the 1990s, and then to the rise of the Internet and digital communication networks. In those chapters I ask what is the relationship of globalization and the Internet to the trends toward concentration, conglomeration, and hypercommercialism.

The Corporate Media Cartel

The striking structural features of the U.S. media system in the 1990s are concentration and conglomeration. It may seem ironic that these are the dominant structural features when, to the casual observer, the truth can appear quite the opposite. We seem inundated in different media from magazines and radio stations to cable television channels and, now, websites. But, in fact, to no small extent, the astonishing degree of concentrated corporate control over the media is a response to the rapid increase in channels wrought by cable, satellite TV, and digital media. Media firms press to get larger to deal with the uncertainty of the changing terrain wrought by new media technologies. "If you look at the entire chain of entities — studios, networks, stations, cable channels, cable operations, international distribution — you want to be as strong in as many of those as you can," News Corporation president Peter Chernin stated in 1998. "That way, regardless of where the profits move to, you're in a position to gain."[1] Yet, any explanation of media concentration and conglomeration must go beyond media technologies. They also result from changes in laws and regulations that now permit greater concentration in media ownership. But the bottom line, so to speak, is that concentrated media markets tend to be vastly less risky and more profitable for the firms that dominate them.

In fact, media concentration is not a new phenomenon. Classically, it has assumed the form of *horizontal integration,* where a firm attempted to control as much of the output in its particular field as possible. The ultimate form of horizontal integration, therefore, is monopoly. Horizontal integration has two great benefits for firms. First, as firms get a bigger share of the market it permits them to have lower overhead and to have more bargaining power with suppliers. Seagram, for example, estimates cost savings of $300 million for its music division from its purchase of PolyGram in 1998.[2] Second, as a firm gets a larger share of a specific market, it gains more control over the prices it can charge for its products.[3] Firms operating in oligopolies — meaning markets dominated by a handful of firms each with significant market share — tend to do what monopolists do: they cut back on output so they can charge higher prices and earn greater profits. Hence, when Bertelsmann bought Random House for $1.4 billion in 1998 to become the dominant U.S. book publisher, fears of canceled authors contracts spread throughout the literary community.[4] Stable oligopolies are very desirable for large firms, because despite their potential for profits, it can be quite difficult for a new player to enter an oligopolistic market. All of this not only drives the firms to use mergers and acquisitions to get bigger and more powerful but it also drives them to lobby for ownership deregulation and to generate new technologies that make concentration more feasible.

The U.S. mass media industries have been operated along noncompetitive oligopolistic lines for much of the twentieth century. In the 1940s, for example, broadcasting, film production, motion picture theaters, book publishing, newspaper publishing, magazine publishing, and recorded music were all distinct national oligopolistic markets, each of them dominated by anywhere from a few to a dozen or more firms. In general, these were *different* firms dominating each of these industries, with only a few exceptions. Throughout the twentieth century there have been pressing concerns that these concentrated markets would inhibit the flow and range of ideas necessary for a meaningful democracy.[5] For a variety of reasons, however, these concerns rarely spilled over into public debate.[6] In particular, the rise of the notion of professional journalism in the early twentieth century — which became widespread, even dominant, by mid-century — attempted to disconnect the editorial process from the explicit supervision of the owners and advertisers of the mass media, thus making the editorial product seem more credible as a "public service." To the extent that this process was seen as successful, the corporate commercial domination of the media seemed a less pressing, perhaps even insignificant, matter.[7]

Concentration has proceeded in specific media markets throughout the 1990s, with the proportion of the markets controlled by a small number of firms increasing, sometimes marginally and at other times dramatically. The U.S. film production industry has been a tight-knit club effectively controlled by six or seven studios since the 1930s. That remains the case today; the six largest U.S. firms accounted for over 90 percent of U.S. theater revenues in 1997.[8] All but sixteen of Hollywood's 148 widely distributed (six hundred or more theaters) films in 1997 were produced by these six firms, and many of those sixteen were produced by companies that had distribution deals with one of the six majors.[9] The newspaper industry underwent a spectacular consolidation from the 1960s to the 1980s, leaving a half-dozen major chains ruling the roost.[10] The emerging consolidation trend in the newspaper industry is that of "clustering," whereby metropolitan monopoly daily newspapers purchase or otherwise link up with all the smaller dailies in the suburbs and surrounding region.[11] Clustering permits newspapers to establish regional and/or broadly metropolitan newspaper monopolies and is quite lucrative. In 1997 it accounted for 25 percent of the record $6.2 billion in U.S. newspaper transactions.[12] Two major 1998 deals further concentrated U.S. book publishing and music production. With Bertelsmann's purchase of Random House, the U.S. book publishing industry is now dominated by seven firms.[13] And with Seagram's $10.4 billion purchase of PolyGram, the five largest music groups account for over 87 percent of the U.S. market.[14]

Media sectors that were once more competitive and open have seen the most dramatic consolidation in the past decade. In cable television systems, six firms now possess effective monopolistic control over more than 80 percent of the nation, and seven firms control nearly 75 percent of cable channels and programming.[15] As Time Warner's Ted Turner puts it, "We do have just a few people controlling all the cable companies in this country."[16] *Variety* notes that "mergers and consolidations have transformed the cable-network marketplace into a walled-off community controlled by a handful of media monoliths."[17] Radio station ownership, which I return to at the end of this chapter, has gone through a stunning transformation in the late 1990s, leaving four newly created giants with one-third of the industry's annual revenues of $13.6 billion.[18] With no small amount of irony, even the "alternative" weekly newspaper market — which was established to provide a dissident check on corporate media and journalism — has come to be dominated by a few chains.[19]

Concentration arguably has been most dramatic in the 1990s at the retail end of the media food chain. In motion picture theaters, for example, the era of the independent or even small chain theater company has gone the way of the passenger pigeon. In 1985 the twelve largest U.S. theater companies controlled 25 percent of the screens; by 1998 that figure was at 61 percent and climbing rapidly.[20] The largest chain, co-owned by the leveraged-buyout firms Kohlberg, Kravis, Roberts and Co. and Hicks, Muse, Tate and Furst, controls around 20 percent of the nation's movie screens.[21] U.S. book retailing has undergone a revolution to such a degree that more than 80 percent of books are sold by a few huge national chains like Borders and Barnes & Noble.[22] The share of books sold by independent book dealers fell from 42 percent to 20 percent from 1992 to 1998.[23]

But concentrating upon specific media sectors fails to convey the extent of concentrated corporate control. The dominant trend since the 1970s or 1980s, which has accelerated in the 1990s, is the conglomeration of media ownership. This is the process whereby media firms began to have major holdings in two or more distinct sectors of the media, such as book publishing, recorded music, and broadcasting. So it is that each of the six main Hollywood studios are the hubs of vast media conglomerates. Each of the six owns some combination of television networks, TV show production, television stations, music companies, cable channels, cable TV systems, magazines, newspapers, book publishing firms, and other media enterprises. The vast majority of the dominant firms in each of the major media sectors are owned outright or in part by a small handful of conglomerates. And this has all come about seemingly overnight. Published in 1983, Ben Bagdikian's seminal, even shocking, *The Media Monopoly* chronicled how some fifty media conglomerates dominated the entirety of U.S. mass media, ranging from newspapers, books, and magazines to film, radio, television, cable, and recorded music. Today that world appears to have been downright competitive, even populist. After the massive wave of media mergers and acquisitions since 1983, Bagdikian has reduced the number of dominant firms, until the most recent edition of *The Media Monopoly* in 1997 put the figure at around ten, with another dozen or so firms rounding out the system.[24]

The "first tier" of media conglomerates includes Time Warner, Disney, Viacom, Seagram, Rupert Murdoch's News Corporation, and Sony, all connected to the big six film studios. The remaining first-tier media giants include General Electric, owner of NBC, and AT&T, which in 1998 purchased TCI, the cable powerhouse with vast holdings in scores of other media enterprises.[25] GE (1998 sales: $100 billion), AT&T-TCI (1997 sales: $58 billion), and Sony (1997 sales: $51 billion) all are enormous firms, among the largest in the world. Their media holdings constitute a distinct minority of their assets.

These media empires have been constructed largely in the 1990s, with a rate of growth in annual revenues that is staggering. In 1988 Disney was a $2.9 billion per year amusement park and cartoon company; in 1998 Disney had $25 billion in sales. In 1988 Time was a $4.2 billion publishing company and Warner Communications was a $3.4

billion media conglomerate; in 1998 Time Warner did $28 billion in business. In 1988 Viacom was a measly $600 million syndication and cable outfit; in 1998 Viacom did $14.5 billion worth of business. The figures are similar for the other giants.[26] In chapter 2 I provide a detailed list of the media holdings of News Corp., Time Warner, and Disney, the most important media conglomerates in the world. For present purposes, consider the holdings of Viacom to get a sense of how one of these giants looks. Viacom owns Paramount Pictures, Simon and Schuster book publishers, Spelling Entertainment, MTV cable network, VH1 cable network, Nickelodeon cable network, TV Land cable network, Showtime cable network, eighteen U.S. television stations, the UPN network, the Blockbuster video rental chain, five theme parks, retail stores, and a vast movie theater empire outside of the United States.

The "second tier" of U.S. media giants includes the great newspaper-based conglomerates like Gannett, Knight-Ridder, and the New York Times Company, cable-based powerhouses like Comcast and Cox Enterprises, as well as broadcast-based powers like CBS. These fifteen or so "second-tier" firms are all conglomerates, but they are smaller than the first-tier firms, with annual sales ranging from $2 billion to $7 billion. They also all tend to lack the film, TV, and music production capacities of the first-tier giants. These second-tier firms have all grown quickly over the past decade and they, too, have been swallowing up smaller firms.

It is unclear how much more upheaval will occur in the U.S. media system, but there is no reason to think that more major mergers and acquisitions are not on the horizon. AT&T's purchase of TCI left its subsidiary Liberty Media in former TCI CEO John Malone's hands, with Malone in complete control and flush with up to $20 billion in liquidity. "When the smoke clears," Malone said when announcing the TCI sale to AT&T, "Liberty is going to have tons of cash."[27] By most accounts, Liberty Media will aggressively move to structure a new media empire in the near future.[28] At any rate, all of the media firms are actively juggling assets to improve market power, even if only a minority will engage in major mergers. As one media analyst puts it, "consolidation among distribution and content players rages on."[29] What is clear is that the option of being a small or middle-sized media firm barely exists any longer: a firm either gets larger through mergers and acquisitions or it gets swallowed by a more aggressive competitor.

Why is that the case? To some extent this trend has been fueled by a desire to create an extremely lucrative *vertical integration,* meaning that media firms would not only produce content but would also own the distribution channels that would guarantee places to display and market their wares. For decades U.S. laws and regulations forbade film studios from owning movie theaters and television networks from producing their own entertainment programs because it was well understood that this sort of vertical integration would effectively prohibit newcomers from entering the film or television production industries. Such restrictions have been relaxed or eliminated in these deregulatory times, and some of the merger pandemonium can be attributed to the race by producers and distribution networks to link up with each other formally rather than be squeezed out by their competitors. Hence Disney owns ABC while News Corp. owns Fox. Viacom and Time Warner have launched their own U.S. television networks as well, the UPN and WB networks respectively. The vast majority of the fifty leading cable television channels, too, are owned outright or in part by the first-tier conglomerates, and the rest are all affiliated with a few of the second tier of media giants. Sony has moved aggressively into U.S. movie theater ownership while Viacom owns Blockbuster video rentals.[30]

These vertically integrated media conglomerates have not necessarily established exclusive arrangements such that their films only appear on their own TV stations and networks, or that their films get first crack in their movie theaters or movie rental stores. For the most part the largest conglomerates are increasingly interdependent, competing in some markets while they are customers for each other in other markets. But when vertical integration can be applied effectively, it is logical to expect media conglomerates to keep production directed to their own distribution outlets.

The first market where full vertical integration looks plausible is with the production of television shows for the TV networks. Television show production had already become increasingly concentrated in the hands of the big six Hollywood studios by the mid-1990s. According to one report, they accounted for thirty-seven of the forty-six new primetime shows on network TV in fall 1998. The four studios which also own TV networks produced twenty-nine of the programs.[31] Fox supplied over 40 percent of its 1998 programs whereas CBS had a stake in 57 percent of its prime-time lineup, a 20 percent increase over 1997.[32] What is new is the demand by the six

TV networks — the four affiliated with Hollywood studios plus NBC and CBS — to own a piece of shows that appeared on their networks. "Each and every one of these networks," one studio executive stated in 1998, "are going to endeavor to own and control as much content as they possibly can." CBS, for example, produced or coproduced six of its seven new shows in 1998.[33]

Some expect that the logical trajectory will be for networks eventually to produce nearly all of their own programs, something that would have been illegal just a decade ago. Hence Viacom CEO Sumner Redstone fired an executive who did not mind seeing programs produced by Viacom's Spelling Entertainment (like *Frasier*) being sold to other networks if they paid more than UPN, although UPN was languishing in the ratings. "I think you are going to see a lot more Spelling shows on UPN," Redstone commented in 1998.[34] The exact same process is taking place with cable TV channels, where most of them are now owned wholly or in part with a major production studio.[35] If this process does continue at this pace, NBC and CBS logically would become part of deals to formally link up with production studios.

But the pressure to become a conglomerate is also due to something perhaps even more profound than the need for vertical integration. It was and is stimulated by the desire to increase market power by cross-promoting and cross-selling media properties or "brands" across numerous, different sectors of the media that are not linked in the manner suggested by vertical integration. "Cross-promotion offers incredible efficiencies, while cross-selling promises major opportunities," *Variety* notes, in explaining the drive to conglomeration.[36] Hence, if a media conglomerate had a successful motion picture, it could promote the film on its broadcast properties and then use the film to spin off television programs, musical CDs, books, merchandise, and much else. "When you can make a movie for an average cost of $10 million and then cross promote and sell it off of magazines, books, products, television shows out of your own company," Viacom's Redstone said, "the profit potential is enormous." (Viacom's) Paramount *Beavis and Butt-Head Do America* film, for example, based on Viacom's MTV cartoon series, cost $11 million but generated a *profit* of $70 million. When Viacom released its *Rugrats* movie — based on its Nickelodeon TV program — in December 1998, it provided extensive editorial programming to promote the movie on Nickelodeon, its VH-1 and Showtime cable networks, and the syndicated television program *Entertainment Tonight,* which is produced by Viacom's Paramount Television.[37] In the new world order of conglomerated media, as an MTV executive put it, "the sum is greater than the parts."[38] "These firms no longer make films or books," Paine Webber's media analyst Christopher Dixon observes, "they make brands."[39]

Disney, more than any media giant, is the master at figuring out "new synergistic ways to acquire, slice, dice and merchandise content."[40] Its 1994 animated film *The Lion King* generated over $1 billion in profit. It led to a lucrative Broadway show, a TV series and all sorts of media spin-offs. It also led to 186 items of merchandising.[41] Wall Street analysts gush at the profit potential of animated films in the hands of media conglomerates; they estimate that such films on average generate *four times more profit* than their domestic box-office take.[42] A look at some of Disney's recent operations shows how it employs the logic of synergy to all of its endeavors. Its *Home Improvement* show is a big hit on its ABC television network. So Disney then has *Home Improvement* star Tim Allen take roles in Disney movies and write books for Disney's book-publishing firms. The other giant media conglomerates are increasingly emulating this pattern.[43] In another example, Disney takes its lucrative ESPN cable channel and uses the name to generate other properties, including an ESPN radio network.[44] In 1998 Disney launched *ESPN Magazine* to compete directly with Time Warner's *Sports Illustrated.*[45] Using incessant promotion on ESPN, the magazine exceeded initial estimates with a circulation approaching five hundred thousand after only a few months.[46] Likewise, Disney is launching a chain of ESPN Grill restaurants to appeal to those who wish to combine sports with dining out.[47]

Murdoch's News Corp. exploits its *X-Files* TV program in the same manner. It produces the show, airs it over its Fox network, and then shows reruns on its twenty-two Fox TV stations and its FX cable network. News Corp. has generated *X-Files* books and extensive merchandising, and Twentieth Century Fox (owned by News Corp.) released a movie version of the *X-Files* in 1998.[48] News Corp. even has a traveling *X-Files* Expo that visited ten U.S. cities in March 1998 with active promotion through all other News Corp. media properties. Organized by the News Corp. licensing and merchandising division and sponsored by General Motors, the Expo is "part rock concert and part fan festival," with the avowed aim of "extending the life cycle" of the *X-Files* property.[49] (Not surprisingly, News

Corp. also uses the *X-Files* on its worldwide television channels.) This is synergy indeed, and it works. Time Warner, too, is aggressively working to have the parts in its massive empire work more closely together. In 1998 it began promoting new releases from its music companies on the videotapes for Warner Bros. films.[50]

If synergy is the principle that makes becoming a media conglomerate more profitable and, indeed, mandatory, the other side of the coin is *branding*. All media firms are racing to give their media properties distinct brand identities. Although the media system has fewer and fewer owners, it nonetheless has a plethora of channels competing for attention. Branding is the primary means of attracting and keeping audiences while also offering new commercial possibilities. Cable channels and even broadcast networks each strive to be regarded as brands by the specific demographic groups desired by advertisers. Hence Viacom's Nickelodeon cable network battles its new competition from News Corp.'s Fox Kids Network and the Disney Channel by incessantly hammering home the Nickelodeon brand name on Nickelodeon and in its other film, television, and publishing holdings.[51] Take, for one fairly minor example of the rise of branding to preeminence as a business strategy, News Corp.'s HarperCollins book-publishing division. In the past few years, HarperCollins has developed *The Little House on the Prairie* from the 1930s and 1940s into a contemporary book series aimed at 8–12 year olds, and has added several new books to the series. HarperCollins has also generated ninety related products, ranging from paper dolls and cookbooks to picture books, all bearing the "Little House" logo.[52]

As this suggests, branding opens up for the media giants the entire world of selling retail products based on their branded properties, and it is a course they have been pursuing with a vengeance.[53] In 1997, $25 *billion* of Disney merchandise was sold, more than twice the global sales of Toys 'R' Us.[54] Disney's own licensing revenue in 1997 was $10 billion, while Time Warner's was more than $6 billion. In 1998, for one example of branded products, Disney introduced a "Mickey Unlimited" fragrance line for men and women in Germany, following the successful release of a "Mickey for Kids" perfume there in 1997. Disney plans to roll out the perfumes across Asia and into the United States.[55] Murdoch's News Corp. generated a paltry $1 billion in licensing revenue, leading to a major shakeup in the Fox hierarchy in early 1998.[56] Disney now has 660 retail stores to sell its branded products; Time Warner has 160 stores. Some of the other media giants are moving in the same direction.[57]

In sum, the logic and trajectory of the media market is such that firms that do not have the cross-selling and cross-promotional opportunities of the media giants are finding it ever more difficult to survive or prosper. As Diane Mermigas, one of the leading observers of the media industry, put it in 1998: "The bottom line is that a handful of sprawling giants like Time Warner and Disney have more options for building out their brands in many different ways across all their business lines that smaller players don't have. The options for generating additional earnings can make all the difference in difficult times that may prove even brand kings — like Disney — are vulnerable."[58]

One important qualification needs to be made concerning media conglomeration and synergy. Not all media sectors mesh equally well with all others. The major newspaper chains have almost all found it lucrative to extend their holdings to radio and television stations, and sometimes to magazine or book publishing. The core unifier for these synergies is news-oriented content and facility with advertisers. Television stations have also been made parts of conglomerates that include TV networks, cable channels, film studios, and music studios. The core unifier for this set of synergies is entertainment content production combined with distribution, cross-selling, and cross-promotion. But there is little evidence, as yet, that newspaper chains and film studios or newspaper chains and music studios offer each other significant "synergies." Hence Disney sold the newspaper interests it acquired as part of its 1995 purchase of ABC and ESPN. And in 1998 Viacom sold all aspects of its Simon and Schuster book publishing that pertained to the business and educational markets. It is worth noting that Viacom kept its general "trade"-book-publishing interests, so it can continue to publish odes to Beavis and Butt-Head. When giant firms sell off assets like these, some observers jump to the conclusion that this proves synergy does not work and that large firms are ultimately too large for their own competitive good. In fact, what it establishes is that smart firms get bigger and bigger, but they carefully assess their holdings to see that they complement each other well. And the trajectory of the 1990s is that the field of media assets that can complement each other for a media conglomerate is growing.

Nor is the media system entirely closed. Despite the ravages of concentration, independent record labels and book publishers have proliferated in recent years, albeit getting a minuscule share of the market. Some argue that the concentration in music and book retailing makes it easier for these independents to establish distribution networks and that this will lead to more competitive markets down the road.[59] That remains to be seen. What is clear right now is that small independent publishers and recording companies play an indispensable part in the overall system of providing content that is too risky for the giants to consider. Then, if the fare proves successful, the big firms can begin to produce it, or even buy up the independent. This is the case in the film industry, where independents account for only 5 percent of industry revenues but serve an important creative function for the giants.[60] By 1998 almost all of the Hollywood "indies" were either owned outright by a major studio or effectively affiliated with one otherwise. Independents have become a source of low-risk profit-making for the media giants, giving the latter near total control over the industry.[61] "Lone wolf production companies," *Variety* noted in 1998, "have become integral to the corporate studio filmmaking process."[62] The notion that independents might sprout up to challenge the existing giants is dead.

Will new first-tier media giants emerge from the woodwork? It is possible if some second-tier firms merge, or if a huge nonmedia firm elects to buy its way into the market, as General Electric, Sony, AT&T, and Seagram have done over the past decade. With the convergence of media with telecommunication and computering, this is an increasing prospect, a point I return to in chapter 3.

The one clear effort to establish a new media giant is DreamWorks, the new Hollywood studio formed by Steven Spielberg and David Geffen, among others, and backed with billions of dollars in investment capital from the Korean heiress Miky Lee and Microsoft cofounder Paul Allen. Can it succeed, becoming, for example, the first successful new Hollywood studio since the 1930s? The connection to Spielberg and Geffen may provide some hope, but otherwise the venture looks like an absurd deployment of capital. One look at animation, one of DreamWorks's main areas of development, shows why: whereas media giants Disney, Time Warner, Viacom, and News Corporation can generate profit from animated films that do lackluster box office by exploiting their numerous other revenue streams, DreamWorks must rely disproportionately on the film's theatrical success. DreamWorks also does not have an arsenal of other media on which to promote its animated films. In 1998 its first animated film, the critically acclaimed *Prince of Egypt,* struggled at the box office compared to concurrent animated films released by Viacom and Disney, each of which were heavily promoted on their various media aimed at children.[63] All of this puts DreamWorks at a distinct disadvantage. It suggests that DreamWorks will either become part of a larger media conglomerate or establish a close relationship with a media conglomerate, making it a de facto subsidiary at some point down the road.[64] This is what the independent computer animation firm Pixar did in 1996, when it formally allied with Disney.[65]

This is not to say that the media market is at all stable. In just three years in the late 1990s the leveraged buyout specialists Hicks Muse spent billions of dollars to build up an empire in radio stations, sports teams, television stations, book publishing, billboards, and movie theaters.[66] According to a *Forbes* profile of Hicks Muse, its goal "is to blanket entire areas for advertisers, with radio, TV and billboards — one-stop advertising."[67] Hicks Muse is now a multibillion-dollar second-tier media conglomerate, having quickly exploited the opportunities for entering media markets that presented themselves with deregulation following the 1996 Telecommunications Act. Whether those opportunities remain in place for others is questionable, unless they want to pay a prohibitive price. But the experience with Hicks Muse underlines the overall logic of the media market: it only makes sense to be a player if you are a very, very big player with a broad stable of media assets to exploit.

Market concentration and conglomeration are necessary for profitability, but they do not assure it. The creation of these empires brought considerable debt to may of these firms, and it was only in the late 1990s that Viacom, Time Warner, and News Corp. returned to profitability. Gordon Crawford, who manages the $400 billion Capital Research mutual fund that has large holdings in all of the media giants, believes the short-term profit difficulties were and are exaggerated, especially if the problem is due to increased corporate debt to finance acquisitions.[68] "Most of these decisions make sense long term, and 20 years down the road, they're going to be all right."[69] Moreover, not all mergers and acquisitions pan out, so benefits accrue to the shrewder and/or more fortunate media giants. But the overarching trajectory for the media system is rapid growth for the largest firms well into the next century. Ironically, in the eyes of investors, the main problem with the existing media system is that there is *too much* competition. "The problem is that too many players are at the table," *Business Week* concludes in its analysis of the media industry, "and it's ruining everyone's hand."[70] Gordon Crawford forecasts that the eventual outcome will be a global media oligopoly dominated by six firms: Time Warner, Disney, Viacom, News Corporation, Sony, and Seagram. Crawford is more than a silent investor; he works quietly but persistently to coordinate deals among the media giants to increase profitability for all of them.[71]

Despite the seeming excess of "competition," the media system is anything but competitive in the traditional economic sense of the term. Not only are all of the markets oligopolies, where almost all of the main players are owned by a handful of firms, the media giants also tend to work quite closely together. The CEOs of Crawford's select six — together with all the other media giant CEOs (and now computer industry CEOs like Bill Gates and Andy Grove) — meet annually at a by-invitation-only retreat in Idaho to discuss the future of their industry.[72] Regardless of what actually happens in Idaho, these interactions bear many of the earmarks of a cartel, or at least a "gentleman's club."

And this barely begins to indicate how noncompetitive the media market is becoming. In addition to their oligopolistic market structure and overlapping ownership, the media giants each employ equity joint ventures with their "competitors" to an extraordinary extent. These are media projects where two or more media giants share the ownership between them. They are ideal because they spread the risk of a venture and eliminate the threat of competition by teaming up with potential adversaries.[73] Each of the eight largest U.S. media firms have, on average, joint ventures (often more than one) with five of the other seven media giants.[74] Rupert Murdoch's News Corp. has at least one joint venture with every single one of them. While competition can be fierce in specific markets, the same firms are often the best customers for each other's products, and the overall effect is to reduce competition and carve up the media pie to the benefit of the handful of giants. According to most theories of market performance, this degree of collaboration can only have negative consequences for consumers.

Finally, when one looks at the membership on the U.S. media giants' boards of directors — the people who legally represent the shareholders and therefore run the companies — the notion that this is a collaborative industry is even more justified. Crawford's select six, less the Japanese Sony and Seagram and adding CBS and GE, have eighty-one directors on their boards. These eighty-one hold 104 additional directorships on the boards of Fortune 1000 corporations. Indeed, the boards for these six firms plus the five largest newspaper corporations (New York Times, Washington Post, Times-Mirror, Gannett, and Knight-Ridder) have directors who also serve on 144 of the Fortune 1000 firms. The eleven media giants also have thirty-six *direct* links, meaning two people who serve on different media firm boards of directors and also serve on the same board for another Fortune 1000 corporation. Each of the eleven media giants has at least two such interlocks. GE has seventeen direct links to nine of the other ten media giants; Time Warner has direct links to seven of them. In combination, this suggests that the corporate media are very closely linked to each other, and to the highest echelons of the corporate community. The point is not that the corporate media are necessarily more intertwined with other large firms than any other industrial sector but, rather, that the media are full participants in the corporate community. As the most recent study of this issue concluded, "The media in the United States effectively represent the interests of corporate America."[75]

Finally, for what it is worth, many of the very wealthiest Americans generated their bounty through their holdings in media properties. Some 17 percent of the Forbes 400 list of the richest Americans derived their wealth primarily from media, entertainment, or computer software. Exactly 20 percent of the fifty largest family fortunes were derived therefrom.[76] Nor are the owners the only beneficiaries of media prosperity. The average compensation in 1997 for the CEOs of General Electric, Viacom, Disney, Time Warner, Universal Studios, the New York Times, CBS, Times-Mirror, Comcast, Cox, TCI, AT&T, Tribune Company, the Washington Post, and Gannett was approximately $4,500,000.[77] In short, those that sit atop our media empires are at the very pinnacle of success as it is measured in a capitalist society.

Corporate Media Culture

The implications of this concentration and conglomeration for media content are largely negative. On the one hand, media fare is ever more closely linked to the needs and concerns of a handful of enormous and powerful corporations, with annual revenues approaching the GDP of a small nation. These firms are run by wealthy managers and billionaires with clear stakes in the outcome of the most fundamental political issues, and their interests are often distinct from those of the vast majority of humanity. By any known theory of democracy, such a concentration of economic, cultural, and political power into so few hands — and mostly unaccountable hands at that — is absurd and unacceptable. On the other hand, media fare is subjected to an ever-greater commercialization as the dominant firms use their market power to squeeze the greatest possible profit from their product. This is, in fact, the most visible trend in U.S. media today.

My argument is institutional. It is understandable why so many observers focus on the personalities of the individuals who dominate the largest media firms as the decisive factor in explaining the nature of the system.[78] Of the eight dominant U.S. media firms, four have owners with enough stock to wield absolute control over their firms: These are Viacom (Sumner Redstone), News Corporation (Rupert Murdoch), Seagram (Edgar Bronfman), and AT&T's Liberty Media (John Malone). This is a far higher percentage than most industries, probably reflecting the recent genesis of the corporate media system. "The mogul style of leadership," one management consultant notes, "is the only one that can work in an industry where the playing field is constantly changing."[79] As the system settles down, and as Murdoch, Redstone, and Malone age, in time at least one or two of those enterprises likely will turn to a more traditional form of corporate management mostly independent of shareholders. And even the media giants with traditional management, like Disney, Time Warner, and GE, have long-standing and strong CEOs in Michael Eisner, Gerald Levin, and Jack Welch respectively. Indeed, Eisner has been accused of stacking the Disney board of directors so that he enjoys an almost unchallengeable grip on Disney operations.[80]

But even with this much CEO autonomy, the problem with the corporate media system is not that the people who own and manage the dominant media firms are bad and immoral people. Their individual traits are mostly irrelevant. The owners and managers do what they do because it is the most rational conduct to pursue in the market context they face. Were, say, frequently maligned media moguls like Rupert Murdoch or John Malone to leave their jobs, their replacements would pursue similar courses, though perhaps with greater or lesser success. And those media CEOs occasionally suspected of humane thought and behavior, like Eisner or Levin or Ted

Turner, resolutely keep a wall between their do-gooder activities and their business activities. (As for those politicians and policy makers who aggressively advance the interests of the giant media firms in Washington, D.C., and elsewhere, I am decidedly less charitable. It may be understandable why most politicians effectively whore for powerful media and communication firms, but it is still a violation of public trust. And when we no longer expect elected officials to meet even rudimentary standards of public integrity, then, indeed, our use of the term "democracy" to describe this system becomes almost Orwellian.)

Let me offer a few provisos to my critique of the U.S. media system. When one assesses the effects of the nature of the media system upon media content, it is usually difficult to isolate one variable as determinative. The core structural factors that influence the nature of media content include the overall pursuit of profit, the size of the firm, the amount of direct and indirect competition facing the firm and the nature of that competition, the degree of horizontal and vertical integration, the influence of advertising, the specific interests of media owners and managers, and, to a lesser extent, media employees. In combination these factors can go a long way to providing a context (and a trajectory) for understanding the nature of media content; but even then this is always a context. This "institutional" or "political economic" approach to understanding media can only rarely provide a detailed understanding of specific media content.

It is also true that the system does produce much of value. In those areas that are especially commercially lucrative — for example, sports, action films, business news, light comedies, "news coverage" of celebrities and royalty, and certain types of popular music — the system is quite productive. For the more favored (meaning affluent) demographic groups, there is considerable choice within these genres, thanks to burgeoning growth in the number of media channels. And sometimes the system even produces remarkable documentaries, drama, and investigative journalism. When compiled into one list it can make for an impressive advertisement for the status quo. Hence John Leonard, after providing such a list in the *Nation,* praises U.S. commercial television as "weirdly democratic, multicultural, utopian, quixotic and more welcoming of difference and diversity than much of the audience that sits down to watch it with a surly agnosticism about reality itself."[81] But this caliber of analysis is akin to traveling to Brazil or India, observing how affluent are the lifestyles of the sizable upper-middle classes, and then concluding that the social orders of Brazil or India are fair and just. (Leonard also reveals a patronizing contempt for popular taste and attitudes, but that is another matter.) The real way to assess the content of the media system is to judge it in its entirety. By that standard, I believe the output is woeful in view of the massive resources these firms command.

Why does the system produce good stuff? There are two closely related reasons. First, the media giants are required to utilize the talents of some very creative people, and in doing so some good material gets produced. These creative talents often have quite different views of the world, and of desirable media content, from media owners and managers. Sometimes creative people have enough commercial success so as to earn a degree of freedom and independence from corporate media norms. Hence a Hollywood star can use her or his marketability to make a film like Warren Beatty's 1998 *Bulworth,* something that would be unthinkable for a Hollywood studio to produce otherwise. Likewise, Michael Moore has carved out a nice niche on the margins of the corporate media system, following the success of his *Roger and Me* documentary.[82] But the extent of this creative freedom is unclear, and those who exercise it like Beatty or Moore usually do so by willingly sacrificing considerable income. So for every Beatty or Moore there are many more prominent artists who internalize the dominant commercial mores — which is not especially difficult to do when one is a millionaire — and young creative people entering the industry learn early on the necessary values to achieve success. While creativity is a factor that breathes continual life into the media system, it is always an uphill fight. By its very nature the commercial system mitigates against creativity and has a difficult time establishing original commercially successful fare. It has 20/20 hindsight, always aping what has worked in the past or for competitors and then re-creating it without the initial spark. Hence U.S. cable television, with its plethora of channels, basically consists of each of the largest media conglomerates offering the same family of commercial-laden channels: business news, sports, reruns, movies, shopping, and music videos.

The second reason for the good fare is that commercial media giants strive to satisfy audience desires and audiences often want quality fare. In popular mythology the corporate media giants, in their pursuit of profit, eagerly and willingly "give the people what they want," or face economic peril. In fact, corporate media are hardly the obedient servants of this mythology. I have laid out a systematic critique of this notion elsewhere, so let me add just one point here.[83] As much as demand creates supply, supply creates demand. Media conglomerates are risk-averse and continually return to what has been commercially successful in the past. Over time, this probably creates a demand in the fare that is commonly presented. There is little incentive in the system to *develop* public taste over time. (Often, so-called audience research is a circular process where consumers are permitted to choose from a narrow slate of the sort of commercially lucrative selections that are already widely distributed.)[84] Even media moguls are aware of this problem but powerless to address it. Richard Branson, founder of Virgin Records, chastised U.S. radio stations in 1998 for continually playing the same old material, hence making in nearly impossible to launch new musical genres or original acts.[85] "Classic rock didn't die — it was murdered by the consultants," a longtime New York radio figure commented. "Instead of playing a hundred of the great things that the Stones have done, they would pick five and wear them out."[86] Even classical music enthusiasts are despondent as classical stations largely play "greatest hits" or "lite" formats, leaving a new generation uneducated in the broader traditions. "The educational approach only leads to the graveyard," one classical radio station music director stated.[87]

Perhaps the clearest example of the complex relationship of audience demand and media supply is shown by the decline in foreign films in U.S. motion picture theaters in the last two decades of the twentieth century. In the mid-1970s, foreign films accounted for over 10 percent of the box office at U.S. theaters. Every decent-sized city had one or more theaters specializing in foreign films, and Manhattan alone had two dozen such theaters. By the mid-1980s the percentage of box office accounted for by foreign films was around 7 percent, and by the late 1990s it is down to under .5 percent. By the logic of the "give the people what they want" thesis, this development would reflect the fact that the American people decided that they were no longer interested in seeing non-U.S. films. But it was nothing like that at all. Instead, what this reflected was the rise to dominance in the United States of the chain-owned megaplex movie theaters. With far lower costs, these multiscreen cinemas drove nearly all the one-screen theaters out of business, the very theaters that had specialized in foreign fare. Megaplex chain theaters would only grant screens to foreign films if the filmmakers were as willing to devote massive amounts to U.S. marketing as U.S. studios could, something wholly unrealistic for them to do. As a result foreign films stopped being exhibited and a new generation has come along with no idea that foreign films even exist. This new generation is therefore highly unlikely to rent foreign film videos, either, as they have no familiarity with them. In short, supply has been the determinative factor in the collapse of demand.[88]

With tremendous pressure to attract audiences but to keep costs down and not take chances, the standard route of the media giants is to turn to the tried and true formulas of sex and violence, always attention getters. In what the trade publication *Variety* termed one of "the biggest political gaffes of the decade," in 1994 the broadcast industry agreed to subsidize detailed studies of TV content to ward off the potential for congressional hearings on the matter. In 1998 the study, conducted by the University of California at Santa Barbara's Center for Communications and Social Policy, concluded that for the third year in a row "violent TV shows account for 60% of TV programming, and that the amount of violence has steadily increased each year."[89] The most comprehensive economic analysis of violent programming on television concludes that violent fare results logically from the workings of the commercial broadcasting system. To the extent that the system factors in audience desires, it does so in a quite limited and commercially exploitable manner.[90] Likewise, the *New York Times* concluded in 1998 that "mainstream television this season is flaunting the most vulgar and explicit sex, language and behavior that it has ever sent into American homes."[91] Programming that features lurid and infantile discussions of sexual behavior, like talk shows hosted by Howard Stern or Jerry Springer, costs virtually nothing to produce and does not need to "develop" an audience. Indeed, when Stern's TV show plummeted in the ratings in 1998, the "racy" program, which featured Stern imploring his female guests to take off their clothes, remained on the air nonetheless. It was still profitable for CBS because "it costs next to nothing to produce."[92]

I would argue that the weaknesses in commercial media fare are long term, but that concentration and conglomeration have encouraged speed-up to what I term hypercommercialism throughout both the media system and the society writ large. Concentrated media control permits the largest media firms to increasingly commercialize their output with less and less fear of consumer reprisal. And conglomerated media control opens the door to vastly greater opportunities for commercial exploitation, the much ballyhooed synergies. The end result is that the integrity of the editorial fare produced by the media giants is greatly compromised, and it has become increasingly difficult to distinguish editorial from explicitly commercial fare, even from advertising. Of course nothing could ever indicate the folly of the notion that the commercial media system "gives the people what they want" more than the rise of this commercial carpetbombing. If there is anything people do not want or have not wanted, it is to be pummeled by commercialism at every turn. Or perhaps that is an exaggeration. Although people may have once been critical of hypercommercialism, perhaps they are becoming inured to it. In a political culture where commercialism appears to be a force of nature rather than something subject to political control, that would be a rational response over time.

This hypercommercialism is apparent across the media landscape. For generations, the nature of the music industry has had ambiguous effects on the content of popular music. At its best, commercialism has allowed musicians to be paid and has permitted the widespread dissemination, cross-pollination, and flowering of popular music. Rock 'n' roll, itself, was the result of this creative combination of commercialism with popular music genres in the late 1940s and early 1950s.[93] But commercial values, when they rule the roost, have proven deadly for artistic creativity. As the seminal jazz critic Sidney Finkelstein put in 1948, commercialism appears acceptable if it refers to musicians earning income or to audiences having access to music, but in the end commercialism leads "to what is really destructive in culture: the taking over of an art by business."[94] More recently, a popular music scholar noted: "It is ironic that the music industry seeks to capitalize on such mixtures [of different musical genres], yet, in producing an organization to take advantage of this, the industry has a tendency to build walls within which 'creativity' can be contained."[95] Many of the great creative waves in rock 'n' roll have come from musicians eschewed by the corporate music companies at the time.[96]

Today, the "windows" of opportunity for exciting new popular music genres to develop before being incorporated into the commercial web have been shortened. If the original rock 'n' roll went a decade before Madison Avenue wised up to its promise, if the 1960s rock renaissance went years before meeting the same fate, and if the 1970s punk, reggae, and hiphop movements also were launched outside the corporate orbit and stayed there for a decisive incubation, by the 1990s the system was geared toward exploiting any "new" trend — or creating the trend if possible so as to have ownership — long before it could establish any artistic integrity. The logic of the corporate media system is to draw everything into the commercial web and to use marketing principles to maximize profit. The implications for popular music have been disastrous. Popular music and its attendant institutions like MTV and commercial radio, a *New York Times* critic wrote in 1998, "have become increasingly reliant on market research, primarily because ratings and circulation are so important to their advertisers. As a result," he concluded, "the mall rules" and "music is in a lull."[97] It is certainly ironic that this compulsive corporate behavior may have the ultimate effect of making the music industry much less important in the long run, and thereby hurting long-term commercial growth, but that is a matter outside the control of the individual giant media firm which must pursue its course or face competitive ruin.

Indeed, the 1990s have seen a systematic rationalization of the commercialization of the music industry into every possible aspect of its operations. Music has increasingly become a crucial area for "branding," and popular artists exploit themselves as brands to capitalize upon their names.[98] Gloria Estefan, for example, is building a "global entertainment franchise" that hawks Estefan-oriented merchandise, restaurants, and collectibles in addition to films, TV shows, and (almost incidentally) music.[99] But the Spice Girls make Estefan look like a piker; in November 1997, to accompany their new CD, they launched a "wave of endorsements and merchandising unprecedented in the music industry." There are Spice Girls bomber jackets, books, potato chips, calendars, key chains, and files. Marketers see the Spice Girls as a unique brand to reach the desirable four-to-six-year-old-girl market, among others.[100] Polaroid even created the SpiceCam as part of its "Expressions" line of cameras, promoted in advertising by the Spice Girls and targeting nine- to twelve-year-old girls.[101]

Increasingly these hypercommercial activities are seen as mandatory for commercial success in the music industry. This is not merely so that artists and recording companies can generate additional revenues; it is to ensure that they remain in the public eye, or ear. "We are looking for any way to enhance their visibility to any consumer who is a potential record buyer," a Time Warner music executive stated regarding his roster of recording artists. "Not long ago," the *Wall Street Journal* observed in 1998, "a star could stay a star by getting a song played on the radio or a music video aired on MTV. . . . Now it's flashy commercialism and marketing alliances that keep a star bright (and richer by the minute)."[102] The "alternative" British band The Verve only made a splash in the United States (making the cover of *Rolling Stone* magazine, among other things) after one of its songs was the theme for a 1998 Nike television advertising campaign.[103] The same thing happened to the British group Republica, which only had a breakthrough by providing a song for a Mitsubishi Motors commercial. By the end of 1998, the *Wall Street Journal* observed that "hip, edgy rockers who once kept their distance from advertising now see commercials as a great promotional vehicle."[104] It does not require a genius to see the limitations for the art of music when commerce permeates it to such an extent. "The music industry is worse than ever," singer Patti Smith stated in a 1997 interview. "Rock 'n' roll is great because it's the people's art," she added. "But it's not ours anymore. Right now, rock 'n' roll belongs to business. We don't even own it."[105]

Book publishing, even more than music, has seen the greatest change as a result of concentration and conglomeration. Only a generation ago, U.S. book publishing was, for better or for worse, a moderately concentrated industry. Since the early 1980s there has been a shakeout in the number of firms, and now most of the remaining publishers are part of corporate media conglomerates. This has changed their operating logic considerably. In addition to shaping what manuscripts are considered market-worthy and what authors "bankable," there is increased pressure to publish and record writers and artists whose work complements products produced in other branches of these far-flung empires.[106] Viacom's Simon and Schuster, for example, has published a Nickelodeon imprint and a Beavis and Butt-Head series to "synergize" other Viacom properties. Although more titles than ever are being published — often due to the work of marginalized and struggling "independent" publishers — the big commercial publishers are emulating the Hollywood model of seeking out super-profitable blockbuster bestsellers and eschewing titles that might sell moderately well but have little chance of attaining blockbuster status.[107] Moreover, concentration within the industry has been accompanied by a sharp decrease in the attention given to book quality. While the number of books published has increased 42 percent since 1991, the number of book editors has declined by 11 percent over the same period, and by 16 percent in New York, where all the giants are headquartered. In sum, the brave new world of corporate publishing has "become a big, fat, screaming, mean, vicious, greedy, rude and crude fest," a senior editor at News Corp.'s HarperCollins commented in 1998.[108]

Concentration at the retail level is an important factor as well. The few chains that dominate bookselling are mostly interested in the biggest and best-selling books — books that have lots of promotion and commercial tie-ins — and this discourages publishers from handling the types of books that were more common on the lists of the big U.S. publishers twenty years ago.[109] The chains eject slow-moving books in as little as 120 days, making success very difficult for smaller presses, noncelebrity authors, or original topics.[110] Indeed, some publishers consult the chain retailers to see if they will carry a prospective book before they even authorize a contract for the author.[111] A similar shakeout among magazine distributors has had the effect of seeing small- and middle-circulation magazines increasingly dropped from newsstands, as it is more profitable for distributors with semimonopolistic holds on local and regional markets to concentrate on the handful of mass circulation titles that generate the most sales.[112]

Hypercommercialism has exploded in the film and television industries as well, no small feat in the latter considering its commercial pedigree. In 1998 NBC violated its long-standing stricture and began selling videos of its programs over the air during broadcasts. "NBC sold 100,000 copies of its 'Merlin' drama with just two 30 second spots," a media executive noted with astonishment. "The network created a new revenue stream."[113] "There is an untapped opportunity for networks in transactions," NBC executive Don Ohlmeyer stated. "This is about the future."[114] CBS broke another taboo in December 1998 when the fourteen stations it owns aired an infomercial during the "prime access" time slot, the period between the evening news and prime time.[115] "Product placement" within films and television shows has moved from being a fringe activity to becoming an important source of revenues.[116] Formally aligning a TV show or film with a number of marketers for cross-promotion has become standard operating procedure. A show like News Corp.'s *The Simpsons,* for example, has such tie-ins with four major firms, including Pepsi-Cola and Subway sandwiches.[117] Likewise, Time Warner inked a three-year deal with Frito-Lay in 1997, in which Warner Bros. characters will be used exclusively in Frito-Lay point-of-purchase displays the world over.[118] It also can penetrate the content of TV shows and films directly, in a much more ambitious version of product placement. In 1998 Disney's Miramax Films signed a deal with Tommy Hilfiger where the characters in a Miramax film will wear Hilfiger clothing and also appear, in character, in ads for Hilfiger jeans. According to Mr. Hilfiger, he will assist Miramax to "create personalities" for "the characters in the movie." "There is a very strong movement toward blending fashion and entertainment," he stated, as his company and Disney "are targeting the identical audience."[119]

It is difficult to exaggerate just how important the ties between global product marketers and media firms are becoming. The 1997 James Bond film, *Tomorrow Never Dies,* for example, had global promotional tie-in deals with Heineken, Avis Rent a Car, BMW of North America, Ericsson Corp.'s cellular phones, Heublein's, Smirnoff vodka, L'Oreal, and Visa.[120] This is now the norm. When Sony released *Godzilla* in 1998 it had a raft of promotional tie-in deals with literally scores of marketers, many of whom featured Godzilla themes prominently in major advertising campaigns. Taco Bell alone, for example, spent $60 million peddling Godzilla merchandise in its 7,000 restaurants. When the lame and formulaic movie atrophied at the box office, it sent shudders down Wall Street, as so many firms had partnered with it.[121] Disney came up with the title for its 1998 *Armageddon* even before it had a story. The point was to produce a live action film with the same sort of profit as *The Lion King.* Disney spent well over $60 million promoting a film that cost $140 million to make.[122] What does this mean for the art of filmmaking? The answer is self-evident. As one industry analyst put it, for the giant media conglomerate, "the movie is almost incidental."[123]

The hypercommercialism of the system increases exponentially when one considers the role of advertising. The sheer number of television ads has increased considerably on broadcast television in the past decade. All of the TV networks have increased the percentage of time devoted to advertising in the 1990s, with Disney's ABC the champion, having increased the amount of time give to commercials by 34 percent since 1989.[124] Some $120 billion is being spent by advertisers on U.S. media in 1998, and around $200 billion is being spent on U.S. advertising overall.[125] Television increasingly appears marinated in advertising and commercialism. As one advertising industry observer put it: "It should be noted that advertising clutter isn't confined to paid advertisements. From talk show hosts plugging their books to race car drivers wearing sponsor logos over every body part, clutter is everywhere."[126] This commercial deluge is taking a toll. As noted by one study, consumer "believability" in advertising dropped from 61 percent to 38 percent between 1987 and 1997.[127] To cut through the clutter, advertisers have resorted to "a new vulgarity and tastelessness" that is "transforming the content of advertising," as a 1998 *New York Times* report concluded. "The push to get noticed" has led advertisers "to do the advertising equivalent of dropping one's pants."[128]

Advertisers are not wed to media, and this clutter has them scurrying about attempting to locate new methods to brand their names on the public's mind. In 1997 Wal-Mart began showing ads on TV monitors to all its customers waiting in line to purchase products.[129] To promote home video release of its 1997 film *Liar, Liar,* Universal Pictures purchased sticker ads that were placed on twelve million Granny Smith and Fuji apples in U.S. supermarkets. "People look at 10 pieces of fruit before they pick one," stated the ad executive responsible for the idea, "so we get multiple impressions."[130] In 1998 Disney and Gillette both began putting advertising on the supermarket "adsticks" that separate customers groceries from each other's while they wait in the checkout line.[131] Some companies are beginning to play advertisements to their customers who are on hold.[132] One Florida-based long-distance telephone company even offered free calls if customers listened to advertising before being connected.[133] Movie theaters, too, are getting into the act: over one-half of the twenty-seven thousand U.S. movie screens now show advertisements before films, more than doubling the number of U.S. theaters that showed ads in 1993.[134] By 1997 the enormous Sony megaplex took the logic the furthest to date: one of its suburban Detroit theaters not only ran General Motors ads prior to feature films but also turned over the lobby and grounds to displays of GM products. Even sections of the theater's parking lot are identified not by row numbers but by the names of GM products.[135]

To capture public attention, some major advertisers are turning to having their brands incorporated into the structure of buildings so as to be indelibly stamped on the public mind.[136] Outdoor advertising (i.e., billboards) has enjoyed a renaissance in this environment.

Deals involving U.S outdoor advertising firms totaled $4.5 billion in 1997, up 80 percent over 1996. Outdoor advertisers have *doubled* their share of ad spending in the 1990s. The newest trend is "street furniture," where municipal governments let private interests provide bus shelters and newsstands permanently draped in the firm's advertising. New York awarded a $1 billion street furniture deal in 1998.[137] Another new trend is "bus wraps" and "building wraps," where entire vehicles or building walls are covered with a vinyl advertisement.[138] Along these lines, ad agencies now do "wild postings" for clients, where they plaster reams of poster-sized ads everywhere from construction sites to toll booths.[139] Another growing area of operations for advertising agencies is staging publicity stunts for corporations, as when General Motors sent a convoy of its new Corvettes on a journey across U.S. Route 66.[140] Other new locales for advertising include floors in public places, rental car audio tapes that greet customers, cash machines, and bathroom stall doors. In short, anything goes in the effort to capture the consumer's attention. As the *New York Times* concluded in 1998, we are in the midst of "an onslaught of ads that accost Americans at every turn."[141]

The media are well aware that clutter is a problem, but their concern is exclusively with satisfying advertisers, not viewers. NBC's solution is to run fewer but longer commercial breaks, so as not to lose viewers to channel-surfing. "The network is trying to figure out how to maximize retention while at the same time maximize revenue," a media executive stated. Its main solution has been to reduce the *number* of advertisers, not the amount of advertising. This leads to greater retention and pleases advertisers.[142] To address the complaints about the incessant advertising on its 1998 Winter Olympics telecasts, CBS began exploring the idea of running advertising continually during the programming in a portion of the screen, rather than reducing the number of commercial breaks.[143]

Moreover, to appease advertisers, media firms are increasingly giving them greater identification with and control over the programming. Procter & Gamble, one of the world's largest advertisers, has signed major production deals with both Sony's Columbia TriStar Television and with Viacom's Paramount to coproduce television programs.[144] P & G has already been coproducer of the TV programs *Sabrina, the Teenage Witch, Clueless,* and *Real TV.*[145] Some media executives say the P & G coproduction deals "may be the sign of things to come."[146] On television, there has been the beginning of a return to a formal "corporate sponsor" system of sponsorship, whereby a single company sponsors an entire program and is identified accordingly.[147] Interpublic, one of the three advertising corporations that dominates the global advertising agency business, has aggressively moved into working on program content to the benefit of its clients. As Interpublic's CEO put it, "We've always felt that longer term, there's going to be a closer relationship between agency, client and programming."[148]

The irony of media in the 1990s is that the vast expansion in cable channels was supposed to increase the power of consumers to control the fare: they would be free to pick and choose from a broader range of shows. Whether that has taken place is subject to debate, but it is clear that the increase in channels has given major advertisers far more negotiating leverage, and they can use their power to demand an increased role in the programming, so that their commercials cannot be as easily ignored by the viewers. Hence the expansion of channels has increased the commercialization of media, rather than decreasing it. (This is a point worth remembering when contemplating the future of the Internet and its alleged ability to liberate users from commercial influences.)

There are two aspects of media hypercommercialism, and both are key contributors to the general commercialization of U.S. culture. First is the trend within the media to ratchet up commercialism internally and therefore increasingly to subordinate editorial fare to commercial values and logic. This is what much of the discussion in this chapter has addressed. It may be symbolic that Barry Diller, creator of the Fox Network and widely regarded as one of the true media visionaries, has established a new TV network based on low-budget programming with an emphasis on sex and featuring infomercials and direct selling worked directly into the editorial content.[149] This trend is also revealed subtly by the increase in the number of prominent actors and musicians who now perform in television commercials. Until recently, this was something respected performers like Daniel Day-Lewis, Harrison Ford, or Jodie Foster only did in far-off Japan, so their "integrity" would not be compromised in the West.[150] Many "have since shed their scruples," the *Financial Times* observes, in view of the riches involved. And, increasingly, one might ask, what is the difference between starring in a film or TV show and appearing in an advertisement?[151]

The practice at Viacom, owner of MTV, is illustrative of this trend as well. MTV explicitly provides editorial coverage — and ample promotional tie-ins — only to those film studios that purchase large amounts of advertising on MTV. MTV even requires the studios to pay the production costs for the special shows on MTV about their movies. "Some magazines and newspapers have come under fire for blurring the line between paid advertising and editorial content," the *Wall Street Journal* observes. "At MTV and its sister networks, VH1 and Nickelodeon, the line has simply disappeared."[152] The Disney-Comcast cable channel E! ventured into similar territory in 1998 when it incorporated sponsor Miller Lite beer directly into the editorial content of its hit show *Talk Soup*.[153] Perhaps the most explicit signal of this direction has been the return of "payola," the process whereby music companies paid radio stations to play their label's artists. Fiercely prosecuted and reviled from the 1950s onward, the process has become legal today, as long as there is an over-the-air acknowledgment of the practice.[154] The British capitalist Richard Branson captured the irony of the situation: "It used to be called payola, and if they got caught, DJs used to get fired. But now the money goes to [station] owners and it's legitimate."[155] By the end of 1998 the *Los Angeles Times* and the *Orlando Sentinel* published evidence that the largest radio station groups were skirting the on-air acknowledgment of payola, yet effectively engaging in the process. "Industry mergers have shifted the balance of power to radio groups, which today have the clout to launch a song simultaneously in scores of markets across the country — or consign it to oblivion."[156]

The second trend is the spread of media conglomerates externally to new areas of social life. This spread is not entirely new — media firms have ventured out of their traditional domain for generations — but the rise of conglomeration has made the prospect increasingly lucrative and hence accelerated the process considerably. Take amusement parks, and the broader area of leisure and recreation for example. Commercial amusement parks have been around for most of the century, but it was Disneyland in the 1950s that showed what a huge market it could provide. Today several of the media giants, including Time Warner and Seagram, have amusement parks, though none approach Disney's empire. They all aspire to exploit every moment for its commercial potential.[157] Disney has even established a commercial zoo, "Animal Kingdom," at its Orlando, Florida, complex.[158] Disney also launched twenty DisneyQuest "virtual reality" mall entertainment centers in 1998, all of which will play upon

Disney "brands."[159] The notion of public parks and recreation is rapidly giving way to a world of privatized and commercialized leisure, conducted under the masterful touch of the media giants.

Even more striking is the aggressive move of the media conglomerates and advertisers to dominate U.S. spectator sports. Prior to the 1950s spectator sport and media had a symbiotic relationship, where sports coverage in the press increased fan interest and fan interest in sports sold magazines and newspapers. But with the rise of commercial broadcast sports in the 1950s the economics and relationship began to change. Over time broadcast rights payments became the most dynamic and important component of sport revenues, and these payments were based entirely upon what advertisers were willing to pay to reach sport viewers and listeners.[160] By the 1990s, U.S. professional (and, arguably, major collegiate) sport leagues were effectively part of the commercial media and advertising industries.[161]

The change was reflected in the number of major media conglomerates that purchased sports teams to be certain to assure content for their media properties. These include Time Warner (Atlanta Hawks, Atlanta Braves), Disney (Anaheim Angels, Anaheim Mighty Ducks), News Corp. (Los Angeles Dodgers, minority stakes in the New York Knicks and the New York Rangers, option to rights in the Los Angeles Lakers and the Los Angeles Kings), Tribune Company (Chicago Cubs), and Hicks Muse (Texas Rangers, Dallas Stars), among others. In all, some twenty-eight U.S. major league sport franchises are now controlled by media companies.[162] Media conglomerates have even contemplated establishing new sports leagues if they were boxed out of TV rights to existing leagues. In 1998, for example, GE and Time Warner discussed the launch of a new pro football league, after losing out in the bidding rights to the NFL.[163] Likewise, News Corp. and CBS contemplated launching a men's basketball league to compete with the NBA, when it looked like a management lockout might create an opening to grab the most marketable players.[164] And Disney, Viacom, and News Corp. have each established versions of "extreme" sports competitions, specifically designed to hit the youth market desirable to advertisers.[165] Explicit ownership of teams and especially leagues makes the most sense for media giants; then they can fully exploit the synergies and commercial possibilities of sport without having to make extravagant rights-fee payment to team owners, who contribute nothing but earn "rent" by having ownership over valuable franchises.[166] At any rate, the face of sport has been commercialized almost beyond recognition in the past generation. For those who are not immediate financial beneficiaries of this process, it is difficult to see how it has improved the sport experience at all.

Even the Broadway theater industry, for example, which was once the locale of promoters independent of the balance of the entertainment industry, is becoming incorporated into the webs of the media giants and commercial sponsors. Stage productions fit naturally into the synergistic world of conglomerates. Disney, again, is the leader of the pack, with a Broadway theater next to its Disney Store in New York's Theater District.[167] The box office for its *Beauty and the Beast* stage play has been $500 million, generating an operating income of $200 million. Its subsequent stage version of *The Lion King* is producing similar numbers. Other Hollywood studios are making plans for their own stage forays.[168]

All of these trends culminate in the rampant commercialization of U.S. childhood. Children and young people are seen as singularly important for advertisers. "More and more companies are realizing," the head of the Fox Family Channel stated, "that if you develop a loyalty with the kids of today they eventually become the adults of tomorrow."[169] Moreover, children are seen as determining a significant number of their family's purchases. "If you have kids, I guarantee you go home and ask the kids, 'What do you want to eat?' or 'What do you want at the store?'" one marketing consultant explains. "The parent doesn't want to get anything the kid is going to complain about. It's not efficient."[170] Moreover, children aged four to twelve are a formidable market in their own right. They spent $24 billion in 1997, three times the figure a decade earlier.[171] And no better medium exists for the delivery of the youth market than television. By age seven, the average American child is watching fourteen hundred hours and twenty thousand TV commercials per year, and by age twelve his or her preferences are stored in massive data banks maintained by marketers of consumer goods.[172] In the 1990s commercial television for children may well have been the most rapid growing and lucrative sector of the U.S. industry, with 1998 ad revenues pegged at approximately $1 billion.[173] Each of the four largest U.S. media giants has a full-time children's cable TV channel to capture the thirty-nine million viewers aged two to eleven.[174] Opening another frontier in 1997, Disney launched a nationwide children's radio network to meet the "great demand by advertisers for kid media." Surveys show that 91 percent of U.S. kids under age twelve listen to radio every week.[175]

Although advertisers see television as the golden path to gaining children's attention, the overall clutter of TV programming puts extreme pressure on each advertisement to distinguish itself from all the others. By the end of 1997, the use of graphic violence — always an attention getter — was growing more common in TV ads aimed at children and youth.[176] In 1998 broadcasters began targeting one-year-olds to get a toehold on the youth market. In a moment of candor, one Time Warner children's television executive conceded that "there's something vaguely evil" about programming to kids that young.[177] While advertisers and media giants have major incentives to exploit the children's market, they have no incentive to consider the social implications of their combined efforts. One thing that is certain is that they are training a generation of world-class shoppers. A 1997 survey showed that 80 percent of girls aged thirteen to seventeen stated they "loved to shop," and they made 40 percent more trips to the mall than other shoppers.[178] And we are also training a generation of couch potatoes; as one exercise physiologist put it, American young people "are dying for some exercise."[179] Commercial television is certainly not to be held responsible for all the afflictions of America's youth, but it figures in any explanation.

Both advertisers and corporate media have also set their sights on expanding externally into the one children's institution that has traditionally remained off-limits to commercialism, schools.[180] The commercialization of education is taking place on several fronts, assisted by the fiscal crisis that has placed many schools, public and private, in dire economic straits. Firms are now paying to have their brands advertised in student textbooks.[181] Fast food, snack, and soft drink firms have launched a successful head-on assault on school cafeterias, where they establish brand identities and make immediate sales as well.[182] By the late 1990s Coca-Cola and Pepsi were locked in a pitched battle to gain contracts to be the exclusive soft drink providers to public schools, using the schools to aggressively promote their product to students.[183] This trend reached the point of absurdity in 1998 when a Georgia high school student was suspended for wearing a Pepsi shirt to school on a day when all students were told to wear Coke shirts for a Coke promotional campaign in which the school was participating.[184]

As a result of its own study, *Business Week* magazine concluded in

1997 that "Corporations are flooding schools with teaching aids — and propaganda."[185] Channel One, an advertising-supported television program for use in schools, is now shown in twelve thousand U.S. schools — some 40 percent of the total number of schools. It bills itself as the leading advertising vehicle to reach "tweens," meaning kids aged nine to fourteen.[186] Major advertisers like Pepsi and Reebok are using Channel One to run promotions with students and to connect their school advertising to their other media activities. In the late 1990s Channel One has become much more aggressive; it now uses teachers and principals in promotional campaigns with major advertisers.[187] In December 1998 Channel One signed a five-year contract with Nielsen Media Research. Nielsen will provide detailed information on Channel One's eight million daily viewers for the firms that pay $200,000 for thirty-second commercials on its program.[188]

The thoroughgoing commercialization of U.S. education is far from complete, and many parents' and teachers' groups continue to oppose it. But the free market political right, led by aging market advocate Milton Friedman, has made the elimination of traditional commercial-free public education the centerpiece of its political agenda for the coming generation.[189] The goal is school vouchers, with public monies paid to private schools. This would almost certainly enhance commercialism at public schools, as their need for money would increase as students take their vouchers to private schools. It would also reduce the role of public education dramatically in the United States, resulting in a tiered educational system, with the best education going to the most accomplished children and, more important, those with the most affluent parents.[190] "We need the same revolution in education that we have had in television and telecommunications," Ralph Reed said in 1998.[191] In the investment community there is already speculation that traditional education as a public service is collapsing, and a hybrid of educational high technology and commercial entertainment will eventually become the primary means of "educating" American kids — as prospective workers and potential consumers. In that case, Disney and the other media giants are poised to capitalize upon the new market.[192]

At any rate, the cultural landscape of the United States is vastly more commercial at the end of the 1990s than it was a generation earlier, and all signs point to further commercial expansion into every nook and cranny of social life. The media giants are not the only participants in this commercial charge; the conversion of traditional high culture, for example, from mostly noncommercial status to the "mega-exhibition, complete with helium-filled hype, souvenir soap and corporate sponsorship," is not the work of the media giants but rather of the major advertisers themselves.[193] As one scholar of high culture concluded, in the 1980s and 1990s "businesses successfully transformed art museums and galleries into their own public-relations vehicles, by taking over the function, and exploiting the social status, that cultural institutions have in our society."[194]

And, indeed, commercialism is not something entirely new; it has been an important theme in the United States throughout its history. But this assertion must be qualified: there is an enormous difference between the degree and nature of commercialism in the United States in, say, 1830 or 1880 or even 1950 or 1970, and what is emerging today. At the dawn of the twenty-first century, the quantitative increase in commercialism may be producing a qualitative change in its role and impact in our society. Along these lines, one of the fastest areas of growth in the 1990s has been the rise of corporate brand licensing — valued at $16 billion in 1997 — where firms lease or use their own trademarks and logos on other unrelated products. The markers of our culture are increasingly those of big business.[195] This should be no surprise, since large corporations and their values so dominate the U.S. economy and polity. It is fitting, then, that GE's NBC found a large market when it decided to market versions of its "Must See TV" slogan to other merchandisers.[196]

Farewell to Journalism

The other side of the coin of commercialization is the decline and marginalization of any public service values among the media, placing the status of notions on nonmarket public service in jeopardy across society. As much as earlier U.S. societies were driven by commerce and profit-seeking, they also tolerated nonprofit and noncommercial institutions and values. In today's hypercommercialized society, on the other hand, the commercial values of maximum profit and sales ballyhoo *über alles* have overwhelmed the vestiges of public service in the media. In chapter 5 I review the decline of U.S. public service broadcasting, and in the next section of this chapter I review the deterioration of Federal Communications Commission (FCC) regulation designed to force commercial broadcasters to provide public service programming. But these attempts at public service in the United States have never amounted to much in any case. In what follows I focus on the one area that traditionally has been regarded as the defining public service of the U.S. media system — its commitment to strong, trustworthy, and reliable journalism.

Journalism has been regarded as a public service by all of the commercial media throughout this century. In particular, commercial broadcasters displayed their public service through the establishment of ample news divisions. These were largely noncommercial during broadcasting's early years and did not become a "profit center" until the 1970s. Historically, journalism is something that newspapers, magazines, broadcasters, and journalism schools regarded as an activity directed toward noncommercial aims that are fundamental to a democracy — aims that could not be bought and sold by powerful interests. Professional journalism was predicated on the notion that its content should not be shaped by the dictates of owners and advertisers, or by the biases of the editors and reporters, but rather by core public service values. For much of the twentieth century the media corporations have brandished their commitment to the high ideals of journalism as their main explanation for why they deserve First Amendment protection and a special place in the political economy.

Of course, in practice, professional journalism has never enjoyed the independence from corporate or commercial pressure suggested by its rhetoric. It did not develop in the early twentieth century as the result of a philosophical effort to improve the caliber of journalism for democracy. To the contrary, professional journalism emerged as a pragmatic response to the commercial limitations of partisan journalism in the new era of chain newspapers, advertising support, and one-newspaper towns. In such an environment, partisanship only antagonized much of the market, upset advertisers, and called into question the entire legitimacy of the news product. As Bagdikian has shown, professional journalism is severely compromised as a democratic agency in numerous ways. To avoid the controversy associated with determining what is a legitimate news story, professional journalism relies upon official sources as the basis for stories. This gives those in positions of power (and the public relations industry, which developed at the exact same time as professional journalism) considerable ability to influence what is covered in the news. Moreover, professional journalism tends to demand "news hooks" — some sort of news event — to justify publication. This means that long-term public issues, like racism or suburban sprawl, tend to fall by the wayside, and there is little emphasis on providing the historical and ideological context necessary to bring public issues to life for readers. Finally, professional journalism internalizes the notion that business is the proper steward of society, so that the stunning combination of ample flattering attention to the affairs of business in the news with a virtual blackout of labor coverage is taken as "natural." In combination these trends have had the effect not only of wiring pro–status quo biases directly into the professional code of conduct but also of keeping journalists blissfully unaware of the compromises with authority they make as they go about their daily rounds.[197] It is far from politically neutral or "objective."

Professional journalism is arguably at its worst when the U.S. upper class — the wealthiest 1 or 2 percent of the population, the owners of most of the productive wealth, as well as the top corporate executives and government officials — is in agreement on an issue. In such cases (for example, the innate right of the United States to invade another nation or the equation of private property and the pursuit of profit with democracy), media will tend to accept the elite position as revealed truth and never subject the notion to questioning. The classic example of this phenomenon today is the virtual blackout of media coverage of the CIA, to be discussed below, and of the military budget. There is no known explanation for the $250–300 billion annual military budget in the post–cold war world and, interestingly, the media never press politicians to provide one. Why is this? Military spending is the one form of government largess that directly harms no notable upper-class interests, while at the same time actively promoting some elite interests. So while the media on occasion will analyze school budgets, public broadcasting proposals, and health care and welfare spending in detail to see if the monies are being spent wisely, there is barely any media examination of the military budget, which is in effect a cash cow for powerful elements of the corporate community.[198] Members of the press, to the extent they even recognize the problem, defend their lack of interest in military spending by noting that the dominant political parties are not debating the matter so therefore it is not a legitimate issue. (So it was in 1999 that the Clinton administration proposed to *increase* the annual military budget by $100 billion over six years to the hearty approval of Republican leaders. The tenor of the press coverage was to emphasize that this was the first *real* increase in the military budget since 1991 — as if that, alone, justified the increase — precisely as the Pentagon, the military-industrial complex, the Clinton administration, and the Republicans wished the issue to be framed.)[199] But such a defense points exactly to the limitations of professional journalism as a democratic force, particularly in a society where commercial forces dominate the political culture.

Professional journalism is arguably at its best, then, when elites disagree on an issue — such as whether a specific U.S. invasion was tactically sound or not — or when the issue does not affect upper-class interests directly (e.g., abortion rights, school prayer, flag burning, gay rights, affirmative action). In some circumstances, too, domestic non-elite constituencies can be so strong, like organized labor, as to have some mitigating effect on elite pressures and the logic of the system. In instances like these, professional journalism has been capable of producing commendable work.[200] After World War II this caliber of professional journalism prospered and developed a certain amount of autonomy from the dictates of owners and advertisers, and from the corporate sector as a whole. At times, this journalism has thrived and produced exemplary coverage. But journalism has always been a struggle, and even in the best of times journalists have had to contend directly and indirectly with powerful corporate, commercial, and government forces that wanted to neuter or corrupt their enterprise. By the 1990s, traditional professional journalism was in marked retreat from its standards of the postwar years, due to the tidal wave of commercial pressure brought on by the corporate media system.

The decline, even collapse, of journalism as a public service is apparent in every facet of the media.[201] For network and national cable television, news has gone from being a loss-leader and a mark of network prestige to being a major producer of network profit. At present, NBC enjoys what is regarded as "the most profitable broadcast news division in the history of television," with annual advertising revenues topping $100 million.[202] NBC is renowned not so much for the quality of its news as for its extraordinary success in squeezing profit from it. NBC uses QNBC, a high-tech statistical service, to analyze its news reports to see exactly how its desired target audience is reacting to different news stories, and to the ads. Its goal is to have a "boundaryless" flow across the program so as to satisfy those paying the bills.[203] Arthur Kent, the NBC correspondent who gained fame for his coverage of the 1990–91 Gulf War, left the network and has published a damning exposé of GE's ongoing efforts to cheapen, degrade, and censor the news. "The people who constitute the conscience of the broadcast news discipline — working journalists — now have less real influence on the daily news agenda than ever before," Kent wrote, "and they face harsh treatment from management if they speak out."[204] In particular, Kent chronicles GE's opposition to NBC News examining any of GE's business operations. This is emerging as a significant problem in the age of conglomerate-controlled journalism. In 1998, Disney-owned ABC News rejected a report by its leading investigative correspondent exposing labor and safety practices at Disney World in Florida. Although ABC News claimed the cancellation was due to factors other than the identity of the subject, the stench of conflict-of-interest could not help but fill the air.[205]

Nor is Kent alone in his assessment. Whereas only ten or fifteen years ago prominent journalists were among the staunchest defenders of the commercial media system, today, in what amounts to almost a sea change, journalists have emerged as among its foremost critics. "Our big corporate owners, infected with the greed that marks the end of the 20th Century, stretch constantly for ever-increasing profit, condemning quality to take the hindmost," observes Walter Cronkite. They are "compromising journalistic integrity in the mad scramble for ratings and circulation."[206] "In any honest appraisal of the state of the press," David Broder, veteran *Washington Post* columnist, noted in a eulogy for journalist Ann Devroy in 1998, "the values that defined Ann Devroy's life are increasingly in jeopardy. Media companies — especially those which are part of mega-corporations — show little respect for that responsibility and professionalism Ann demonstrated every day in her work."[207] Richard Reeves concluded in 1998 that after a decade of corporate concentration and commercialism, the United States could be characterized as being in an era of the End of News. Reeves defined "real news" as what "you and I need to keep our freedom — accurate and timely information on laws and wars, police and politicians, taxes and toxics." As Reeves notes, what has been regarded as good journalism is seen as very bad business by those who rule the media world.[208]

Of course many, perhaps most, working journalists remain dedicated to providing a public service independent of the commercial needs or political aims of their owners and advertisers. And even in the horrid context we are describing some superb journalism is produced. Disney's ESPN, for example, which counts Nike and Reebok among its major advertisers, aired an extraordinary exposé of Asian shoe manufacturing sweatshops in 1998. In November 1998 *Time* ran a magnificent and unprecedented investigative series exposing corporate welfare. CNN and CBS's *60 Minutes* periodically do investigative reports, too, that remind one of what journalism is supposed to be. But regrettably these are the exceptions that go against the trajectory, and most journalists who remain in the commercial news media come to internalize the dominant values if they wish to be successful and to be at peace with themselves.

Indeed, the overriding commercialism of contemporary journalism has been adapted as well by the leading editors and reporters. As James Fallows chronicles in depressing detail in *Breaking the News,* the superstars of journalism are increasingly those who do fairly mindless TV shows, give lectures for exorbitant fees, and generally earn annual incomes approaching seven figures.[209] One almost had to feel sympathy for the CNN correspondent who was reprimanded in 1997 after he did a television commercial as a spokesperson for Visa USA; his role in the commercial had been originally cleared by CNN and it certainly seemed in keeping with the commercial thrust of television journalism. His crime, it would seem, was being caught, or being a small fry.[210] In 1998, recently retired ABC news anchor David Brinkley began doing advertisements for the Archer Daniels Midland corporation that ran on his old *This Week* program.[211] ABC stopped running the spots only after controversy erupted, after having aired them initially so as not to antagonize one of its most important sponsors.[212] (Archer Daniels Midland is the agribusiness firm that had to pay a $100 million fine for price-fixing and that has shown a distinct self-interest in the outcome of environmental, regulatory, and agricultural policy debates.)[213] *Advertising Age* captured the irony of the Brinkley situation: "Journalists have raised the biggest racket about Mr. Brinkley's new job, even as they solicit paid speeches from groups they could be reporting on."[214]

If, as mentioned above, media conglomerates discourage their news divisions from examining their corporate operations, these giants have fewer qualms about using their control over journalism to promote their other media holdings. In 1996, for example, the news story that NBC gave the *most* time to was the Summer Olympics in Atlanta, an event that did not even rank among the top ten stories covered by CBS, ABC, or CNN. What explains NBC's devotion to this story? NBC had the television rights to the Olympics and used its nightly news to pump up the ratings for its prime-time coverage.[215] According to the *New York Times,* "various shows on ABC, now owned by Disney, have devoted a great deal of time to several movies produced by Disney, although the network has maintained in each instance that there was justified journalistic interest in the films."[216]

But the main concern of the media giants is to make journalism directly profitable, and there are a couple of proven ways to do that. First, lay off as many reporters as possible. The corporate news media has been doing this in spurts since the mid-1980s, and several of the network TV news operations made major layoffs again in 1998.[217] Second, concentrate upon stories that are inexpensive and easy to cover, like celebrity lifestyle pieces, court cases, plane crashes, crime stories, and shootouts.[218] Not only are such stories cheaper to cover and air, they hardly ever enmesh the parent corporation in controversy, as do "hard" news stories. Consider network TV news. International news has declined from 45 percent of the network TV news total in the early 1970s to 13.5 percent in 1995. Most of this drop took place in the 1990s after the end of the cold war, but since this was also the period of the rise of the global economy, one might reasonably expect TV's international coverage to remain at earlier levels if not increase.[219] What replaced the expensive international news? The annual number of crime stories on network TV news programs *tripled* from 1990–92 to 1993–96.[220] In one revealing example, CNN addressed a decline in ratings in the summer of 1997 by broadcasting a much-publicized interview with O. J. Simpson.[221]

As bad as this seems, local television news is considerably worse. One recent detailed content analysis of local TV news in fifty-five markets in thirty-five states concludes that local news tends to feature crime and violence, triviality, and celebrity, and that some stations devoted more airtime to commercials than to news.[222] Another detailed study, this time a content analysis of the local news on 102 stations in fifty-two markets on March 11, 1998, reported that 40 percent of the news was "about crime, disaster, war, or terrorism." This was generally visually stimulating material taken inexpensively off a satellite feed that had no public policy implications for local communities. Another 25 percent of the local news was deemed "fluff," including "stories about hair tattoos, beer baths, a dog returning home and a horse rescued from mud in California."[223] In the winter of 1997–98, local TV news programs in Los Angeles turned the airwaves over to the live coverage of several prolonged car chases à la O. J. Simpson, though the significance of the chases seems to have eluded even the broadcast news anchors.[224] As a writer for the *New York Times Magazine* concluded in 1998: "Most anyone in the press and academia who has given it much thought has concluded that while there are exceptions, local television news is atrocious."[225] Besides making it ever more difficult, even impossible, to have an informed citizenry, lame local news can have stark material consequences. A 1998 study of local television news in Baltimore concluded that the extreme focus on crime stories, with a strong racial twist, was an important factor in a declining general perception of the quality of life in Baltimore, leading to business exodus and job loss.[226]

The attack on journalism is every bit as pronounced in the nation's newspapers. Newspaper coverage of international news, for example, declined by an even greater percentage than that of network TV news between the 1970s and 1990s.[227] The concentration of ownership into local monopolies that are part of large national chains gives the media corporations considerable power to reduce the resource commitment to journalism, thus fattening the bottom line. Gannett showed the genius of this approach as it built its empire over the past thirty-five years. Since purchasing the *Des Moines Register* in the 1980s, for example, it has slashed the paper's once-extraordinary coverage of state affairs to the bone.[228] To cut costs, these corporate giants are increasingly using temporary labor to serve as reporters and photographers.[229] In addition, there is implicit pressure on editors and reporters to accept marketing principles and to be "more reader friendly."[230] This means an emphasis upon lifestyle and consumer issues that strongly appeal to sought-after readers and advertisers.[231] "Marketing," one reporter stated in 1997, "these days means spending more time focusing on the things that concern the people who have all the money and who live in the suburbs."[232] A telling indication of this turn came in Detroit, where the city's last full-time labor reporting position at the *Detroit Free Press* was eliminated in 1998, while the newspaper added fifteen new editorial positions in the suburbs.[233] In 1998 the massive Times-Mirror newspaper chain asked three of its most prominent reporters to write portions of its annual report, a task usually assigned to accountants and public relations officials.[234]

In perhaps the most publicized new measure, the Times-Mirror's flagship *Los Angeles Times* in 1997 appointed a business manager to be "general manager for news" and directly oversee the editorial product to ensure that it conformed to the best commercial interests of the newspaper.[235] *Times* publisher Mark Willes informed *Forbes* magazine that he intended to tear down the "Chinese wall between editors and business staffers" with "a Bazooka if necessary." In June 1998 Willes authorized his editorial staff to participate in an unprecedented "Day with the *Los Angeles Times*" sponsored by the local public relations community. This session included having local PR officials learn more about Willes's plans for increasing the editorial-business cooperation at the newspaper and how this could work to their clients' advantage.[236] A sense of what this leads to came in 1998 when Willes wrote a memorandum to his editorial staff saying that the paper could attract more women readers by offering more emotional and less analytical articles. He later apologized for the stereotyping of women, but not for his attitude toward journalism.[237] Investors are wild about Willes and his plans for journalism; "Wall Street has loved Willes from the first," *Forbes* notes.[238] The editor of the trade publication *Advertising Age* applauded Willes's reforms wholeheartedly: "Is it a sin to try to come up with ideas advertisers respond to? Are editorial people selling out when they work with ad people to . . . attract more advertisers? I don't think so; in fact, that's their job."[239] It may say a great deal about the state of journalism that among publishers Willes sometimes is held up as the "liberal" protector of journalism values, in contrast to the CEO of Cowles Media, who argues that newspapers should have no qualms about writing favorable pieces about major advertisers.[240]

What is happening at the prestigious *Los Angeles Times* in fact only makes explicit a growing trend in journalism: the need to serve commercial needs first and foremost. On balance, magazine journalism has had less concern with keeping a formal separation between advertising and editorial content for years; in 1997 the *Wall Street Journal* reported that some major national advertisers demanded to know the contents of specific issues of magazines before they would agree to place ads in them.[241] In the immediate aftermath, reports described numerous other incidents of advertiser scrutiny, implying censorship of magazine editorial content.[242] This caused a public outcry, with magazine editors and publishers formally denouncing the practice.[243]

By the end of the 1990s major magazine publishers like Time Warner and Newhouse's Condé Nast have "corporate marketing departments" whose purpose is to help their magazines work with advertisers so that the magazine becomes "an integral part of the [advertising] message," and to help "advertisers adjust their image in hopes of increasing their sales." The logic is such that major advertisers are increasingly in a position to demand favorable treatment. "Let's be honest," the president of Chanel confessed, "I think you want to support those magazines which — from an editorial point of view — support you."[244] In 1998 both *Time* and *Martha Stewart Living* featured special sections or entire issues with just one advertiser and permitted the advertiser to participate to varying degrees in the editorial planning for the issue.[245] But even if advertisers are not officially vetting the contents of magazines, and even if publishers are not explicitly ordering their editors to serve advertisers first and foremost, the message has been underlined and bold-faced: what editors and reporters do will directly affect both their own and their magazine's fortunes.

Perhaps some sense of the general commercialization of editorial content came in 1998 when Tina Brown quit her position as editor of the *New Yorker,* perhaps the most respected U.S. commercial publication, to go to work on a new magazine and other projects for Disney's Miramax subsidiary. "I feel the kind of movies [Miramax] makes are the kind of journalism we try to do," Brown stated. They "have this incredible gift for making good things commercial." Brown's partner in the new venture is Ron Galotti, former publisher of *Vogue.* Galotti and Brown will produce a magazine explicitly designed to produce synergies, that is, to generate stories that will turn into good TV programs and movies.[246] And the synergies extend to advertisers. As Galotti put it, he and Brown will be able to help major magazine advertisers get their "tentacles into the Hollywood area." "I think clients are looking for out-of-the-box ideas and ways to position products and brand their products." Galotti said that advertisers in Brown's new magazine could look for product placements in Miramax films, among other things. But there is no need to worry, according to Galotti, because "the editorial aspect of the magazine will have no commercial overtone at all."[247] This, then, would seem to be the nature of editorial integrity in the era of commercialized journalism.

There are some who argue that this turn to trivia and fluff masquerading as news is ultimately going to harm the media corporations' profitability. As more and more people realize they no longer have any particular need to read or watch the news, and news is competing with the entire world of entertainment for attention, its readership and audience may simply disappear. Whether that is true or false is impossible to say, but the media corporations, by their actions, have made it clear that they prefer to take their profits now rather than make a lot less money now for a chance at pie-in-the-sky profits far down the road. In fact, it would be highly irrational business conduct for the dominant media firms to approach journalism in any manner other than the way they presently do.

Several incidents surrounding major news stories and journalists in 1998 point to the severe limitations of contemporary journalism as a democratic agency. On the one hand, the corporate sector is increasingly exempt from any sustained critical examination *from a public interest perspective.* (Serious examination of certain aspects of corporate behavior to provide information to the investment community, of course, is one of the main functions of the business press.) In May 1998, for example, the *Cincinnati Enquirer* ran an eighteen-page investigative report on Cincinnati-based Chiquita Brands International that chronicled in detail the unethical and illegal business practices of Chiquita overseas. The factually based story seemed a potential Pulitzer Prize winner. Chiquita, however, determined one of the reporters had gleaned some of the information for the report from illegally obtained voice mail messages and sued the newspaper. The *Enquirer* folded, giving Chiquita $10 million, formally retracting the series, and firing the reporter in question. It is worth reiterating that the truth of the story itself has never been disproven.[248]

This threat of libel is often pointed to as an explanation for commercial media's unwillingness to go after wealthy corporations, and there is an element of truth to this.[249] But this can only partially explain the seeming hostility to the very notion of investigative journalism. A News Corp. station fired two television reporters in December 1997 for refusing to water down and create a misleading impression of their investigative report on Monsanto. The report never aired.[250] And CBS's leading consumer reporter, Roberta Baskin, who was responsible for an acclaimed 1996 exposé of Nike's labor practices in Vietnam, was demoted and stripped of her support staff in 1998. What was her apparent crime? She had protested too loudly when CBS on-camera correspondents wore the Nike logo and Nike gear during the CBS telecasts of the 1998 Winter Olympics, for which Nike was a major sponsor.[251]

On the other hand, in 1998 the corporate news media faced — and failed — their moment of truth with regard to how they cover those government agencies that primarily serve elite interests — the CIA and the military. This is not a new development, as I noted above, and the media have had a distinct double standard as they investigate the affairs of state. Those government activities that serve primarily the poor or the middle class (e.g., welfare and public education) are often subject to close scrutiny, whereas those operations that serve some powerful interests and harm others can also receive vigorous coverage (e.g., tobacco subsidies and regulations against smoking). But intelligence, foreign policy, and military operations are conducted primarily to serve the needs of the elite, and while some powerful interests may not benefit as much as others, none are penalized by these activities and all benefit from having the government commissioned to act in defense of corporate power abroad. The extent of the debate on these issues historically has reflected the extent to which the elite itself was split over specific military actions, such as the Vietnam War after 1967 or 1968. During the cold war this clear double standard that journalists applied toward different types of government activities was justified — for better or, in my opinion, for worse — on grounds of national security. It was fueled by an intense anti-Communism that made it "natural" to apply vastly different standards to the U.S. government and its official enemies. But since the demise of the communist "threat," this justification for treating with kid gloves what some call the national security state has evaporated. It was only a matter of time until some principled mainstream journalists began applying the same standards to the CIA and the military that they were encouraged to apply to welfare spending and onerous business regulations.

That moment came in 1996 when the *San Jose Mercury News* ran Gary Webb's exposé on the CIA's connection to drug dealing in U.S. inner cities. The balance of the media ignored the story, until pressure from the African-American community forced a response. The main gatekeepers — the *New York Times, Washington Post,* and *Los Angeles Times* — all published attacks on the *Mercury News* story. After all, if a story like this was true, it called into question the entire "free press" that had been asleep at the switch for decades while all of this was going on. Finally, the *Mercury News* published a retraction for the story and Webb was demoted and ultimately forced to leave the paper. What received little attention, however, was that extensive subsequent research effectively supported the thrust of Webb's allegations, and, indeed, suggested they were only the tip of the iceberg.[252] Moreover, due to pressure from the congressional Black Caucus, the CIA agreed to do an internal investigation of Webb's charges. The in-house report did not disprove and, indeed, effectively supported Webb's claims, acknowledging that the CIA had relations with drug dealers throughout the 1980s. Yet, aside from brief mention, the matter was ignored in toto in the commercial news media.[253]

Another 1998 incident also reveals this trend. In June Time Warner's CNN formally retracted an investigative story it had run concerning the possible use of sarin, a nerve gas, by the U.S. military on deserters in the Vietnam War. Although the exact truth of the story has yet to be determined, what was striking was how quickly the CNN executives folded to pressure from the military-industrial complex. A story that took nearly a year to produce, was reviewed by scores of CNN officials along the way before being broadcast, and was the work of several of CNN's most respected and experienced producers was shot down in two weeks without the producers having a bona fide chance to defend themselves. The producers, April Oliver and Jack Smith, refused to resign, insisting on the report's truth, and were fired.[254] As *The Times of India* noted, the incident "raises troubling questions about press freedom" in the United States. "While U.S. journalists routinely speculate about the crimes of other governments on the flimsiest of evidence, they are evidently not free to point fingers at their own."[255]

There is no reason to believe the corporate news media will reverse course and begin directing journalism toward corporate or national security state activities. In fact, the way these examples from 1998 played out — with journalists fired, demoted, or pressured into resignation in every case — almost assures that few journalists will venture down this path in the future. This is the classical "chilling effect," much talked about in First Amendment law when the issue is government, not corporate, intervention in the affairs of the press. Journalists who wish to do investigations of corporations or the national security state will have to use all their leverage and then some to get clearance from their bosses, while they will build up their leverage by doing the tried-and-true formula pieces that cost little, mesh well with the commercial aims of the news operation, and do not antagonize elite interests. Over time, successful journalists simply internalize the idea that it is goofy and "unprofessional" to want to pursue these controversial stories that cause mostly headaches.[256] In addition, journalists will find it ever more difficult to get the go-ahead for these types of stories from their editors and bosses. Time Warner's largest shareholder, Ted Turner, insisted that the CNN story lacked "evidence to convict."[257] In the future, it would seem, prospective stories on the military and intelligence agencies (or powerful corporations that have the resources to make a counteroffensive) will require "evidence to convict" before they are even *opened* to journalistic examination, a preposterous standard. "By this standard," April Oliver noted, "there would have been no Watergate."[258]

The 1998 incidents also highlight something perhaps even more insidious, the lack of any follow-up for critical investigative journalism. For journalism to be effective, a single reporter or story cannot be the extent of treatment of an issue. The initial report can only open up an area of inquiry, into which some other journalists must pour their attention, unleashing a very healthy journalistic competition. A good example of how it can work was in Watergate, where several top journalists followed up the *Washington Post* revelations with their own important exposés. In all of the above episodes, however, there was no follow-up, no echo, so the stories floundered while the journalists were flame-broiled. This is now pretty much standard operating procedure in journalism toward controversial investigative reporting, especially when the target is a powerful corporation. Former *Washington Post* reporter Norman Mintz counted *five* major news stories that were published about corporate malfeasance in the summer of 1998, but he noted that the stories were rarely reprinted in other media, especially the elite media, and certainly not investigated any further. The stories died on the vine.[259] Moreover, in 1998 journalists themselves, like Howard Kurtz of the *Washington Post,* emerged as the primary attackers of journalists like Webb, Oliver, and Smith. "Aggressive reporting always has been risky business, but most disgusting about recent assaults are not the predictable onslaughts of corporate lawyers," one observer noted, "but the venom with which other journalists have turned on their colleagues." As Daniel Schorr put it, "Attack a government agency like the CIA, or a Fortune 500 member like Chiquita, or the conduct of the military in Southeast Asia and you find yourself in deep trouble, naked, and often alone."[260] In sum, time-consuming and expensive investigative journalism looking into subjects that raise any questions about the ultimate legitimacy of our ruling institutions is not welcome in the domain of corporate media and the professional journalism it spawns.

But the drift of journalism to a more explicitly procorporate position is only partially determined by the institutional factors discussed heretofore. It also reflects the rightward movement in elite and mainstream political culture over the past two decades. As commercial journalism almost always stays within the parameter of mainstream opinion, the tenor of journalism has become less conciliatory toward ideas critical of capitalism and the "free market" and less receptive of ideas laudatory of social spending, poor people's social movements, and regulation of business. I do not wish to exaggerate the range of mainstream or journalist opinion prior to, say, the 1980s — even at its best journalism has been fundamentally flawed as a democratic institution — but nonetheless there has been a notable shift. This rightward drift in the political culture is largely due to broad factors, not the least of which is the aggressive right-wing campaign to tame and direct ideological discourse since the mid-1970s. And, of course, a media system more closely tuned in to the greatness of the "free market" and the notion that all deviations from the market are dubious at best serves to reinforce the probusiness thrust of our times.

The evidence of the rightward bias is compelling. Studies of the sources and guests used on mainstream news programs like *Nightline* or the *MacNeil-Lehrer News Hour* show a heavy bias toward conservatives, with scarcely anyone who would have qualified as a liberal in the 1960s or 1970s, let alone the 1940s.[261] Some of the corporate media owners maintain their journalism holdings not merely to make profit but also to promote their probusiness, antilabor view of the world. Rupert Murdoch, for example, is an outspoken proponent of the view that the main problems with the world are the prevalence of taxation on business and the wealthy, the regulation of business, government bureaucrats, and labor unions.[262] He willingly subsidizes the right-wing *Weekly Standard* to see that those views get a constant plug before the political elite. As Liberty Media (and former TCI) CEO John Malone stated, Murdoch would be willing to keep his Fox News Channel on the air even if it was not profitable because Murdoch wants "the political leverage he can get out of being a major network."[263] Both Murdoch and Malone are board members of the Cato Institute, one of the leading right-wing probusiness think tanks in Washington, instrumental in advancing deregulation and privatization policies.[264] "It is curious," the famous graphic designer Milton Glaser wrote in 1997, "that after the triumph of capitalism, American business is embracing the politburo practice of censoring ideas it deems unacceptable."[265]

The Quashing of Public Debate

Allowing the deterioration of journalism and broader media culture makes perfect sense for media owners, but the degree to which it has been enacted reflects also the absence of organized and coherent public protest about these trends. Until media owners feel some political heat, they have little reason to alter course. As it is, the dominant mood in the United States is one of resignation and demoralization, not only about media but about other political issues as well. Even among those who deplore corporate concentration and conglomeration, hypercommercialism, and the decline of public service and journalism, and who regard the social and political implications of these trends as extremely negative, there is a fatalistic sense that this is the way it must be. After all, the United States is, always has been, and always will be a business-run society.

But this is not necessarily so. In fact, the nature of the U.S. media system is the result of a series of *political* decisions, not natural law or holy mandate. Even when media are regulated preponderantly by markets, it remains, in the end, a *political* decision to turn them over to a relative handful of individuals and corporations to maximize profit. The U.S. media system of the late twentieth century looks substantially different from the media system of the late nineteenth century, and it is diametrically opposed to the press system of the Republic's first two generations. All modern U.S. media (including the advertising industry) are affected directly and indirectly by government policies, regulation, and subsidies. Specifically, the development of radio and television broadcasting has been and remains the province of the political system. At any time the American people might have chosen to establish a truly nonprofit and noncommercial radio and television system; they have always had the constitutional right to do so.[266] The seminal law for U.S. broadcasting was the Communications Act of 1934; it was only recently superseded by the Telecommunications Act of 1996.

What is most notable about media policy making in the United States is not that it is important and that it exists, but, rather, that virtually the entire American population has no idea that it exists and that they have a right to participate in it. In 1934, for example, there was considerable opposition to corporate commercial domination of radio broadcasting, but those who led the opposition had barely any influence on legislative or regulatory issues in Washington. In fact, the striking feature of U.S. media policy making is how singularly undemocratic it has been — and remains. Crucial decisions are made by the few for the few behind closed doors. Public participation has been minuscule, virtually nonexistent.[267]

This was not an accident — not in the 1930s, and not since. The primary reason for this lack of public debate has been that the media and communication industries covered by these laws have unusually powerful lobbies that effectively control the debate and impose boundaries on the "legitimate" range of discussion. The commercial broadcasters, as represented by the National Association of Broadcasters (NAB), have been a powerhouse since the 1930s and are stronger than ever today. The NAB's lobbying team is so immense, it is barely noticed that it includes Kimberly Tauzin, daughter of Rep. Billy Tauzin (Rep., La.), chair of the crucial House Telecommunications Subcommittee.[268] The most important commercial broadcasters are now part of the giant media conglomerates like GE, Time Warner, Disney, and News Corporation, which each have their own lobbying machines. The *Wall Street Journal* calls the commercial broadcasters the "most powerful lobby in Washington," and most other analysts place broadcasters in the top tier of influence.[269] Likewise, the other main communication industry trade associations are also Capitol Hill lobbying powerhouses.[270]

A look at Rupert Murdoch's Washington, D.C., lobby provides concrete evidence of the corporate media's political power. Murdoch's lobby had a budget of $800,000 for the first half of 1997 alone. It is directed by Peggy Binzel, who had worked previously for Rep. Jack Fields, then the chair of the House Telecommunications Subcommittee, which handles the relevant legislation. Binzel has several staffers, including Maureen O'Connell, a former special counsel at the FCC. Murdoch also hired Daren Benzi for his lobbying team. Benzi is a close personal friend of recently retired FCC commissioner James Quello, the man who at all times championed the interests of both News Corporation and the commercial broadcasters during his stint of "public service." The list of Murdoch's lobbyists goes on and on, seeming to include a who's who of influential lobbyists on Capitol Hill. In 1998, when Murdoch's efforts to become a part of the Primestar satellite TV operation were being stymied by the Justice Department, he deployed ten lobbyists to work full-time on the matter. To top it off, Murdoch is a generous campaign contributor. He gave nearly $1 million in "soft money" donations between 1991 and mid-1997, all but $75,000 going to the Republicans. But while Murdoch is an outspoken right-winger, he will do what is necessary to get his way. In November 1997 Murdoch wrote two checks for $25,000, one for the Republican Party and one for the Democrats.[271] And Murdoch is not alone; all the other media and communication giants have similar lobbying arsenals.[272]

The NAB and the other corporate media lobbies are so strong not merely because they are rich and give lots of money to politicians' campaigns, though they are and they do. Far more importantly, the corporate media control news and access to the media — something politicians respect even more than money. This also means the media are in the enviable position of being able to cover political debates over their own existence. Consequently, ideas critical of corporate or commercial domination of the media are basically verboten in the commercial news media, and discussions of key laws and regulations are restricted to the business pages and the trade press, where they are regarded as issues of importance to investors, not as public issues of importance to citizens. The last thing the NAB or the corporate media want is for the American people to get the crazy idea that they have a right to create whatever type of broadcasting or media system they desire.

The corporate media also aggressively subsidize a continuing public relations offensive to promote the view that they are the natural democratic stewards of the airwaves and the media, selflessly "giving the people what they want" and battling to protect the First Amendment.[273] The extent to which this mythology is accepted or internalized by academics, journalists, "liberals," "progressives," politicians of all stripes, and the public at large is the extent to which public debate about communication policy making will be nonexistent or tangential.

This does not mean that the NAB or the corporate media always get their way; it only means they get their way when their conflict is with the general public. Otherwise, the media lobbies sometimes battle with each other and sometimes with other powerful communication lobbies. Indeed, were the media and communication corporations battles only with the general public, their massive lobbies would be absurdly unnecessary. The deliberations leading up to the passage of the Telecommunications Act of 1996 featured battles between long distance carriers and local telephone companies and between cable and satellite broadcasters, to mention just a couple. Since 1996 these sectors are squaring off before the FCC and the Justice Department; they have serious conflicts as they struggle to obtain the most favorable regulations in their related enterprises. For the public, these struggles are not inconsequential. But it is almost an iron law of modern politics that when the media and communication lobbies march in lockstep, or when there is no clear opposition to one of their pet projects, they are very difficult to defeat. Whatever their disagreements, the one thing they all agree upon is that the corporate sector should rule U.S. media and communication to maximize profit — and that this precept should not be the subject of debate by Congress or the general public.

Nor does this mean that dissatisfaction with the effects of corporate commercial control over media, especially broadcasting, is altogether eliminated. But the discontent is reined in and neutered, consigned to being the province of a largely ineffectual "consumer" special interest group. In that capacity, citizens on rare occasions can have some impact protesting the worst abuses of monopolistic media power, as in 1992 when Congress passed a law limiting the ability of cable companies to jack up their rates. But such successes happen rarely, and are fairly easy for powerful lobbies to circumvent over time. As two industry observers put it, the cable industry finds "ways to thwart Congress's will."[274] By 1998 cable rates were increasing at four times the rate of inflation, causing Congress to rattle its sabers and grumble about such direct and undisguised monopolistic attacks upon voters' wallets. But in the end Congress produced "a lot of smoke and not much fire."[275] (It should be noted that Congress usually pays more attention to such inequities during election years.)[276] At no time, however, are citizens invited to ponder an issue like cable television, for example, from the perspective of being citizens rather than mere couch potatoes.

There have long been numerous organized "public interest" groups working to weigh in on the public's behalf — as citizens, not just as consumers — and to influence media legislation and regulation in Washington. In order to be taken seriously by legislators and regulators, these groups are compelled to accept the corporate system as it is, immutable and all-powerful. Then, and only then, may they seek what a liberal at the FCC termed "market friendly" reforms. "Market friendly" is a euphemism for a reform that will not hurt a firm's bottom line in any appreciable manner, with all that that suggests about the range of possibilities. There is tremendous pressure on these consumer groups to be regarded as "legitimate" and "realistic"; if they are not, they will instead be seen as ineffectual and therefore lose their institutional and foundation funding. And as these inside-the-beltway reformers gravitate to minor and largely inconsequential "market friendly" reform proposals, any hope of inspiring popular enthusiasm and widespread support for media reform is sacrificed. If these are the "solutions," a citizen would be right to conclude, this must not be much of a problem. But dealing with the citizenry is not much of a concern for these reformers, as they receive virtually no press coverage and have negligible support among the general population, which is largely unaware of their existence.

In the 1960s and 1970s these public interest activities achieved a modicum of success. By the 1990s, however, with the advent of the free market theology as reigning civic religion and the collapse of even moderately progressive politics, they have less leverage than ever before. Their only hope for success is to pick the strongest side in a conflict between corporate communication sectors or firms, hoping thereby to get a few crumbs tossed their way from the victor. So it was in 1998 that civil rights and media activists worked with Rupert Murdoch on his proposal to let his Fox group increase the percentage of the nation its television stations cover to 45 percent, above the legal limit of 35 percent. Maintaining a strict 35 percent maximum coverage level for television station owners is actually endorsed by the NAB, since all but the five or six giants who are at the 35 percent level would find it ever more difficult to compete with the giants were they permitted to grow even larger. In exchange for getting this concession by the FCC, Murdoch would donate up to $150 million to a fund that would support minority investment in broadcast stations.[277] That media reformers are reduced to this level is in many respects tragic, because some of these groups, like the Media Access Project and the Citizens for Media Education, are run by very smart, talented, and dedicated democratic activists.

With all this in mind, the bankruptcy of U.S. regulation of commercial broadcasting makes perfect sense. In theory, commercial broadcasters receive their access to the publicly owned spectrum at no charge because they provide a public service, namely, they do things that they would not do if they were solely interested in maximizing profit. And broadcast regulation can provide an important way for a nation to establish public service values in the commercial portion of the broadcast system. The operating logic has been that for-profit broadcasters supported by advertising will tend to concentrate on light entertainment fare regardless of the social value. Since broadcasting plays such a dominant role in a nation's media culture, and since broadcasters are licensed to use scarce channels, the public has a right to demand that commercial broadcasters do that which is socially valuable but would not be commercially attractive otherwise. Perhaps the best example of effective public regulation of commercial broadcasters has been in Britain, where until recently the commercial broadcasters were held to standards similar to those of the BBC. Some observers argue that at times the British commercial broadcasters were in fact providing a superior public service to the BBC.

U.S. broadcast regulation has never been even close to the British standard. Very early in the FCC's existence, it internalized the notion that it had to assure the profitability of the industry it was regulating before it could make public service demands; such a dynamic meant that public service demands were by definition limited and easily undermined or quashed by the commercial interests. This process was encouraged by the extraordinary political and economic power of the commercial broadcasters. As such, the regulation of the U.S. broadcasting industry has been an abject failure. In many respects the FCC has become the classic example of what is called the "captive" regulatory agency. FCC members and officials sometimes come from the commercial broadcasting industry and often go there for lucrative employment after their stints in "public service."

This is hardly some sort of conspiracy. Periodically, a maverick gets on the FCC who might want to press the issue of public service. Usually even the mavericks are harmless enough and are permitted to blow off enough steam to get a job teaching at a university once their FCC stint is completed, like 1960s rebel Nicholas Johnson. Sometimes they actually propose a public service requirement that might appreciably affect the bottom line. In cases like these, the broadcasters can use their leverage with key members of Congress to force the maverick to back down and to leave controversial matters to "elected officials," even though the reforms are invariably within the letter and spirit of the law. In 1994, for example, a proposed FCC investigation into Rupert Murdoch's broadcast empire was dropped when Murdoch's good friend Rep. Jack Fields, the ranking Republican on the relevant House committee, threatened to conduct a "top-to-bottom review" of the FCC if it proceeded with its investigation.[278] Most recently, sparks flew when new FCC chair William Kennard had the temerity to suggest that commercial broadcasters should be required to provide free airtime for political candidates. With U.S. electoral politics wallowing in an almost universally recognized spending crisis that tends to limit involvement to the super-rich and those who represent the super-rich, Kennard argued that it was absurd for candidates to have to pay for TV commercials — some $500 million in 1998 — to commercial broadcasters to have access to the public airwaves.[279] Kennard backed down from this attack on the broadcast industry's biannual cash cow when members of Congress told the FCC to do so or face full hearings on whether the FCC deserves to remain in existence.[280] Likewise, when Kennard suggested that the FCC might want to roll back some of its own mandated deregulation that had permitted concentrated radio and TV station ownership, the NAB's friends on Capitol Hill announced that it might be time again for congressional hearings on whether the FCC was "overstepping its bounds."[281]

For the most part, then, the FCC's notion of regulation owes more to its support of the commercial interests than to its being the public's watchdog of their activities. The commercial broadcasters have become de facto owners of the public airwaves, and challenges to broadcast licenses on the grounds that a commercial broadcaster has failed to provide a public service are virtually impossible to win. In 1998, for example, the FCC rejected a license challenge in Denver, despite evidence that the Denver stations had provided appalling trivia and violence-laden news, with virtually no local public affairs coverage.[282] If there is no viable threat that a station-owner might lose its license if it fails to provide a public service, or if such failure is not otherwise severely punished, there can be no meaningful enforcement standards for public service on commercial broadcasters.

Yet even in this barren landscape there has been a clear devolution of how commercial broadcasters can fulfill their commitment to public service. In the 1920s, for example, it was widely accepted that radio broadcasting could not provide a public service at all if its primary means of support came through advertising.[283] When the Communications Act of 1934 was passed, creating the FCC, commercial broadcasters fulfilled their public service obligations with what were called "sustaining" programs, meaning shows that had no advertisers. At one time, sustaining shows occupied as much as 40 percent of the schedule (most of it during periods which advertisers expressed no interest in purchasing). When advertisers finally came to purchase the entire day, public service programming "ghettos" were established — late at night and very early in the morning, and especially on weekends. The quality of these programs tended to be so deplorable that hardly anyone could advocate their continuation, and commercial broadcasters were able to have the regulations relaxed. Even more importantly, they were able gain approval for the idea that public service programs could include advertising.

By the 1990s, public service on commercial television had been reduced to the occasional do-gooder public service announcement (PSA) from the Advertising Council, a public relations group underwritten by the advertising industry. And even here, the commercial broadcasters have fought to limit their commitment to what has remained of public service. In 1997 the NAB argued that its members could run fewer PSAs because they were running so many commercial advertisements with public service messages, like Budweiser's "Know When to Say When" campaign.[284] That same year the commercial networks insisted that the Advertising Council tailor spots that would feature each network's stars, so the PSAs would promote not only safe sex or moderate drinking but also the network's upcoming shows. At first the Advertising Council protested this distortion of public service, but eventually it caved in.[285] "We're going backwards in terms of media opportunity," Ruth Wooden, the Ad Council president, stated in 1998. In addition to promoting media fare in Ad Council PSAs, Wooden has begun to link nonprofit groups to corporate marketers, so advertisers will sponsor PSAs for nonprofit groups and causes. These PSAs will, of course, also mention the corporate sponsor. "Good nonprofits have great credibility and ruboff value" for advertisers, Wooden enthuses. "Talk about brands!"[286] Notions of public service in U.S. commercial broadcasting may have never been sublime, but by now they have certainly become ridiculous.

The plight of U.S. public interest media lobbyists becomes even clearer when one looks at what has now come to constitute a "victory" for them. In 1998, U.S. television sets began to be equipped with "V-chips," so that parents could ostensibly block out sexual and violent fare from their children, or themselves.[287] A similar reform, following congressional pressure, has been to have music CDs rated for the nature of their content and to have television programs rated on-screen to alert viewers to the nature of the content, like the film rating system used for decades. As Professor George Gerbner, one of the leading communication scholars of the late twentieth century, commented, "the movie style rating system is an uninformative scheme that deceives the public and protects the industry from parents rather than the other way around." Gerbner, who attended the TV industry meetings with educators to determine a ratings format in 1997 and 1998, saw the meetings as little more than a public relations ruse. The ratings system, he wrote, was "patched up and rammed down the public's throat."[288] In all these reforms the corporate control and commercial marination of the industry is sacrosanct; the onus falls on "consumers" to avoid the lousy shows. As Gerbner points out, the amounts of violence and of alcohol advertising will not be lessened. What cannot be broached, however, is why do we have a media system that produces so little of value and so much that is garbage?

Perhaps the greatest recent victory of the inside-the-beltway media public interest lobbyists came in 1996 when, after years of lobbying in one form or another, the FCC instituted a new policy whereby commercial television networks were required to begin doing three hours of children's educational programming per week, starting in September 1997. This sounds like a dramatic gain, until one realizes that these three hours of kids' TV are advertising-supported and determined by the same business minds that created the current monstrosity that is commercial children's television. Those conditions were nonnegotiable from the get-go. The *Wall Street Journal* observed that many advertising agencies regarded the deal for "educational" children's television as providing a "marketing bonanza" for Madison Avenue, which is always on the lookout for new ways to round up the "littlest consumers." One advertiser targeting the children's market enthused that the FCC's educational TV requirement would mean that "advertisers will take a bigger role in co-producing TV shows."[289]

The early returns on the FCC's new educational kids' deal range from proponents claiming it makes the best of a bad situation to critics who view it as an outright farce. CBS, for example, simply informed all of its children's shows that they were now "educational" programs. "Weird" Al Yankovic expressed surprise, for example, when notified that his program qualified as meeting the CBS educational standards.[290] The striking tendency has been to co-promote "educational" programs with commercial partners, who use the shows as a means to "brand" with the youth market.[291] Two of the most publicized shows established to meet the new "educational" requirement, for example, are *The Sports Illustrated for Kids Show* and Home Depot's *Homer's Workshop*. Both of these were thinly veiled efforts to establish brand names on youth television under the false colors of "public service."[292] Fox's solution to the problem was to purchase *The Magic School Bus* (an award-winning series) from PBS. Now the school bus travels with a full complement of commercial advertisements.[293] "Despite the three-hour rule," the Children's Television Workshop CEO noted in 1998, "we don't see a lot of heavy demand [by broadcasters] for real educational programming."[294] Indeed, in 1998 the Annenberg Public Policy Center's third annual assessment of children's programming concluded that, despite the FCC three-hour rule, the educational quality of children's TV shows continues to decline.[295]

Although the communication lobbies have successfully neutered any and all political challenges to their control over broadcasting and the media, the legislative process makes it impossible to keep the public entirely shut out. During those rare instances in which Congress is considering legislation for the overall regulation of broadcasting and communication, it is customary that there be congressional committee hearings on what the public interest is and how it might be served by the proposed legislation. Hence in 1934 and again in the mid-1990s the great fear of the NAB was that these hearings might generate publicity and provoke formerly uninterested Americans into a newfound interest in media policy. The industry's goal on both occasions was to push to get the laws passed without any congressional debate, leaving the "controversial" matters to be discussed behind closed doors at the FCC or some other toothless advisory body — in other words, out of the "glare" of public attention.

In 1934, as I discuss in chapter 4, there was an organized campaign to have a significant sector (25 percent) of U.S. radio broadcasting channels turned over to nonprofit organizations. The NAB managed to get the relevant congressional committee to reject the idea of discussing the matter itself and, instead, to authorize the new

FCC to hold advisory hearings after the law had been passed. Two of the three FCC members responsible for the hearings told the NAB in advance that there was no way they would approve the idea. The hearings were held without any publicity in the autumn of 1934 and were flooded with material generated by the NAB. Some of the most principled activists for public service broadcasting refused to participate, or else made token appearances simply so they could protest the kangaroo court nature of the proceedings. Afterwards — to no one's surprise — the FCC reported that commercial broadcasting was doing a superior job of meeting the public interest and that nonprofit broadcasting was unnecessary.[296]

It will seem tragic or comical, depending upon one's mood and perspective, that these sham hearings of 1934 were *the only instance of a formal public deliberation on the matter of who should own and control broadcasting in the United States and for what purpose it should be conducted.* This is a "deliberative process" worthy of the old Soviet Union or the type of corrupt police state exemplified by Suharto's Indonesia or Mobutu's Zaire.

In 1996 there was nowhere near the organized opposition to corporate commercial broadcasting that existed in 1934, but the NAB wanted to leave nothing to chance. Just as the emergence of radio broadcasting had demanded a new federal code, so now the emergence of digital technologies necessitated a new statute to accommodate the convergence of communication industries. Once momentum built for a new law by the early and middle 1990s, each of the corporate sectors wanted to get the best deal it could, but none wanted the law to linger in Congress, risking public notice. Just weeks before the law was passed, most observers predicted that due to severe fights between the various corporate interests, it would be impossible to get the bill through. But the communication lobbies all decided to bury the hatchet, and they pushed the law through at breakneck speed. The last thing the communication corporations would want was to have this remain a live issue through a presidential election, especially with a gadfly like Ross Perot capable of piping up about the type of corporate welfare and special-interest politics this law exemplified. In the 1992 presidential campaign, Perot had thrown a monkey wrench into the best-laid bipartisan plans to sneak NAFTA and GATT through Congress by raising a stink about the issue.

The wording of the Telecommunications Act of 1996 is accordingly void of detail on many issues, for these are matters to be determined down the road by the FCC and others. The core premise of the bill was to eliminate restrictions on firms moving into other communication areas — for example, phone companies moving into cable television and vice versa, or long distance phone companies moving into local service and vice versa — and then to eliminate as many regulations as possible on these firms' behavior. A few crumbs were tossed to "special interest" groups like schools and hospitals, but only when they didn't interfere with the probusiness thrust of the legislation.

Proponents of the Telecommunications Act promised that deregulation would lead to genuine market competition, the result being much better service and lower prices. Market forces would serve the consumer where regulation had failed. The notion that the bill had something to do with encouraging actual competition was of course a public relations ploy designed to mask the nature of capitalism and conceal how these markets actually work. Had this bill been structured to establish competitive industries, the corporate communication lobbyists who pushed for the bill — and who, it is rumored, actually wrote portions of it — would have never let it see the light of day. There may well be some increased competition as a result of the law in some markets; but the end result will certainly be tightly controlled oligopolistic markets. No sane firm would ever make a multibillion dollar investment to enter a new area unless it thought the result would be that it would be a member in good standing in a mature oligopoly with high barriers to entry to protect the firm's and the industry's profitability. Indeed, when more than a few firms look like viable players in communication markets, Wall Street ordinarily calls for a "shakeout" to establish a more profitable semimonopolistic market.[297]

Unless they think they are operating from a position of such strength that they can deliver punishing blows to the competition, the most rational move for these firms when considering new markets is to merge and/or to establish joint ventures. They thereby sacrifice some potential market share, but they seriously reduce risk and competition. Thus the precepts of the Robber Barons live on. In the immortal words of Rupert Murdoch, "We can join forces now, or we can kill each other and then join forces."[298] And the relaxation of restrictions on ownership in the Telecommunications Act — ostensibly to encourage competition — has led instead to a massive wave of corporate consolidation throughout the communication industries. "The urge to merge," the *Wall Street Journal* noted in its 1998 evaluation of the Telecommunications Act, "has overwhelmed the compulsion to compete."[299] There are now four regional telephone companies instead of the seven Baby Bells of pre–Telecom Act days. MCI was sold to WorldCom and the trend in telecommunications is toward more mergers, acquisitions, and market concentration. And so on.

The effects of the Telecommunications Act on media were evident in the discussion of the contemporary media market earlier in the chapter. "The 1996 Telecommunications Act," the *Economist* notes with understatement, "has served the media companies well."[300] One trade publication observes that the Telecommunications Act of 1996 has "fueled a consolidation so profound that even insiders are surprised by its magnitude."[301]

The one media sector most thoroughly overturned by the Telecommunications Act has been radio broadcasting. The Telecommunications Act relaxed ownership restrictions so that a single firm can own up to eight stations in a single market. In the twenty months following enactment of the new law, there has been the equivalent of an Oklahoma land rush as small chains have been acquired by middle-sized chains, and middle-sized chains have been gobbled up by the few massive giants who have come to dominate the national industry. Since 1996 some one-half of the nation's eleven thousand radio stations changed hands, and there were over one thousand radio firm mergers.[302]

Deregulation has made it possible for giant radio firms to establish "superopolies" that control enough of a market to compete with television and newspapers for advertisers.[303] This sort of consolidation also permits the giant chains to reduce labor costs by "down-sizing" their editorial and sales staffs and coordinating programming from national headquarters. According to *Advertising Age,* by September 1997 in each of the fifty largest markets, three firms controlled over 50 percent of the radio ad revenues. And in twenty-three of the top fifty markets, three companies controlled more than 80 percent of the ad revenues.[304] In each of the thirty largest U.S. markets, the largest radio-station-owning firm controls around 40 percent of the radio revenues.[305] Four rapidly growing chains, including Hicks Muse, account for over 33 percent of the industry's almost $14 billion in annual revenues.[306] CBS, formerly Westinghouse, ranks as one of the four national leaders with 175 stations, predominantly in the fifteen largest markets, where it has "maxed out" to the new legal limit.[307] As the *Wall Street Journal* puts it, these deals "have given a handful of companies a lock on the airwaves in the nation's big cities."[308]

When one ponders these developments in radio, the implications for media of the Telecommunications Act of 1996 become more starkly evident. Relative to television and other media technologies, radio is inexpensive for both broadcasters and consumers. It is also ideally suited for local control and community service. Yet radio has been transformed into a engine for superprofits — with greater returns than any other media sector — for a small handful of firms so that they can convert radio broadcasting into the most efficient conduit possible for advertising. As one Wall Street analyst put it, "we're not sure what radio could do for an encore." Another called the 1998 U.S. radio industry "the best of all worlds today." Yet another Wall Street analyst enthused, "Nobody knows how big these companies can get. That plays very well [on Wall Street]."[309] Across the nation, these giant chains use their market power to slash costs, providing the same handful of formats with only a token nod to the actual localities in which the stations broadcast. On Wall Street, the corporate consolidation of radio is praised as a smash success, but by any other standard this brave new world is an abject failure.[310]

And worse may be on the way. One leading "industry guru" predicted early in 1998 that a similar consolidation would soon take place in TV station ownership, as the FCC extends the relaxation of ownership restrictions in accord with the 1996 Telecommunications Act.[311] The leading station-owning company not associated with a network — the Sinclair broadcast group — plans to more than double its number of stations to over one hundred by 2000. Like the new radio giants, Sinclair's recipe for profit is slashing costs to the bone and giving the advertisers what they want.[312] One media researcher projects that the number of TV station owners will fall from 658 in 1994 to around one hundred by 2000 or 2001. And, as in radio, a small handful, all but one or two owned by first-tier media giants, will dominate the twenty-five to fifty largest markets.[313]

Conclusion

The clear trajectory of our media and communication world tends toward ever-greater corporate concentration, media conglomeration, and hypercommercialism. The notion of public service — that there should be some motive for media other than profit — is in rapid retreat if not total collapse. The public is regarded not as a democratic polity but simply as a mass of consumers. Public debate over the future of media and communication has been effectively eliminated by powerful and arrogant corporate media, which metaphorically floss their teeth with politicians' underpants. It is, in short, a system set up to serve the needs of a handful of wealthy investors, corporate managers, and corporate advertisers. Its most important customers are affluent consumers hailing from the upper and upper-middle classes. The system serves the general public to the extent that it strengthens and does not undermine these primary relationships. Needless to say, the implications for democracy of this concentrated, conglomerated, and hypercommercialized media are entirely negative. By the logic of my argument, the solution to the current problem of U.S. media demands political debate and structural reform. But before we turn to that topic there is much else to discuss.

CHAPTER 2

THE
MEDIA
SYSTEM
GOES
GLOBAL

By the end of the 1990s a major turning point was reached in the realm of media. Whereas media systems had been primarily *national* before the 1990s, a *global* commercial media market has emerged full force by the dawn of the twenty-first century. "What you are seeing," states Christopher Dixon, director of media research for the stockbroker PaineWebber, "is the creation of a global oligopoly. It happened to the oil and automotive industries earlier this century; now it is happening to the entertainment industry."[1] In the past, to understand any nation's media situation, one first had to understand the local and national media and then determine where the global market — which largely meant imports and exports of films, TV shows, books, and music — fit in. Today one must first grasp the nature and logic of the global commercial system and then determine how local and national media deviate from the overall system. The rise of a global commercial media system is closely linked to the rise of a significantly more integrated "neoliberal" global capitalist economic system. To some extent, the rise of a global media market is encouraged by new digital and satellite technologies that make global markets both cost-effective and lucrative. It is also encouraged by the institutions of global capitalism — the World Trade Organisation (WTO), the World Bank, the International Monetary Fund (IMF) — as well as those governments, including that of the United States, that advance the interests of transnational corporations (TNCs). Moreover, during the past thirty years, media and communication more broadly have become a much more significant sector for business activity.[2] And this is just the beginning. As Ira Magaziner, the Clinton administration's Internet policy adviser put it in 1998, worldwide electronic commerce will be "the primary economic driver over the next 25 years."[3]

The rise to dominance of the global commercial media system is more than an economic matter; it also has clear implications for media content, politics, and culture. In many ways the emerging global media system is an extension of the U.S. system described in chapter 1, and its culture shares many of the attributes of the U.S. hypercommercial media system. This makes sense, as the firms that dominate U.S. media also dominate the global system and the system operates on the same profit maximizing logic. But there are also some important distinctions. On the one hand, a number of new firms enter the picture as one turns to the global system. On the other hand, and more important, a number of new political and social factors enter the discussion. There are scores of governments, and regional and international organizations that have a say in the regulation of media and communication. There are also a myriad of languages and cultures, which makes establishing a global version of the "U.S. system" quite difficult. But even if the U.S. media system and culture will not be punch-pressed onto the globe, the trajectory is toward vastly greater integration, based on commercial terms and dominated by a handful of transnational media conglomerates.

In this chapter I briefly chronicle the rise of the global media system and its core attributes. It is a system dominated by fewer then ten global TNCs, with another four or five dozen firms filling out regional and niche markets. I examine the activities and holdings of the three most important global media firms — Time Warner, Disney, and News Corporation — in detail. I then consider what the rise of the global media means for traditional notions of cultural imperialism, and for culture and journalism writ large. In my view, the general thrust of the global commercial media system is quite negative — assuming one wishes to preserve and promote institutions and values that are conducive to meaningful self-government. Such a global media system plays a central role in the development of "neoliberal" democracy; that is, a political system based on the formal right to vote, but in which political and economic power is resolutely maintained in the hands of the wealthy few.

The Rise of the Global Media System

The global markets for film production, TV show production, book publishing, and recorded music have been oligopolistic markets throughout much of their existence. Although there are important domestic companies in many of these industries, the global *export* market is the province of a handful of mostly U.S.-owned or U.S.-based firms. These not only remain important markets but are also tending to grow faster than the global economy. The motion picture and TV show production industries are absolutely booming at the global level.[4] The major film studios and U.S. TV show production companies (usually the same firms) now generate between 50 and 60 percent of their revenues outside the United States.[5] A key factor that makes these global oligopolies nearly impenetrable to newcomers is the extent of their distribution systems.[6] The rational choice for someone wishing to enter this market is either to buy one of the existing giants or, if one does not have a spare $10 or $20 billion or does not wish to spend it, to set up as an "independent" and forge a link with one of the existing giants.[7] The global film industry is the province of seven firms, all of which are part of larger media conglomerates. Likewise, the global music industry is dominated by five firms, all but one of which (EMI) are part of larger media TNCs.[8] These five music giants earn 70 percent of their revenues outside of the United States.[9]

What distinguishes the emerging global media system is not transnational control over exported media content, however, so much as increasing TNC control over media distribution and content within nations. Prior to the 1980s and 1990s, national media systems were typified by nationally owned radio and television systems, as well as domestic newspaper industries. Newspaper publishing remains a largely national phenomenon, but the face of television has changed almost beyond recognition. The rise of cable and satellite technology has opened up national markets to scores of new channels and revenue streams. The major Hollywood studios — all part of global media conglomerates — expect to generate $11 billion alone in 2002 for global TV rights to their film libraries, up from $7 billion in 1998.[10] More important, the primary providers of these channels are the media TNCs that dominate cable television channel ownership in the United States and have aggressively established numerous global editions of their channels to accommodate the new market.[11] Neoliberal "free market" policies have opened up ownership of stations as well as cable and satellite systems to private and transnational interests. As the *Wall Street Journal* notes, "the cable colonialists continue to press on in Europe, Asia and Latin America, betting on long-term profit."[12] Likewise, the largest media TNCs are invariably among the main players in efforts to establish digital satellite TV systems to serve regional and national markets.[13]

Television also is rapidly coming to play the same sort of dominant cultural role in Europe, Asia, and worldwide that it has played in the United States for two or three generations. After reviewing the most recent research, one observer noted in early 1998: "Europe hasn't caught up to American TV consumption levels, but Europeans are spending more time than ever watching television."[14] In 1997 French children aged four to ten years old watched on average nearly two hours of television per day, up 10 percent from the previous high in 1996; but this remains only one-half the amount of TV watching for children in the United States.[15]

The close connection of the rise of the global media system to the global capitalist political economy becomes especially clear in two ways. First, as suggested above, the global media system is the direct result of the sort of "neoliberal" deregulatory policies and agreements (e.g., NAFTA and GATT) that have helped to form global markets for goods and services. (It is worth noting that the actual negotiations surrounding communication issues in these international trade agreements are so complex, and the language employed in the deals is so technical and legalistic, that one expert estimates that no more than a few dozen people in the entire world — mostly lawyers — can intelligibly explain the media and cultural terms they include. A less inclusive discourse over global media policy would be difficult to imagine.)[16] At the global level, for example, the WTO ruled in 1997 that Canada could not prohibit Time Warner's *Sports Illustrated* from distributing a Canadian edition of the magazine.[17] In Australia, for another example, the High Court ruled against the legality of Australian domestic media content quotas in April 1998, stating that "international treaty obligations override the national cultural objectives in the Broadcasting Services Act."[18]

Although there is considerable pressure for open media markets, this is a sensitive area. There are strong traditions of protection for domestic media and cultural industries. Nations ranging from Norway, Denmark, and Spain to Mexico, South Africa, and South Korea, for example, have government subsidies to keep alive their small domestic film production industries.[19] Over the coming years it is likely that there will be periodic setbacks to the drive to establish an open global media market. In the summer of 1998 culture ministers from twenty nations, including Brazil, Mexico, Sweden, Italy, and Ivory Coast, met in Ottawa to discuss how they could "build some ground rules" to protect their cultural fare from "the Hollywood juggernaut." Their main recommendation was to keep culture out of the control of the WTO.[20] A similar 1998 gathering sponsored by the United Nations in Stockholm recommended that culture be granted special exemptions in global trade deals.[21] In India, in 1998, a court issued an arrest warrant for Rupert Murdoch for failing to appear in court to defend himself on the charge that his Star TV satellite service broadcast "obscene and vulgar" movies.[22]

Nevertheless, the trend is clearly in the direction of opening markets to TNC penetration. Neoliberal forces in every country argue that cultural trade barriers and regulations harm consumers, and that subsidies even inhibit the ability of nations to develop their own competitive media firms.[23] There are often strong commercial media lobbies within nations that perceive they have more to gain by opening up their borders than by maintaining trade barriers. In 1998, for example, when the British government proposed a voluntary levy on film theater revenues (mostly Hollywood films) to provide a subsidy for the British commercial film industry, the British commercial broadcasters reacted warily, not wishing to antagonize their crucial suppliers.[24] In November 1998 the British government declared the proposal dead after lobbying pressure from British commercial broadcasters.[25]

The European Union (EU) and European Commission (EC) provide an excellent case study of the movement of media policy making toward a largely procommercial position, and of the complexities involved in such a position. Historically, European nations have enjoyed prominent and well-financed national public broadcasters as well as a variety of other mechanisms to protect and promote domestic cultural production. The EU and EC are scarcely commissioned to advance the interests of U.S.-based media TNCs, but they are devoted to establishing strong European firms and a regional open commercial market. "If the European market doesn't become a single market," an Italian film director stated, "there's no way it can compete against America."[26] The powerful European media giants want the EU to advance their interests in the same way the U.S. government invariably lobbies and pushes for the interests of its media TNCs.[27] In 1998, for example, the EC officially moved to break up the European distribution company co-owned by Viacom, Seagram, and MGM–United Artists, arguing that it gave U.S. film producers too much ability to overwhelm potential European competitors.[28]

The EU and EC also see their mission as encouraging more competitive media markets between European firms.[29] Pressure from the EU Competition Commission was a factor in derailing the prospective merger between Reed Elsevier and Wolters Kluwer in 1998.[30] Accomplishing competitive markets, while helping build strong pan-European firms, sometimes produces conflict, as in 1998 when the EU opposed the efforts of Bertelsmann and Kirch to merge their German digital TV operations. In this case, some voices in the European business community argued that the EU was undermining the "emergence of a strong European business."[31] But the EU and EC, like regulators everywhere, are less likely to act on behalf of the public interest if it is aligned against the entirety of the business community. So it was with the Bertelsmann-Kirch deal — the dominant European media groups as well as Rupert Murdoch were urging the EU to block the merger, since they all wanted to have a shot at the German TV market as well.[32] Bertelsmann, too, was rumored not to be displeased that the deal was kiboshed, as it cripples the debt-laden Kirch and leaves Bertelsmann with an even better chance of dominating German digital television — all by itself.[33]

The nature of the EU system's media policies and values were revealed in several other developments in the late 1990s. To address the concern that U.S.-based media firms would quickly overwhelm Europe unless regulations to protect European content were enacted, the EU nearly passed a law in 1997 requiring that 50 percent of TV content be European-made. This drive fell short after a "ferocious" lobbying campaign by the largest European media interests, who are linked with U.S. media firms and dependent upon U.S. fare. Eventually the wording of the law was watered down to become virtually meaningless.[34] The EU system has been more effective in spreading commercial values; on two occasions in 1997 the European Court of Justice ruled that member states could not prohibit cable TV channels that featured advertising aimed at children, even though this violated national statutes.[35] Even when, in response to massive pressure from health authorities and educators, the EU banned tobacco advertising and sports sponsorship in 1998, there was a reasonable chance the law could be overturned by the European Courts of Justice.[36]

Increasingly lost in the shuffle are the fates of European public broadcasters. As the political power of public broadcasters recedes in Europe, the market-oriented EU and EC find the traditional notion of public service media, meaning nonprofit media with public subsidy, something of a square peg. By 1998, for example, a coalition of European commercial broadcasters and publishers were lobbying the EU to stop state subsidies of public broadcasters, when the public broadcasters were using the funds to enter into commercial television ventures.[37] (I will discuss this tension and what it means for public service broadcasting in greater length in chapter 5.) An indication of the shifting terrain of European policy making came in June 1997 when the European Summit found it necessary to include a protocol to the EU treaty formally acknowledging that public service broadcasters had a right to exist.[38] A generation earlier such a protocol would have been considered not just unnecessary but absurd.

Advertising is the second way that the global media system is linked to the global market economy. Advertising is conducted disproportionately by the largest firms in the world, and it is a major weapon in the struggle to establish new markets. The top ten global advertisers alone accounted for some 75 percent of the $36 billion spent by the one hundred largest global marketers in 1997.[39] For major firms like Procter & Gamble and Nike, global advertising is a vitally important aspect of their campaigns to maintain strong growth rates.[40] In conjunction with the "globalization" of the economy, advertising has grown globally at a rate greater than GDP growth in the 1990s.[41] The most rapid growth has been in Europe, Latin America, and especially East Asia, although the economic collapse of the late 1990s has slowed what had earlier been characterized as "torrid ad growth."[42] Advertising in China is growing at annual rates of 40 to 50 percent in the 1990s, and the singularly important sector of TV advertising is expected to continue to grow at that rate, at least, with the advent of sophisticated audience research that now delivers vital demographic data to advertisers, especially TNC advertisers.[43]

It is this TNC advertising that has fueled the rise of commercial television across the world, accounting, for example, for over one-half the advertising on the ABN-CNBC Asia network, which is co-owned by Dow Jones and General Electric.[44] And there is a world of room for growth, especially in comparison to the stable U.S. market. In 1999, the United States still accounted for nearly one-half of the world's approximately $435 billion in advertising.[45] Even in the developed markets of western Europe, for example, most nations still spend no more than one-half the U.S. amount on advertising per capita, so there remains considerable growth potential.[46] Were European nations, not to mention the rest of the world, ever to approach the U.S. level of between 2.1 and 2.4 percent of the GDP going toward advertising — where it has fluctuated for decades — the global media industry would see an almost exponential increase in its revenues.[47] As it is, European commercial television is growing at more than a 10 percent annual rate, twice the U.S. average.[48]

The advertising agency business itself has consolidated dramatically on a global basis in the 1990s, in part to better deal with the globalization of product markets and also to better address the plethora of commercial media emerging to serve advertisers. The largest advertising organizations now include several major brand agencies and countless smaller formerly independent agencies in nations around the world. The largest ad organization, Omnicom (1997 revenues: $4.2 billion), has fourteen major agencies in its portfolio, including BBDO Worldwide and DDB Needham Worldwide.[49] Omnicom dominates the global advertising agency industry along with two other massive giants — WPP Group (1997 revenues: $3.6 billion), and Interpublic Group (1997 revenues: $3.4 billion). They have a combined income greater than that of the ad organizations ranked fourth through fourteenth; and the size of ad organizations falls precipitously after one gets past the first fourteen or so. For example, number fifteen (Carlson Marketing, 1998 revenues: $285 million) does less than half the business of the firm ranked number fourteen, Cordiant Communications. And the fiftieth-largest advertising organization in the world — Testa International (1997 revenues: $60 million) — does around 1.5 percent of the business of the Omnicom Group.[50]

The wave of global consolidation among advertising agencies is far from over. The four most active ad agency acquirers spent $1.25 billion to buy other agencies in 1997, up over 250 percent from what they spend in 1996. Industry surveys suggest that most agency executives expect the agency merger and acquisition boom to increase in momentum in coming years.[51] Interpublic budgeted $250 million in 1998 for the purchase of other advertising companies.[52] The consolidation is encouraged by globalization, as the largest advertisers increasingly prefer to work with a single agency worldwide.[53] When Citibank consolidated its global advertising into one agency in 1997, an observer noted that "they want to have one brand with one voice — that's their mantra."[54] "We're not going to get a shot at [major clients]," one agency owner said, "without being global."[55] Global consolidation is also encouraged because the larger an ad agency, the more leverage it has getting favorable terms for its clients with global commercial media.[56] An agency needs worldwide "critical mass" to be competitive, the president of the French Publicis stated when Publicis purchased the U.S. Hal Riney and Partners in 1998.[57] The largest advertising organizations are scurrying about purchasing almost all of the remaining viable independent agencies around the world.[58] Even Japan, until recently effectively off-limits to foreign ad agencies, is being incorporated into the global networks of these giant agencies, as its main advertisers want global expertise for their brands.[59] In 1998 Omnicom and the WPP Group each purchased stakes in major Japanese agencies.[60] In combination, all of this suggests increased advertising influence over media operations.

But the most important corporate concentration concerns the media industry itself, and here concentration and conglomeration are the order of the day. There is increased global horizontal integration in specific media industries. Book publishing, for example, has undergone a major shakeout in the late 1990s, leading to a situation in which a handful of global firms dominate the market. "We have never seen this kind of concentration before with global ownership and the big getting bigger," a mergers and acquisitions lawyer who specializes in publishing deals stated in 1998.[61] But much more striking have been the vertical integration and conglomeration of the global media market. In short order the global media market has come to be dominated by the same eight TNCs that dominate U.S. media, as I presented in chapter 1, plus Bertelsmann, the German-based conglomerate. The dominant advertising firms are featherweights in comparison to the first tier of media firms, all of which rank among the few hundred largest publicly traded firms in the world in terms of market value. They are General Electric (#1), AT&T (#16), Disney (#31), Time Warner (#76), Sony (#103), News Corp. (#184), Viacom (#210), and Seagram (#274).[62] Bertelsmann would certainly be high on the list, too, were it not one of the handful of giant firms that remain privately held. In short, these firms are at the very pinnacle of global corporate capitalism. This is also a highly concentrated industry; the largest media firm in the world in terms of annual revenues, Time Warner (1998 revenues: $28 billion), is some fifty times larger in terms of annual sales than the world's fiftieth-largest media firm.[63] But what distinguishes these nine firms from the rest of the pack is not merely their size but the fact that they have global distribution networks.

I spelled out the rapidity with which these giants have emerged in the 1990s in chapter 1. There, too, I explained the strong pressure for firms to get larger and larger (and fewer and fewer). Likewise, and probably lost to most Americans who do not travel abroad, the media giants have moved aggressively to become global players. Time Warner and Disney, for example, still get the vast majority of their revenue in the United States, but both firms project non-U.S. sales to be a majority of their revenues within a decade, and the other media giants are all moving to be in a similar position. The point is to capitalize on the potential for growth — and not get outflanked by competitors — as the U.S market is well developed and only permits incremental growth. As Viacom CEO Sumner Redstone puts it, "companies are focusing on those markets promising the best return, which means overseas."[64] Frank Biondi, former chair of Seagram's Universal Studios, says "ninety-nine percent of the success of these companies long term is going to be successful execution offshore."[65] Another U.S. media executive stated that "we now see Latin America and the Asia-Pacific as our twenty-first century."[66] Sony, to cite one example, has hired the investment banking Blackstone Group to help it identify media takeover candidates worldwide.[67]

But this point should not be exaggerated. Non-U.S. markets, especially markets where there are meddlesome governments, are risky and often require patience before they produce profit. The key to being a first-tier media powerhouse is having a strong base in the United States, by far the largest and most stable commercial media market. That is why Bertelsmann is on the list; it ranks among the top U.S. recorded music, magazine publishing, and book publishing companies. It expects to do 40 percent of its $16 billion in annual business in the United States in the near future.[68] "We want to be a world-class media company," the CEO of the U.K.'s Pearson TV stated, "and to do that, we know we've got to get bigger in America."[69]

It is also mandatory to be a conglomerate, for the reasons presented in chapter 1. The essence of the first-tier firms is their ability to mix production capacity with their distribution networks. These nine firms control four of the five music firms that sell 80 percent of global music. The one remaining independent, EMI, is invariably on the market; it is worth considerably more merged with one of the other five global music giants that are all part of huge media conglomerates, or to another media TNC that wants a stake in the music market.[70] All of the major Hollywood studios, which dominate global film box office, are connected to these giants too. The only two of the nine that are not major content producers are AT&T and GE's NBC. The former has major media content holdings through Liberty Media and both of them, ranking among the ten most valuable firms in the world, are in a position to acquire assets as they become necessary. Such may soon be the case for GE. NBC was forced to scale back its expansion into European and Asian television in 1998, in part because it did not have enough programming to fill the airwaves.[71]

The global media market is rounded out by a second tier of four or five dozen firms that are national or regional powerhouses or have strong holds over niche markets, such as business or trade publishing. About one-half of these second-tier firms come from North America; most of the rest, from western Europe and Japan. Each of these second-tier firms is a giant in its own right, often ranking among the thousand largest firms in the world and doing over $1 billion per year in business. The list of second-tier media firms from North America includes, among others, Dow Jones, Gannett, Knight-Ridder, Newhouse, Comcast, the New York Times, the Washington Post, Hearst, McGraw Hill, Cox Enterprises, CBS, Advance Publications, Hicks Muse, Times-Mirror, Reader's Digest, Tribune Company, Thomson, Hollinger, and Rogers Communication. From Europe the list of second-tier firms includes, among others, Kirch, Havas, Mediaset, Hachette, Prisa, Canal Plus, Pearson, Carlton, Granada, United News and Media, Reuters, Reed Elsevier, Wolters Kluwer, Axel Springer, Kinnevik, and CLT. The Japanese companies, aside from Sony, remain almost exclusively domestic producers. I will discuss the handful of "third world" commercial media giants below.[72]

This second tier has also crystallized rather quickly; across the globe there has been a shakeout in national and regional media markets, with small firms getting eaten by medium firms and medium firms being swallowed by big firms. Many national and regional conglomerates have been established on the back of publishing or television empires, like Denmark's Egmont Group.[73] The situation in most nations is similar to the one described in the United States in chapter 1: a smaller number of much larger firms dominate the media in comparison to the situation only ten or twenty years ago. Indeed, as most nations are smaller than the United States, the tightness of the media oligarchy can be even more severe. In Britain, for example, 90 percent of the newspaper circulation is controlled by five firms, including Murdoch's News Corporation, while mergers have turned British cable into a fiefdom dominated by three firms.[74] In Canada, vocal right-winger Conrad Black — who owns 437 newspapers globally in an empire that generated revenues of $2.2 billion in 1997 — owns 61 of that nation's 101 daily newspapers, and over one-half of Canada's newspaper circulation.[75] The second-largest chain controls another one-quarter of Canadian newspaper circulation.[76] The situation may be most stark in New Zealand, where the newspaper industry is largely the province of the Australian-American Murdoch and the Irish Tony O'Reilly, who also dominates New Zealand's commercial radio broadcasting and has major stakes in magazine publishing. Two of the four terrestrial (over-the-air) television channels are owned by the Canadian CanWest. Murdoch controls pay television and is negotiating to purchase one or both of the two public TV networks, which the government is aiming to sell.[77] In short, the rulers of New Zealand's media system could squeeze into a closet.

Moreover, as the New Zealand example implies, the need to go beyond national borders applies to second-tier media firms as well as first-tier giants. Australian media moguls, following the path blazed by Rupert Murdoch, have the mantra "expand or die." As one puts it, "you really can't continue to grow as an Australian supplier in Australia."[78] Mediaset, the Berlusconi-owned Italian television power, is desperately seeking to expand in Europe and Latin America.[79] Perhaps the most striking example of second-tier globalization is provided by Hicks, Muse, Tate and Furst, the U.S. radio-publishing-TV-billboard-movie theater power discussed in chapter 1 that has been constructed almost overnight. In 1998 Hicks Muse spent well over one billion dollars purchasing media assets in Mexico, Argentina, Brazil, and Venezuela.[80]

In combination, these sixty or seventy giants control much of the world's media: book publishing, magazine publishing, music recording, newspaper publishing, TV show production, TV station and cable channel ownership, cable/satellite TV system ownership, film production, motion picture theater ownership, and newspaper publishing.[81] They are also the most dynamic element of the global media network. But the system is still very much in formation. New second-tier firms are emerging, especially in lucrative Asian markets, and there will probably be further upheaval among the ranks of the first-tier media giants. And firms get no guarantee of success merely by going global. The point is that they have no choice in the matter. Some, perhaps many, will falter as they accrue too much debt or as they enter unprofitable ventures. But the chances are that we are closer to the end of the process of establishing a stable global media market than we are to the beginning of the process. And as that happens, there is a distinct likelihood that the leading media firms in the world will find themselves in a very profitable position. That is what they are racing to secure.

Corporate growth, oligopolistic markets, and conglomeration barely reveal the extent to which the global media system is fundamentally noncompetitive in any meaningful economic sense of the term. As I mentioned in chapter 1, many of the largest media firms share major shareholders, own pieces of each other, or have interlocking boards of directors. When *Variety* compiled its list of the fifty largest global media firms for 1997, it observed that "merger mania" and cross-ownership had "resulted in a complex web of interrelationships" that will "make you dizzy."[82] The global market strongly encourages firms to establish equity joint ventures in which the media giants each own a part of an enterprise. In this manner, firms reduce competition and risk, and increase the chance of profitability. As the CEO of Sogecable, Spain's largest media firm and one of the twelve largest private media companies in Europe, put it to *Variety,* the strategy is "not to compete with international companies but to join them."[83] In 1998, for example, Prisa, another large Spanish media conglomerate, merged its digital satellite television service with the one controlled by state-owned telecommunications firm Telefonica to establish a monopoly in Spain.[84] Almost all of the second-tier companies have joint ventures or important relationships with each other and with first-tier media giants. Indeed, it is rare for first-tier media giants to launch a new venture in a foreign country unless they have taken on a leading domestic media company as a partner. The domestic firm can handle public outreach and massage the local politicians.

News Corporation heir Lachlan Murdoch expressed the rational view when explaining why News Corporation is working more closely with Kerry Packer's Publishing and Broadcasting Ltd., the company that with News Corp. effectively controls much of Australian media. It's better, contends Murdoch the younger, if we are not "aggressively attacking each other all the time."[85] In the global media market the dominant firms compete aggressively in some concentrated oligopolistic markets, are key suppliers to each other in other markets, and are partners in yet other markets. As the headline in one trade publication put it, this is a market where the reigning spirit is to "Make profits, not war."[86] In some respects, the global media market more closely resembles a cartel than it does the competitive marketplace found in economics textbooks.

The Holy Trinity of the Global Media System

The nature of the global media system seems less abstract when one examines the recent growth, activities, and strategies of its three most important TNCs: Time Warner, Disney, and News Corporation. Time Warner and Disney are the two firms with the largest media and entertainment operations. News Corporation is in contention with Viacom for the status of fourth largest, with sales around one-half those of Time Warner and Disney, but under Rupert Murdoch it has led the way in media globalization. These global empires were mainly constructed in the 1990s, and they are a long way from completion.

Time Warner is the outgrowth of the 1989 merger of Time and Warner Communications and the 1996 acquisition of Turner Broadcasting. It did around $28 billion in business in 1998, and its sales are expected to continue to grow at double-digit rates for the foreseeable future. With two hundred subsidiaries worldwide, Time Warner is also a strikingly dominant global player in virtually every important media sector except newspaper publishing and radio broadcasting. Time Warner's challenge is to develop its *synergies* (the process of taking a media brand and exploiting it for all the profit possible), that is, to mesh its extremely lucrative parts to increase the size of the profit whole.[87] It has an unparalleled combination of content production and distribution systems to work with.

Here are some of Time Warner's holdings:

- majority interest in the U.S. WB television network;
- largest cable broadcasting system operator in U.S., controlling twenty-two of the one hundred largest markets;
- controlling interest in cable TV channels CNN, Headline News, CNNfn, CNN International, TNT, TBS, Turner Classic Movies, CNNSI, Cartoon Network, Court TV, HBO, HBO International, and Cinemax;
- partial interest in cable TV channel Comedy Central;
- minority stake in U.S. satellite TV service Primestar;
- Warner Bros. film studios, one of the half-dozen studios that dominate the global market;
- Warner Bros. TV production studios, one of largest TV show production companies in the world;
- New Line film studios;
- the largest U.S. magazine publishing group, including *Time, People, Sports Illustrated,* and *Fortune;*
- Warner Music Group, one of the five firms that dominate the global recorded music industry;
- leading global book publisher, with 42 percent of sales outside the U.S.;
- 150 Warner Bros. retail stores;
- the Atlanta Hawks and Atlanta Braves U.S. professional sports teams;
- Hanna-Barbera animation studios;
- 10 percent stake in France's Canalsatellite, a digital TV service;
- 100 percent of Citereseau and 49 percent of Rhone Cable Vision, two French cable television system companies;
- 90 percent of Time Warner Telecom, which offers telephone service over Time Warner cable lines;
- 37 percent stake in Road Runner, the cable Internet Access service;
- one of the largest movie-theater-owning companies in the world, with over one thousand screens, all outside the U.S.;
- 20 percent of Midi Television, first private South African television network;

- over 40 percent stake in Towani, a joint venture with Toshiba and Japan's Nippon Television to produce movies and TV programs for Japanese market and export;
- 4.5 percent stake in Enic, owner of four European football teams, and, in fifty-fifty joint venture with Time Warner, proprietor of a worldwide chain of Warner Bros. restaurants;
- 23 percent stake in Atari;
- 14 percent stake in Hasbro;
- minority stakes in the following non-U.S. broadcasting joint ventures: Germany's N-TV, European music channel VIVA, and Asian music channel Classic V;
- 31 percent stake in U.S. satellite television company Primestar;
- 25 percent stake in Japanese cable company Titus;
- 19 percent stake in Japanese cable company Chofu;
- 50 percent stake in Columbia House record club.

Yet even this formidable list fails to do justice to Time Warner's global reach. CNN International is the dominant global TV news channel, broadcasting in several languages to some two hundred nations.[88] HBO is a global powerhouse as well, having expanded successfully into both eastern and western Europe, Latin America, and most of Asia. As one observer notes, HBO's International division "gobbles up new countries."[89] The Warner Bros. film studios coproduces films with Australian, German, French, Japanese, and Spanish companies, often times not in English.[90] Warner Bros. International Television Production has joint ventures to coproduce TV series with partners in Canada, France, Germany, and Britain.[91] Even the U.S.-based magazine division is going global, with non-U.S. editions of its publications and planned acquisitions of European magazines.[92]

What really distinguishes Time Warner, and what gives it such leverage in the global market, are two related things. First, in addition to arguably *producing* more media content than any other firm, Time Warner also has the world's largest library of music, films, TV shows, and cartoons to exploit. This makes Time Warner extremely attractive to national media firms for joint ventures or simply major contracts, such as it has with Canal Plus, the satellite television power in France, Spain, and Italy.[93] Second, Time Warner has perhaps more recognizable media *brand names* than any firm in the world. Branding is considered the most crucial determinant of market success and the one factor that can assure success in the digital world, with its myriad of choices — even though the choices are controlled by a small number of owners. Branding also lends itself to extensive licensing and merchandising of products related to media characters, channels, and programming. Time Warner considers its *Looney Tunes* cartoons alone a $4 billion worldwide brand; Batman is a mere $1 billion worldwide brand. With 150 Warner Bros. retail stores and scores of licensing agreements, merchandising has become a multi-billion-dollar segment of Time Warner's annual income — and what is more, it is among the fastest-growing branches of its global operations.

But nobody understands branding and merchandising better than Disney, which runs neck-and-neck with Time Warner for the honor of being the world's largest media firm. With some 660 Disney retail stores worldwide as well as merchandising and licensing deals with numerous manufacturers and retailers, Disney is evolving into what one industry observer characterizes as "the ultimate global consumer goods company."[94] Disney has moved aggressively into China; it has seven stores in Hong Kong and plans to open several more on the mainland before the century ends.[95] Disney has also carefully intertwined its media brands with its retail activities, and has done so on a global basis. There are major Disney theme parks in Japan and France as well as in the United States, a Disney passenger cruise ship line, and the company is launching DisneyQuest, a chain of "location-based entertainment" stores — that is, high-tech video arcades — centered around Disney brands.[96] Disney has even launched a planned community near its Disney World resort in Orlando, Florida, replete with Disney-run schools and social services. Disney is the master of synergies. Its animated films routinely generate vastly more income and profit from merchandising and other sources than they do from box-office receipts.

Here are some of Disney's holdings:

- the U.S. ABC television and radio networks;
- ten U.S. TV stations and twenty-eight radio stations;
- U.S. and global cable TV channels Disney Channel, ESPN, ESPN2, ESPNews, ESPN International, and major stakes in Lifetime, A&E, E! Entertainment, and History Channels;
- a stake in Americast, an interactive TV joint venture with several U.S. telephone companies;

- 43 percent of InfoSeek, an Internet portal service;
- major film studios, Miramax, Touchstone, and Walt Disney Pictures;
- TV production and distribution through Buena Vista;
- magazine publishing through its Fairchild and Chilton subsidiaries;
- book publishing holdings including Hyperion Press;
- music recording, including the Hollywood, Mammoth, and Walt Disney labels;
- world's largest theme parks and resorts, including Disneyland, Disney World, and a stake in EuroDisney;
- Club Disney, chain of children's restaurants and entertainment locations;
- Disney cruise line;
- DisneyQuest, chain of high-tech arcade game stores;
- controlling interest in Anaheim Mighty Ducks and Anaheim Angels, U.S. professional sports teams;
- 660 Disney stores worldwide;
- 50 percent stake in Super RTL, a joint venture with Bertelsmann;
- 20–33 percent stakes in the following commercial media companies: Eurosport TV network, the Spanish Tesauro SA, the German terrestrial channel RTL2, the German cable TV channel TM3, and the Brazilian TVA, a pay-TV company;
- 33 percent stake in Patagonic Film, Argentine film studio.

Disney, like Time Warner, has globalized its production and has signed production and distribution deals with firms in France, Japan, and Latin America, to mention but a few.[97] Disney's Miramax is launching a European film studio to be based in Britain.[98] Disney also has distributed its Disney TV Channel in numerous nations around the world, customizing it to local cultures and languages. Most important, Disney's ESPN International has become the world leader in televised sports. It is broadcast on twenty networks in twenty-one languages to 155 million TV households in 182 nations outside the United States. It is even available in Antarctica.[99]

Sport is arguably the single most lucrative content area for the global media industry, a point understood best of all by Rupert Murdoch, the swashbuckling CEO of News Corp. Sport was crucial in making his British Sky Broadcasting (BSkyB) the most successful satellite TV service in the world and in making the U.S. Fox TV network a full-fledged competitor of ABC, NBC, and CBS. Murdoch, more than any other figure, has been the visionary of a global corporate media empire. Using as a base his newspaper empires, first in his native Australia where he controls 70 percent of the daily circulation, and later in Britain where he is the largest newspaper publisher, Murdoch has expanded into film, publishing, and, especially, television worldwide.[100] He has established a major film studio in Australia to serve the global market.[101] Murdoch remains the most aggressive media mogul, and he has turned to joint ventures to expand his empire without using much of his own capital. "We don't see ourselves as a large corporation," Murdoch informed a closed meeting of investors in 1997. "We see ourselves as tiny compared to the world-wide opportunities for media." Murdoch has devoted inordinate attention to developing media properties in Asia and Latin America, even though News Corp. will receive the majority of its income from the United States for at least another decade. "He views these investments in multiyear terms," states a securities analyst, "even multigenerational."[102]

Here are some of News Corp.'s holdings:

- the U.S. Fox television network;
- twenty-two U.S. television stations, covering 40 percent of the U.S. population;
- Fox News Channel, U.S. and international TV network;
- 50 percent stake in fx, fxM, Fox Sports Net, Fox Kids Worldwide, Family Channel TV channels;
- 33 percent stake in Golf TV Channel;
- film studio Twentieth Century Fox;
- Twentieth Television, U.S. and international TV production and distribution group;
- over 130 daily newspapers, including *The Times* (of London) and the *New York Post,* controlling 70 percent of Australia's newspaper circulation;
- 23 magazines;
- 40 percent stake in United Video Satellite Group, publisher of *TV Guide* and interactive TV technology company;
- 30 percent stake in Echostar, U.S. satellite television company;
- book publishing, including Harper-Collins;

- the Los Angeles Dodgers professional baseball team;
- minority stake in the New York Knicks and the New York Rangers;
- option to purchase 40 percent stake in Los Angeles Kings NHL hockey team and 10 percent of Los Angeles Lakers NBA basketball team;
- controlling interest in British Sky Broadcasting (BSkyB) satellite TV service;
- through BSkyB, 32.5 percent stake in British Interactive Broadcasting, interactive television service;
- numerous Sky TV channels distributed across Britain and parts of Europe including Sky News;
- partial stake in Music Choice Europe TV channels;
- Latin American TV channels El Canal Fox and Fox Sport Noticias;
- 30 percent stake in Latin Sky Broadcasting satellite TV service to Latin America, joint venture with AT&T-TCI, Televisa, and Globo;
- following additional Latin American TV holdings: 20 percent stake in Cinecanal, pay-TV service; 12 percent stake in Telecine, Brazilian pay TV service;
- 66 percent stake in Munich TV station TM-3;
- 50 percent stake in German Vox TV network;
- controlling interest in Italian pay-TV venture, Stream;
- minority stake in Taurus, holding company that owns German Kirch media group (pending);
- Fox TV Channel (the Netherlands);
- the following European radio interests: 71 percent stake in Sky radio; 42 percent stake in Radio 538; 28 percent stake in Sky radio Sweden;
- 80 percent stake in New Zealand's Natural History Unit, the world's leading producer of nature and wildlife documentaries;
- Heritage Media, leading U.S. direct marketing company, with 1996 revenues over $500 million;
- partial stakes in two eastern European telecommunication companies: PLD Telekom (30.2 percent) and PeterStar (11 percent);
- Asian Star TV satellite TV service;
- pan-Asian TV channels: ESPN and Star Sports (four Asian

channels), Channel V music channel (four Asian channels) joint venture with major record companies, Star World, Star Plus, Star Movies (nine Asian channels);

- 50 percent stake in Indian TV channels Zee TV, El TV, and Zee Cinema;
- partial stake in Indian cable TV company Siti Cable;
- partial stake in Indonesian pay TV venture Indovision and Film Indonesia pay TV channel;
- 11.375 percent stake, with Sony, Fuji TV, and Softbank, in Japan SkyPerfecTV Broadcasting satellite TV system;
- Star Chinese Channel, broadcast across Taiwan;
- 45 percent interest in Phoenix Chinese Channel, satellite TV service for mainland China;
- partial interest in Golden Mainland Productions, TV joint venture with Taiwan Sports Development;
- Australian TV channel FoxTel;
- controlling interest in New Zealand's Independent Newspapers Ltd., controls 52 percent of New Zealand's newspaper circulation, and owns 40 percent of New Zealand's Sky Television.
- partial interest in ChinaByte, website joint venture with China's *People's Daily*;
- India Sky Broadcasting, satellite TV service;
- 50 percent stake, Australian National Rugby League;
- British First Division soccer team, Manchester United (pending approval).

The defining feature of Murdoch's global push is the establishment of satellite television systems, along with the channels and programming to be displayed on them. By 1998 Murdoch claimed to have TV networks and systems that reached more than 75 percent of the world's population. As Murdoch contends, "The borderless world opened up to us by the digital information age will afford huge challenges and limitless opportunities."[103] The archetype will be BSkyB, which not only dominates British pay television but also has launched film and program production facilities and has channels to be broadcast not only in Britain but also on European TV systems and eventually across the world.[104] Murdoch's two other main TV "brands" are the Fox channels, connected to his U.S. TV network, cable channels, and major film and TV production studios, and his Star Television service, which News Corp. purchased in 1993, for all of Asia.

The list above barely gives a sense of how quickly Murdoch's News Corporation has made Asian television its fiefdom. In India, for example, it has equity stakes of either 50 or 100 percent in eight different networks, constituting 45 percent of the nation's total viewership in cable and satellite homes. News Corp. has six networks in China, and its Phoenix joint venture has already been cleared in 36.2 million Chinese cable TV households. In Taiwan, News Corp. has seven channels and dominates the market.[105]

In 1997, when Prince Al-Waleed invested $400 million to purchase a 5 percent stake in News Corp., he commented that "News Corp. is the only real global media company that covers the world."[106] Whether News Corp. ever fulfills its ambitions remains to be seen, and it faces numerous obstacles along the way. In India, for example, the government in 1997 cracked down on foreign ownership of media after Murdoch hired scores of former government employees to be his top local executives.[107] News Corp. has enjoyed tremendous successes and its persistence has paid off just about everywhere it has gone. But in China, Murdoch got in hot water in 1993 by remarking that new communication technologies "were a threat to totalitarian regimes everywhere."[108] And as firms like News Corp. expand through mergers and acquisitions, they run the risk of taking on large levels of debt that leaves them exposed, especially if there is a business recession.

There is no indication that Murdoch is slowing down his march across the planet. He negotiated, albeit unsuccessfully, in 1998 to purchase stakes in leading media companies in Germany, Italy, and Argentina.[109] In 1998 Murdoch established an Italian-based subsidiary, News Corp. Europe, to coordinate News Corp.'s expansion into continental television, especially in Italy, Germany, Spain, and France. As one business analyst put it, "It's D-Day and the invasion has begun."[110] Murdoch has shown a remarkable capacity to use his media properties to curry the favor of political leaders, and use that favor to advance his interests. In chapter 1 I reviewed his massive U.S. lobbying armada. It is no less impressive elsewhere. His British newspapers' surprise support for Tony Blair in the 1997 election has put him in the prime minister's very good graces, to the extent that Blair spoke on Murdoch's behalf to the Italian government when Murdoch was negotiating to buy Mediaset in 1998.[111] This conduct has not settled well with all Britons. "We have a Prime Minister," Nick Cohen observed in the *New Statesman,* "who cannot control his tongue when Rupert Murdoch's posterior passes by."[112]

All of the media giants are emulating News Corp.'s strategy of getting bigger and going global with a vengeance. In the current political environment, the global media giants are in position to make dramatic strides in short order. Thus the world is being remade before our eyes by the executives of gigantic corporations, in dogged pursuit of profit.

Global Media Culture

When turning to the implications of the emerging global media system for journalism, politics, entertainment, and culture, the same caveats provided for the discussion of U.S. commercial media culture in chapter 1 apply again. Although fundamentally flawed, the system produces much of value for a variety of reasons. Commercial entertainment can be very appealing and often plays on very attractive themes. In addition, the global media system can be at times a progressive force, especially as it enters nations that had been tightly controlled by corrupt crony media systems, as in much of Latin America, or nations that had significant state censorship over media, as in parts of Asia. But, as we will see, this progressive aspect of the globalizing media market should not be blown out of proportion; the last thing the media giants want to do anywhere is rock the boat, as long as they can do their business. The global commercial media system is *radical,* in the sense that it will respect no tradition or custom, on balance, if it stands in the way of significantly increased profits. But it ultimately is politically *conservative,* because the media giants are significant beneficiaries of the current global social structure, and any upheaval in property or social relations, particularly to the extent it reduced the power of business and lessened inequality, would possibly — no, probably — jeopardize their positions. Indeed, in this regard, the logic and trajectory of global media culture is quite similar to that of the U.S. product.

It may be a bit misleading to call the emerging system "global." As India proved with News Corporation, nations can erect huge barriers against the intrusion of transnational media corporations, whether for political, cultural, or economic reasons. As mentioned at the outset of this chapter, there is widespread concern that regulations and subsidies are necessary to protect local content.[113] Therefore, to make sense of any particular national media scene, one must take into account local laws and regulations, as well as the contours of the domestic commercial media industry. Nevertheless, the momentum is clearly in the opposite direction. Even China has put its media on a largely commercial basis, and is in the process of opening its doors to media TNCs in a manner unthinkable only two or three years ago.[114] In addition, the global commercial media system is far more developed in some parts of the world than in others. As a profit-driven enterprise, it devotes most of its attention to the wealthier sectors. In the so-called developing world, the system is accordingly oriented toward middle- and upper-class consumers. In India, this relevant market contains perhaps at the outside 300 or 400 million people — a large number, to be sure, but not overwhelming in a nation of almost one billion. Not surprisingly, an area like sub-Saharan Africa receives minimal global media attention in comparison to almost anywhere else in the world. Nor does this mean sub-Saharan nations (or the poor of India) enjoy a wealth of indigenous media, for these poorest populations have scarcely any public funds to develop media.

Presented in this manner, the logical question traditionally has been: Does the global media system represent the highest form of "cultural imperialism"? Or to put it another way: Are the largely U.S.-owned and/or U.S.-based media giants inculcating the world's peoples with western consumer values and undermining traditional cultures and values?[115] (One thinks of Disney CEO Michael Eisner's delight when someone presented him with a photograph of a woman from Timbuktu wearing a cap for Disney's Anaheim Mighty Ducks hockey team. "Now that's the definition of global reach!" Eisner enthused.)[116] The answers to these questions are yes and sort of. One of the problems with the way the issue often has been framed is that it regards culture in a static manner and assumes that corporate commercial culture equals "American" culture. As the *Economist* put it, "people who see America as a cauldron of self-obsessed, TV-centred, have-it-all sensation" fail to understand "that the country still contains deeper hungers and a respect for cultural attitudes which address them."[117] "There is nothing particularly American," the *Economist* noted in reference to the themes of Hollywood blockbuster films, "about boats crashing into icebergs or asteroids that threaten to obliterate human life."[118] The flip side of this reductionism toward U.S. culture is to regard non-U.S. cultures as pristine.

In addition, viewing the global media system in terms of national geopolitical domination may have made some sense in the 1960s and 1970s, but it is no longer an especially satisfactory construct. It is true that the U.S. government remains the steadfast advocate of the transnational media corporations worldwide. Media and computer software — the "copyright" industries — are the leading exports of the United States, to the tune of $60 billion in 1997.[119] This figure has doubled during the course of the 1990s.[120] The U.S. government therefore harasses and threatens with sanctions nations that do not respect media firms' copyrights.[121] It also uses its diplomatic leverage to get barriers to media imports reduced. President Clinton, for example, during his June 1998 China trip, pressured the Chinese government to increase its quota for U.S. films from 10 to 20 within two years.[122] In 1998, the U.S. government led the fight in the negotiations among the largest economic powers over the new multilateral agreement on investment — a bill of rights for global investors to protect them from national government regulations — to see that the MAI included all media, communication, and "cultural" activities within its province.[123] In that same year the U.S. government pressured the WTO to declare the Internet a "duty-free area," so as to encourage its commercial development.[124] In addition, the U.S. government has further relaxed its anemic antitrust standards for media mergers and acquisitions, thus permitting them to become "stronger worldwide player[s]."[125] The U.S. government even subsidizes a program to train bureaucrats and business persons around the world in how to construct commercial broadcasting systems.[126]

It is also true that the expansion of media TNCs generally greases the wheels for global markets in general — which has long been a general aim of the U.S. and other western governments. It is notable that in 1998 a leading member of the U.S. business community argued that the United States should relax its efforts to establish a global commercial media market and accept that nations might have legitimate concerns about "cultural imperialism." Such a tack, he argued, would undercut the movements against global free trade and "even bolster America's ability to export its ideas and ideals for the long haul."[127] But regardless of what the U.S. government does, U.S. firms have always enjoyed a tremendous advantage in the global media market because their huge domestic market gives them economies of scale such that their media exports can be sold at rates well below cost of production for a smaller nation. They also have the advantage of the principal international language, English. It is telling that in 1998 several leading French film directors began working in English, as that was understood as the only way "to reach a wider international audience."[128] U.S. firms can also take advantage of their historic ability to define the terms of commercial entertainment.[129] Naturally there is a strong taste for U.S. commercial entertainment around the world: in the global marketplace, the U.S. is the 500-pound gorilla.[130]

But the impetus behind the global media system is far more corporate and commercial expansion than national geopolitics, and, as the system evolves, the material basis for providing "American" entertainment lessens. On the one hand, the "geopolitical" element of the global communication system prior to the 1990s was connected to some extent to the ideological aspect of the cold war, which is no longer a pressing concern. On the other hand, the system is moving away from direct attachment to a particular nation-state. The British film industry enjoyed a boom of sorts in the late 1990s, but did so through a series of deals with the major Hollywood studios that provided both financing and the global distribution networks necessary for success.[131] When Time Warner, for example, is earning over half its income outside the United States, when its shareholders come from all over the world, and when its production is globalized, it will still have important ties to the United States and the U.S. government; but those ties will be weakened. It will be bad business for a U.S.-based media giant to be nationalistic. "Today, the media's responsibility for helping us see the world in all its complexity is greater than ever," Time Warner CEO Gerald Levin stated in 1998. "Yet too often we are left with a superficial impression of a global village that resembles an American suburb, in which the values and viewpoints fit into familiar categories."[132] Moreover, the always dubious notion that the product of the corporate media firms represents the essence of U.S. culture appears ever less plausible as the media system is increasingly concentrated, commercialized, and globalized.

The global media system is better understood, then, as one that advances corporate and commercial interests and values, and denigrates or ignores that which cannot be incorporated into its mission. Four of the eight largest media firms are headquartered outside of the United States, but all of them — Bertelsmann, News Corp., Sony, and Seagram — are major U.S. players, indeed owning three of the major Hollywood film studios. They rank among the seventy largest foreign firms operating in the United States, based on their U.S. sales, and all but Bertelsmann rank in the top thirty.[133] There is no discernible difference in the firms' content, whether they are owned by shareholders in Japan or Belgium or have corporate headquarters in New York or Sydney. Bertelsmann CEO Thomas Middelhoff bristled when, in 1998, some said it was improper for a German firm to control 15 percent of the U.S. book publishing market. "We're not foreign. We're international," Middelhoff said. "I'm an American with a German passport."[134] Bertelsmann already generates more income from the United States than from any other nation;[135] Middelhoff's immediate goal is to boost the U.S. percentage of Bertelsmann's revenues from 31 to 40 percent.[136] "The soul of the whole entertainment business is in the U.S.," stated Bertelsmann's second-ranking executive.[137] Indeed the output of the global media giants is largely interchangeable, as they constantly ape each other's commercial triumphs.

In this light, the notion that the transnational media conglomerates ultimately will fail because people tend to prefer their local media and cultures appears wide of the mark. For one thing, the evidence is mixed, and people's tastes are malleable. There is significant indication that Hollywood-type fare is popular worldwide, and that the taste for it is growing with increased exposure. In France, arguably Europe's most culturally nationalistic nation, U.S. films account for 60 percent of box-office revenues. In Britain, U.S. films account for 95 percent of the box-office revenue.[138] In April 1998, for example, U.S. films dominated the lists of top ten box-office movies for most European nations: in France, seven of ten; in Britain, nine of ten; in Spain, ten of ten; in Italy, nine of ten; and in Germany, nine of ten. In 1996 the United States claimed 70 percent of the EU film market, up from 56 percent in 1987. Growth was comparable in Japan.[139] Indeed the trade deficit between the EU nations and the United States in films, television programs, and videos has grown steadily in the 1990s, and stood at nearly $6 billion in 1996.[140] The German market, by far Europe's largest, provides a further indicator of Hollywood dominance. Of its fifty top grossing films in 1997, forty-two were made by first-tier global media giants.[141] Nine of Germany's ten leading video rentals and nine of its top ten best-selling videos in 1997 were also produced by the Hollywood giants.[142]

Moreover, as the global media system spreads its tentacles and deepens its reach, there is reason to believe this will then shape popular tastes toward that with which they are becoming more familiar. *Variety* editor Peter Bart concluded in 1998, based upon his conversations with Hollywood executives, that "there's also growing evidence that the world filmgoing audience is fast becoming more homogeneous." Whereas "action" movies had once been the only sure-fire global fare — and comedies had been considerably more difficult to export — by the late 1990s comedies like *My Best Friend's Wedding* and *The Full Monty* were doing between $160 and 200 million in non-U.S. box office.[143] A 1998 survey of thirty-five thousand consumers in thirty-five countries, conducted by the venerable Roper Starch Worldwide research group, provided "additional evidence that consumers around the world are more similar than different." As Martha Farnsworth Riche, former director of the U.S. Census Bureau who consulted on the study, put it, certain factors once deemed crucial to understanding consumer behavior, particularly overseas, had become less important. "People aren't all that different. Their tastes are very similar," Riche stated. "When selling Whirlpools in Korea," for example, "you've got to make sure you that you don't use the taboo color, but the cultural stuff is just a wrinkle."[144]

At the same time, there is countervailing evidence. Although U.S. films dominate the European market, the box office revenues of European films in Europe are beginning to rebound, especially with the rise of the multiplex theater. In music, non-U.S. fare has been the most rapidly growing element of the global market.[145] The CEO of a Spanish media firm only stated what is virtually received wisdom across the media industries: "The most successful content in most countries is local content."[146]

But this is hardly a contradiction. To the extent that most audiences prefer locally made fare if it is of adequate quality, the global media giants, rather than flee in despair, have globalized their production.[147] This globalization of production is spurred by economic and political factors, such as the desire to establish stronger relationships with domestic broadcasters who may be required to air locally produced content.[148] When U.S. magazine publishers expand overseas they cheerfully adjust the content and language to appeal to Germans, Japanese, or Russians.[149] As the discussion above of the "holy trinity" suggests, all of the media TNCs are establishing production on a global basis.[150] Universal Pictures, for example, spent much of 1997 "busily forging international acquisition and co-production deals with a raft of filmmakers in Europe, Latin America and Asia." As *Variety* notes, "there's moolah to be made from foreign films."[151] Time Warner has found that it can enhance the appeal of its Warner Bros. films in Asia by having local musicians do a song in the native language for the film's promotional campaigns in each nation.[152] Indeed, the media TNCs' global television channels all emphasize a mixture of English-language material with a heavy dose of local languages and programming as well as programming dubbed in local languages. Time Warner's Cartoon Network is dubbed in numerous languages, including those of smaller nations like Sweden and Denmark.[153]

Animation is, in fact, ideal for dubbing; hence the children's television and entertainment market is more easily dominated by the media TNCs.[154] Viacom's Nickelodeon has a commanding presence in Latin America and parts of Europe, and launched a major expansion into Asia in 1998.[155] "For all children, the Disney characters are local characters and this is very important. They always speak local languages," a Disney executive stated. The Disney strategy, he added, is to "think global, act local."[156] This principle applies beyond animation, however, to the entire global media system: "The right mix for Western media," Rupert Murdoch informed a United Nations conference on television in the autumn of 1997, "is taking the best international programming and mixing it with local content. Localization is playing an increasingly crucial role."[157] In the case of Latin America, then, its TV media capital has become Miami, where English- and Spanish-language fare easily co-exist.[158]

The traditional notion of media or cultural imperialism also tended to regard the existing non-TNC domestic commercial media as some sort of oppositional or alternative force to the global market. That was probably a dubious notion in the past, and it does not hold true at all today. Throughout the world, media consolidation and concentration have taken place in national markets, leaving a handful of extremely powerful media conglomerates dominating regional and national markets. These firms have found a lucrative niche teaming up with the global media giants in joint ventures, offering the "local" aspect of the content, and handling the local politicians. As the head of Norway's largest media firm put it, "We want to position ourselves so if Kirch or Murdoch want to sell in Scandinavia, they'll come to us first."[159]

The notion of non-U.S. or non-TNC media firms being "oppositional" to the global system is no less far-fetched when one turns to the "Third World." Mexico's Televisa, Brazil's Globo, Argentina's Clarin, and the Cisneros group of Venezuela, for example, rank among the sixty or seventy largest media firms in the world.[160] They have extensive ties and joint ventures with the largest media TNCs, as well as with Wall Street investment banks.[161] These firms tend to dominate their own national and regional media markets, which are experiencing rapid consolidation in their own right.[162] The commercial media powerhouses of the developing world tend, therefore, to be primary advocates for — and beneficiaries of — the expansion of the global commercial media market.[163] And these Third World media giants, like other second-tier media firms elsewhere, are also establishing global operations, especially to nations that speak the same languages.[164] And within each of their home nations these media firms have distinct probusiness political agendas that put them at odds with large segments of the population.[165] In short, the global system is best perceived as one that best represents the needs of investors, advertisers, and the affluent consumers of the world. In wealthy nations this tends to be a substantial portion of the population; in developing nations, a distinct minority.

All of these trends converge in the global music industry. Music has always been the least capital-intensive of the electronic media and therefore the most open to experimentation and new ideas. U.S. recording artists generated 60 percent of their sales outside of the United States in 1993; by 1998 that figure was down to 40 percent.[166] Rather than fold their tents, however, the five media TNCs that dominate the world's recorded music market are busy establishing local subsidiaries across the world, in places like Brazil where "people are totally committed to local music."[167] Sony, for example, has led the way in establishing distribution deals with independent music companies from around the world.[168] In places like India and Japan, there has been a huge expansion of interest in traditional western pop music, combined with a maintenance of domestic musical traditions and the rise of local pop traditions that merge elements of each.[169]

This development of new and exciting forms and genres of popular music underscores the point that commercial culture is a complex process that does not always lend itself to categorical analysis. In one sense these developments demonstrate just how flexible capitalism and commercialism can be in allowing new trends and even "countercultural" patterns in the pursuit of profit.[170] But this point should not be exaggerated. Commercial imperatives put distinct (and often quite negative) limits on the nature and range of what music gets produced, as the long U.S. experience with the corporate music industry reveals.[171] (I discuss this point in chapter 1.) And to the extent that Viacom's global MTV Networks, which reach 300 million homes or one-quarter of the world's TV households, influence music, commercialism is clearly in the driver's seat.[172] As one trade publication noted approvingly, MTV provides a "seamless blend of hip music and sponsors' messages."[173]

The corporate media culture is hardly the result of some abstract value-free media market that "gives the people what they want." Highly concentrated, it gives the dominant corporations market power to give their shareholders what they can make the most profit from. That means linking media fare to all sorts of products and merchandising, as described in the discussion of the "holy trinity" above. As one observer noted, Hollywood films now have so many promotional tie-ins and deals that their competition "extends from theaters to fast-food chains to grocery aisles."[174] Disney and McDonald's have a ten-year exclusive agreement to promote each other's products in 109 nations, a relationship so detailed that the *Wall Street Journal* termed the two firms "McDisney."[175] Music labels, for example, increasingly link musical genres to clothing fashions that can also be exploited. The rise of "hip-hop" clothing in the middle 1990s has increased music industry revenues by as much as 20 percent.[176] On the other hand, and most important, the media firms devote their activities to providing advertisers with the audiences and content they want. Hence, aside from sports with its "killer" demographics of middle- and upper-class males aged eighteen to forty-nine, the other main focus of the global media system is children's television programming and its product-conscious audience.[177]

The hallmark of the global media system is its relentless, ubiquitous commercialism. At the most explicit, TV shopping channels are one of the primary growth areas around the world.[178] Similarly, "infomercials" are positively booming on global commercial television systems. Mike Levey, the U.S. "king of the infomercial," sells goods in sixty countries and in fourteen languages. Virtually unknown in his own land, Levey has become a television superstar, the "heartthrob to the world."[179] Advertising not only dominates media, it is beginning to be used on telephone and paging systems.[180] In this commercially saturated environment, audiences barely raised their eyebrows when former Soviet premier Mikhail Gorbachev did a TV commercial for Pizza Hut in 1997.[181] In Japan, where the commercial competition to influence the teen market is intense, agencies now exist that will hire teenagers to undertake surreptitious "word-of-mouth" advertising for their corporate clients to create an artificial "buzz" about them.[182] Although media scholars can study and debate the exact nature of media effects upon people, it should be no surprise that account after account in the late 1990s documents the fascination, even the obsession, of the world's middle-class youth with consumer brands and products.[183]

Being a global market also influences the nature of film content, since the U.S. market only accounts for about 40–45 percent of Hollywood studio revenues. This may be the one area where Americans can sense how a global media market changes things; otherwise, the rest of the world is getting a taste of what has been the U.S. situation for generations.[184] Of course, globalization has some positive attributes; for example, it makes films less likely to portray Arabs or Asians in a racist manner that would undercut crucial markets. (Sometimes this effort to avoid giving offense reaches almost comic dimensions. For example, the world hockey championships in *D2,* the Disney *Mighty Ducks* sequel, depicted the thuggish "bad guys" as being from *Iceland* — a nation with probably fewer movie theaters than most U.S. suburban shopping malls!) Hollywood films are also more likely to employ international casts so as to have global box office appeal.[185] But globalization has also meant that violent films (and TV shows) receive massive attention, "while comedy and drama languish."[186] As has been well documented, violent "action" fare is the genre that crosses borders most easily and makes the most commercial sense. The result is, when filmgoers are exposed to more and more "action" films and begin to develop a taste for them, the studios piously claim they are "giving the people what they want." Violent fare also has a certain de-evolutionary logic to it. Over time, films and TV programs need to become ever more grisly to attract attention.[187] Even animal documentaries have found a worldwide niche because they feature numerous "kill sequences" and blood fights among the animals.[188]

Global Media and Neoliberal Democracy

With this hypercommercialism and corporate control comes an implicit political bias regarding the content of the media system. Consumerism, the market, class inequality, and individualism tend to be taken as natural and often benevolent, whereas political activity, civic values, and antimarket activities tend to be marginalized or denounced. This does not portend mind-control or "Big Brother," for it is much more subtle than that. (For example, Hollywood films and television programs may not present socialism in a favorable light, and will rarely criticize capitalism as an economic system overall, but they frequently use particular businesses or business persons to serve as the "bad guys." Since businesses of one kind or another rank high on many peoples' lists of disreputable operators, to avoid using them as "bad guys" in entertainment would leave the studio to resort to science fiction.)[189] Indeed, the genius of the commercial media system is the general lack of overt censorship. As George Orwell noted in his unpublished introduction to *Animal Farm,* censorship in free societies is infinitely more sophisticated and thorough than in dictatorships because "unpopular ideas can be silenced, and inconvenient facts kept dark, without any need for an official ban."[190] The logical consequence of a commercial media system is less to instill adherence to any ruling powers that be — though that can and does of course happen — than to promote a general belief that politics is unimportant and that there is little hope for organized social change.

As such, the global media system buttresses what could be termed "neoliberal" democracy, that is, the largely vacuous political culture that exists in the formally democratic market-driven nations of the world. As I mentioned in the introduction, neoliberalism operates not only as an economic system but as a political and cultural system as well. Neoliberalism works best when there is formal electoral democracy, but when the population is diverted from the information, access, and public forums necessary for meaningful participation in decision making. As neoliberal theorist Milton Friedman put it in his seminal *Capitalism and Freedom,* because profit making is the essence of democracy, any government that pursues antimarket policies is being antidemocratic, no matter how much informed popular support they might enjoy. Therefore it is best to restrict governments to the job of protecting private property and enforcing contracts, and to limit political debate to minor issues. The real matters of resource production and distribution and social organization should be determined by market forces.[191]

Equipped with this peculiar understanding of democracy, neoliberals like Friedman had no qualms over the military overthrow of Chile's democratically elected Allende government in 1973, because Allende was interfering with business control of Chilean society. After fifteen years of often brutal and savage dictatorship — all in the name of the free market — formal democracy was restored in 1989 with a constitution that made it vastly more difficult, if not impossible, for the citizenry to challenge the business-military domination of Chilean society. That is neoliberal democracy in a nutshell: trivial debate over minor issues by parties that basically pursue the same probusiness policies regardless of formal differences and campaign debate. Democracy is permissible as long as the control of business is off-limits to popular deliberation or change; that is, so long as it isn't democracy.

Neoliberal democracy therefore has an important and necessary by-product — a depoliticized citizenry marked by apathy and cynicism. If electoral democracy affects little of social life, it is irrational to devote much attention to it. The United States provides the preeminent model of "neoliberal" democracy and shows the way for combining a capitalist economy with a largely toothless democratic polity. Sometimes these points are made explicit. Jaime Guzmán, principal author of Chile's 1980 constitution, believed that private property and investors' rights needed to be off-limits to popular debate or consideration, and he crafted Chile's "democracy" accordingly. Consider Guzmán's thoughts. "A democracy can only be stable when in popular elections . . . the essential form of life of a people is not at play, is not at risk," Guzmán explained. "In the great democracies of the world, the high levels of electoral abstention do not indicate, as many erroneously interpret them, a supposed distancing of the people from the reigning system." Noninvolvement by the bulk of the population is in fact a healthy development. Guzmán concludes that in the best form of capitalist democracy, "if one's adversaries come to power, they are constrained to pursue a course of action not very different than that which one would desire because the set of alternatives that the playing field imposes on those who play on it are sufficiently reduced to render anything else extremely difficult."[192]

Chile is held up as the greatest neoliberal success story in Latin America, perhaps even the world. As the *New York Times* put it,

Pinochet's coup "began Chile's transformation from a backwater banana republic to the economic star of Latin America." And while there has been strong overall economic growth over the past decade, Chile has also seen a widening of economic inequality such that it ranks seventh worst in a World Bank study of economic stratification in sixty-five nations. But what is the caliber of political and social life in this neoliberal miracle? Prior to the 1973 coup, Chile was legendary for the intense politicization of its population, reflected by voter turnouts as high as 95 percent of the adult population. One U.S. researcher found in 1970 that Chilean teenagers were among the three least alienated, most optimistic groups of youth on earth. In the 1990s Chile is a very different nation. As one observer puts it, "Chile is perhaps the one place on earth where idolatry of the market has most deeply penetrated." In the most recent elections 41 percent of the population either did not vote, defaced their ballots, or left them blank. Voter participation among Chileans under twenty-five was considerably lower. By the canons of neoliberalism, then, Chile is a success both economically and politically.[193] Chile has seen its political life reduced to a placid, tangential spectator sport.

This hollowing out of democracy is a worldwide phenomenon in the age of the uncontested market. As a Greek peasant put it following Greece's 1996 elections: "The only right we have is the right to vote and it leads us nowhere." The very term democracy has been turned on its head so its very absence in substance is now seen as what constitutes its defining essence. The *Washington Post* noted that modern democracy works best when the political "parties essentially agree on most of the major issues."[194] Or, more bluntly, as the *Financial Times* put it, capitalist democracy can best succeed to the extent that is about "the process of depoliticising the economy."[195] (Is it even necessary to note that in a genuine democracy, the matter of who controls the economy and for what purposes would be at the *center* of political debate and consideration?)

Let me be clear about my argument. I am not stating that the global media or commercial media are solely or even primarily responsible for the type of depoliticized and demoralized political environment that exists in the United States or that has developed in Chile. My argument is that this depoliticization responds most directly to the rise of the market and commercial values to preeminence in those societies. But I am obviously generalizing; in any given nation any number of other important factors are going to influence the nature and trajectory of its political culture, and that is true for both the United States and Chile as well. That being said, however, the global commercial media system is integrally related to neoliberal democracy with its attendant depoliticization at two levels. At the broadest institutional level, the rise of a global commercial media system has been the result of and necessary for the rise of a global market for goods and services dominated by a few hundred TNCs. Both the global commercial media system and the growth and emergence of this "global" economy are predicated upon probusiness neoliberal deregulation worldwide. On the other hand, the marketing networks offered by global media system are essential for the creation of global and regional markets for TNC goods and services. To the extent, therefore, that the neoliberal global economic order thrives upon a weak political culture, the global media system is a central beneficiary as well.

But the global media system plays a much more explicit role in generating a passive, depoliticized populace that prefers personal consumption to social understanding and activity, a mass more likely to take orders than to make waves. Lacking any necessarily "conspiratorial" intent, and merely following rational market calculations, the media system simply exists to provide light escapist entertainment. In the developing world, where public relations and marketing hyperbole are only beginning to realize their awesome potential, and where the ruling elites are well aware of the need to keep the rabble in line, the importance of commercial media is sometimes stated quite candidly. In the words of the late Emilio Azcarraga, the billionaire head of Mexico's Televisa: "Mexico is a country of a modest, very fucked class, which will never stop being fucked. Television has the obligation to bring diversion to these people and remove them from their sad reality and difficult future."[196]

The global journalism of the corporate media system reinforces these trends, with devastating implications for the functioning of political democracies. Here the trends mirror the collapse of U.S. journalism discussed in chapter 1. Again, I do not wish to exaggerate the decline of journalism to the extent that I imply the existence of some previous glorious golden age that most certainly did not exist. Privately owned press systems historically have been conservative forces, and for logical reasons: they tended to reflect the values of their owners. That bias remains: in 1998 Sweden's three largest newspapers, all Swedish-owned, take explicit "free market" editorial positions, despite the fact that Sweden continues to have significant support for prolabor, welfare state, and socialist politics.[197]

But as in the United States, journalism worldwide is deteriorating, as it has become an important profit source for the media giants.[198] Because investigative journalism or coverage of foreign affairs makes little economic sense, it is discouraged as being too expensive.[199] On the one hand, there is a relatively sophisticated business news pitched at the upper and upper-middle classes and shaped to their needs and prejudices. CNN International, for example, presents itself as providing advertisers "unrivalled access to reach high-income consumers."[200] But even in "elite" media there is a decline. The *Economist* noted that in 1898 the first page of a sample copy of the *Times* of London contained nineteen columns of foreign news, eight columns of domestic news, and three columns on salmon fishing. In 1998 a sample copy of the *Times,* now owned by Rupert Murdoch, had one international story on its front page: an account of actor Leonardo DiCaprio's new girlfriend. "In this information age," the *Economist* concluded, "the newspapers which used to be full of politics and economics are thick with stars and sport."[201] On the other hand, there is an appalling schlock journalism for the masses, based upon lurid tabloid-type stories. For the occasional "serious" story, there is the mindless regurgitation of press releases from one source or another, with the range of debate mostly limited to what is being debated among the elite. "Bad journalism," a British observer concluded in 1998, "is a consequence of an unregulated market in which would-be monopolists are free to treat the channels of democratic debate as their private property.[202]

As with entertainment, at times the media giants generate first-rate journalism, but it is a minuscule fraction of their output and often causes just the sort of uproar that media firms prefer to avoid. It is also true that some well-organized social movements and dissident political views can get coverage in the world of commercial journalism, but the playing field is far from level. And, as John Keane noted, "in times of crisis" — meaning when antibusiness social movements gain *too much* political strength — "market censorship tends to become overt."[203]

Just how bogus this commercial journalism is, when measured by any traditional notion of the communication requirements necessary for a democracy, becomes especially clear when one looks at China. There, a full-scale dictatorship with a long tradition of suppressing dissident or prodemocratic political viewpoints has no particular problem with business news or tabloid journalism, the two main products of the so-called "free press."[204] The Chinese government media has lost most of its subsidy, and has turned to advertising as the primary means of support, with all that that suggests about content. So far the marriage of commercial media and communism has been considerably less rocky than most analysts had anticipated.[205] Indeed, it appears increasingly that the Chinese government can co-exist with the corporate media giants quite comfortably. Chinese president Jiang Zemin went so far as to praise the 1997 U.S. film *Titanic* in a speech before the National Peoples Congress. "Let us not assume we can't learn from capitalism."[206]

The relationship of the media giants to China is highly instructive about their commitment to democracy as well. In 1997, when Disney had the temerity to produce *Kundun,* a film biography of the Dalai Lama, Disney's numerous media projects in China were "frozen" by the Chinese government.[207] Disney responded by working with the Chinese government to show them how to use public relations to ride out the controversy. Disney even hired super-lobbyist Henry Kissinger to go to China and "to keep China open to the Walt Disney Company."[208] The advertising that Disney was contractually obligated to provide for *Kundun* virtually eliminated any reference to Disney.[209] In the summer of 1998, Disney appointed a special executive, John J. Feenie, to coordinate its Chinese activities. Feenie observed that Disney had made "great strides toward smoothing things over with the Chinese" and it hoped to distribute more films and even build a theme park in China. Disney CEO Michael Eisner "is very serious about wanting meaningful progress in that market," Feenie stated.[210] Eisner finally made a visit to Beijing to meet the head of state in December 1998, and indications were that Disney would soon be able to resume its Chinese operations.[211] The message is clear: Disney, and any other firm that is attempting to maximize profit, will never again produce a film like *Kundun* concerning China. Nor will such a firm countenance the caliber of journalism that could significantly undermine the firm's capacity to maximize profit.

Far more striking have been the activities of Rupert Murdoch and News Corporation in China. Since Rupert Murdoch fell into the Chinese leadership's bad graces by suggesting in 1993 they would not survive the rise of satellite communication, he has bent over backwards to appease them. In 1995 he eliminated the BBC from his Star Television bouquet because the Chinese leaders thought the BBC too critical of their activities. Then, in 1996, he launched an Internet joint venture with the Chinese *People's Daily* newspaper. He also published what one critic termed a "fawning biography" of Chinese leader Deng Xiaoping, written by no less an authority than Deng Xiaoping's youngest daughter.[212] Then in 1998 Murdoch's Harper-Collins canceled its contract to publish former Hong Kong governor Chris Patten's book, which was expected to be highly critical of the Chinese government. Murdoch personally ordered the cancellation — leading the HarperCollins editor to resign in protest — describing the Patten book as "boring" and beneath his standards. (Those standards had apparently been determined after the publication of the Deng Xiaoping biography.) After an extraordinary public brouhaha, Murdoch and News Corporation apologized for the cancellation and reached a settlement with Patten, but his book would be published by another press.[213] (It may be worth noting that this incident was ignored in the newspapers and news media owned by News Corporation.)[214] Following this episode, Murdoch was appointed to be one of fourteen "captains of industry" who would advise the new Hong Kong government on how to lure international investment.[215]

But Murdoch hardly will be deterred by a little bad publicity. Mandarin-language Phoenix Television, in which News Corp. has a 45 percent stake, signed major deals to gain clearance on Chinese cable television systems in 1997 and 1998, with the tacit approval of the Chinese leadership.[216] And industry observers claim Phoenix "has made significant progress in capturing advertising."[217] As the *Financial Times* put it, Phoenix "enjoys rare access into China, which has been denied to other foreign broadcasters."[218] In May 1998 Murdoch won another major victory when his Chinese partners in Phoenix Television won effective control of Hong Kong's second (of two) terrestrial broadcast stations.[219] Some sense of Phoenix's "journalism" came when a Phoenix reporter prefaced a question to Chinese premier Zhu Rongji with the words: "You are my idol."[220] In December 1998, Murdoch had a well-publicized visit with Jiang Zemin, worthy of a head of state. As a result, observers noted that Murdoch's fortunes were "rising fast in the East."[221] In stunning contrast, at the exact moment Murdoch was breaking bread with the Chinese leadership, three of China's foremost prodemocratic activists — who advocated free elections, new political parties, free speech, and independent trade unions — were given long prison sentences in the toughest crackdown on political dissidents since 1989.[222]

Compare this corporate behavior with that of Baruch Ivcher, the Peruvian whose TV station's numerous exposés of the Fujimori government's corruption and criminal activity led to the seizure of his station and caused him to flee Peru.[223] Or compare Murdoch and Eisner to Jesús Blancornelas, the Mexican newspaper editor who has faced assassination attempts for refusing to back down on his investigation into that nation's drug trade and its links to the highest echelons of Mexican society.[224] Or compare Murdoch and Eisner to Larisa Yudina, the Russian editor savagely murdered in a contract killing, whose crime was reporting the corruption of her local government.[225] Across the world there are numerous examples of heroic journalists, risking life and limb to tell the truth about the powers that be. The Brussels-based International Federation of Journalists reports forty-one journalists murdered worldwide in the line of duty in 1997, and 474 since 1988.[226] The U.S.-based Committee to Protect Journalists reported twenty-six journalists murdered worldwide in 1997, with another 129 cases of journalists wrongly imprisoned for going about their work.[227] But only in rare instances are these murdered and imprisoned journalists in the direct employ of the media giants.[228] One might posit that thugs and tyrannical governments are afraid to mess with reporters from powerful media corporations, so they concentrate on hassling the small fry. But if that was the case, why don't the types of stories that these martyrs were investigating get sustained attention in the corporate giants' media? The truth is that Baruch Ivcher, Jesús Blancornelas, Larisa Yudina, and their ilk may be courageous journalists valiantly advancing the public interest, but they lack what it takes to become successful in the brave (new) world of commercial journalism.[229]

It was ironic, indeed, when the World Bank in 1998 attributed the economic crisis in Asia to the lack of a "freer, more aggressive and more critical news media in the region" that would "put a brake on government corruption and so-called crony capitalism." The bank's own policies had been instrumental in assuring that no such media and no such journalism could possibly exist.[230]

Conclusion

As with the United States, it does not have to be this way. The "wild card" in the global media deck are the people of the world —

people constituted as organized citizens rather than as passive consumers and couch potatoes. It may seem difficult, especially from the vantage point of the United States and other wealthy nations, to see much hope for public opposition to the global corporate media system. As one Swedish journalist noted in 1997, "Unfortunately, the trends are very clear, moving in the wrong direction on virtually every score, and there is a desperate lack of public discussion of the long-term implications of current developments for democracy and accountability."[231] And, as discussed above, this political pessimism is precisely the type of political culture necessary for a neoliberal economic order to remain stable.

But there are indications that progressive political forces in nations around the world are increasingly making media issues part of their political platforms. (I discuss some of these activities in the conclusion.) As the global media system is increasingly intertwined with global capitalism, their fates go hand in hand. And despite much blathering about the "end of history" and the triumph of the market in the commercial media and among western intellectuals, the actual track record is quite dubious. Asia, the long celebrated tiger of twenty-first-century capitalism, is now mired in an economic depression. Latin America, the other vaunted champion of market reforms since the 1980s, has seen what a World Bank official terms a "big increase in inequality."[232] The ecologies of both regions are little short of disastrous. "The international economy, outside of the United States and Europe — perhaps 50% of the world," one economist noted in 1998, "is already experiencing a downturn that is worse than any that has occurred since the 1930s."[233] If this generates anything remotely like the political responses that emerged in the 1930s, all bets will be off concerning the triumph of neoliberalism and the global media market.

CHAPTER 3

WILL
THE
INTERNET
SET US
FREE?

The picture I present in chapters 1 and 2 is one of a starkly antidemocratic media system. Dominated by a handful of massive firms, advertisers, and the firms' billionaire owners, the system is spinning in a hypercommercial frenzy with little trace of public service, or public accountability. For decades, in the United States at least, the antidemocratic implications have been downplayed or ignored by the commercial media system's defenders. We should rejoice with this system, we have been told, because the government's role is minimal and this is exactly what the Founding Fathers intended with the First Amendment to the Constitution. Or, we are told, this is a truly fair and democratic media system that is ultimately controlled by the people because competition in the marketplace forces the media giants and advertisers to "give the people what they want." I address both of these arguments elsewhere in this book, especially chapters 1 and 6.[1]

In the 1990s a new argument has emerged, the effect of which is to suggest that we have no reason to be concerned about concentrated corporate control and hypercommercialization of media. This is the notion that the Internet, or, more broadly, digital communication networks, will set us free. This is hardly an unprecedented argument; every major new electronic media technology this century, from film, AM radio, shortwave radio, and facsimile broadcasting to FM radio, terrestrial television broadcasting, cable TV, and satellite broadcasting, has spawned similar utopian notions. In each case, to varying degrees, visionaries have told us how these new magical technologies would crush the existing monopolies over media, culture, and knowledge and open the way for a more egalitarian and just social order. But the Internet is qualitatively the most radical and sweeping of these new communication technologies, and the claims about it top earlier technological visions by a wide margin.

One factor that distinguishes the Internet from previous new communication technologies is its all-encompassing nature. "What people have not grasped is that the Internet will change everything," the CEO of Cisco Systems stated in 1998. "The Internet will change how people live, work, play and learn. . . . And it will have every bit as much impact on society as the Industrial Revolution. It will promote globalization at an incredible pace. But instead of happening over 100 years, like the Industrial Revolution, it will happen over 7 years."[2] Writers from Nicholas Negroponte and Douglas Rushkoff to George Gilder and even Newt Gingrich inform us that we are entering a period of fundamental social change the likes of which may occur once in a millennium, with the very essence of human social life and cognition undergoing qualitative change.[3] Many predict a future where individuals will have vastly greater power over their own lives than was ever dreamed.[4]

The claims for what the Internet will do to media and communication are no less sweeping.[5] "The Internet is wildly underestimated," Negroponte states. "It will grow to be the enabling technology of all media — TV, radio, magazines and so on."[6] The Internet, the argument goes, holds the potential to undermine corporate and commercial control of media. If everything is in the process of becoming digital, if anyone can produce a website at minimal cost, and if it can be accessed worldwide via the World Wide Web, it is only a matter of time (e.g., expansion of bandwidth, improvement of software) before the media giants find themselves swamped by countless high-quality competitors. Their monopolies will be crushed. John Perry Barlow, in a memorable comment from 1995, dismissed concerns about media mergers and concentration. The big media firms, Barlow noted, are "merely rearranging deck chairs on the Titanic." The "iceberg," he submitted, would be the Internet with its five hundred million channels.[7] As one *New York Times* correspondent put it in 1998: "To hear Andy Grove [CEO of Intel] and Reed Hundt [former chair of the U.S. Federal Communications Commission] talk, the media industry is about where the horse-and-buggy business was when Henry Ford first cranked up the assembly line."[8]

In this chapter I try to untangle the claims, even mythology, about the Internet from the observable record. It is not an easy task to do justice to this topic. On the one hand, the Internet is a quite remarkable and complex phenomenon that cannot be categorized by any previous medium's experience. It is two-way mass communication, it uses the soon-to-be-universal digital binary code, it is global, and it is quite unclear how, exactly, it is or can be regulated. On the other hand, the Internet is changing at historical warp speed. Any attempt at prediction during such tumultuous times is nearly impossible; something written on the Internet as recently as 1992 or 1993 has about as much currency in 2000 as discourses on the Wars of the Roses do for understanding contemporary British military policy. But I believe enough has happened in cyberspace that we can begin to get a sense of the Internet's overarching trajectory, and a sense of what the range of probable outcomes might be.

Although I agree that the Internet will be part of massive social changes, I do not share the optimism of the Gilders and Negropontes.[9] Their utopianism is based not just upon a belief in the magic of technology but, more important, upon a belief in capitalism as a fair, rational, and democratic mechanism. The latter I find mythological. (Combining a belief in technological magic with a faith in the magical markets makes for a heady brew. So it is that those most devoted to the privatization and commercialization of education often also advocate the ability of technology to solve the problems of education. In the next five years, Newt Gingrich stated in 1998, "a main goal" should be to "replace all textbooks with a PC.")[10] I also agree that the Internet is changing the nature of our media landscape radically. As Barry Diller, builder of the Fox TV network and a legendary corporate media seer, put it in December 1997, "We're at the very early stages of the most radical transformation of everything we hear, see, know."[11] What I wish to examine in this chapter, specifically, is whether these changes will alter the core tendencies mentioned in chapters 1 and 2 and pave the way for a qualitatively different media culture and society. Or will the corporate, commercial system merely don a new set of clothing?

I should add one caveat to what follows. The Internet is a truly global medium, arguably the first in history.[12] By all accounts, the

Internet is crucial to the global integration of the economy, and many accounts see it as having extraordinary social implications for global culture and politics as well.[13] At the very least, as *Business Week* notes, "It's a nifty way to expand a company's markets without spending a bundle on foreign subsidiaries."[14] For this reason as well, the Internet is becoming more and more important to giant media firms as they expand their operations globally. Those points notwithstanding, I concentrate upon the U.S. experience herein, only bringing in the global dimension where necessary to provide accuracy or to color a point. The global aspect of the Internet's development is so complex (and, still, underreported) as to require a book of its own to do it justice and to avoid oversimplification. For a variety of reasons, not the least of which is the U.S. creation of and current dominance of cyberspace, I believe a focus on the United States can generate a reasonably accurate understanding of the phenomenon. But, to the extent a U.S.-centric approach to the Internet is even plausible in 2000, that will not be the case in the future.

This chapter has five main parts. In the first section I look at the evolution and nature of U.S. Internet policy making, and locate the Internet in the historical tradition of communication policy making. One of the striking features of the Internet is that for something roundly proclaimed to be so millennial, it has enjoyed virtually no public debate over how it should be organized and deployed. This is especially noteworthy because the Internet is a public sector creation. In the 1990s the Internet has been deemed something to be developed by the private sector, with the guiding principle being whoever makes the most money wins. Besides being determined in a supremely undemocratic manner, this Internet policy is predicated, at least outwardly, on a notion of capitalism that is dubious. I devote the second section of the chapter to an explanation of why the current corporate development of cyberspace will almost certainly not lead to the sort of competitive, rational, and fair environment that politicians and pundits promise. I then proceed from the abstract to the concrete, by taking a close look at the policy debates and industrial developments surrounding U.S. digital television. With the shift of television to digital format in the next decade, it will become virtually interchangeable with the Internet. Hence those firms that come to dominate digital television may well be poised to play a major role in the age of the Internet. Given the stakes, the battles over digital TV have been especially intense in Washington, D.C. This shift has also opened the window, albeit only one one-hundredth of an inch, for public debate concerning what the public service obligations of digital broadcasters should be. Barring a change in the political climate, these discussions, conducted in 1997 and 1998 by a group called the Gore Commission, may well be the only thing close to citizen participation in determining the future of the Internet.

The fourth section continues on this path and assesses the way the Internet is being developed in the current profit-driven context. I first look at how the dominant firms in the relevant sectors — telecommunications, computer software, computer hardware, media — are addressing the Internet. Each of these firms and sectors is threatened by the Internet and is compelled to act defensively, and each also sees the Internet as a route to long-term growth and profitability. A key theme I touch on is *convergence,* which refers to the manner in which digital technology eliminates the traditional distinctions between media and communication sectors; for example, telephone companies and cable companies can provide each other's services. In conventional thinking, this convergence provides the basis for highly competitive markets, as firms can now invade formally irrelevant markets. I argue that the more telling consequence has been a wave of unprecedented mergers and alliances of the largest media, telecommunication, and computer firms. I also examine where it appears most likely for profit to be found in cyberspace, through electronic commerce and what are called portals, meaning the Internet locations users must access to get anywhere else on the web.

I conclude the chapter by turning to the crux of the matter, looking specifically at the media giants and how they have approached the Internet since the mid-1990s. I show how these firms have tremendous assets that should assist them in avoiding any prospective "icebergs." I assess what the prospects are for the Internet upsetting the media and corporate communication applecart, and/or providing the basis for a qualitatively different media, journalism, politics, and culture. As should be already evident, I think the evidence points in a very different direction from that suggested by the Internet utopians.

The Evolution of Internet Policy Making

Before considering the nature of U.S. Internet policy making, it is best to first provide context for the basic policy issues that surround any major new communication technology, including what the U.S. tradition has been prior to the Internet in formulating basic communication policy.

Two sets of fundamental political questions emerge when we discuss the development of any major communication technology. The first set asks who will control the technology and for what purpose? The corollary to this question is who will *not* control the new technology and what purposes will *not* be privileged. In the case of U.S. television, for example, it was determined that a few enormous corporations would control the medium for the purpose of maximizing profits, which would be realized by selling advertising time. Thus the United States put the development of television on a very distinct trajectory, a path rather unlike that which was adopted in most parts of Europe.

The second set of questions deals with the social, cultural, economic, and political impact of the new communication technology on the overall society and explores why the new communication technology is important. The institutional structures created to answer the first set of policy questions will generally determine the answers to the second set. In fact, much of communication policy making at this second level consists of trying to coerce the communication system — its owners and operators — into behavior they ordinarily would not pursue. The classic case in point would be the constant discussion about reducing the level of television violence. At the same time, however, the second set of policy questions cannot be reduced entirely to structural issues, otherwise it would not need to be considered fundamental. Regardless of how a communication technology is owned and operated, this will have consequences that are often unintended and unanticipated, and only related in varying degrees to its structural basis. Thus television dramatically altered the domestic culture of U.S households in the postwar years and it has arguably had a strong effect upon the nature of journalism and public discourse.[15]

The process by which society answers these questions can be regarded as policy making. The more a society is genuinely democratic, the more that society's policy debates concerning the application and development of paramount communication technologies will be open, informed, thoughtful, and passionate. But regardless of how democratic the policy-making process may be, these questions still emerge and will be answered in one form or another. As a general rule, if certain forces thoroughly dominate a society's political economy they will thoroughly dominate its communication system, and the first set of policy questions will not even be subject to debate. So it is and so it has been with the Communist Party in various "people's republics," and, for the most part, with big business interests in the United States.

The current communication revolution demands answers to both sets of policy questions, but it is not unprecedented. It corresponds most closely to the situation in the 1920s, when the emergence of radio broadcasting forced society to address the two sets of political questions mentioned above. Like the Internet in the 1990s, radio broadcasting was a radically new development, and there existed great confusion throughout the 1920s concerning who should control this powerful new technology and for what purposes. There was little sense of how radio could be made a profitable enterprise and much discussion of how liberating and democratic it could be. Much of the impetus for radio broadcasting in the first decade came first from amateurs and then from nonprofit and noncommercial groups that immediately grasped the public service potential of the new technology. It was only in the late 1920s that capitalists began to sense that through network operation and commercial advertising, radio broadcasting could generate substantial profits. Through their immense power in Washington, D.C., these commercial broadcasters were able to so dominate the Federal Radio Commission that the scarce number of air channels were effectively turned over to them with no public and little congressional deliberation on the matter.

It was in the aftermath of this commercialization of the airwaves that elements of U.S. society coalesced into a broadcast reform movement that attempted to establish a dominant role for the nonprofit and noncommercial sector in U.S. broadcasting. I referred to this movement in chapter 1 and I chronicle this episode in detail in chapter 4. The reform movement disintegrated after the passage of the Communications Act of 1934, which established the FCC. The 1930s reformers did not lose to the commercial interests, however, in any fair debate on a level playing field. The radio lobby dominated because it was able to keep most Americans ignorant of or confused about the communication policy matters then under discussion in Congress through its control of key elements of the news media and its sophisticated public relations aimed at the remainder of the press and the public. In addition, the commercial broadcasters became a force that few politicians wished to antagonize; almost all of the congressional leaders of broadcast reform in 1931–32 were defeated in their reelection attempts, a lesson not lost on those who entered the next Congress. With the defeat of the reformers, the industry claims that commercial broadcasting was inherently democratic and American went without challenge and became internalized in the political culture.

Thereafter the only legitimate way in which to criticize U.S. broadcasting was to assert that it was uncompetitive and therefore needed aggressive regulation. The basis for the "liberal" claim for regulation was that the scarce number of channels necessitated regulation, *not* that the capitalist basis of the industry was fundamentally flawed. This was a far cry from the criticism of the 1930s broadcast reformers, who argued that the problem was not simply one of lack of competition in the marketplace as much as it was the rule of the marketplace per se. Such limitation also means that with the vast expansion in the number of channels in the current communication revolution, the scarcity argument has lost its power and liberals are at a loss to withstand the deregulatory juggernaut.[16]

This constricted range of policy debate was the context for the development of subsequent communication technologies including facsimile, FM radio, and television in the 1940s. That the communication corporations had first claim to these technologies was unchallenged, even to such public-service-minded New Dealers as James Lawrence Fly, Cliff Durr, and Frieda Hennock. In comparison to the public debate over radio in the 1930s, there was almost no public debate concerning alternative ways to develop these technologies. By the 1940s and thereafter liberals knew the commercial basis of the system was inviolate, and merely tried to carve out a nonprofit sector on the margins. This was problematic, since whenever these nonprofit niches were seen as blocking profitable expansion, their future was on thin ice. Thus the primary function of the nonprofit sector in U.S. communications has been to pioneer the new technologies when they are not yet seen as profitable — e.g., AM radio in the 1920s, FM radio and UHF television in the 1950s — and then to be pushed aside once they have shown the commercial interests the potential of the new media. This has already been the fate of the Internet's computer networks, which after substantial public subsidy were turned over to private operators.

What would be a truly democratic manner to generate communication policy making? The historical record points to two basic principles which should be made operational. First, in view of the revolutionary nature of the new communication technologies, citizens should convene to study what the technological possibilities are and to determine what the social goals should be. At this point several alternative models of ownership and control should be proposed and debated, and the best model selected. In short, the structural basis of the communication system should be decided after the social aims are determined. *The key factor is to exercise public participation before an unplanned commercial system becomes entrenched.* Is such public participation an absurd idea? Hardly. In the late 1920s, Canada, noting the rapid commercialization of the U.S. and Canadian airwaves, convened precisely such a public debate over broadcasting that included public hearings in twenty-five cities in all nine provinces. The final decision to develop a nonprofit system was adopted three years later after a period of active debate.[17] Is this a ridiculous extension of democracy? One hopes not. If the shape of the emerging communication system that stands to alter our lives radically for generations is not fair game for democratic debate, one must wonder just what is.

Second, if such a public debate determines that the communication system needs a significant nonprofit and noncommercial component, the dominant sector of the system must be nonprofit, noncommercial, and accountable to the public. The historical record in the United States and globally is emphatic in this regard. In addition, it is arguable that commercial interests, too, must always be held to carefully administered public service standards. There are justified reservations about government involvement with communication. The purpose of policy making, in this case, should be to determine how to deploy these technologies to create a pluralistic, decentralized, accountable nonprofit and noncommercial sector, one that can provide a viable service to the entire population. Fortunately, communication technologies seem to be quite amenable to such an approach. One suspects that if our society devoted to this problem only a fraction of the time that it has devoted to commercializing communication, then we could find some workable public service models.

The U.S. policy-making experience with the Internet follows the undemocratic historical pattern prevalent since the mid-1930s. A crucial difference between the Internet and the previous new communication technologies since AM radio has been that the Internet's interactive decentralized structure has not lent itself to any existing regulatory model, making it more difficult to know exactly how the Internet should be handled.[18] This environment should have called for deliberation, study, experimentation, and debate; instead the door has been opened to letting commercial interests exploit the new medium to see where the most money could be made. The key decisions to do this have been and are essentially made by self-interested (commercial or procommercial) parties behind closed doors with minimal public or even congressional participation. A policy "consensus" emerged early on among industry and government officials in favor of privatization and commercialization, so there was nothing for the public to debate.

The ultimate importance of the corrupt Telecommunications Act of 1996 was and is to establish that the private sector would determine the future of U.S. electronic media and digital communication. Although the debates surrounding the Telecom Act rarely mentioned the Internet, with that law, Congress (and the public) effectively washed their hands of that matter, apparently for all time. As I described in chapter 1, the powerful corporate communication lobbies have no interest in public debate over whether or not their control of communication serves the public; they feel the same way about the commercialization of the Internet. In addition, the computer industry has established itself as a formidable lobbying force in Washington.[19] The leading media, telecommunication, and computer firms also have lobbying groups specifically commissioned to advance their interests on the Internet.[20] And it is not a case of the computer industry giants finding an unresponsive audience in Washington, quite the contrary. Vice-President Gore has actively cultivated computer firm CEOs, forming a "cyber-cabinet" of these "Gore-Techs" to meet monthly so he can stay on top of industry policy concerns.[21] By 1998 leading congressional Republicans were making almost weekly sojourns to Silicon Valley to convince the powers of the computer industry that they, more than the Democrats, would advance their interests on Capitol Hill and elsewhere.[22]

The goal of the corporate sector is unambiguous; it wants to entrench a commercial system before there is any possibility of public participation. Once such a system is entrenched, regulatory codes can then be enacted to lock it in for all time. This is entirely contrary to the democratic notion of public determination of policy *before* a commercial system gets entrenched. Once a communication system is established, and has powerful lobbies behind it, the difficulty in changing it through public policy increases exponentially. The necessity of the privatization and commercialization of cyberspace is also the official position of the Clinton administration, the Republicans, and indeed the entirety of the mainstream political spectrum. As one reporter put it, we live in "a climate where any regulation of the Internet in its commercial infancy is considered high treason."[23] It is now axiomatic, as one publication put it, that the "fundamental consideration" in all Internet policy making "must be how to transform the Net into a reliable and stable commercial tool which businesses and consumers know they can trust."[24] By the late 1990s, the sentiment of many, perhaps most, "Internet experts" was that "the government had little choice but to leave the meatiest decisions up to private industry."[25]

Although this crystallization of opinion — and utter lack of debate — concerning the Internet accords with the general trajectory of U.S. communication policy making over the past sixty-five years, it is nonetheless striking when one considers the origins of the Internet. All historians of the Internet recognize that it is a product of the public sector, and that it was closely associated with the military. But every bit as important, many, perhaps most, of the university scientists who designed the architecture of the Internet did so with the explicit intent to create an open and egalitarian communication environment. They had a vision of a noncommercial sharing community of scholars and, eventually, all citizens of the world. It was to be a public utility.[26] The Internet could have never been produced by the private sector; not only would the long-term wait for a payoff have been unacceptable but the open architecture would have made no sense for a capitalist to pursue, since it makes "ownership" of the Internet and profitability much more difficult. As recently as the early 1990s, cyberspace was a largely noncommercial preserve, with notable egalitarian and almost anarchistic characteristics, chock full of hackers flaming the efforts of those who dared bring commerce to the Net.

Some associate the commercialization of the Internet with the rise of the World Wide Web in 1993–95, and that was a contributing factor. But the crucial determinant was the decision of the U.S. government to privatize its portion of the Internet backbone, which began in 1993 and made possible the elimination of the earlier prohibition against commercialism in cyberspace. One feature of almost all discussions of the commercialization and privatization of the

Internet is the use of the passive voice. Nobody did anything, apparently, it just happened. So the *Economist* wrote concerning the metamorphosis of cyberspace governance: "When Cyberia was a small, academic country, such an informal arrangement worked well. But now it has been colonised by commerce, a more businesslike approach is felt to be necessary."[27]

So who decided to privatize the Internet? The detailed history of this shadowy process has yet to be written, but one reputable Internet history argues that the basic plan for a "transition of the network from a government operation to a commercial service" was hammered out at a by-invitation-only meeting in 1990 at Harvard University. The meeting was attended by government officials and representatives of the largest telecommunication and computer firms. A decisive point was the argument that it would be "unfair" to private providers of network services to have to compete with the government, so the government should just get out of the Internet. The conference summary report acknowledged that private control of the Internet would change the nature of the system, moving it away from a public service, with private vendors most interested in providing services to affluent consumers and businesses, but that did not alter the report's recommendation for privatization.[28] "Sure [the government] created the technology through their funding," an official of the Internet Society conceded, "but the baby has grown up and left home."[29]

It is perhaps not entirely accurate to say that there was no public participation in the decision to privatize the Internet. Some obscure and mostly unreported congressional hearings broached the subject, but usually in the sort of techno-jargon that rendered the core issues incomprehensible. The already weak and battered media public interest lobby, discussed in chapter 1, had little to contribute to whatever Internet debate might have taken place in the early and mid-1990s. In fairness to them, few if any critical thinkers had much of a notion of a progressive way to structure the Internet; it *is* a new form of communication to which old models of control cannot be applied categorically. No one really had a firm sense, for example, of what exactly, if anything, the privatization of the Internet would mean for individual users.

In the end, the only stratum that could provide organized opposition to the privatization of the Internet and to the elimination of any public debate concerning the Internet would have to come from the

"user" community, those who helped build up the noncommercial
Net culture of the late '80s and early '90s. But politics proved not to
be a comfort zone for most hackers and netizens, and few had a very
sophisticated appreciation for how corporate media and communication systems operate. Many of them, including those who detested
the idea of commercialized cyberspace, were open to the idea that
the government was the main enemy. Attacking the government is
hardly a controversial position in contemporary U.S. society. Electronic Freedom Foundation cofounder Mitchell Kapor captured this
sentiment in a 1993 piece in *Wired* magazine. Kapor argued that the
cable and telephone companies would be the proper groups to bring
the Internet to American homes, and that this was consistent with
the "Jeffersonian vision of diversity, openness and decentralization
of control." Kapor acknowledged that private control might lead to
some undermining of the Jeffersonian vision, and if it did the government might have to begin modest regulation. But, on balance,
Kapor argued that the private sector — not the government — was
the friend of a democratic Internet.[30]

Along these lines, most hackers and netizens ignored the deliberations leading up to the passage of the 1996 Telecommunications Act,
but they were up in arms when Congress attached the Communications Decency Act to it. This absurd statute — a proverbial red her-
ring — would have permitted such grotesque state censorship of
Internet content that even its backers knew it had no chance for success once it was challenged in the court system. And, indeed, it was
shot down as unconstitutional shortly after its passage. So long as the
government was out of the way, much of the hacker and netizen reasoning went, then individuals could "do their own thing" on the
Internet thanks to its open architecture, regardless of commercialization otherwise. The notion that the Internet is a super-powerful
technology that can override any nongovernmental (or, even, governmental) effort to tame it was and is quite prevalent, especially
among those immersed in computer culture.

Curiously, there was one public forum where the National Telecommunications Information Administration (NTIA) solicited opinions from Internet users on the prospective privatization of the last
government-owned portion of the Internet backbone, scheduled
for May 1995. Taking place online from November 14 to November
23, 1994, the "virtual" conference generated many long and thoughtful posts objecting to commercializing the Net and favoring the

maintenance of government ownership of the backbone to guarantee public access. Many of the participants demanded that there be many more public hearings, with much greater publicity so many more could participate. "[I am] hoping that no irreversible decisions are made on the basis of this conference," one participant posted. "There needs to be a much wider opportunity for public comment." The government proceeded with the privatization as planned and no more public hearings were ever held on the matter.[31] It may be worth noting that a 1995 advertising industry survey showed that some two-thirds of Americans did not want to have advertising on the Internet.[32]

The Clinton administration has aggressively promoted commercialization of the Internet, proclaiming that the commercial development of cyberspace is the key to current and long-term economic growth.[33] "It is in the best interest of the Internet and the United States for this medium to grow and become ubiquitous," Clinton administration Internet adviser Ira Magaziner stated. "And the Government's getting out of the way of its management is the best way to achieve that."[34] The Clinton administration has pressed to see that there be a "tax-free, self-regulated digital marketplace."[35] In December 1998 Magaziner turned over his formal interagency policy report on electronic commerce to the White House, with its recommendation in favor of maintaining the administration's "laissez-faire policy on Internet commerce."[36] An Internet industry group, representing fifty large corporations and marketers, the Online Privacy Alliance, has been formed to provide the sort of industry self-regulation that the Clinton administration has been calling for. "I think the enforcement mechanisms they are putting in place," Magaziner commented regarding their voluntary privacy standards, "are what we have been calling for."[37] The old informal Internet governance system based in universities and among scientists — the system dedicated to an open architecture and, at one time, to the noncommercial democratic development of cyberspace — is giving way to a system where corporate interests have more and more say.[38] Business interests are coming to play the dominant role in establishing Web technical standards, which are crucial to expediting electronic commerce.[39] What is clear to the business community is that if the Internet is to become central to business, then commerce has to be the raison d'être of cyberspace; it cannot prosper if it has to piggyback onto a noncommercial architecture and unsympathetic governance structure.[40]

In 1998 the Clinton administration decided that the U.S. government would abandon the management of the Internet's address system, turning it over to an international nonprofit group that would represent elements of the Internet industry.[41] The core telecommunication companies that now own the Internet's backbone, including MCI, GTE, and AT&T, have formed the Global Internet Project to provide "longer-term solutions" to Internet self-regulation.[42] The Clinton administration also led the bipartisan campaign which resulted in Congress passing a series of laws enhancing Internet commerce in October 1998. Perhaps most important, Congress approved the global treaty extending strict copyright standards to the Internet.[43] This copyright measure was opposed by educators, librarians, civil libertarians, and even some consumer electronics firms — all of whom feared for various reasons the privatization of Internet content and the chilling effect that it might have on the free flow of ideas — but the measure had the overwhelming support of the "large media and computer software companies" that would be its direct beneficiaries.[44] "This might surprise you coming from a Republican," the CEO of Cisco Systems stated in November 1998, "but this administration really gets it — the major impact that the Internet will have on job creation and the economy."[45]

This does not mean there are no battles over the future of the Internet, but the most important policy fights are at the global level. Although a global medium, the Internet still has a "made-in-USA" trademark. In 1997, U.S. business accounted for 90 percent of Internet commerce in 1997, 70 percent of commercial websites, and 93 percent of web revenues.[46] Some forecast that the United States, which accounts for a clear majority of global Internet traffic in 1999, may have no more than one-third of the total by 2005.[47] But one study forecasts that in 2002 only 13 percent of Europeans will be online compared to 34 percent of Americans.[48] This sends shudders down the spines of European policy makers, who fear the U.S. rush to promote "self-governance" of the Internet by its users will keep it primarily in service to U.S. interests.[49] In 1998 the Organization for Economic Cooperation and Development (OECD), which represents the world's richest twenty-nine nations, prepared a report "condemning the U.S.-centric nature of the Internet as a barrier to the development of electronic commerce."[50] These tensions bubbled over late in 1998 when the United States and the EU negotiated how to establish global Internet governance.[51] In October 1998 the largest U.S. Internet firms, in combination with Internet firms from Europe, Australia, and Japan, established the Internet Corporation for Assigned Names and Numbers (ICANN). The purpose of ICANN is to provide global private sector leadership for Internet governance, as the United States desired and about which the EU was wary.[52] At the same time the largest U.S. Internet firms launched an online privacy awareness campaign, to allay EU fears that commercial interests might disrespect privacy and to demonstrate "to policy makers that the industry can regulate itself." Finally, in January 1999, one hundred of the largest global media and telecommunications companies launched "Global Dialogue on e-Commerce," the point of which was to discourage any national attempts to regulate the Internet. Bertelsmann's CEO, Thomas Middelhoff, said the point was to have the Internet be directed by "industry-led, market-driven, self-regulatory" policies to "encourage private investments." As the group's initial statement concluded: "We as entrepreneurs look forward to taking up the challenge of actively shaping the policy framework for the internet of the next century."[53]

The exact contours of global Internet governance will be determined in the next few years, probably with little or no public awareness or participation. For the purposes of our discussion, two points are noteworthy about this global battle over Internet policy. First, it establishes clearly where notions of the "public interest" vis-à-vis corporate power fit into U.S. government conceptions of cyberspace: nowhere, except in rhetoric, if even there. Such is also the case in other global communication forums, where FCC officials openly lobby for deregulation so that U.S. transnational firms can exploit and dominate foreign markets.[54] Second, while the EU opposes the U.S. domination of the Internet, it does not oppose its commercial development otherwise.[55] Its goal is to slow down the self-regulation momentum long enough to permit European firms time to develop and be major participants. The EU, for example, supported the U.S. campaign in 1998 before the World Trade Organization to keep electronic commerce duty-free.[56] The EU and EC also oppose the application of national regulation to the Internet in Europe — they want a single continental market — as that would "crimp electronic commerce before it has a chance to start."[57] Hence the trajectory of all the dominant business, governmental, and regulatory agencies is toward greasing the wheels for a commercialized global Internet. The EU and the United States both work with the global corporate communication sector to encourage the "modernization" of the International Telecommunications Union (ITU), the body that regulates global telecommunication and that historically has had a pronounced public service element in its operations.[58] Modernization means two things: First, the ITU should increasingly work with Internet engineers to develop global standards.[59] Second, and more important, the ITU should become more "business-friendly" in its conduct. In 1998 the ITU's new leader received a warm response from the corporate sector when he announced the ITU would give business "a stronger say in the policy-making process." The ITU also proposed to reduce the number of elected posts in its permanent administration.[60]

Within the United States, there are tremendous struggles between firms and sectors to dominate the Internet; these are often fought out before regulatory agencies outside of the public eye. But the paltry U.S. public debate that does exist presupposes as legitimate the corporate commercial exploitation of cyberspace and proceeds from there to smaller issues that do not challenge that framework. Perhaps the biggest issue, because it pits the law enforcement establishment against the corporate community, deals with police opposition to the sort of strong encryption that protects electronic commerce, as police see strong encryption providing a harbor for criminal activity.[61] Similarly, the public is allowed to be involved to the extent of being spectators in the row between the Justice Department and Microsoft, which will determine whether Microsoft can have a possible monopoly over certain markets or will have to share them with two or three other massive firms like Oracle or Sun Microsystems.[62]

As for the media public interest lobby today, it enjoys the same leverage on Internet policy that it has on broadcasting and other communication policy, as I described in chapter 1. The one Internet issue that public interest lobbyists pursued in the early 1990s — assuring Internet access to poor and working-class citizens — has been effectively swept aside in the tidal wave of commercial Internet development. Public officials still mouth platitudes about universal access, but there is no effort to make it a reality, as it would cost billions and benefit the least important members of the U.S. polity.[63] Two minor measures have been developed to appease universal access advocates. One is an FCC program to wire the nation's schools and libraries, a program President Clinton has repeatedly praised.[64] Such praise notwithstanding, the FCC cut the funding for the program in half in 1998, to $1.28 billion.[65] Another measure is the proposal to establish an "Internet 2," to do what the original Internet did prior to privatization. But the Internet 2 is hardly intended to provide widespread public access, or even to be a "public service" alternative to the commercialized Web. To the contrary, the point of Internet 2, as much as anything, is to expedite research links between the corporate sector — especially the high tech sector — and universities. As such, Internet 2 is arguably more part of the process of corrupting the integrity of higher education than of protecting it.[66]

Public interest lobbyists have gravitated to the margins of legitimate debate on the Internet, sadly grasping for a legitimate straw to hang on to. So it was in 1998 that a leading public interest activist, once an advocate of noncommercial cyberspace, urged the government to regulate Internet marketing practices to children, because they "threaten not only children's privacy, but also the future of e-commerce." "Clear rules," she wrote, "would create a safe harbor for companies that practice responsible marketing" to children on the Internet.[67] The difference in tone of the late 1990s activists from the early 1990s hackers and netizens, or, better yet, the 1930s opponents of commercial broadcasting, could not be more striking. Corporate dominance and commercialization of the Internet have become the undebated, undebatable, and thoroughly internalized truths of our cyber-times. It is a clear reflection of the strength of corporate power in the United States, of the unanimity of sentiment for privatizing and commercializing the Internet on Wall Street and in elite circles, and of the weakness of democratic and progressive forces.

The Mythology of the Free Market

The antidemocratic nature of Internet policy making is explained or defended on very simple grounds: The Internet is to be and should be regulated by the free market. This is the most rational, fair, and democratic regulatory mechanism ever known to humanity, so by rights it should be automatically applied to any and all areas of social life where profit can be found. No debate is necessary to establish the market as the reigning regulatory mechanism, because the market naturally assumes that role unless the government intervenes and prevents the market from working its magic. Indeed, by this logic, any public debate over Internet policy can only be counterproductive, because it could only lead us away from a profit-driven system. Public meddling would allow unproductive bureaucrats to interfere with productive market players.

Combining the market with the Internet, we are told, will allow entrepreneurs to compete as never before, offering wonderful new products at ever lower prices. It will provide a virtual cornucopia of choices for consumers, and empower people all over the world as never before imaginable. Enterprise will blossom as the multitudes become online entrepreneurs. It will be a capitalist paradise. Nowhere will the cyber-market revolution be more apparent than in the realm of media and communication. When anyone can put something up on the Internet, the argument goes, and when the Internet effectively converges with television, the value of having a television or cable network will approach zero. Eventually the control of any distribution network will be of no value as all media convert to digital formats. Production studios will have less leverage too as the market will be opened to innumerable new players. And even governments, in the end, will find its power untamable.[68] As a consequence, the likely result of the digital revolution will be the withering, perhaps even the outright elimination, of the media giants and a flowering of a competitive commercial media marketplace the likes of which have never been imagined, let alone seen. Indeed, the rise of the Internet threatens not only the market power of the media giants but also the very survival of the telecommunication and computer software giants, as their operations are directly undermined by the Internet as well.[69]

These are very powerful claims about the market. It is ironic that as the claims about the genius of the market have grown in conventional discourse over the past two decades, the need to provide empirical evidence for the claims has declined. The market has assumed mythological status, becoming a totem to which all must pledge allegiance or face expulsion to the margins. The mythology of the market is so widely embraced because it has some elements of truth, and, more important, because it serves the interests of the most dominant elements of our society. And the free market mythology harms few if any powerful interests, so increasingly it goes unchallenged. As this mythology is the foundation of almost the entire case for the absence of any public debate on the course of the Internet, and therefore in favor of the privatization and commercialization of the Internet, it demands very careful scrutiny. And when we have a demythologized vision of the market and capitalism, we will be able to see through the hoopla to grasp what is actually transpiring in cyberspace.

The claim that the market is a fair, just, and rational allocator of goods and services is premised on the notion that the market is based on competition. This competition constantly forces all economic actors to produce the highest quality product for the lowest possible price and it rewards those who work the hardest and the most efficiently.[70] Therefore, these new technologies will permit hungry entrepreneurs to enter markets, slay the corporate dinosaurs, lower prices, improve products, and generally do good things for humanity. And just when these newly successful entrepreneurs are riding high on the hog, along will come some plucky upstart (probably with a new technology) to teach them a lesson and work the magic of competition yet again. This is the sort of pabulum that is served up to those Americans who lack significant investments in the economy. It provides an attractive image of the way our economy works — making it seem downright fair and rational — but it has little to do with the reality. Corporate executives will invoke this rhetoric in dealing with Congress or the public and, at a certain level, they may even believe it. But their actions speak louder than words.

The simple truth is that for those atop our economy success is based in large part on *eliminating* competition.[71] I am being somewhat facetious, because in the end capitalism is indeed a war of one against all, since every capitalist is in competition with all others. But competition is also something successful capitalists (the kind that remain capitalists) learn to avoid like the plague. The less competition a firm has, the less risk it faces and the more profitable it tends to be. All investors and firms rationally desire to be in as monopolistic a position as possible. (Only an idiot would want to be in the type of competitive market pictured by introductory economics textbooks and incessantly invoked by the likes of Jack Kemp, Newt Gingrich, Steve Forbes, and Dan Quayle. In that nightmare world, every time a capitalist makes an above-average profit along comes a horde of new competitors to try to take it away!) In general, most markets in the United States in the twentieth century have gravitated not to monopoly status but to oligopolistic status. This means that a small handful of firms — ranging from two or three to as many as a dozen or so — thoroughly dominate the market's output and maintain barriers to entry that effectively keep new market entrants at bay, despite the sort of profitability that Milton Friedman tells us would create competition. In pricing and output, oligopolistic markets are far closer to being monopolistic markets than they are to being the competitive markets described in capitalist folklore.

To be sure, despite all this concentration these firms still compete — but not in the manner the mythology suggests. As one business writer put it, "Companies in some industries seem to do everything to win customers, apart from cutting prices."[72] Advertising, for example, arises to become a primary means of competition in oligopolistic markets. It provides a way to protect or expand market share without engaging in profit-threatening price competition. On occasion, foreign competition or economic crisis or new technologies or some other factor may break down a stable oligopoly and lead to a reshuffling of the deck and a change in the cast of corporate characters. But the end result will almost always be some sort of stable oligopoly; otherwise, no sane capitalist would participate. Yet even the notion of oligopoly is somewhat insufficient, because widespread conglomeratization along with pronounced involvement by the largest financial institutions in corporate affairs has reduced the level of autonomy of distinct industries, bringing a degree of instability if not much more direct competition to the system. Rather than concentrate on specific oligopolistic industries, then, it is perhaps better to recognize the economy as being increasingly dominated by the few hundred largest firms. This certainly is the best context for understanding developments in media and communication.

So how should we expect the Internet to develop in this model of the free market? Exactly as it has so far. Despite now having the technological capacity to compete, the largest firms are extremely reticent about entering new markets and forcing their way into existing and highly lucrative communication markets. Thus the local telephone companies have tended to avoid providing pay television over their wires, and the cable companies have avoided providing telephone services over their lines. This is no conspiracy. There have been a few, and will no doubt be more, attempts by these firms and others to cross over and compete in new markets. But it will be done selectively, usually targeting affluent markets that are far more attractive to these firms.[73] Most important, none of the giants will attempt to enter another market unless they are reasonably certain that they will have a chance to win their own monopoly, or at least have a large chunk of a stable oligopoly with significant barriers to entry. A less risky option for these firms, rather than venturing on entrepreneurial kamikaze missions into enemy territory, is to merge to get larger so they have much more armor as they enter competitive battle, or to protect themselves from outside attack. Short of mergers, the other prudent course is to establish joint ventures with prospective competitors, to reduce potential competition and risk. In short the rational behavior is to attempt to reduce the threat of competition as much as humanly possible, and then to engage in as little direct competition as can be managed.

When capitalism is viewed in this light, the "iceberg" thesis is considerably less plausible. After all, the corporate media giants have significant weapons in their arsenal not only to confront but also *to shape* the new technologies. Moreover, once we have a realistic understanding of how capitalism operates, we can see why, instead of shrinking, the dominant corporate media firms are in fact growing rapidly in the United States and worldwide. In the United States, the media industry (and the largest media firms) is growing much faster than the overall economy, experiencing double-digit growth in consecutive years in 1997 and 1998 for the first time since the 1980s.[74]

But what about new firms? Will they provide the competitive impetus the giants rationally attempt to avoid? In general, new firms are ill-equipped to challenged giant firms in oligopolistic markets due to barriers to entry. The role of small firms in the classic scenario is to conduct the research and development and experimentation that large firms find insufficiently profitable, and then, when one of them finds a lucrative new avenue, they sell out to an existing giant. Some of the impetus for technological innovation comes from these small firms, eager to find a new niche in which they can grow away from the shadows of the corporate giants in existing industries. It is in times of technological upheaval, as with the Internet and digital communication, that brand new industries are being formed and there is an opportunity for new giants to emerge.

It is safe to say that some new communication giants will be established during the coming years, much as Microsoft attained gigantic status during the 1980s. But most of the great new fortunes will be made by start-up firms who develop a profitable idea and then sell out to one of the existing giants. (Witness Microsoft, which spent over $2 billion between 1994 and 1997 to purchase or take a stake in some fifty communication companies.) Indeed, this is conceded to be the explicit goal of nearly all the start-up Internet and telecommunication firms, which are founded with the premise of an "exit scenario" through their sale to a giant.[75] As an Internet stock manager put it in 1998, Internet company stock prices were "driven by speculation about who will be the next company to get snapped up by a much bigger company from another medium as a way of buying their way on to the Internet."[76] Hence the traditional function of start-up firms is still the rule. For every new Microsoft, there will be a thousand WebTVs or Starwaves or Netscapes, small technology firms that sell out to media and communication giants in deals that make their largest shareholders rich beyond their wildest dreams. And for every WebTV or Starwave, there are thousands and thousands more that go belly up.

What should be clear is that this market system may "work" in the sense that goods and services are produced and consumed, but it is by no means fair in any social or political or ethical sense of the term. Existing corporations have tremendous advantages over start-up firms. They use their power to limit the ability of new firms to enter the fray, to limit output and keep prices higher. But the unfairness extends beyond the lack of competitive markets. Wealthy individuals have significant advantages over poor or middle-class individuals in terms of participating as capitalists. A tremendous amount of talent simply never gets an opportunity to develop and contribute to the economy. It is unremarkable that "self-made" billionaires like Bill Gates, Ted Turner, Michael Eisner, Rupert Murdoch, and Sumner Redstone all come from privileged backgrounds. And, on the "demand" side of the market, power is determined by how much money an individual has; it is a case of one dollar, one vote, rather than one person, one vote. In this sense, then, the political system to which the market is most similar is the limited suffrage days of pre-twentieth-century democracies, where propertyless adults could not vote and their interests were studiously ignored.

In truth, this is what a defense of the market system in terms of fairness boils down to: new firms *can* start and they *can* become giants, and to do so they probably have to do something quite remarkable, or be very lucky. All it means is that the system holds open the slightest possibility of a nonwealthy person becoming a multimillionaire, that success is extremely difficult to attain in this manner, and that the hope of being rich will drive countless people to their wits' end.

There are a couple of other aspects of capitalism that do not comport to the mythology. First, and this is well understood by capitalists even if their rhetoric goes in the opposite direction, the government is scarcely a nonfactor in the economy, nor is its role merely to harass hard-working business people through onerous regulations and heavy-handed taxation. When free market mythologists criticize the heavy hand of government, what they really mean by the heavy hand is that government might actually represent the interests of the citizenry versus those of business. When governments spend billions subsidizing industries or advocating the interests of business, not a peep can be heard about the evils of Big Government. A 1998 investigative report in *Time* magazine noted that the U.S. government pays out some $125 billion annually in "corporate welfare," primarily to a few hundred very large corporations. As the series chronicles, little if any of this spending can be justified as a public expense.[77] Few corporate sectors have been recipients of government largess as much as the communication industries.

Most of the communication technologies associated with this revolution, particularly the Internet, grew directly out of government subsidies. Indeed, at one point fully 85 percent of research and development in the U.S. electronics industry was subsidized by the federal government, although the eventual profits accrued to private firms.[78] The free distribution of the publicly owned electromagnetic spectrum to U.S. radio and television companies has been one of the greatest gifts of public property in history, valued as high as $100 billion. One study of government spending places the annual "welfare" subsidies to commercial broadcasters and the advertising industry at $8 billion per year. (To give some sense of proportion, for $8 billion the U.S. government could subsidize a totally noncommercial public radio and television system with national networks, in-house production facilities, and multiple local channels that would be the equal of any public or commercial network in the world. The current federal subsidy for public broadcasting is $260 million.)[79] This self-serving notion of government explains why someone like AT&T-Liberty Media's John Malone can constantly bellyache about government intervention in the free market when it puts restrictions on his firm's activities. It would never occur to Malone to point out that his entire wealth came through cable company TCI, which grew powerful on the back of state-authorized legal monopolies that had zero competition.

Moreover, it is entirely misleading to submit that in this neoliberal, promarket era of "deregulation" the government is playing a smaller role than in earlier times. In fact, the government role is as large as ever, at least during this formative stage of digital communication systems. Extremely crucial decisions about the Internet and digital communication are being considered and will be implemented in the next few years that will effectively determine the course of the U.S. media and communication system for at least a generation, perhaps longer. The exact manner in which the Internet and digital communication develop will be determined by technological specifications, as well as by who controls the commercial digital industry.[80] The government will be singularly responsible for these activities, and what it does and who it favors will go a long way toward determining which firms and which sectors get the inside track on the information highway. What is different from earlier times is that under "deregulation" there is no pretense that the government should represent the public interest vis-à-vis commercial interests. The government is supposed to expedite commercial domination, which, ipso facto, serves the public interest.

Understanding the crucial importance of the government undercuts also the myth that the market exists "naturally," independent of the government, blindly rewarding the most efficient performers. Government policies are instrumental in determining who the winners will and will not be, and those policies are often derived in an antidemocratic and corrupt manner. More broadly, the notion that capitalism is the natural "default" economic or regulatory system for the human race, one that can only be messed with by meddling governments or trade unions, does not comport at all to the world as we know it. Establishing capitalism was a remarkable historical accomplishment. Capitalism as an economic system, based on the centrality of investment in pursuit of maximum profit, only developed in a small corner of the world after centuries of social transformation. It required massive changes in morals, laws, religions, politics, culture, and "human nature," not to mention economics. A recent indication of the absurdity of capitalism being humanity's "default" system comes from postcommunist Eastern Europe, where the attempt to let capitalism develop "naturally" has been nothing short of a disaster, in all but a few central European nations where the market had made strong inroads prior to communism.[81]

Another flaw in the mythology of the free market is that it posits that market-driven activities always produce the optimum and most rational social outcome. To some extent this argument for the market is based on the almost nonexistent model of pure competition;

in economic theory the degree of market concentration that exists across the economy undermines the claims for producing rational and socially optimal results. But the flaw in this argument is much deeper than that, and would even apply in mythological free markets. The simple truth is that markets often produce highly destructive and irrational results.[82] On the one hand, what is a rational course of action for an individual investor can easily produce negative results when pursued by many investors. For example, it is rational for an investor to withdraw an investment during a recession, since the chances for profit are small or nil. But if many investors take this same rational step, they may well turn the recession into a depression in which everyone loses out. The economic collapse of many so-called tiger economies of East Asia in 1998 highlights this distasteful aspect of markets to a painful degree.

On the other hand, markets produce what are called "externalities." These are the unintended social consequences of markets that are set up to reward individual pursuit of utility and, most important, profit. To put it bluntly, in their pursuit of profits there are things capitalists do that have important effects but capitalists do not care — cannot care — because these effects do not alter their bottom lines. Some externalities can be positive, such as when a corporation builds an especially beautiful office building or factory. It receives no material benefit from all those in the community who enjoy gazing at the structure, but the community clearly gains. Most externalities are negative, such as air pollution. Unless public policy interferes with the market there is no incentive within the market to address the problem. For extreme examples of this phenomenon, one need only travel to cities like Santiago or Delhi, where unregulated markets have produced air that is nearly unbreathable and where the market "solution" is to have the wealthy move to the high-priced areas with the least amounts of pollution.

The media system produces clear externalities. On the positive side, media can produce educational and civic effects through their operations, though the benefits will not accrue to media owners. The negative side of media externalities is well-catalogued. In their rational pursuit of profit, media firms produce vast quantities of violent fare, subject children to systematic commercial carpetbombing, and produce a journalism that hardly meets the communication needs of the citizenry. The costs of the effects of this media fare will be born by all of society. Commercial media also find it most profitable to use the new technologies to slice and dice the American people demographically to maximize their revenues; as a result, in our media-centric society, Americans have fewer shared cultural experiences common to all or most of us, especially with people outside their specific marketing peer group. One of the main trends in television over the past two decades, for example, has been for African Americans and white Americans to increasingly watch entirely different programs, except for sports. This logic, as it continues to develop, suggests that our ability to think of the United States as a community of people with diverse backgrounds may be compromised, as we increasingly have little exposure to the cultural experiences of broad sectors of society.[83] Democratic media policy making, then, should systematically attempt to create a system that produces large positive externalities and the smallest possible amount of negative externalities.

But media externalities are not simply the result of the market; they also result from how the market interacts with new technologies, or just from the technologies themselves. In the case of television, for example, regardless of the content per se, when viewing became ubiquitous and dominant, it changed the way people socialized and interacted. It led, for better or, in my view, for worse, to greater social isolation. All communication technologies have unanticipated and unintended effects, and one function of policy making is to understand them so we may avoid or minimize the undesirable ones. The digitalization and computerization of our society are going to transform us radically, yet even those closely associated with these developments express concern about the possibility of a severe deterioration of the human experience as a result of the information revolution. As one observer notes, "Very few of us — only the high priests — really understand the new technologies, and these are surely the people least qualified to make policy decisions about them."[84]

For every argument extolling the "virtual community" and the liberating aspects of cyberspace, it seems every bit as plausible to reach dystopian, or at least troubling, conclusions. Is it really so wonderful or necessary to be attached to a communications network at all times? Is sitting in front of a computer or digital television for hours per day really such a great thing for humans to do, even if it is "interactive"? Why not look at the information highway as a process that encourages the isolation, atomization, and marginalization of people in society? One controversial and hotly debated study at Carnegie

Mellon University in 1998 reached precisely these conclusions.[85] In fact, cannot the ability of people to create their own "community" in cyberspace have the effect of terminating a community in the general sense? In a class-stratified, commercially oriented society like the United States, cannot the information highway have the effect of simply making it possible for the well-to-do to bypass any contact with the balance of society altogether? These are precisely the types of questions that need to be addressed and answered in communication policy making and precisely the types of questions in which the market has no interest. We should look, and think, before we leap.

In sum, the mythology of the free market serves to protect the interests of the wealthy few, those who benefit from having the market rule near and far without popular "interference." The purpose of the mythology is not to clarify or guide or contribute to public debate but to obfuscate matters and to eliminate the desirability or need for public debate and democratic policy making. It is wrong to posit that the market should automatically rule unless massive evidence of specific "failures" can be produced; even when the market is working at its best, it can and does produce antisocial and antidemocratic outcomes that must be addressed by a democratic polity. My point is not that the market is an entirely inappropriate regulatory mechanism in a democracy; whatever its flaws there may well be some — even many — areas where the market can be deployed effectively. My point is that to the extent the market rules in communication, it should be as the result of public debate based upon informed and wide-ranging participation, not as the result of secretive deliberation wrapped in a bogus mythology.

Digital Television: Beginning of Convergence

Perhaps the most concrete way to reveal the relationship of corporate power and government policies to the way in which the Internet will develop is to look at digital television. In 1998 the United States began in earnest the process of converting from analog to digital television. It is a process expected to be completed between 2005 and 2010.[86] When television goes fully digital, it effectively becomes interchangeable with a personal computer, becoming an entry point to the Internet.[87] The converging possibilities became ever more clear with Microsoft's WebTV, which made it possible to browse the World

Wide Web on a conventional analog television set.[88] Then, in 1998, Broadcom introduced a single computer chip that made it possible to meld Internet pages and television pictures on TV screens.[89] Likewise, software made it possible to watch television over a PC.[90] In 1998 two cable television channels even launched spin-off channels on the Internet to begin building an audience for them, as they thought that would be as effective as being among the expanded offerings on digital cable systems.[91] Conversely, a popular Internet website, "Comedy Net," went the other way, launching digital TV channel versions of its websites in 1999.[92]

All of this is just the tip of the iceberg. Nobody knows how digital television will develop or what its relationship will be with the Internet. This much is clear: In 1999, only 27 percent of U.S. homes have online connections, and only 45 percent of U.S. homes have personal computers in them. Moreover, PC penetration has plateaued as many Americans find them too expensive and complicated. As the *Wall Street Journal*'s technology writer put it, "The Web is imprisoned in the PC."[93] The situation is ripe for a new inexpensive "network" computer, that could appeal to the 50–75 percent of the U.S. population that is presently not online. The situation is also ripe for digital television to become the primary conduit to the Internet for a significant number of Americans. As one Internet expert noted, the commercial broadcasters' "evolving digital platform could provide them with an Internet jump-start." As an Internet executive stated in 1998, the big broadcasters "could be sitting on an answer to Internet competition."[94] In short, the digital TV winners may have the inside track to dominating the commercialized Internet *writ large*.

The three routes to digital television are satellite television, digital cable television, and digital terrestrial television. Digital satellite TV is growing but nevertheless a minor player, and few think it will ever make a major dent in the cable industry's 70 percent penetration of the U.S. market. The digital satellite TV industry is already down to two main competitors, General Motors's DirecTV and Echostar, in which Rupert Murdoch's News Corp. has a large stake.[95] The appeal of digital satellite systems is the vast number of channels compared to standard cable TV, but that advantage is rapidly being eliminated. In 1998, five of the six largest cable systems companies that effectively control most of the United States rolled out a digital set-top box that will permit viewers to access hundreds of channels and eventually the World Wide Web over their analog television sets. "This is a watershed for the cable industry," states CEO John Malone of AT&T's Liberty Media.[96] It will also be a very expensive proposition, so the cable industry is courting partnerships with the likes of Microsoft, Oracle, and AT&T to provide capital and technical expertise. Microsoft purchased an 11.5 percent stake in cable giant Comcast in 1997 for $1 billion.[97]

What will fill these hundreds of channels? Almost all of the new program channels will be occupied by offerings from the same eight or nine firms that at the end of 1997 owned outright or in part forty-eight of the fifty leading cable channels.[98] All of the media giants have developed plans for an expansion in cable channels (almost always offering multiple channels of their tried and true formats) to meet the increase in channel capacity.[99] Viacom's Showtime, for example, has established eight channels, including Showtime Extreme, which will feature action films.[100] Time Warner's HBO and Viacom's Nickelodeon also have digital platforms of ten channels each.[101] "New cable services are everywhere," the *New York Times* observed in 1998, "but they all seem to be owned by the same big companies."[102] This much is already clear about digital television: the vast increase in channels does not mean more competition or fresh new players. As one industry observer concluded, the rise of digital means the "Ma and Pa days" of television are over.[103] Or, as one cable executive put it in 1998, "Most entrepreneurs have already gotten the word that the cable field is closed."[104]

But merely offering vastly more channels is not necessarily a recipe for increased profitability. Research shows that when people have forty-eight channels to choose from, they basically use eleven; with seventy-five choices, they use twelve on average; when the number jumps to two hundred channels, people still only use thirteen.[105] Just offering more channels, then, may not even be especially appealing to consumers. In the void the cable giants are offering plenty of pay-per-view films, sports events, and music concerts. The initial response to AT&T-TCI's pacesetting digital cable package in 1998 was called "astounding," with one million subscribers signing up in less than a year. The firm expects to convert 80 percent of its customer base within five years.[106] The other cable giants aggressively launched their digital platforms in 1999.

Two related areas are regarded by cable industry executives as important new revenue streams opened up by the conversion to digital.

First, the possibilities for extending and enhancing advertising are considerable. According to Liberty Media's Malone, digital cable television also will be "a bombshell for Madison Avenue."[107] On the one hand, digital will permit advertisers to pinpoint specific target audiences so that two households watching the same program could see "radically divergent" spots from the same advertiser.[108] "It's a big thing," says Malone, whose TCI has worked to design the digital format so it would "work best for the advertising community."[109] The key for digital cable's success, according to one advertising executive, will be whether firms like AT&T-TCI "focus on applications that help advertisers target consumers rather than those requiring consumers to interact with the advertising."[110] To that end, Malone convened an "off-the-record brainstorming session" for forty top marketing and ad agency executives in November 1998. The purpose of the meeting was "to get advertisers' input on how they can benefit from the upcoming generation of advanced digital set-top boxes."[111]

The second new revenue stream will come from electronic commerce, which means selling merchandise during programs and commercials. This is closely related to the expansion of advertising because it means viewers can click on ads to make immediate purchases. But it means much more than that. There will be numerous channels available for infomercials and interactive marketing. The capacity to sell merchandise during programs is particularly attractive.[112] Microsoft's WebTV has already shown how easy it is to offer "enhanced content" to accompany traditional TV programs.[113] "In enhanced TV," a new media analyst noted, "the brand takes on a new life — as advisor, as co-creator, even as a playmate. The opportunity here is to protect and position a brand while extending it."[114] At their most hopeful, cable executives aspire to siphon off a considerable portion of the electronic commerce business that would otherwise go to the Internet. As I discuss in the next section, estimates vary wildly over how quickly U.S. e-commerce will grow, but even conservative forecasts place it at well over $60 billion by 2003. Considering that *all* of U.S. broadcasting and cable advertising amounted to $45 billion in 1998, one can see why e-commerce has attracted the attention of cable executives.[115]

What type of media culture should we expect from a system with this operating logic? As one of the leading business writers on media wrote, not disapprovingly at all, in the age of digital television, "the ability to cross-promote products and services will be too great for any content provider to resist." The opportunity for consumers to solicit data about products and purchase them "will routinely be integrated at all points into all TV programs." The "winning paradigm for program producers," she went on to say, "will be in building and exploiting core franchises and brands by endlessly 'layering in' related products and services." In short, digital television offers the opportunity to supercharge commercial synergies, "an incessant stream of pitching and peddling."[116] Perhaps this writer's forecast is too starkly commercial, but at any rate the route to digital television profitability is pointed toward intensified commercialization. And if digital cable is any sort of dry run for the Internet, what is emerging is a far cry from the sort of Jeffersonian ideal that Mitchell Kapor argued was on the horizon at the hands of the cable and telephone companies.

But digital cable television does not have a clear path to success. It is in some ways a stopgap measure, though if successful it may go a long way toward determining what will follow. Eventually, over-the-air (terrestrial) television broadcasting will convert from analog to digital. At the outset, viewers will be able to use a converter — like the familiar "box" of cable conversion — to show digital signals on their analog TV sets; but down the road all television transmission and reception will be done purely on a digital basis. And when all television sets are digital, convergence will be complete as they will permit access to the Internet. When over-the-air broadcasting switches to digital format, the possibilities are seemingly boundless. Using the same amount of spectrum as presently used for five to seven channels, a community could receive anywhere from fifteen to twenty high-definition channels to as many as sixty or seventy channels similar in quality to the current analog, instead of the current five to eight terrestrial channels available in most U.S. communities. Digital terrestrial television also has commercial potential like that of digital cable. In 1998 the largest media and computer firms agreed on its technical specifications. A main benefit of the interactive television digital terrestrial television can provide, it was reported, is that it will permit marketers to gain extensive information about consumers and give advertisers more ability to sell their wares over the air.[117]

The transition from analog to digital television poses fundamental policy questions for the United States. Who will get to own and control these channels and for what purposes? What will be the relationship of digital terrestrial broadcasting to cable television and to the

World Wide Web? The government alone ultimately determines who can use the limited spectrum, and for what purposes. This is one area where Congress traditionally weighs in with formal policy guidelines for the FCC. In view of the importance of television — and now the Internet — in our society, this should be a political issue worthy of the greatest possible study, debate, and public participation. And given the vast qualitative difference between digital and analog television, there has been no reason to assume that the old broadcasters are automatically entitled to rule the new millennium without review. Indeed, such debate might have raised the question of how and why the commercial broadcasters had won the right to rule the old millennium. Moreover, even if one grants corporations the right to dominate the digital age, it is already clear that the market is a very poor regulatory mechanism for developing a new technology. Manufacturers do not think there will be a market for expensive new digital TV sets until there are high-quality digital channels that people want to see; and broadcasters do not want to invest in high definition digital television until there are large numbers of people who own digital TV sets.[118] In short, any way one slices it, the government will play a central role in determining the contours and trajectory of digital television.

It is in relation to digital television that the corrupt and antidemocratic nature of the Telecommunications Act of 1996 becomes most evident.[119] The commercial broadcasters wanted to control digital television, but they did not wish to have any public debate over who should get the new channels and under what terms. In 1995, the NAB and the top executives in the broadcasting industry used their influence to have a clause quietly added to the prospective act that would require the FCC to *give* each existing television broadcaster an additional six megahertz of spectrum so they could begin broadcasting simultaneously in digital and cable. Rupert Murdoch, owner of Fox television interests, and his lobbying machine were instrumental in the process. Murdoch's close relationship with Rep. Jack Fields, the ranking Republican on the relevant House committee, paid big dividends, as Fields "shepherded the legislation through Congress." As one industry observer put it, "Murdoch's people called the shots for Fields and his staffers, and everyone knew it."[120] It is worth noting that communication firms have to pay to use the scarce spectrum for nonbroadcast purposes like cellular telephony. The spectrum was valued at anywhere from $40 billion to $100 billion. As the NAB intended, this clause received no debate at the committee level. It also received no media coverage to speak of. The public was completely in the dark.[121]

When word leaked about the giveaway, a minor crisis erupted. Conservative columnist William Safire lambasted it as corporate theft that would make the robber barons blush. Senator John McCain (R-Ariz.) termed it "one of the great scams in American history."[122] Senate majority leader Bob Dole, who was then running for president, termed the spectrum giveaway "corporate welfare," and stated he would prevent the telecommunications law from coming to a vote in the Senate as long as the giveaway remained in the bill. Interpretations of Dole's sudden and unexpected concern over "corporate welfare" vary. Some argue that he genuinely "found religion," at least on this one issue. Less sympathetic observers argue that his stance was based on his desire to undercut Pat Buchanan's growing support as a so-called populist in the early Republican presidential primaries. Others argue that Dole was threatening to hold up the corporations' beloved Telecommunications Act mostly to shake down the broadcasters and the other communication corporations for campaign contributions. And still others note that when Dole first voiced opposition to the digital plan, in a private meeting with Murdoch and other broadcasting executives in November 1995, he complained about what he regarded as the negative TV coverage of his presidential campaign.[123] At any rate, Newt Gingrich and some corporate lobbyists pulled Dole aside and told him how much was riding on the law and how important it was to get it passed as quickly as possible. Dole formally backed down, after being given an oral promise that the Senate could hold public hearings on digital television in next session of Congress before the FCC would issue any new licenses.

The Telecommunications Act was then passed by an overwhelming majority in both the House and Senate, with the NAB's clause intact. A few months later, Bob Dole resigned his seat in the Senate to concentrate upon his flagging candidacy for the presidency. His replacement as Senate majority leader, Trent Lott, soon thereafter wrote to the FCC, in a letter co-signed by Newt Gingrich and other Republican leaders, informing the commission that he had no interest in Senate hearings on digital television and wanted the FCC to proceed posthaste with issuing licenses for digital broadcasting to the existing broadcasters. At that point the public's formal right to participate in digital television policy making was forfeited, without a murmur of press coverage. (A cynic might be forgiven for noting that Senator Lott was a college classmate and is a close friend of NAB president Eddie Fritts.)

Some people at the FCC and the White House shared Dole's and McCain's reluctance to turn the spectrum over without any strings attached; although the law required the FCC to assign the spectrum at no charge, it was permitted to negotiate public interest standards otherwise. Here the FCC found allies among other corporate media sectors in their negotiations. A major issue was (and is) the pace at which the broadcasters would convert to being fully digital. The theory was that in around ten years, when most Americans have digital TV sets or converters, and all signals are digital, analog broadcasting would be discontinued and the spectrum would be returned to the FCC and auctioned off for nonbroadcast purposes. The consumer electronics industry and the computer software industry were gung ho for a rapid transition to digital, since that would open up a huge new market for digital equipment and also speed up the convergence of television and the Internet. Commercial broadcasters, on the other hand, were in no such hurry. Once the licenses for digital broadcasting were safely in their hands, they had no particular incentive to go headfirst into digital; it would cost money without necessarily bringing in new revenues, and to the extent that it brought convergence with the Internet, it might introduce competition to their markets.[124] (At the same time, the broadcasters could not drag their heels on digital conversion indefinitely. If digital communication, digital television, and the Internet took off and the broadcasters did not have a viable presence, there might be the possibility that they would be pushed to the margins of the system. As one industry report put it, "Broadcasters who do not jump on the digital conversion bandwagon will be out of business in 10 years."[125] So they had to do something, they just did not know what that was.) In April 1997, after much pressure from NAB sympathizers in Congress, the FCC formally issued the licenses for digital broadcasting. The best it could do was get an informal commitment from the broadcasters to roll out digital broadcasting in a "timely" manner. *Variety* characterized it as a stunning victory for the broadcast industry.[126]

By the summer of 1997 the industry was already making noises that it could not afford to develop digital broadcasting as quickly as the government desired. "With HDTV," states one TV executive, "nobody has any goddamned idea if anybody can make a nickel on it."[127] "Where is the incremental increase in revenues that justifies the investment?" a broadcasting executive asked about HDTV. "We don't see it out of an HDTV single channel, advertiser-supported business in the early years."[128] Similarly, executives at Disney's ABC and some other commercial broadcasting firms stated that rather than do one high-definition channel in digital, it would be better business to provide six to ten channels — or "multicasting" — with the same six megahertz using lower definition.[129] NBC announced that it, too, was pondering the notion of multicasting its cable networks digitally through all of its own stations and its affiliated stations.[130] At the same time, deregulation and the shift to digital were encouraging a wave of consolidation among TV station owners. Sinclair Broadcasting, for example, spent $3 billion acquiring stations in 1997–98 and planned to have over one hundred stations by 2000.[131] "In the digital world," one trade publication noted, "it's better to big."[132] Indeed, if a company multiplexed six or eight stations in every market where it owned a station, and it owned scores of stations, digital broadcasters could create powerful broadcasting networks all on their own.

There was one basic problem with this scenario for digital terrestrial television: it upset the cable and satellite TV industries that were now facing the prospect of terrestrial broadcasting offering fifty to a hundred channels in a market and providing a "free" alternative to their pay services.[133] It also upset some members of Congress who had been told all along that the digital spectrum giveaway was not a giveaway because the broadcasters would have to invest millions to produce a vastly superior high-definition signal.[134] These members of Congress were egged on by the consumer electronics lobby; without HDTV there was little need to exchange existing analog TV sets for digital TV sets, since a small digital converter would suffice. By the spring of 1998 the cable industry announced it did not plan to carry the new "multicast" digital terrestrial channels on their expanded digital cable systems. This could kill multicasting in the cradle as cable is how most Americans received their television.[135] The conflict between the cable companies and the broadcasters over multicasting was mitigated by the fact that the largest terrestrial broadcasters — for example, Disney, GE, News Corporation, and CBS — also have large stables of cable television channels.[136] As the CEO of Sinclair Broadcasting, the largest TV-station-owning firm in the nation and main proponent of multicasting, put it, "the cable business and the broadcast business can become partners."[137]

In 1999, the industry, the corporate lobbies, the FCC, and congressional leaders remain in intense negotiations to have the broadcasters give a "speedy rollout" to digital and at least make a partial commitment to providing some high-definition channels in every market.[138] The FCC has assumed a more direct role in pushing the broadcasters, cable companies, and computer/Internet firms to make their digital formats compatible and to resolve their differences amicably.[139] "Until the three industries get together," stated Bud Paxson, CEO of Paxson Communications, in 1998, "and figure out how to incentivize [sic] and educate consumers, we are on a path to nowhere."[140] At this point in time, the "vision for digital" is "still blurry," as one trade publication put it.[141] In the end, it is likely that broadcasters will indeed provide some combination of high-definition and multicasting digital broadcasting.[142] So communities that currently have five or six terrestrial channels will eventually have at least twenty or thirty digital channels, all owned by the same five or six companies that currently rule their markets. And they will have paid not one penny to the government for their increase in holdings.

This would seem to be a classic case of powerful lobbies fighting it out and cutting deals behind closed doors to determine the most profitable course with zero concern for any noncommercial or broadly defined public interest values. But that is not the entire story. When the FCC found itself pressured to turn over spectrum to the broadcasters before it had an opportunity to develop any nonmonetary public service conditions, as it was permitted to do by the Telecommunications Act, it convinced the White House to appoint an advisory committee to propose recommendations for what public service the broadcasters could provide in exchange for the gift of a free spectrum. The twenty-two members of the so-called Gore Commission, named after its honorary chair, Vice President Al Gore, were appointed in October 1997. After a series of public meetings, they delivered a report with recommendations to President Clinton in December of 1998. The Gore Commission report consisted of "watered-down voluntary measures on political advertising and on educational or public-affairs programs."[143] Even elements of the trade press were underwhelmed by the commission and its report. The Gore Commission, *Mediaweek* observed, recommends "in the wimpiest way possible that the broadcasters adopt *some* voluntary standards of conduct . . . in return for these expensive digital airwaves."[144] *Electronic Media* reported that the immediate response to the report was "that its overall impact will be minimal."[145] The *Los Angeles Times,* in one of the rare commentaries on the Gore Commission not in the business or trade press, characterized the commission's report as "a national scandal."[146] In 1999 the Gore report was sent along to the FCC for review, where it almost certainly will be buried. The prospect of the FCC aggressively developing the sort of viable public interest standards that the Gore Commission had so clearly avoided was close to nil. In late 1998, the FCC had been forced to back down from a modest attempt to tighten broadcast ownership rules when Wall Street executives and broadcast industry executives used their influence in Congress to force FCC chairman William Kennard to withdraw the proposals. If the FCC's autonomy is so limited on modifications of ownership regulations, it is nonexistent when the subject turns to viable public interest standards that might effectively cost broadcasters in the hundreds of millions or billions of dollars.[147]

Since scholars, regulators, and communication industry officials may well point to the Gore Commission in future generations as the one moment in which the United States formally pondered the social implications of its emerging digital media culture, this episode in communication policy making merits at least a brief postmortem. The commission was cochaired by Les Moonves, the president of CBS Television, and included six commercial broadcasting executives as well as several stellar public interest advocates, including Peggy Charren, the founder of Action for Children's Television, and Gigi Sohn of the Media Access Project. However, the commission was severely compromised from the beginning. It was advisory, so on the off chance that it did make some strong suggestions, the NAB would be able to shoot them down fairly easily behind closed doors in Congress and at the FCC. In addition, the Gore Commission had no *leverage* over the broadcasters, since the FCC has already issued the licenses for digital broadcasting. For a group like this to have teeth, such deliberation needs to precede licensing. Perhaps most important, even if Moonves and the other commercial broadcasters were the most public-spirited members of the business community in U.S. history, their basic allegiance is to their industry, and they probably could not conceive of public service if it in any way harmed the commercial prospects of their industry.

This strong presence of the commercial broadcasters during the deliberations of the Gore Commission gave their operations an almost surreal quality. "Panel members repeatedly dismissed recommendations that would not fly with the politically formidable commercial TV industry," one observer noted. Although the commission finally did recommend that broadcasters, at some point off in the future, should be required to meet some minimal standards for public service, it avoided stating what those requirements might be. *Any* specification of public service obligations for commercial broadcasters, one commercial broadcaster on the commission stated, would be nothing short of "a declaration of war" on the industry.[148] And, indeed, the NAB and the industry's pit-bull trade publication, *Broadcasting and Cable,* were going to oppose any public service recommendations by the Gore Commission categorically. The NAB produced documentation at the third commission meeting showing that commercial TV stations already provided $6.85 billion worth of public service annually to their communities at no charge, making additional public service requirements unnecessary. This was a claim that even industry trade publications had trouble taking very seriously.[149] "Broadcasters don't need the government — listen up, Gore Commission — telling them what to do or how to do it," an editorial in *Broadcasting and Cable* intoned.[150]

Moreover, the Clinton administration was never comfortable with the idea of the Gore Commission making a full-scale study and report on public service for digital television. "The White House has made it known," *Variety* reported, "the sole reason for the Gore panel's existence is to nail down a free airtime recommendation for the 2000 presidential election."[151] But the industry representatives on the Gore Commission quickly kiboshed that idea.[152] Many philosophical reasons were given, but the bottom line was that this is a five-hundred-million-dollar-per-election market for commercial broadcasters. They were not about to give it up unless they got something substantial — something more than the digital spectrum they already had — in return.[153] To extract even a recommendation for a voluntary five-minute-per-night commitment of free time for candidates in the month preceding an election, the Gore Commission recommended that broadcasters be permitted to raise their ad rates for political commercials beyond the rates then legally permissible.[154] The Gore Commission said that no requirement of free time for political candidates on television should be made until Congress passed comprehensive campaign finance reform legislation. The broadcasting industry, Moonves said, "shouldn't be the Lone Ranger."[155] Indeed, the commission's report made all sorts of recommendations concerning issues other than the ones it was commissioned to study. In addition to calling upon Congress to pass campaign finance reform, the report urged the cable industry to accommodate the needs of digital broadcasters, and it proposed recommendations to beef up public broadcasting so it could provide much of the public service currently absent in U.S. television. The fingerprints of the commercial broadcasters were all over the report.

In the final analysis, the best hope for the Gore Commission would have been to become a widely publicized group that held public hearings across the country with no holds barred. At the commission's second meeting, when it was already clear that the group was dead in the water, Peggy Charren recommended that the commission reach out and solicit broad-based public input. Moonves dismissed the idea categorically as inappropriate "grandstanding."[156] Public exposure was the last thing the industry wanted or would countenance; *Electronic Media* warned its readers that Americans were sympathetic to the idea of having public service be a part of television.[157] A public opinion survey conducted in late 1998 found widespread support for public interest requirements for commercial broadcasters that went well beyond anything broached at the Gore Commission.[158] At its best, the Gore Commission might have stimulated formal FCC or, better still, congressional hearings on the subject.

In short, the Gore Commission should have attempted to provide the democratic participation in policy making that has so far been nonexistent. Instead it was not covered in the media aside from trade and business publications, and the range of debate was limited to matters which could not in any way threaten the profits of the dominant players. The recommendations that were debated and ultimately made in the report were trivial in the context of the commission's initial mandate, and could only capture the interest of a commercial broadcaster whose business was affected or of an inside-the-beltway public interest lobbyist so used to being ignored that just seeing the words "public interest" in a government report was a life-defining event. The most important subject of all — why the commercial broadcasters were automatically assumed to be the proper stewards of digital television — was decidedly off-limits. After all, by contemporary political standards, the commercial broadcasters had stolen the digital channels fair and square. It was left to dissident Gore Commission member and former FCC chair Newton Minow to put the matter in historical context: "Our grandchildren will one day regret our failure to meet one of the great communication opportunities in the history of democracy."[159] They will conclude, Minow added, "that our generation believed that from those to whom much is given, nothing much is required in return."[160] The Gore Commission has joined the sham FCC hearings of 1934, discussed in chapter 1 and again in chapter 4, in the rogue's gallery of bogus communication policy making groups.

The Hunt for the Killer Application

It remains to be seen if either digital cable or digital terrestrial broadcasting, or both, will prove commercially successful. Or it even may turn out, as one trade publication put it in 1998, that the development of the "set-top box could even kill off the Internet as an entertainment medium."[161] But the digital broadcasters are joined in the pursuit of Internet riches by a host of other media and nonmedia firms, all of whom act both out of a desire for more profit and out of a fear of being outflanked by their competitors on the Internet if they do not proceed aggressively. The crucial factor that will be necessary for the Internet to become ubiquitous and dominant will be the expansion of "broadband" capability to the bulk of the population; that is, the ability to have material flow as quickly online — even as fast as the speed of light — as signals travel on television. When that happens, the Internet may well become a vast converged communication machine, eliminating traditional distinctions between communication and media sectors as everything goes digital. The president of NBC News, Andy Lack, predicts that it will be at least the year 2008 until full-motion video — television as we know it — is widely available in U.S. homes via the Internet, and others tend to think it could be longer than that.[162] But firms do not have the luxury of sitting back and waiting for that moment: those that dominate cyberspace then will be determined well before the era of widespread broadband access.

The late 1990s, accordingly, has seen a flood of investment to Internet-related enterprises.[163] "It may seem as if the two year old internet industry is mounting a takeover of corporate America," the

Financial Times noted in 1998. "The reality is more like a merger."[164] Huge sums have been squandered already, and more will certainly be lost in the future as firms seek out the "killer application" that will define the Internet as a commercial medium. But by the end of the 1990s the dust is beginning to settle and some inkling of how great wealth can be generated by the Internet is becoming more clear. And as the formal policy is to let the market rule, wherever the most money can be found is how the Internet will develop.

The two most important corporate sectors regarding the Internet are telecommunications and computers. Each of these sectors is more immediately threatened by the Internet than are the dominant media firms. In the case of the seven or eight massive telecommunication firms that dominate the U.S. telephone industry, the Internet poses a threat to the industry's very existence. The new technology of Internet protocol (IP) telephony threatens to open the way to vastly less expensive communication and the possibility of new-found competition.[165] Sprint has gone so far as to revamp its entire network to operate by IP standards.[166] More important, the very notion of voice telephony is in the process of being superseded by the digital data networks that send voice as only a small portion of their data delivery. In this sense, the big telecommunication firms can appear like giant dinosaurs made irrelevant by the Internet.

But the giant telecommunication firms have a few distinct assets to play upon. First, they have wires into people's businesses and homes and these wires are suitable for carrying Internet traffic. Second, the Internet "backbone" of fiber-optic trunk lines is owned by several of the largest U.S. telecom firms, including WorldCom-MCI, AT&T, GTE/Bell Atlantic, and Sprint.[167] These factors make the telecommunication firms ideally suited to become Internet service providers (ISP) to business and consumers, already an area with a proven market.[168] Indeed, with the entry of the large telecommunication companies into the ISP sector, the *Financial Times* noted that the "Internet small fry" were "on the road to oblivion." "The situation is very much like the PC market 10 years ago," it added, "where a lot of smaller PC dealers went out of business."[169]

The third asset the telecommunication firms enjoy is a great deal of cash and cash flow. This liquidity has made it easier for the telecommunication giants to merge and acquire other telecom firms. Such size is seen as a necessity in the competition to offer global services. In 1998 alone, scores of mergers took place in telecommunication, including the merger of Bell Atlantic with GTE and the purchase of Ameritech by SBC Communications.[170] It is also very much a global process.[171] A harbinger of things to come may have been the announced merger of AT&T's global operations with British Telecommunications in July 1998, so that AT&T could better "focus on serving multinational corporations."[172] The consensus of opinion in the business community is that early in the twenty-first century as few as four to six firms will dominate the entirety of global telecommunications.[173] This will almost certainly mean that the market for Internet access will be restricted to a handful of players.

But the telecommunication firms are not alone in the ISP market. The other major contender for providing Internet access is the cable industry; in the United States that means the five or six companies that have monopolies over more than 80 percent of the nation. It is these cable companies, including Time Warner (with Road Runner) and AT&T-TCI-Liberty Media (with @Home), that are the media firms most directly and immediately affected by the Internet. By the summer of 1998 the FCC effectively abandoned the notion that the ISP market could ever be remotely competitive. It began the process of granting the regional Bell companies the right to restrict the use of their wires to their own ISP services, rather than forcing them to make their wires available to all users at a fair price. By doing so, the FCC hopes to encourage at least *two* viable ISP services — one telephone-based, the other cable-based — in each market, rather than have it become a monopoly.[174]

The ISP industry is shaping up as a highly lucrative aspect of the emerging digital system; it may well be the first "killer app." But the key to great Internet wealth may be whether the ISPs can mimic what the U.S. cable companies did (when they demanded partial ownership of cable TV channels if the channels wanted access to their systems and also freely launched their own channels), and use their control over the crucial Internet wires as a means to get a piece of the commercial action that transpires over their systems. This is an issue we turn to below with the discussion of portals.

One of the striking features of having Internet access provided by the private sector is that the notion of universal service to the entire population is — must be — sacrificed to the needs of the market. The most money is made by pitching high quality service to the affluent who can afford it, and who are most attractive to advertisers. As John Malone put it, the best way to conduct the Internet access business is to offer "tiered" service, with high-speed access for the affluent and for businesses, on down to slow clunker Internet access for those who cannot afford better service.[175] In 1998 the average U.S. Internet user had an income double the national average, and there is little reason to expect that to change quickly.[176] The fees expected for high-speed Internet access into the twenty-first century are expected to be around $100 per month, which would all but rule out about half of the U.S. population.[177] The greatest disparity is between African Americans and white Americans, where the difference goes well beyond what one would expect from economic factors alone.[178]

Computer firms, too, are threatened by the Internet. None more than Microsoft, which stands to see its lucrative monopoly on stand-alone computer software eliminated by the rise of digital computer networks. Since recognizing the threat in 1995, Microsoft has used all of its market power and wealth to see that it is not outflanked on the Internet, and that it has a finger (or hand) in the pie of any emerging killer application. Microsoft is a partner with TCI in its digital cable TV operation.[179] It also has its own WebTV, connecting TV sets to the World Wide Web through telephone lines — and that technology may in the end prove superior. Microsoft also has a play in each of the two routes that are competing to establish high-speed Internet access to the consumer personal computer market.[180] Through its 11 percent stake in Comcast, Microsoft has a piece of @Home, the cable modem ISP run by the major cable companies. It also is a partner with Intel, GTE, and the Baby Bell regional phone companies in the venture to offer high-speed Internet access via telephone lines.[181] Microsoft also has a 10 percent stake in Time Warner's Road Runner cable modem service.[182] In 1998 Microsoft purchased major stakes in Qwest, the fourth-largest U.S. long-distance carrier, and Thomson, the biggest maker of television sets in the United States.[183]

Microsoft has major horses in virtually every route that could lead to a commercially viable consumer-oriented Internet, including its Internet Explorer web browser, the Microsoft Network online service, and its MSNBC joint venture website-cable TV channel that it runs with NBC.[184] Many, perhaps most, of these ventures are faltering and will eventually fail, but if only a few of them succeed the losses will appear insignificant.[185] Microsoft's ravenous appetite for dominating the Internet has attracted the attention of the U.S. Justice Department, which advanced an antitrust case against it in 1998 and 1999. The main point of contention is Microsoft's bundling of its

Internet Explorer browser with its Windows operating software, but the issues go well beyond that. Even if Microsoft should lose the case, experts are uncertain what if anything the government can do to effectively address the situation, in the context of the recent antitrust tradition.[186] And even if Microsoft must jump some hurdles with regulators, Paine Webber's chief investment strategist stated in 1998 that Microsoft's strategy would pay off. Microsoft had established a "dominant position across the entire Information Age spectrum," he noted, making Microsoft "the leading beneficiary of convergence."[187]

But the really important corporate activity, as the Microsoft example suggests, is not understood by looking at firms in isolation, or even at sectors as a whole, but rather by looking at the interaction of firms in one sector with firms from other sectors. Although digital convergence is only just beginning, and there remain important distinctions between computer, telecommunication, and media companies, a striking business convergence has emerged due to the Internet.[188] This takes the form of out-and-out mergers and acquisitions, equity joint ventures with two or more partners on specific projects, and long-term exclusive strategic alliances between two firms. On the one hand, this "convergence" is due to the desire to limit risk by linking up with potential competitors or swallowing them. Following the logic of Richard Nixon's memorable phrase, it is better to have your enemy inside pissing out rather than outside pissing in. On the other hand, this "convergence" is explained by the inability of a telecom, computer, or media firm to provide a comprehensive Internet service. And there is indication that there is a market for just this sort of service. According to one 1998 survey, 83 percent of U.S. consumers are willing to receive bundled services — cable, telephone, and Internet access — from a single provider.[189]

So, ironically, the most striking feature of digital communication may well be not that it has opened up competition in communication markets but that it has made it vastly easier, more attractive, and more *necessary* for firms to consolidate and strike alliances across the media, telecommunication, and computer sectors. In the late 1990s there were a series of mergers between large telecommunication and computer equipment companies, due to the Internet.[190] Almost all the media giants have entered into joint ventures or strategic alliances with the largest telecom and software firms. Time Warner is connected to several of the U.S. regional (Bell) telephone giants, as well as to AT&T and Oracle. It has a major joint venture with U.S. West. Disney, likewise, is connected to several major U.S. telecommunication companies, as well as to America Online. News Corp. is partially owned by WorldCom (MCI) and has a joint venture with British Telecom.[191] The media firms most directly implicated in this convergence are the cable companies, since their wires are arguably the best suited of the existing choices. As noted above, Comcast is partially owned by Microsoft while Microsoft cofounder Paul Allen purchased Marcus Cable in 1998. But the truly seminal deal was AT&T's $48 billion purchase of cable giant TCI in 1998. The key to the deal was the linking of TCI's wires to the home with AT&T's trunkline fiber-optic system. The point will be to offer "one-stop shopping" to home consumers of local and long-distance telephony, cable television, and high-speed Internet access via cable modems.[192] Through TCI's Liberty Media, AT&T will now have interests in a large stable of media assets. Criticism of the deal is mostly that it is premature, not improper.

Business analysts expect more mergers between phone, cable, and media companies, a "scramble to control the information pipeline into people's homes." "One way or another," Merrill Lynch's media analyst stated in 1998, cable "companies are going to be affiliated with phone companies. There's going to be consolidation in this industry."[193] (Some business analysts project cable as seizing as much as one-third of the annual $200 billion U.S. telephone market by 2004. As the entire cable industry only generated $25 billion in 1998, such a development would radically transform the economics of the industry and the few firms that dominate it.)[194] "It is inevitable that the industry will consolidate," the CEO of AT&T told the U.S. Senate Judiciary Committee. Time Warner president Richard Parsons concurred, saying the mergers were "absolutely necessary" for true competition to emerge. "Such alliances, joint ventures, mergers, and other combinations are increasingly essential to remain competitive on a global basis," he added.[195] An executive at SBC Communications, following its merger with Ameritech, said that it will only be with the emergence of corporate "scale," that is, the creation of super huge enormous firms, "that you'll get the competition that was envisioned" by the 1996 Telecommunications Act.[196] In due course the global media oligopoly may become a much broader global communication oligopoly, dominated by a small number of massive conglomerates, with a myriad of joint ventures linking all the players to each other. In the battle between the Internet's ballyhooed "decentralizing" bias and the market's tendency toward concentration, the market is winning.

But where, aside from the ISP market, are the killer applications to justify the expense of some of these acquisitions and joint ventures? By the end of the 1990s the market began to crystallize around two commercial Internet applications. The most important is electronic commerce, using the Internet to buy and sell products. In addition to being interactive, the Web permits marketers to generate a superior profile of an Internet user's past purchases and interests through examining the "cookie" file in a user's web browser, among other things.[197] At the low end, one 1998 study predicts that U.S. and European spending online will reach $16 billion by 2002.[198] Other studies, using broader criteria, by private groups and the U.S. government, forecast electronic commerce at a whopping $300 billion by 2002.[199] By all accounts electronic commerce is becoming *the* future of retailing and commerce, and the U.S. government calls it the foundation of the "emerging digital economy."[200] It seems clearly a world historic phenomenon, lacking only improvements in Net security and bandwidth to become the standard for commerce.[201] And as electronic commerce becomes the rule, it will push those not online to get connected.

But how do the communication giants benefit from electronic commerce, unless they are selling their own products? After all, why cannot these transactions be simply between buyer and seller? This leads to the second "killer app" for the Internet: *portals.* Portals refer to the Internet services that people "use to start their treks through cyberspace." They bring order to the Internet experience. More than browser software or the standard ISP, portals organize the entire Web experience and provide a "search" mechanism to bring Internet material to users as painlessly as possible. Portals constitute the link for the user between the ISP and the ultimate destination in the Internet; and they logically may well become ISPs and include many final destinations over time.[202] The key elements for a portal are to have email, a search engine, and easy access to e-commerce. Exclusive or semi-exclusive rights to popular media content does not hurt either.[203] "Portals are transforming the internet from a chaotic collection of thousands of websites into something more manageable and familiar for consumers and investors," the *Financial Times* notes, "by capturing large audiences and establishing themselves as the primary internet 'channels.'"[204] "The search engines have become to the Internet what Windows is to the computer desktop," a technology investment banker stated in 1998. Even if portals per se never assume that lofty perch, something like them looks to be the immediate direction for the Internet.

The archetype of the portal is America Online (AOL), which did $2.5 billion in business in 1998. AOL provides an "Internet on training wheels," with email, chat rooms, and banks of operators to answer any questions users might have. With eleven million subscribers, AOL accounts for 40 percent of all online traffic, and 60 percent of home use.[205] Fully 80 percent of AOL users never venture beyond AOL's sites.[206] AOL has also shown the way to Internet riches, and not only from monthly access fees. In addition, AOL is "drawing advertisers, who sense a mass market taking shape."[207] Even more important, it uses its hold on such a huge section of the Internet population to extract fees from firms that want to do commerce on AOL.[208] In just one of scores of deals, AOL will receive $12 million plus a share of revenues over four years for giving the Fragrance Center a prominent display on AOL's site.[209]

By all accounts AOL is poised to grow dramatically in the coming years. One Wall Street analyst expects AOL to have one-half of the projected fifty-five million U.S. online households in 2003, and AOL will receive annual fees for carrying e-commerce of more than $3 billion, in addition to much greater income from advertising and subscriber fees. If this report is accurate, AOL will become the fourth largest media firm in the United States.[210] In November 1998 AOL purchased Netscape for $4.2 billion, thus acquiring the leading web browser, as well as one of the three most-visited sites in cyberspace. A main aim of the deal was to give AOL a leg up on Microsoft in the battle "to transform the greater part of cyberspace into a vast virtual mall."[211] At the same time AOL announced a strategic alliance with Sun Microsystems, the point of which was, among other things, to make "an end-run around Microsoft's grip on desktop computing."[212] To counteract the threat of digital television to its Internet operations, AOL launched AOL-TV in 1999. It will provide people with the ability to surf the Internet on their televisions, similar to Microsoft's WebTV.[213]

AOL faces two distinct sets of challenges on its course to Internet portal hegemony. First, there are several other portals based on their own search engines competing for market share.[214] Yahoo! and Excite, for example, are linked with AT&T's Worldnet Service and Dell Computer respectively.[215] AltaVista is owned and promoted by Compaq, a computer manufacturer like Dell.[216] Online shopping has become the main focus of these portals. It is "fundamental to our business," Yahoo's chief operating office said, "every bit as important as basic search and directory functions."[217] Microsoft, too, looms large in the portal wars. To complement its Microsoft Network, Microsoft consolidated its massive website activities and launched the portal "start.com," which offers personalized data collection, web-searching, and email for its customers.[218] Microsoft also announced a strategic alliance with Barnes & Noble, in which the two would "weave together their online products and services."[219] Indeed, much of the momentum for portals comes from businesses desperate to find portals to facilitate their electronic commerce activities. "Launching an E-commerce site without a portal partner," one investment analyst noted, "is like opening a retail store in the desert. Sure, it's cheap, but does anybody stop there?"[220]

The second threat to AOL — and, indeed, to all of the portals just mentioned — comes from the cable and telephone companies. As they begin to provide broadband services like @Home and Road Runner, they will displace AOL as an ISP and be in a position to have their portal service automatically serve their customers. If users want to use AOL they will have to pay an additional fee.[221] "The telcos and cable companies are coming after AOL's customers," a Forrester Research analyst stated.[222] AT&T executives have stated that it does not want @Home to be a traditional ISP, offering "dumb-pipes" that others like AOL and Yahoo! use to get rich.[223] "It is clear," the *New York Times* wrote, "that whoever controls the front door that people use to start their Internet surfing — a 'portal' in industry jargon — will control the biggest share of advertising and shopping revenues."[224] AOL understands that if it cannot remain an ISP when the cable and telephone companies offer broadband Internet access, its entire business plan will become very fragile. Hence this is a very crucial fight over the contours of the portal industry. In 1999 the FCC ruled against AOL's complaint that it should be entitled to use cable wires to provide a competitive ISP service at the same price as the cable ISP services, @Home and Road Runner. It granted AT&T the right to "bundle" its portal and ISP, in exchange for AT&T's speeding up its local telephone service to compete with the Baby Bell monopolies.[225] To address its concerns, AOL began negotiations with the major cable companies to see if its service could get some preferential treatment on the broadband cable systems.[226] It has tremendous market leverage, so its future remains rosy. In December 1998, for example, AOL negotiated a deal with Dell, the second largest U.S. computer manufacturer, to have AOL software preinstalled on all Dell Computers.[227]

How exactly the portal market will shake down is unclear at this point in time. Many more major mergers, acquisitions, and strategic alliances will take place in the next few years. By most accounts we will have a "long and brutal war" leading to a crystallization with three to six firms dominating the global market.[228] Michael Parekh, the lead Internet analyst for Goldman Sachs, forecasts a half-dozen major portals until 2000 or 2001, when that number "will shrink to a top three fairly quickly." A major development along these lines came in January 1999 when AT&T's @Home purchased leading Internet portal Excite for $6 billion.[229] But so far our discussion of portals has concentrated upon computer, cable, and telecom firms. It will only be complete when we assess the role the media giants will play in the Internet's development, or, to put it another way, the way the Internet will figure in the media giants' development.

The Internet and the Media Giants

The media firms and media industries are directly involved in both electronic commerce and the establishment of viable commercial portals. But these are best regarded as parts of a broader series of moves, in addition to digital television, made by media firms to extend their empires to cyberspace. "For traditional media companies," the *New York Times* correctly notes, "the digital age poses genuine danger."[230] The great fear for the media firms is that the Internet will breed a new generation of commercial competitors who take advantage of the Internet's relatively minuscule production and, especially, distribution costs. "The entertainment companies are terrified of being blindsided by the Internet," a business consultant said, "as the broadcasting networks were blindsided by cable in the 1980s."[231] At its greatest the fear is that the broadband Internet will lead to an entirely new media regime that makes the corporate media giants irrelevant and obsolete. But it remains to be seen exactly where the Internet and/or any other digital communication network will fit into the global media landscape ten or twenty years down the road. As Time Warner CEO Gerald Levin put it, it is "not clear where you make money on it."[232]

But even if the Internet takes a long time to develop as a commercial medium, it is already taking up some of the time that people used to devote to traditional media.[233] One 1998 marketing study showed 64 percent of regular Internet users reported watching less TV than in their precyberspace days, and 48 percent of them were reading less.[234] An AC Nielsen study conducted late in 1998 determined that Internet homes watched 15 percent less television overall than unwired homes.[235] So even if the Internet does not spawn a new generation of triumphant media industries and giants, it is having a clear impact upon the corporate media, and it is getting their attention. Since the mid-1990s the media giants have been establishing an online presence so, as it does develop, they will not get boxed out of the digital system.

Most of the Internet activities of the traditional media firms have been money losers, and some have been outright disasters. Time Warner's Pathfinder website, for example, began in 1994 with visions of conquering the Internet, only to produce a "black hole" for the firm's balance sheet.[236] Likewise, the New Century Network, a website consisting of 140 newspapers run by nine of the largest newspaper chains, was such a fiasco that it was shut down in 1998.[237] But none of the media firms have lost their resolve to be a factor, even to dominate, cyberspace. As one media executive put it, Internet "losses appear to be the key to the future."[238] And this is one of the distinguishing characteristics of media firms as they approach the Internet in comparison to entrepreneurs who want to use the Internet to become media content providers: the media firms have a very long time horizon and very deep pockets. They simply cannot afford to abandon ship.

By the end of the 1990s, all major media have significant web activities. The media firms use their websites, at the very least, to stimulate interest in the traditional media fare. This is seen as a relatively inexpensive way to expand sales.[239] Some media firms duplicate their traditional publications or even broadcast their radio and television signals over the net, with the commercials, of course.[240] The newspaper industry has rebounded from the New Century Network debacle and has a number of sites to capture classified advertising dollars as they go online.[241] But most media firms are going beyond this on the

Web. Viacom has extensive websites for its MTV and Nickelodeon cable TV channels, for example, the point of which is to produce "online synergies."[242] These synergies can be found by providing an interactive component and additional editorial dimensions to what is found in the traditional fare, but the main way websites produce synergies is by offering electronic commerce options for products related to the site.[243] Several other commercial websites have incorporated Internet shopping directly into their editorial fare. As one media executive notes, web publishers "have to think like merchandisers."[244] Electronic commerce is now seen as a significant revenue stream for media websites; all in all the similarity between digital television and what is happening on the Internet is striking.[245]

Indeed, by the end of the 1990s the possibility of new Internet content providers emerging to slay the traditional media appears more farfetched than ever before. In 1998 there was a massive shakeout in the online media industry, as smaller players could not remain afloat. Forrester Research estimated that the cost of an "average-content" website increased threefold to $3.1 million by 1998, and would double again by 2000.[246] "While the big names are establishing themselves on the Internet," the *Economist* wrote in 1998, "the content sites that have grown organically out of the new medium are suffering."[247] Even a firm with the resources of Microsoft flopped in its attempt to become an online content provider, abolishing its operation in early 1998. "It's a fair comment to say that entertainment on the Internet did not pan out as expected," said a Microsoft executive.[248] As telecom and computer firms work to develop Internet content, they will now turn to partner with the corporate media giants. By May 1998, over three-quarters of the thirty-one most visited news and entertainment websites were affiliated with large media firms, and most of the rest were connected to outfits like AOL and Microsoft.[249]

We can now see that those who forecast that the media giants would smash into the Internet "iceberg" exaggerated the power of technology and failed to grasp the manner in which markets actually work. In addition to having deep pockets and a long time horizon, the media giants enjoy five other distinct advantages over prospective intruders onto their fiefdom. First, the media giants have digital programming from their other ventures that they can plug into the Web at little extra cost. This, in itself, is a huge advantage over firms that have to create original content from scratch. Second, to generate an audience, they can and do promote their websites incessantly on their traditional media holdings. The media giants can bring their audiences to their sites on the Internet. By 1998, it was argued that the only way an Internet content provider could generate users was by buying advertising in the media giants' traditional media. (Yahoo! the portal not only does extensive TV advertising to promote its services, it also has arranged for product placements on primetime TV shows like *Ally McBeal* and *Caroline in the City*.)[250] Otherwise, an Internet website would get lost among the millions of other web locations. As the editor-in-chief of MSNBC on the Internet put it, linking the website to the existing media activity "is the crux of what we are talking about; it will help set us apart in a crowded market."[251] "Offline branding," a trade publication observed, "is also key to generating traffic."[252] It is the leading media "brands" that have been the first to charge subscription fees for their Web offerings; indeed, they may be the only firms for which this is even an alternative.[253]

Third, as the possessors of the hottest "brands," the media firms have the leverage to get premier locations from browser software makers and portals.[254] The new Microsoft Internet Explorer 4.0 offers 250 highlighted channels, and the "plum positions" belong to Disney and Time Warner.[255] Similar arrangements are taking place with Netscape and Pointcast.[256] Indeed, the portals are eager to promote "Hollywoodesque programming" in the competition for users. They have little choice in reality.[257] In 1998, for example, @Home signed a major deal with Viacom's MTV to develop a brand name music content service. The other portals are lining up their arrangements with music websites, recording companies, and retailers as well.[258] Fourth, and this relates to the deep pockets, the media giants are aggressive investors in start-up Internet media companies. Approximately one-half the venture capital for Internet content start-up companies comes from established media firms.[259] The Tribune Company, for example, owns stakes in fifteen Internet companies, including the portals AOL, Excite, and iVillage, which targets women.[260] Some media giants, like Bertelsmann and Sony, have seemingly bypassed new acquisitions of traditional media to put nearly all their resources into expanding their Internet presence. GE's NBC arguably has taken this strategy the furthest. To cover all the bases, GE has made over $2 billion in investments in more than twenty Internet companies, in addition to NBC's own web activities. "It wants to be wherever this thing takes off," an industry analyst said. "But there is no clear strategy."[261] In sum, if some new company shows commercial promise, the media giants will be poised to capitalize upon, not be buried by, it.

Fifth, to the extent that advertising develops on the web, the media giants are positioned to seize most of these revenues. Online advertising amounted to $900 million in 1997, and some expect it to reach $5 billion by 2000. (It is worth noting that this will still be no more than 3 percent of all U.S. ad spending that year, suggesting again how long a path it will be to an era of Internet dominance.)[262] The media giants have long and close relationships with the advertising industry, and work closely with them to make Web advertising viable.[263] The media giants can and do get major advertisers to commit to their online ventures as part of the advertisers' contracts to do advertising on the media giants' traditional media. Internet advertising even surpasses the potential benefits of advertising on digital television. Advertisers can tailor their spots to individuals and very specific markets.[264] At its most effective, Internet advertising merges with e-commerce and uses the immense amount of information on consumers available on the Internet to locate potential customers, pitch a tailored spot to them, and conclude a sale immediately.[265]

This merging of advertising and e-commerce is ideal for certain products, but it is hardly viable for the preponderance of advertising. Most products that are advertised in the traditional media are "low-involvement," meaning people are not interested in the ads and will avoid them if given an opportunity. Much dominant product advertising is for products where there is only marginal difference in product quality or price between the main competitors so the actual advertising emphasizes extraneous factors to win over the consumer. This caliber of "image" advertising, which has been prominent on television for decades, is seen as roadkill on the Internet. The Internet makes it almost impossible to corral consumers to sit through advertising. The initial trend to discrete banner ads on Internet websites, where users could voluntarily "click-through" on banners to get product details, was generally regarded as a dud. One business writer captured the worst fears of the advertising industry when he observed, "All those advertisers who make their living wasting everyone's time may need to find new gigs."[266] "This new medium is more a threat than an opportunity," a Procter & Gamble executive conceded.[267]

In August 1998 Procter & Gamble convened an emergency meeting of four hundred Internet and advertising executives to "brain-storm" on how the Internet could be made suitable for traditional advertisers.[268] "We want to test the proposition of how to make the Internet work for a low involvement brand," a Procter & Gamble executive stated.[269] The portals and commercial websites were eager to cooperate with the aims of the conference. As one Internet trade association official put it, "It's an opportunity for all of us to check our agendas at the door and speak to the higher good of advertising on line."[270] But even if everyone works together, making advertising ubiquitous on the Internet so it can command the attention of millions and millions of users is still a distant proposition. Advertisers have found they could increase the click-through rate dramatically by having "pop-up" banners that appeared on the user's screen until they were clicked closed.[271] Likewise, web advertisers have found they have much more success when their ads are big and complicated. The problem with that is that this uses considerable bandwidth and might send users away from the portal or website altogether. The core problem with both of these solutions is that consumers can still find ways to avoid the ads too easily from the advertisers' perspective.[272]

The apparent solution to this problem on the Internet is similar to the solution to the problem of advertising clutter and multiple channels on television: the melding of commercial and editorial content so users cannot easily separate the two.[273] As one study noted late in 1998: "Increasingly, online advertisers aren't just moving money to the sites they like; they are stepping forward with ideas about how to change the sites into better vehicles for their messages. And the people who run the Web sites aren't taking offense, the way their cousins in print and television might. Instead, they are braiding advertisers' stories into the central message of their sites."[274] A common form of Internet advertising is "sponsorships," whereby for a flat sum ranging from $100,000 to $1 million annually, "the advertiser, its agency and the host Web network work together to develop advertorials."[275] Forrester Research, perhaps the leading Internet research group, cut to the bone in a 1998 report. Internet advertising and e-commerce "will introduce new tensions to the media's perennial balancing act between editorial integrity and the bottom line. The magazine industry recently rejected advertisers' growing demands for advance editorial review. This line won't hold on the Web." The report added that to be successful on the Internet, "Media companies must remove traditional barriers between editorial, advertising sales, and technical staff."[276]

When these five factors are put together, the nature of emerging web content makes sense. "The expansion in channel capacity seems to promise a sumptuous groaning board," TV critic Les Brown wrote, "but in reality it's just going to be a lot more of the same hamburger."[277] Although the nature and logic of Internet content may change in time, there is little on the horizon now to suggest that the most resources will be devoted to anything but sites with an express commitment to a commercialism unusual even for the traditional U.S. media. By the end of the 1990s the Internet was seen as offering media firms "New Synergy," a supercharged version of the process described in chapter 1, whereby media firms offered enhanced websites based on their traditional media brands chock full of commercial applications such as electronic commerce.[278] The most popular areas for Web content are similar to those of the traditional commercial media, and, for the reasons just listed, they are dominated by the usual corporate suspects. Viacom's MTV is squaring off with GE's NBC, AT&T's TCI, and *Rolling Stone* to, as one of them put it, "own the mind share for music." Each website is "slavishly reporting recording industry news and gossip," all to become the, or one of the, "default destinations for people interested in music on the Web." The stakes are high: Forrester Research estimates that online music sales, concert ticket sales, and music-related merchandise sales could reach $2.8 billion by 2002.[279]

The greatest war for market share is with regard to sports websites, where Disney's ESPN, News Corp.'s Fox, GE and Microsoft's MSNBC, Time Warner's CNNSI, and CBS's SportsLine are in pitched battle. Sports is seen as the key to media growth on the web; advertisers, for one, understand the market and want to reach it. Plus sport websites are beginning to generate the huge audiences that advertisers like.[280] To compete for the Internet sports market, it is mandatory to have a major television network that can constantly promote the website. One Forrester Research survey found that 50 percent of respondents visited a sport website as a direct result of its being mentioned during a sport broadcast. Indeed, 33 percent said they visited a web sport site while watching a sports event on TV.[281] The media giants also routinely bring their largest advertisers to their sports websites as part of package deals between the advertiser and the firm's television properties.[282] The media giants can also use their resources to purchase exclusive Internet rights from major sports leagues, as Disney has with the NFL.[283] And, as with music sites, sports offers all sorts of electronic commerce possibilities.[284]

We might want to ponder what all of this means for the nature of journalism on the Internet. This is really a fundamental issue; if the Internet fails to produce a higher caliber of journalism and stimulate public understanding and activity, the claim that it is a boon for democracy is severely weakened. Chapters 1 and 2 chronicled the deplorable state of commercial journalism at the hands of the media giants. Based on the discussion so far in chapter 3, there is little reason to expect a journalistic renaissance online. The most visited websites for news and information are those associated with the corporate media TV news operations and the largest newspaper chains.[285] At present the trend for online journalism is to accentuate the worst synergistic and profit-hungry attributes of commercial journalism, with its emphasis on trivia, celebrities, and consumer news. One observer characterized the news offerings on AOL, drawn from all the commercial media giants, as less a "marketplace of ideas" than "a shopping mall of notions."[286] The increasingly seamless relationship on the Web between advertising and editorial fare is pronounced in its journalism too. "On the web," the West Coast editor of *Editor and Publisher* wrote, "the two [advertising and journalism] often overlap in ways that make it difficult for even journalists and editors to differentiate between the two."[287]

This does not mean there are no considerable advantages to or differences between the emerging digital world and what preceded it. Even if the Internet becomes primarily a commercial medium for electronic commerce, email, and commercial news and entertainment fare, it will also be a haven for all sorts of interactive activities that never existed in the past. It can, at the very least, be an enormous and mostly uncensorable soapbox, open to a plethora of voices to speak, and be heard, worldwide at relatively minimal expense. This is indeed a communication revolution, and one that is being taken advantage of by countless social and political organizations that heretofore were marginalized.[288] In 1998, for example, the global, and largely secretive, negotiations for a Multilateral Agreement on Investment (MAI) were undercut when a flurry of Internet communication created a groundswell of popular opposition. The MAI was barely covered in the commercial media, and to the extent it was the coverage was favorable to a global bill of rights for investors and corporations.[289] "From Mexico to China," the British *Guardian* noted in December 1998, "the Internet is proving an invaluable tool for acts of political defiance, large and small, as governments wedded to traditional media find it hard to quell political dissent channeled through cyberspace."[290] When the Internet is viewed in this manner, it is hard not to see it as constituting the basis for a genuine revolution in information dissemination with striking and world historical implications for politics. This is the Internet that has enthralled the Tofflers and Negropontes and Gilders — the utopian futurologists — for the past decade. And the strength of this vision is that it has an important element of truth.

But this point should not be exaggerated. Having a website does not mean many people will know of its existence and therefore seek it out. We should not extrapolate from the experiences of a small community of activists to think that this will become the heart and soul of the Internet experience. It has not and it will not. Ultimately, the point is unavoidable that if the Internet is going to democratize our societies it will require a journalism quite different from that currently being produced. And, here, the prospects are not encouraging. As a rule, journalism is not something that can be done piecemeal by amateurs working in their spare time. It is best done by people who make a living at it, and who have training, experience, and resources. Journalism also requires institutional support (and protection from commercial and governmental attack) to survive and prosper. The corporate media giants have failed miserably to provide a viable journalism, and as they dominate the journalism online, there is no reason to expect anything different. Those who argue that the Internet may revolutionize mainstream journalism for the better tend to downplay the commercial pressures that have produced the present deplorable situation. They present no plausible explanation for why corporate media's Internet journalism will be qualitatively superior for democracy than what they currently produce elsewhere.[291] In this context, it should be no surprise that the leading product of Internet journalism is none other than Matt Drudge, who, as the *Economist* puts it, "spares himself the drudgery of fact-checking."[292]

To make this discussion more concrete, consider some of the Internet activities of Time Warner and Disney, the world's two largest media firms. What they are doing, it is fair to say, is a good indication of how the other media giants are approaching cyberspace. In addition to its activities as a cable company, Time Warner produces nearly two hundred websites, all of which are designed to provide what it terms an "advertiser-friendly environment," and it aggressively promotes to its audiences through its existing media.[293] Its CNN website is now available in Swedish, with other languages to follow.[294] Time Warner uses its websites to go after the youth market, to attract sports fans, and to provide entertainment content similar to that of its "old" media.[295] It established a major website around the 1998 World Cup, to attract global attention to its Internet activities.[296] The success of the World Cup website led Time Warner to "go ahead with more ad-supported non-U.S. Internet projects." "We've had hits originating from 92 countries with their own Internet suffixes," a Time Warner executive stated. "We now want to take things we learned from this and move on."[297] Also in 1998, it began to develop entertainment content explicitly for the Web, in anticipation of a broadband future.[298] Time Warner is bringing advertisers aboard with long-term contracts, and giving them equity interest in some projects.[299] Its most developed relationship with advertisers is the ParentTime website joint venture it has with Procter & Gamble.[300]

Disney's vision of the digital future also sees a major role for advertising. "With a click of a remote-control button," ABC president Preston Padden enthused in 1997, "customers will be able to tell us if they want a free sample of a new headache remedy or wish to test-drive a new car."[301] Disney has been as aggressive in cyberspace as Time Warner and the other media giants; in 1997, as part of a "blitz by Disney to establish Internet beachheads for many of its products," it launched a subscription website for its "Daily Blast" children's website, exclusively available on the Microsoft Network.[302] In 1998 Disney announced that it was extending its conception of advertising on the Internet to see that Internet commerce was more directly "integrated into Disney's site." Its first major deal was with Barnes & Noble, granting the bookseller exclusive right to sell books across all Disney websites. Disney not only gets a cut of the action, it also gets free promotion of its wares in Barnes & Noble stores and on the Barnes & Noble website. According to Disney, the two websites that offered the most promise for commercial synergy were its ESPN Internet Ventures and ABCNews.com.[303] Disney's ultimate online aim, as the president of Disney's Starwave website producer, stated, is "to create the destination which contains everything someone could want. . . . It's the brand power that we have."[304]

But establishing hegemony over any new media rivals on the Web still does not mean that cyberspace will prove particularly lucrative; one could argue it proves the opposite. Time Warner, for example, was exultant that it had sold enough online advertising to cover nearly 50 percent of its online unit's budget for 1998. For a small start-up venture, this would spell death.[305] This is where we return to our point of departure for this section, to electronic commerce and portals, the two prospective "killer apps" on the Internet. What is the relationship of the media firms to these two phenomena?

With regard to electronic commerce, media firms stand to be major players because a significant amount of what is being sold are media products. In 1998, fully five of the top ten categories for e-commerce were software, books, music, videos, and tickets for sports and entertainment events.[306] This also casts the future of traditional media retailers — bookstores, music stores, video rental stores — in a shadowy light. The way was shown by the rapid emergence of Amazon.com, the online bookseller; its market value in 1998 was greater than the combined market values of Barnes & Noble and Borders, the two chains that dominate U.S. bookselling.[307] By the end of 1998 Amazon.com had expanded into video and music sales and had established operations in Europe.[308] "Our goal is to be an e-commerce destination," Amazon.com CEO Jeff Bezos stated.[309] Others have dubbed it "the Wal-Mart of the Net."[310] But Amazon.com can hardly count on clear sailing to Internet riches. Several other firms, including, as we will see below, some media giants, are coming after it. But Internet e-commerce is an area where size does matter and matter a great deal. Profit margins are very small so selling vast quantities is crucial for survival. In addition, a seller must have a large enough stock so as to deliver the books, videos, or CDs in a reasonable amount of time. So it was in 1998 that the two largest Internet music sellers — CDNow and N2K — merged in order to survive the coming war for preeminence. As a result of the merger they now have almost one-half of the market for Internet music sales. "There is an increasing sense of concern about whether the no. 2 player can survive," a Wall Street analyst said of the music-selling market on the Internet.[311]

Selling music online is by all accounts expected to be one of the next great arenas for electronic commerce. In 1998, online music sales totaled $87 million; in 2005 they are projected to reach some $4 billion.[312] Sales will mushroom because online CD prices can be significantly below those offered in traditional retail stores. Eventually music will be sent digitally to the computer, rather than being mailed as a CD, which should reduce prices dramatically and give a tremendous impetus to sales.[313] Nevertheless the five firms that dominate global music are hardly ecstatic about what the Internet might do to their business. By 1998 the ability to copy and send music digitally by email was becoming widespread through a software format called MP3.[314] Although the music industry got Congress to approve copyright legislation which extended their ownership rights to cyberspace, MP3 makes "piracy" as simple as hitting the "send" button and is a nightmare to police.[315] The industry has responded by working with software and telecommunication companies on methods to track "pirates."[316] It has also been working with IBM and AT&T to develop a secure method to sell music digitally that will make it very difficult, if not impossible, for copyright infringement.[317]

But even if the music giants can eliminate, or at least minimize, the problem with piracy, they are not out of the forest. The Internet allows a whole new group of competitors to come after their market share online, competitors who could never have thought of breaking into the global music market otherwise. Indeed, the music industry will be the first and perhaps only media sector that will test the "iceberg" thesis, the notion that the Internet will introduce massive competition and break up existing oligopolistic media markets. To be more precise: the market power of the five firms that dominate global music is based largely on their extensive distribution networks; with electronic distribution those networks cease to matter. The production of music in and of itself is not a particularly expensive undertaking. On the surface, one might ask what function do the music companies fulfill as distribution goes online?[318] (When bandwidth expands, in a decade or so, and movies can be distributed directly online as well, the media giants will face less threat there because the capital costs of filmmaking are so significantly higher, and their distribution networks will remain important because the role of big screen theater exhibition should not change.) Already in 1998 the Internet Underground Music Archive posts the work of some twenty-five hundred artists, charging 99 cents to users who wish to download it to their computers using MP3 software.[319] The challenge for the music giants — Bertelsmann, Sony, Seagram, Time Warner, and EMI — will be to parlay their existing market strength, during the next decade or so while they still have it, into online market power.

They are already in negotiation with Internet service providers and portals to grease the wheels for selling their wares in a privileged manner online.[320] They combine this with their large promotional budgets to try to establish barriers-to-entry that can survive the Internet.[321] The big five might be able to use these factors to keep start-ups at bay, but media giants like Disney, News Corp., and Viacom — with their own significant market power online and promotional budgets — should find themselves in a position to expand their music activities if they wish to do so. And even more threatening, major recording stars with name recognition may well flee the music giants and sell their music directly online.[322]

The media giants have turned to e-commerce in two ways. First, as major producers of the content being sold online, they are in a superior position to sell it themselves at a profit. They have little reason to let Amazon.com or anyone else get rich selling their wares when they can do it just as easily themselves. In the fall of 1998 Time Warner launched a major push to be a Web retailer — what the *Wall Street Journal* termed an "Internet superstore" — that would begin by selling primarily products relating to its vast media empire. Eventually Time Warner plans to sell the merchandise of its rivals as well.[323] Bertelsmann is an even more striking example. As the world's largest book publisher and one of the big five music companies, Bertelsmann plans to become the leading global Web retailer of music and books.[324] One Bertelsmann publishing executive stated that "Our goal is, quite simply, to eventually offer online all books, from all publishers, in all languages."[325] Bertelsmann has a 50 percent stake in AOL Europe and is AOL's exclusive bookseller in Europe.[326] In October 1998 Bertelsmann paid $200 million for a 50 percent stake in Barnes & Noble's Internet bookstore, the main competitive threat at the time to Amazon.com.[327] In 1999 Bertelsmann went the next step, launching Bertelsmann Online, or bol.com, which will sell books across the world — except in the United States where it will work through Barnes & Noble's website — with services customized by language and content for each country.[328]

The second way media giants pursue e-commerce is to link it to the advertising and commerce they are conducting on their traditional media. NBC, which has pioneered direct selling over network television, in 1998 established "Giftseeker," an online shopping website. NBC has incorporated "Giftseeker" directly into its television advertising sales, so that clients will integrate their NBC advertising with

Giftseeker exposure.[329] NBC's flagship website, NBC.com, was described by *Fortune* magazine as "little more than a colorful marketplace dressed up as entertainment."[330] One Wall Street analyst projects that by 2002 NBC will generate over $200 million in profit from e-commerce, more than offsetting the decline in viewership and revenues at the NBC television network.[331] Chancellor Broadcasting, the largest U.S. radio company with 463 stations, established an Internet venture in 1999 so that its stations could push listeners to their website "where they could purchase merchandise, music recordings or concert tickets."[332]

As we noted in the discussion of e-commerce in the last section, Internet selling has quickly gravitated to portals, those places where web users tend to congregate. And when it comes to portals, the media giants are especially well positioned to participate, since, in effect, portals see themselves as media companies. "Any media company is leveraging their relationship with their audience. Period. End of discussion," an AOL executive said. "You build the audience, you figure out how to extract value. . . . We have a very big ability to control the flow of our audience."[333] GE's NBC led the media foray into portals with its purchase of Snap and partial interest in Snap creator Cnet in June 1998.[334] In December NBC bought a stake in the popular women's website iVillage, in part to build more audience for Snap. "Women are to NBC what kids are to Disney," an NBC executive commented. In January 1999 Snap launched Cyclone to provide a web portal for the high-speed Web services being offered by Bell Atlantic, GTE, and SBC Communications in their competition with @Home and Road Runner.[335] Disney followed the NBC deal for Snap almost immediately by purchasing 43 percent of the portal InfoSeek with an option to take controlling interest. The head of Disney's Internet Group called the deal "mission-critical" to Disney's future growth.[336] "The game is to end up with something bigger and better than AOL," said an ABC executive.[337] In 1999 Disney formally launched its all-purpose portal, the Go Network, a joint venture with InfoSeek. With the Go Network, the *New York Times* observed, Disney "is now making a bigger bet on cyberspace than any other media concern in the world."[338] The Go Network includes five main sections: sports (based on ESPN.com), news (based on ABC.com), entertainment, kids, and financial news. The entire portal has e-commerce options at most every turn.[339] Go offers email and the InfoSeek search engine, but, as one observer put it, "the new service seems primarily intended to feed you willy-nilly into the wonderful world of Disney."[340]

Whether or not the Go Network pans out, business analysts believe this is just the beginning of a formal drive by the media giants into the portal business. Observers expect the other media giants to purchase their own portals, if they are not turned off by the high prices. The remaining independent portals are eager either to get purchased by media giants or to work closely with them.[341] In January 1999, for example, News Corp. and Yahoo announced a major strategic alliance, whereby each would aggressively promote the other on its channels, through advertising and product placements in News Corp. movies and TV shows. They would also offer advertisers joint packages. "The Internet media business," the *New York Times* notes, "is expected to follow the pattern of cable television, where entrepreneurs created CNN, ESPN and MTV and were later bought out by Time Warner Inc., Disney and Viacom Inc. respectively."[342] Whether or not media giants come to own portals outright, they almost certainly will be major players in all of them.

It may turn out, as a few Internet experts suggest, that portals will prove to be a flash in the pan.[343] As the president of InfoSeek put it, "The Internet's still in the Stone Age."[344] But however it develops, the comment of the president of Time, Inc. seems fairly accurate: "I believe the electronic revolution is simply one new form of communications that will find its place in the food chain of communications and will not displace or replace anything that already exists, just as television did not replace radio, just as cable did not replace network television, just as the VCR did not replace the movie theatres."[345] The evidence so far suggests the media giants will be able to draw the Internet into their existing empires. While the Internet is in many ways revolutionizing the way we lead our lives, it is a revolution that does not appear to include changing the identity and nature of those in power.

Conclusion

By 1999 notions of the Internet providing a new golden age of competitive capitalism were quickly fading from view in the business press. The *New York Times* argued that the lesson of the Internet was that "The big get bigger and the small fade away." Indeed, as the newspaper noted, the Internet, rather than having a competitive bias, may in fact stimulate monopoly and oligopoly. "At first glance, the Internet seems to favor David over Goliath, as any upstart can open an on-line store or an electronic publication. But it appears that the first capable pipsqueak to shoot a slingshot in any given area may grow to giant size so quickly tha[t] any new challengers have been kept at bay."[346] The prospects for new giants emerging was even more remote in the area of "content." Despite its much-ballyhooed "openness," to the extent that it becomes a viable mass medium, it will likely be dominated by the usual corporate suspects. Certainly a few new commercial content players will emerge, but the evidence suggests that the content of the digital communication world will appear quite similar to the content of the pre-digital commercial media world.[347] In some ways the Web has even extended commercial synergies and the role of advertising and selling writ large to new dimensions. This does not mean that the Internet will not be a major part in reconfiguring the way we lead our lives; it almost certainly will. Some aspects of these changes will probably be beneficial whereas others may be detrimental.

Nor does this mean that there will not be a vibrant, exciting, and important noncommercial citizen sector in cyberspace open to all who veer off the beaten path. For activists of all political stripes, the Web increasingly plays a central role in organizing and educational activities. But from its once lofty perch, this nonprofit and civic sector has been relegated to the distant margins of cyberspace; it is nowhere near the heart of operating logic of the dominant commercial sector. In a less dubious political environment, the Internet could be put to far greater democratic use than it is or likely will be in the foreseeable future. But the key point is simply that those who think the technology can produce a viable democratic public sphere by itself where policy has failed to do so are deluding themselves. And the dominant forces in cyberspace are producing the exact type of depoliticized culture that some Internet utopians claimed the technology would slay. Indeed, one function of the noncommercial Internet activities in the coming years may well be ideological: if one doesn't like what dominates, the argument will go, they should shut up and start their own website or visit any one of the millions of obscure websites. It is not a political issue.

Aside from the notion of Internet content per se, the notion that the Internet is a democratic medium — that it will remain or become available to the public on anything close to egalitarian terms — seems dubious at best. A market-driven digital communication system seems just as likely to accentuate widening class divisions as to lessen them. In the eighteenth century, Thomas Paine wrote that "The contrast of affluence and wretchedness continually meeting and offending the eye, is like dead and living bodies chained together."[348] In the digital age, however, the affluent can increasingly construct a world where the wretched are unchained and out of sight — a communication world similar to the gated residential communities to which so many millions of affluent Americans have fled in the 1990s.[349] A viable democracy depends upon minimal social inequality and a sense that an individual's welfare is determined in large part by the welfare of the general community. Unfortunately the media system, and digital communication in particular, can accentuate the antidemocratic tendencies of the broader political economy.[350]

More than forty years have passed since the publication of C. Wright Mills's *The Power Elite,* one of the most insightful and prescient critiques of U.S. political culture written in the past half-century.[351] In his book Mills discusses the paradox of the postwar United States. On the one hand, it is a nation abuzz with technology, celebrity, and commercialism, a radical society in which tradition has been torn asunder and all that is solid melts into air. On the other hand, it is a highly depoliticized society — only formally democratic in key respects — where most important political decisions are made by the few for the few, with public relations to massage the rabble should they question their status. The commercial media system plays a major role in maintaining the social order. The final third or so of Mills's book depicts the United States as a fundamentally conservative society and a deeply troubled one at that. To my mind, when one looks at the core argument, it could well have been written in 2000.

Mills also provides us with a useful schema to make sense of what seem like revolutionary changes in our media and communication systems at the dawn of the twenty-first century. On the one hand, we are dazzled by a mind-boggling explosion of new technologies, seemingly lifted from the pages of a science fiction novel, that promise unprecedented consumer choice. On the other hand, the clear tendencies of our media and communication world tend toward ever-greater corporate concentration, media conglomeration, and hypercommercialism. But, as Mills well understood, there is no real paradox in this: the illusions of consumer choice and individual free-dom merely provide the ideological oxygen necessary to sustain a media system (and a broader social system) that serves the few while making itself appear accountable and democratic. The digital revolu-tion seems less a process of empowering the less powerful than a process that will further the corporate and commercial penetration and domination of life in the United States. Following Mills's analy-sis, the logical trajectory of the current patterns is to abet the ongo-ing depoliticization, polarization, and demoralization of social life. And, as Mills understood better than anyone, the way forward — the way out — is for scholars committed to democracy to tell the truth about the system, to the end of assisting citizens to organize to change the system.

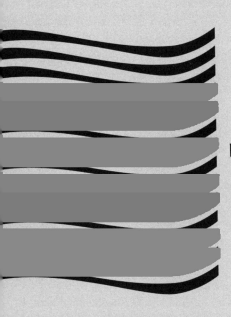

part two

HISTORY

CHAPTER 4

EDUCATORS AND THE BATTLE FOR CONTROL OF U.S. BROADCASTING, 1928–35

It is a core presupposition of contemporary mainstream policy debates about U.S. media and communication that the U.S. broadcasting system has been owned and operated by firms attempting to maximize profit through the sale of advertising since early on, and that this was accepted by almost all Americans as the natural order of things. The privatization and commercialization of the U.S. airwaves has been presented as a democratic, innately American, and mostly benevolent process, and one that gently underscores the historic wisdom of permitting market forces to dominate thoroughly the U.S. (and global) media and communication sectors for all time, or at least as far into the future as we can imagine. Scholars, too, have tended to accept this premise, though sometimes with considerable misgivings about the lack of public service principles in U.S. broadcasting.[1] When one looks closely at the origins of U.S. broadcasting, however, the paltry status of public service broadcasting in the United States was not necessarily inevitable, and it certainly was not regarded as a "given" in the 1920s and early 1930s. When the modern network-dominated, advertising-supported system did emerge, between 1927 and 1932, various elements of U.S. society reacted with outrage and organized to establish a significant nonprofit and noncommercial component to the U.S. system.

The single most important opponent to commercial broadcasting in the 1930s came from the ranks of education. Educators formed the vanguard of a broadcast reform movement that attempted to establish a U.S. broadcasting system where the dominant sector would be nonprofit and noncommercial. The attraction of educators to broadcasting was uncomplicated; many regarded radio and other systems of communication as logically part of the nation's broader educational network and therefore fully within their purview.[2] These educators were enamored of radio's general capacity to promote a democratic political culture far more than they were interested in the medium's potential as a classroom supplement, although these interests were not negligible. They regarded the profit motive as being nearly as inimical to democratic communication as it would be to public education. Their efforts for reform were directed by the National Committee on Education by Radio (NCER), a group supported by the Payne Fund and established in 1930.

Not all educators, however, worked for structural reform. The National Advisory Council on Radio in Education (NACRE), also formed in 1930, advocated that educators should work with the two networks, the National Broadcasting Company (NBC) and the Columbia Broadcasting System (CBS), that dominated U.S. broadcasting. Educators associated with the NACRE shared the NCER's belief in the importance and potential of radio broadcasting for a democratic society, but were either sanguine about the power of NBC and CBS to dictate U.S. broadcasting or resigned to its immutability for the foreseeable future. Subsidized by the Carnegie Corporation and John D. Rockefeller, Jr., the NACRE argued that if educators cooperated with the networks, they would be able to establish public service principles in network business practices while the industry was in its infancy.

In this chapter I address the activities of the NCER and the NACRE during what was the most tumultuous period in the development of U.S. broadcasting. It was between 1927 and 1935 that the basic institutions and regulatory and business practices were established not only for radio but also for television when it would be developed in the 1940s and 1950s. I review the general landscape of the period, the formation of each of the groups, their stances concerning commercial broadcasting, their visions for public service in U.S. broadcasting, and their relationships with each other and educators as a whole. I then discuss how the NCER and the NACRE each fared with their programs. Although they eventually failed, each group had impact upon the debate over broadcast policy in the 1930s. Moreover, each group, in its own manner, attempted to expand the possibilities for public service broadcasting in the United States.

The defeat of the NCER and the NACRE signaled the beginning of the modern era, in which the profit-driven, advertising-supported basis of U.S. broadcasting became politically sacrosanct, as it remains to the present. One cannot grasp the tragedy of public service broadcasting in the United States unless this period is given its due weight. Moreover, given the near ubiquity of advertising and commercial media in our culture and the movement to extend explicit commercial criteria to the educational system, this episode points to a rich and overlooked U.S. tradition of antimarket media criticism provided by educators with a striking commitment to democracy and universal public education. Most important, this episode calls into question one of the main historical arguments used to eliminate any possibility of public debate over the suitability of corporate and commercial control of our media system.

The Emergence of Commercial Broadcasting and Ferment among the Educators

Although large corporations, especially the Radio Corporation of America (RCA), dominated most aspects of the radio industry, broadcasting eluded the corporate net for much of its initial decade. Educational institutions were arguably the "true pioneers" of U.S. broadcasting, establishing over one hundred stations in the early 1920s.[3] Even those stations established by for-profit groups in the 1920s were not intended to generate profits in their own right; rather they were meant to generate favorable publicity for the owner's primary enterprise. Thus, although radio broadcasting was bustling and dynamic in the 1920s, it was uniformly unprofitable for all types of stations and therefore unstable. The core problem was the inability to determine an adequate way to subsidize broadcasting. Direct advertising, meaning advertising with explicit sales messages rather than merely mentioning the sponsor's name, was not even considered prior to the end of the decade. As the American Newspaper Publishers Association reassured its membership in 1927, "Fortunately, direct advertising by radio is well-nigh an impossibility."[4] An American Telephone and Telegraph survey in 1926 determined that only 4.3 percent of U.S. radio stations could be characterized as "commercial broadcasters."[5] Prior to the end of the decade there was no discussion of broadcasting's future in terms of what would soon follow.

Under pressure from all broadcasters and listeners, Congress passed the Radio Act of 1927, which established the Federal Radio Commission (FRC) to provide regulation of broadcasting and bring stability to the ether, as many more stations wished to broadcast than could be accommodated in the scarce electromagnetic spectrum.[6] While there was a general consensus that broadcasting should not be monopolized by the government, as was the case in Britain, the congressional debates over the legislation did not consider advertising nor did they examine the role of NBC, established by RCA in 1926, and CBS, which followed in 1927.[7] Rather, Congress expected the new FRC to determine which stations would be permitted to broadcast and, conversely, which would not. The Radio Act of 1927 only authorized the FRC to favor those stations which best served the "public interest, convenience, or necessity," though it did not attempt to define the terms. With barely any congressional or public oversight and almost no publicity, the pro–commercial broadcasting FRC instituted a general reallocation in 1928 which effectively assigned all stations to new frequency assignments and provided them with new power allowances. This reallocation determined the shape of AM radio for the balance of the century.

NBC and CBS were the clear victors in the reallocation. Whereas they barely existed in 1927, by 1931 they and their affiliated stations accounted for 70 percent of all wattage. By 1935 only four of the sixty-two stations that broadcast at 5000 watts or more did not have a network affiliation; one study showed that fully 97 percent of nighttime broadcasting, when smaller stations were not licensed to broadcast, was controlled by NBC and CBS.[8] Likewise the networks developed commercial advertising as a means of support, even in the teeth of the Great Depression. From virtual nonexistence in 1927, radio advertising expenditures were over $100 million in 1929.[9] Radio advertising continued to grow throughout the 1930s, to the point where it nearly approached the amount of advertising in the U.S. newspaper industry.[10] The development of the networks and advertising was mutually reinforcing as over 80 percent of advertising expenditures went to 20 percent of the stations, all network owned or affiliated.[11] These developments took most Americans by surprise. "Broadcasting today is not what it was expected to be," one observer noted in 1932. "The amount of advertising on the air is beyond any expectation that could have existed five years ago."[12] Another observer stated in 1930 that "Nothing in American history has paralleled this mushroom growth." This has since become a staple insight in U.S. broadcasting history.[13]

The losers in the reallocation were the educational and nonprofit broadcasters. University stations were in an economic crisis prior to the reallocation of 1928; their total number fell from 128 in 1925 to 95 two years later.[14] Most nonprofit broadcasters thought the term "public interest, convenience, or necessity" meant the FRC was supposed to favor nonprofit organizations over commercial enterprises in the allocation of licenses.[15] The FRC determined otherwise, arguing in the legal proceedings that followed the reallocation that it had to favor commercial broadcasters because nonprofit groups were not motivated by profits (i.e., satisfying market demand) and therefore were more likely to spread unwanted "propaganda." The FRC also asserted that advertising was a necessary evil, as it was the only form of material support that did not have ideological strings attached.[16] As a result, the number of college broadcasters continued to plummet in the late 1920s, falling by half between 1927 and 1930. Those nonprofit stations that remained on the air were almost all given limited daytime hours on frequencies shared with commercial stations. Even the University of Wisconsin's WHA, the foremost college station, found its work "practically wrecked" when it was forced for a time to share its frequency with eight other stations.[17] The FRC has "taken away all the hours that are worth anything and left us with hours that are absolutely no good either for commercial programs or educational programs," wrote the director of the soon defunct University of Arkansas station.[18] In this context most university stations had difficulty developing audiences or maintaining budgets from state legislatures. The upshot was that nonprofit broadcasting was effectively nonexistent for most Americans by the early 1930s.

Although the reallocation of 1928 went a long way toward establishing the dominance of network-dominated, advertising-supported broadcasting in the United States, full-fledged consolidation remained years away. On one hand, the FRC had only been established on a temporary basis by the Radio Act of 1927. Congress considered legislation for the permanent regulation of broadcasting at every session until the passage of the Communications Act of 1934, which was only replaced by the 1996 Telecommunications Act. The 1934 Communications Act, which created the FCC to replace the FRC, restated the radio charter of the Radio Act of 1927 virtually verbatim. Nonetheless, in the years between 1927 and 1934 this outcome was anything but guaranteed and this uncertainty granted the opponents of commercial broadcasting a political legitimacy that would vanish after 1934.

Moreover, the system was not yet ideologically entrenched; between 1927 and 1934 commercial broadcasting was not considered innately "American" and "democratic" and therefore immune to fundamental attack. Indeed, the initial public response to commercial broadcasting was decidedly negative, particularly in comparison to later attitudes. Radio advertising was almost uniformly disliked. "I know that dissatisfaction with the present broadcasting system and its results is well nigh universal," one journalist wrote. "Out of one hundred persons you will not find more than five who are satisfied; of the other 95%, more than one-half are ready to support any kind of movement for drastic change."[19] This assessment was shared to varying degrees by the industry and its supporters. "Radio broadcasting," *Business Week* noted in 1932, "is threatened with a revolt of the listeners. . . . Newspaper editors report more and more letters of protest against irritating sales ballyhoo."[20] The challenge for those opposing the status quo was to convert this antipathy to commercial fare into support for structural reform, before the system became fully entrenched and listeners reconciled to its existence.

This was a daunting task, regardless of public opinion, if only due to the strength of the radio lobby. NBC, RCA, CBS, and the National Association of Broadcasters (NAB), the commercial broadcasters' trade association, comprised a lobby that was, as all acknowledged, "one of the most powerful here in Washington."[21] Network presidents could have audiences with members of Congress, even the president, almost at a moment's notice. The industry devoted lavish resources to a public relations campaign to establish the benevolence of commercial broadcasting and utilized the airwaves to further promote this theme.[22] The radio lobby also successfully cultivated the support of the newspaper industry and the legal community.[23] Perhaps most important, the networks had a policy of offering free air time to members of Congress and government officials during this period; between January 1931 and October 1933, for example, U.S. senators made 298 appearances over NBC. Moreover, it was the network lobbyists who were responsible for scheduling members of Congress for their broadcasts.[24] As one frustrated reformer observed, "the politicians are too eager to use radio to come out for reform."[25]

This was the situation facing the national foundations and educational organizations as they became interested in broadcasting in the second half of the 1920s. The political and business climate was such that philanthropies and nonprofit groups determined that it would be incumbent upon them to provide the missing public service component to U.S. broadcasting. The Payne Fund, a small foundation established in 1926, was perhaps the first of these groups to actively pursue the educational potential of radio. The Payne Fund was dominated by its primary benefactor, Frances Payne Bolton, whose grandfather had generated a vast fortune with Standard Oil in Cleveland, Ohio, her hometown. Bolton's husband, Chester, was a Republican U.S. representative, and she, too, was a devoted Republican from the progressive wing of the party. She envisioned the Payne Fund as quietly sponsoring a variety of projects concerning education and communication. The Payne Fund is best known for sponsoring a series of academic studies, under the direction of Ohio State University professor W. W. Charters, on the effects of motion pictures on audiences between 1928 and 1933; these studies remain seminal pioneering works in U.S. mass communication research. Most of the Payne Fund's initial forays into broadcasting were coordinated by its radio counsel, Armstrong Perry, a journalist with a long interest in educational radio, and its secretary, Ella Phillips Crandall, who managed the Payne Fund's New York headquarters.[26]

The fund's initial goal was to create a national "School of the Air," whereby educational programs for children and adults would be broadcast by educators over the commercial networks. The Payne Fund had no qualms about working with NBC and CBS, finding them "friendly" and willing to provide the necessary air time "without charge."[27] The networks also agreed, at the Payne Fund's insistence, that these educational programs should be produced by independent educational authorities and that there should be no commercial interference. The major stumbling block for this project, as it developed, came not from the networks but from educational groups and foundations. Perry spent most of 1928 attempting to find an educational group willing to undertake such a program or a philanthropist willing to underwrite it. "I see no evidence," he concluded in 1929, "that any educational organization will do so on a national basis."[28] By this time the Payne Fund was convinced that with the flood of advertising to radio, the prospects for educational broadcasting were dismal, and that, if anything, the educational programs provided by the networks would be "prepared for advertising purposes rather than educational value."[29]

Using their contacts with the National Education Association (NEA), the Payne Fund convinced Secretary of the Interior Ray Lyman Wilbur in May 1929 to create the Advisory Committee on Education by Radio, known widely as the Wilbur Committee, to examine the crisis in educational broadcasting. Wilbur, a proponent of educational stations, was a former Stanford University president who had been disappointed when Stanford had been forced to close its radio station.[30] Working under the direction of Commissioner of Education William John Cooper, whose Office of Education was part of the Interior Department, the Wilbur Committee was commissioned to report back to Wilbur with recommendations for how to promote education by radio. The Payne Fund helped subsidize the Wilbur Committee and it assigned Perry to work for the committee until it filed its report. Perry spent the balance of 1929 traveling across the United States interviewing educators and broadcasters.

It was during this period that Perry became radicalized. First, he discovered that NBC and CBS were curtailing their commitment to educational programming as they were able to sell more and more of their time to advertisers.[31] There was the distinct possibility, he concluded, that "all the time available on stations covering any considerable territory will be sold for advertising purposes."[32] Second, Perry finally located a group of educators who seemed to grasp the importance of radio for education: the college and university broadcasters. Perry became convinced that the only hope was to protect these stations from extinction and, moreover, to create a viable nonprofit and noncommercial broadcasting sector. These broadcasters convinced Perry that their enemies were the FRC and, above all, the commercial broadcasters, who, in the quest for profit, were attempting to occupy every available channel. "One thing is evident," Perry noted in June 1929, "and that is that commercial radio wants to head off any possibility of the growth and connection of stations owned by the people."[33]

The NBC and CBS executives on the Wilbur Committee successfully deflected Perry's efforts to have the committee recommend that educational stations be protected and invigorated. The networks argued that they remained willing to provide whatever air time was necessary for educational and cultural purposes. The February 1930 report simply called for the educators and commercial broadcasters to work together and for the Office of Education to establish a special radio section to promote educational broadcasting and "attempt to prevent conflicts between various broadcasting interests."[34] Although the networks were elated, this was not a thorough defeat for the proponents of independent educational stations. Since Congress could not fund this new radio section for another year, the Payne Fund "lent" Perry to Cooper to oversee the new office that Wilbur had established upon receipt of the report. Cooper instructed Perry to handle all radio correspondence and keep him "up to date on radio."[35] NBC and CBS attempted, unsuccessfully, to undercut Perry's influence with Wilbur and Cooper. By the end of the summer Perry had convinced them both of the limitations of the Wilbur Committee's recommendations and the need to protect the college stations. His case was buttressed when twenty-three more university broadcasters went off the air between January and July of 1930.[36]

At first the Payne Fund was reluctant to formally enter "prolonged and obstinate opposition" to commercial broadcasting.[37] By July 1930, however, Bolton and Crandall accepted the wisdom of Perry's approach, advising him to "lay out a new plan of action more valuable than the original project." Crandall acknowledged that the cause of education on radio could only be served by nonprofit stations and therefore required "a direct blow against the monopolistic intentions and efforts of commercial broadcasters."[38] Perry argued that all the major national educational organizations needed to join forces to lobby Congress on behalf of reform, and that he had generated considerable interest in the idea in his work in the Office of Education.[39] Bolton's resolve to enter the fight for broadcast reform stiffened when conversations with her husband's colleagues "clearly indicated the intense resentment and distrust of Congress toward the radio interests."[40] In September the Payne Fund confidentially informed Perry that it had set aside a five-year, $200,000 grant to support an educator broadcast reform organization. Working with Perry and the Payne Fund, Cooper convened a meeting in Chicago, to be closer to the more radical midwest land-grant universities, to formally establish such a group.[41]

The October 13 meeting established the NCER as an umbrella

organization of the NEA, the American Council on Education, the National Association of State Universities, and six other national educational organizations.[42] Cooper arranged for Joy Elmer Morgan, editor of the NEA's *Journal*, to chair the NCER. Since the NCER was formally chartered to lobby Congress for legislation to set aside 15 percent of the channels for educational stations, Cooper had nothing further to do with the group, stating it would be inappropriate for a government official to work with a partisan organization.[43] The NCER was established as a "fighting committee," as the Payne Fund put it. There was no pretense at the Chicago meeting or thereafter that it was possible for educators to work with commercial broadcasters; that approach was presupposed to be bankrupt.[44] In November and December the Payne Fund negotiated with Morgan and other education leaders to determine the precise nature of the NCER and the NCER's relationship to the Payne Fund. The Payne Fund eschewed publicity for itself, and was especially bashful about a public role with the NCER so as not to embarrass Bolton's congressman husband. Bolton informed Morgan that the fund "emphatically" disavowed "the least intention to influence the policies of your Committee when our judgments may be at variance."[45] As Crandall informed Perry, the fund established the NCER so educators could defend their own interests, not to go about "fighting their fight for them."[46]

The Payne Fund honored this commitment, particularly during the five years covered by the initial grant. Funding an explicitly antiestablishment organization like the NCER was an extraordinary, perhaps even unprecedented, step for a U.S. foundation like the Payne Fund to take. Whereas the Payne Fund was highly critical of the film industry, it made no attempt to wrestle control of that industry away from the major studios. The Payne Fund effectively resolved that Hollywood was, more or less, "giving the people what they want," and therefore the primary duty of the educational community was to train a more sophisticated audience for films. Such a tactic was not even considered for radio, where the public nature of the scarce airwaves along with the networks' seeming adherence to advertisers before listeners propelled the Payne Fund in a distinctly radical direction. As Perry observed, this was mostly a coincidence since the fund "happened to be organized at a critical moment" in the development of U.S. broadcasting.[47] The irony of the Payne Fund, which had entered the field planning to cooperate with the networks, subsidizing a political assault on the capitalist basis of U.S. broadcasting was not lost on Perry. As he wrote to one CBS executive in March 1931: "I certainly am aware that your company holds a very vigorous opinion against the setting aside of certain channels for educational broadcasting. The opinion has helped to turn hundreds of thousands of dollars of philanthropic money, which was appropriated for the purpose of developing public interest in your educational programs and those of other companies into other channels where it is developing a nationwide reaction against commercial broadcasting."[48]

The Payne Fund was well aware of the magnitude of the NCER's task and anything but hesitant about challenging the corporate domination of U.S. broadcasting once it had made the commitment to the NCER. Radio reform became a consuming passion for Bolton and Crandall, "the most impressive example" of what the Payne Fund could accomplish, as Crandall informed one Payne Fund board member.[49] In 1931, to supplement the NCER, the Payne Fund surreptitiously bankrolled an eighteen-month campaign under the aegis of the *Ventura* [Calif.] *Free Press* to mobilize newspaper, congressional, and popular support for broadcast reform. "The objective of the campaign, as I understand it," noted the journalist hired to direct publicity in the $50,000 campaign, "is the complete overthrow of the present system."[50] Although the *Ventura Free Press* radio campaign failed to accomplish its goals, it alarmed the networks and helped rouse some newspaper publishers to oppose commercial broadcasting in 1932 and 1933.[51]

The NCER and the Broadcast Reform Movement

The NCER formally commenced operations in January 1931. The nine member organizations each provided one representative for the NCER's board, which met to determine basic policy four times annually. Morgan was the NEA representative and served as NCER chair until 1935. Based in Washington, D.C., the NCER was directed on a daily basis by Tracy F. Tyler, a Columbia Ph.D. who managed the office and edited the NCER newsletter, *Education by Radio.* Tyler also coordinated the NCER's research program and he arranged a clearinghouse so educational stations could share their programs. Perry left the Office of Education to direct the NCER's Service Bureau, which was responsible for representing educational and nonprofit stations in their hearings before the FRC. Nonetheless, it was the campaign for broadcast reform that was the NCER's raison d'être. In its first week the NCER sent an open letter to Congress criticizing U.S. radio as "the dollar sign's mightiest megaphone."[52] Between 1931 and 1934 Tyler, Perry, and the other educators associated with the NCER made hundreds of speeches and wrote scores of articles promoting the cause.

It was Morgan, however, more than anyone else, who gave the NCER its public identity. A devotee of Horace Mann, Morgan embraced Mann's maxim to "be ashamed to die until you have won some victory for humanity."[53] Morgan had worked for public ownership of utilities during the Progressive Era, when he honed his hatred of the "power trust" and the large corporations, like RCA, that would come to dominate radio.[54] Morgan believed accessible public education was the foundation of genuine democracy; he derided college admissions tests as a "crime," claiming they created an "intellectual aristocracy."[55] He regarded education as "the most fundamental activity of the state" and defined it in the broadest terms imaginable. "Education is no narrow academic affair. It is not confined to children. It concerns the entire population. It involves the whole life of the individual, on the one side, and the whole life of society, on the other."[56] In his capacity with the NEA Morgan became convinced that the commercial broadcasters would never provide adequate time for educational programming. "That practice has been tried for nearly a decade and proved unworkable," he stated in 1931. "It is no longer open to discussion."[57] Moreover, radio broadcasting had emerged as the most important educational influence in the United States, "more important than home, school, and church combined in the formation of human character," he asserted in 1933.[58]

Given these sentiments, Morgan regarded the fight for broadcast reform as indispensable to the battle for political and social democracy, casting the struggle in urgent, almost apocalyptic, terms: "As a result of radio broadcasting, there will probably develop during the twentieth century either chaos or a world-order of civilization. Whether it shall be one or the other will depend largely upon whether broadcasting be used as a tool of education or an instrument of selfish greed. So far, our American radio interests have thrown their major influence on the side of greed. . . . There has never been in the entire history of the United States an example of mismanagement and lack of vision so colossal and far-reaching in its consequences as our turning the radio channels almost exclusively into commercial hands."[59] Morgan argued that "whoever controls radio will in the end control the development of the human race."[60] In the depths of the Depression he wrote that the United States cannot "solve any of its major political problems without first solving the radio problem."[61]

Not surprisingly, the NCER generated an ice-cold response from the commercial broadcasters. The trade publication *Broadcasting* characterized the NCER as "a group of misguided pedagogues" who were "professional reformers" with "silly demands." One editorial described the NCER as "childish" and as "a racket by which a few zealots want to justify the jobs they are holding."[62] The industry displayed no interest in taking the NCER's concerns seriously; rather, the NAB characterized the NCER as trying to "invade the broadcast band at the expense" of the commercial stations that had been willing "to bear the trials of pioneering."[63] Morgan, in particular, was a target of derision and ridicule. *Broadcasting* dismissed him as "coming from the ranks of primary school men," and possessed by an "unreasoning sort of crusading."[64]

The NCER and the *Ventura Free Press* radio campaign were not the only groups pursuing broadcast reform, though they were the best financed. Organized labor, religious groups, and the American Civil Liberties Union (ACLU), among others, worked throughout the early 1930s for legislation to establish a significant nonprofit and noncommercial component to U.S. broadcasting.[65] In addition to organized reform efforts, the cause of broadcast reform received the nearly unconditional support of the U.S. intelligentsia.[66] As Morgan observed, it was virtually impossible to find any intellectual in favor of the status quo unless that person was receiving money or air time from a commercial station or network.[67] Among these intellectuals was John Dewey, who in 1934 stated that "radio is the most powerful instrument of social education the world has ever seen. It can be used to distort facts and to mislead the public mind. In my opinion, the question as to whether it is to be employed for this end or for the social public interest is one of the most crucial problems of the present."[68] Dewey argued that freedom of the press was structurally impossible as long as broadcasting was under "concentrated capitalist control."[69]

Dewey's critique of radio was similar to that of the NCER. Indeed, there was a striking consistency in the criticism of commercial broadcasting made by all the various elements of the broadcast reform movement. Three themes dominated this critique. First, the reformers emphasized that the system was structurally flawed on free expression grounds; a for-profit, corporate-dominated system would be inherently biased against broadcasting material critical of big business and the status quo. "Freedom of speech is the very foundation of democracy," one *Education by Radio* article stated. "To allow private interests to monopolize the most powerful means of reaching the human mind is to destroy democracy. Without freedom of speech, without the honest presentation of facts by people whose primary interest is *not* profits, there can be no intelligent basis for the determination of public policy [their emphasis]."[70]

Second, the reformers detested radio advertising and its influence over programming. In the early 1930s advertisers generally provided the programs in addition to the commercial announcements that appeared during the programs.[71] "It is a trite but ever truthful saying that he who pays the piper calls the tune," *Education by Radio* observed. "Where has it been shown to better advantage than in radio?"[72] Most commercial programs were regarded as trivial and inane, and it was seen as inevitable that advertisers would downplay educational, cultural, or controversial fare to favor inexpensive, unoriginal entertainment programs. One college president associated with the NCER stated that "it is inevitable that a commercial concern catering to the public will present a service as low in standard as the public will tolerate and will produce the most profit."[73] The NCER emphasized that radio advertising was distinct from print advertising as the listener was "helpless" to avoid it, and, to enjoy radio programs, the public was forced to have "its homes turned into salesrooms."[74] Moreover, the public showed no desire for radio advertising. To the NCER, if the commercial broadcasters were genuinely interested in "giving the public what it wants," as they often proclaimed, the first thing that would happen is advertising would be stricken from the airwaves.[75]

The NCER took this critique of radio advertising one step farther than the other reformers. Morgan argued that radio advertising "is making great efforts to get into the schools."[76] He contended that "one reason why commercial interests have sought to destroy independent educational stations has been their ambition to broadcast radio advertising into the schools themselves."[77] The NCER carefully monitored incidents of commercial educational programs being used in public schools, arguing that it must "be kept out of the schools just as advertising has been kept out of textbooks."[78]

The NCER's critique of advertising harbored an element of elitism and, at times, academic contempt for the mere notion of entertainment programming. This left the educators in stark contrast to organized labor, which insisted that entertainment had to play a large role on a nonprofit working-class radio station, whether or not advertising was present.[79] It also undercut the populist appeal of the balance of their critique, damaging their prospects for generating popular support. "It is much more important that people be informed than that they be entertained," Morgan argued.[80] Morgan informed one 1931 audience that for the commercial broadcasters "to get the large audiences, they cultivate the lower appeals. The educational stations realize that the finer things of life have always appealed first to the few."[81] This point should not be exaggerated, however. Most of the college and nonprofit broadcasters regarded their survival as dependent upon their ability to cultivate and satisfy audiences in order to win the budgets necessary to stay on the air. In their minds, they were appealing directly to listeners while the commercial broadcasters were concerned primarily with advertisers. Moreover, the broadcast reformers regarded themselves as representing the legitimate desires of the vast majority of U.S. listeners in the early 1930s; it was only later, as the system became entrenched, that educators accepted their role as one of attempting to establish a noncommercial beachhead in a popularly embraced commercial system.

The third theme of the reform movement critique was that the commercial system had been the result of a mostly secretive process in which the public and even Congress had played almost no role. This violated the reformers' democratic sensibilities. More broadly, the reformers thought the very notion of turning a vital public resource over to private interests for profitable exploitation was nothing short of "an incredible absurdity for a democracy," as one NCER member put it.[82] "So the question really is," Perry noted, "do we want to submit to the regulation of radio by the people we elect to rule over us, or do we want to leave our radio channels in the hands of private concerns and private individuals who wish to use these public radio channels for their own profit?"[83]

In sum, this was explicitly radical criticism; the reformers were unified in their belief that the FRC experience established beyond doubt that it was absurd to think a government agency could regulate private broadcasters to act against their interests and in the public interest. Structural reform was mandatory. It is "a fact that radio channels belong to the people," one NCER organizer stated, "and should not be placed in the hands of private capital."[84] While most reformers looked to basic capitalist economics to explain the seeming mad rush of capital to dominate the airwaves, they all saw this as a classic struggle of the people versus the plutocrats, where those in power were well aware of the stakes in the outcome. Some were inclined to more sinister explanations. "Candidly," one educational broadcaster observed, "I believe there is a definite, organized conspiracy within big business to keep radio out of the hands of those who would put it to use for the people. It is such a potent agent of enlightenment that special privilege cannot tolerate its public uses."[85] But if there was unanimity among the reformers regarding the core weaknesses of commercial broadcasting and the need for structural reform, the opposite was the case when it came to generating an alternative plan for U.S. broadcasting. The NCER was never enthusiastic about the proposal to reserve 15 percent of the channels for educational broadcasters; Morgan characterized it as merely "an emergency and not a final measure."[86] As Perry noted, it left unresolved the pressing question of how to pay for quality noncommercial programming.[87]

All of the NCER officers individually were enthralled by the British Broadcasting Company (BBC), a nonprofit, noncommercial, quasi-governmental agency that held a monopoly over broadcasting in the United Kingdom. While none wanted to see such a monopoly in the United States, most major NCER figures thought a publicly funded nonprofit system, with a dominant though not exclusive role, was a rational alternative.[88] To Perry, the BBC provided the "ideal" example of a "broadcasting service maintained primarily for the benefit of all radio listeners" and was the solution to "the whole world problem of broadcasting."[89] The NCER and the other reformers determined that it would be politically impossible to achieve such a system in the United States, so it was never formally proposed or advocated. At the same time, the reformers never could agree on one specific plan to subsidize a nonprofit broadcasting sector for the United States and then coalesce to work on that plan's behalf on Capitol Hill. After canvassing the various broadcast reform lobbyists in 1932, a frustrated Payne Fund official commented that "every son-of-a-gun and his brother has a definite idea about the way it should be handled."[90]

If the NCER could not apply the BBC model to the United States, it came to regard Canada as "leading the way" for the balance of North America.[91] (I discuss the Canadian reform movement again and in greater detail in chapter 5.) In 1932 the Canadian House of Commons formally resolved to establish a nonprofit, noncommercial, government-subsidized broadcasting system after studying both the British and U.S. experiences with radio. The movement for radio reform in Canada had been led by Graham Spry and the Canadian Radio League, which successfully painted the alternative as one of radio to "be operated by big business or to be operated by the government."[92] The fear of U.S. commercial domination also propelled the Canadians in a radical direction. "If the fear of the United States did not exist," Spry confided to an American in 1931, "it would be necessary, like Voltaire's God, to invent it."[93] Spry spent a month in the United States in 1931, mostly meeting with NCER members and discussing their mutual interests.[94] He was impressed by the "universal criticism of the advertising element in broadcasting" in the United States.[95] At the House of Commons hearings in 1932, Spry used the rising opposition to commercial broadcasting in the United States as prima facie evidence that it would be absurd for Canada to go the commercial route.[96] Moreover, Morgan was the only American to testify in Ottawa that spring and his criticism of commercial broadcasting was unequivocal. "Until your appearance," Spry later congratulated Morgan, "the committee had regarded the American situation as largely satisfactory."[97]

Spry believed that Canada's noncommercial system "would seriously weaken the whole advertising basis of American broadcasting."[98] The NCER shared this hope that Canada would expose Americans near the border to the possibilities of public service broadcasting. More important, the NCER became convinced that if the U.S. Congress established a full-blown independent study of broadcasting like Canada had done, it, too, would resolve to establish a nonprofit and noncommercial system. The notion that individuals without a material stake in the outcome could possible endorse the existing U.S. system as the best one possible was simply inconceivable to the NCER. Hence a few months after Canada's decision, the NCER formally dropped the call for reserving 15 percent of the channels from its platform and adopted a plank calling for Congress to establish an independent study of broadcasting to determine how best to promote the public interest.[99] This plank also permitted the NCER to avoid dealing directly with the thorny question of how nonprofit broadcasting could be supported; it would now become the task of the proposed federal study to make that determination.

The NACRE and the Contest for the Educational Community

The Carnegie Corporation began to explore the educational potential of broadcasting a few months after the Payne Fund did. Founded in 1911 and based upon a $135 million endowment provided by steel magnate Andrew Carnegie, the New York–based foundation was arguably the most important in the United States.[100] The Carnegie Corporation, under its president Frederick P. Keppel, regarded the Radio Act of 1927 as implicitly calling for "a group of public spirited citizens, including prominent educators . . . that could cooperate with broadcasters" in developing educational and cultural programs.[101] Keppel began discussions with his friend Owen D. Young, president of General Electric and founder of RCA, to establish such a group in 1928. Young was a visionary capitalist who believed that RCA's new NBC had a public service obligation that went beyond what could be expected from simply pursuing profit maximization.[102] In December 1928 the Carnegie Corporation provided $20,000 to conduct a study with NBC to determine how an independent group could provide quality noncommercial programming that the network would then broadcast at no charge.[103] The study was canceled when the Wilbur Committee was established in May 1929; the Carnegie Corporation then offered its time and money to assist the Wilbur Committee with its work.[104]

Once the Wilbur Committee completed its work, the Carnegie Corporation established the NACRE in early 1930, after a series of meetings between Keppel and Carnegie Corporation officers, Young, Young's son-in-law Everett Case, and network executives.[105] Keppel regarded the recommendations of the Wilbur Committee as a virtual mandate for the NACRE's existence. When Cooper went on to coordinate the founding of the NCER later that year, it was regarded as an "inexplicable stab in the back." The Carnegie Corporation provided annual grants of $30,000 for the next several years; John D. Rockefeller, Jr., also provided the NACRE annual grants of $25,000 in these years before the formal establishment of the Rockefeller Foundation.[106]

The NACRE's mission was to provide the broadcasting industry with a "representative organization to which it can turn for advice and counsel in educational matters."[107] The Carnegie Corporation and Case determined the membership of the NACRE's prestigious board of directors. It included, among others, Young, Charles Evans Hughes, Elihu Root, and university presidents Robert Millikan of the California Institute of Technology, Walter Dill Scott of Northwestern University, and Robert M. Hutchins of the University of Chicago. The NACRE's primary function was to arrange for noncommercial educational programs that would be aired over CBS or NBC during the evening hours when there were large adult audiences. The networks would provide the NACRE this air time at no charge. Accordingly, the NACRE's success was predicated on a healthy relationship with the networks. Indeed, the meeting which established the NACRE was marked by repeated statements praising the networks for their commitment to broadcasting educational programs.[108] NBC, which received the bulk of the NACRE's programs, came to informally regard the NACRE as its educational "branch."[109] NBC president Merlin Aylesworth praised the NACRE's work as being "of the greatest importance in the educational field."[110] The industry and the trade press routinely praised the NACRE as the "able" and legitimate representative of educational broadcasting, often in the process of attacking the NCER.[111] In short, to the commercial broadcasters, the NACRE was the solution to the problem of education by radio.

Perhaps the most important member of the NACRE's board of directors was the thirty-one-year-old Hutchins, who had already generated unusually widespread publicity for an academic due to his youth and his commitment to educational reform and education by radio.[112] Hutchins's participation in the NACRE was problematic. On one hand, he was capable of delivering a speech damning the asininity of commercial broadcasting. Yet this criticism was always tempered by his belief that the status quo was entrenched. "I do not believe that the existing situation can be materially affected at this time," he wrote to one reformer in 1931, while stating his support for reform if it ever became feasible.[113] In addition, the University of Chicago had a working relationship with NBC's WMAQ in Chicago. This was generally acknowledged "as the single experience of successful cooperation between educational institutions and radio stations."[114] This relationship also left Hutchins in NBC's debt. As

WMAQ began to sell more advertising and have less time for educational programs, however, Hutchins increasingly attacked the commitment of the networks to educational broadcasting.[115] NBC monitored his activities closely. "Hutchins is a bug for the use of Radio for Education," Aylesworth wrote to RCA president David Sarnoff in a 1933 memorandum regarding some of Hutchins's critical comments.[116] Hutchins never did support broadcast reform during this period. Even in 1934, when he began to regard commercial broadcasting in a most disparaging manner, he argued that educators had no alternative but to work with the existing networks.[117]

Keppel appointed Levering Tyson, an adult educator from Columbia University who had coordinated Columbia's educational broadcasts over NBC's WEAF between 1925 and 1928, to be the NACRE's director. Tyson quickly became the public face of the NACRE, as Morgan was for the NCER. Ironically, Tyson acknowledged that the WEAF-Columbia program collapsed because "changes in the policy of the station after the commercial side of broadcasting became so highly developed, resulted in a complete abandonment of the whole educational experiment idea which we had."[118] Despite this "great disappointment," Tyson unconditionally advocated the NACRE philosophy that educators had to work through the auspices of NBC and CBS if they were to have any success with broadcasting.[119] Tyson argued that "undoubtedly, the American system is a commercial one," the matter having been settled in the early 1920s.[120]

To Tyson, the purpose of the NACRE was explicitly "to work with the existing broadcasting facilities," not to engage in a "fruitless and unwarranted . . . destructive attack upon the American broadcasting system."[121] The NACRE refused to take a formal position on broadcast reform legislation. Tyson professed "absolute neutrality" on the political questions surrounding broadcasting, characterizing the NACRE as "the sole American organization which is non-partisan in its attitude and purely objective in its approach to the many baffling problems that have arisen in educational broadcasting."[122] Tyson argued that only the NACRE would courageously "sit on the fence and be shot at from both sides."[123] At the same time, Tyson always publicly exonerated the commercial broadcasters when discussing the admittedly dismal fare on the radio; in his mind the fault lay with educators who had not learned to prepare high quality programs to which the public would want to listen, or with a public which demanded tripe.

Although Tyson and Keppel were resigned to the permanence of commercial broadcasting, in private they regarded the system as producing moronic programs. "Because of the inane advertising," Tyson confided to Keppel in 1933, "there are few countries in which so many poor programs are broadcast."[124] While the NACRE's public rhetoric extolled the networks in no uncertain terms, Tyson and Keppel had no illusions about the commitment of commercial broadcasters to noncommercial educational and cultural programs. Tyson acknowledged that NBC and CBS "are not interested" in the NACRE "from any educational motive."[125] Keppel concluded that NBC "will be useful to the NACRE just as long as the NACRE is useful to it."[126]

For Tyson or Keppel to publicize these sentiments would have been counterproductive; the implicit quid pro quo was that the networks would broadcast NACRE programs and in return the NACRE would use its prestige to confer legitimacy upon the fledgling industry. "Broadcasting's position in this country is not overly secure," Tyson reminded one NBC executive concerning the NACRE's role in network operations. "I have no hesitation in stating to you that many influential members of the Council were supporters of the theory of government broadcasting until the success of our programs convinced them the American system is and can be workable."[127] Others at the Carnegie Corporation had no qualms about buttressing the status quo in radio. If the NCER contained some remnant of the populist and progressive traditions, the Carnegie Corporation was unequivocally linked to the dominant interests in U.S. society, albeit often on the liberal wing. Indeed, a significant left critique of major U.S. foundations along these lines emerged in the 1930s.[128] As Carnegie Corporation educational advisor Henry Suzzalo informed Keppel, the purpose of the NACRE was not only to conduct educational broadcasting but also to rightfully squash the "demand for public ownership . . . of the land-grant college crowd" and assure that "radio under private ownership succeed in this country."[129]

Moreover, the NACRE assisted the networks as they infiltrated the organizations affiliated with the NCER, thus undercutting the sentiment for broadcast reform in the educational community. "Every one of the educational organizations connected with the Committee is being besieged by the radio trust outfit," one Payne Fund memo observed, "and Brother Morgan knows it well."[130] In 1932 Morgan called an emergency meeting with Crandall to address the "attempts of the radio interests to interpenetrate their organization."[131] Nowhere was this more apparent than in Morgan's own NEA, which had developed a regular series on NBC in conjunction with the NACRE, leaving NEA officials in debt to the network. Perry observed that Morgan was "constantly in a somewhat ridiculous position, not being supported by his own organization."[132]

Beneath a cordial public veneer, relations between the NCER and the NACRE were quite bitter. Tyson regarded the NCER as "a belligerent and propagandistic organization which has allied itself with every disgruntled element appearing in the field." To Tyson, the NCER obsessively "attempted in every way to throw sand into our machinery."[133] The NCER, for its part, commended the NACRE for its success in developing "a very credible program that has become well known and approved by many educators and others."[134] At the same time, the NCER regarded the program as flawed since it would "subordinate education to the management of commercial stations."[135] *Education by Radio* argued that "people who believe that education by radio can accomplish its work in an occasional hour over a commercial chain, utterly fail to comprehend the magnitude of our educational needs."[136] Most educators associated with the NCER conceded that the NACRE was motivated by a genuine interest in educational radio. One college broadcaster termed NACRE educators the "unwitting patsies" of the networks, who "just couldn't turn down all the good money" and air time offered to them to work through the existing system.[137] Nevertheless, questions of intent aside, all NCER educators and broadcast reformers regarded the NACRE as "a smoke screen to further the efforts of the radio monopolists in gobbling up broadcasting," as one Payne Fund official put it.[138] To the NCER, the NACRE's professed neutrality on broadcast reform legislation was a ruse. In sum, each of these groups saw the prospects for its own success as inversely related to the success of the other.

In a broader sense, the tension between the NACRE and the NCER reflected the conflict between the Carnegie Corporation and the Payne Fund over which organization, and which approach, would prove dominant in determining the course of education by radio. Before funding the NCER, Bolton had studied the NACRE, concluding that the NACRE "is not particularly popular with the educators of this country."[139] To the Payne Fund, the NCER was premised on the notion that legitimate educational organizations should be responsible for educational broadcasting, not "privately-appointed committees in New York."[140] The NCER characterized the Carnegie Corporation as "the enemy of free democratic education," and the contest between the two foundations as "the same old struggle of greed and autocracy on one hand against democracy and opportunity on the other."[141] The Payne Fund was angered by what it regarded as the Carnegie Corporation's apparent ambition to become "the mouthpiece of all education" with regard to radio, thus leaving the NCER and the Payne Fund in the lurch.[142] Tyson, conversely, regarded the Payne Fund as the cause of all dissension about the NACRE in the educational community. "If Payne Fund money was not available," he wrote to Keppel, "this whole agitation . . . would die from lack of nourishment."[143] Accordingly, Tyson spent considerable time in the early 1930s attempting, unsuccessfully, to "shut off this source of Payne Fund money" by "bringing Mrs. Bolton into our camp."[144]

As much of this hostility remained subterranean, many educators were puzzled by the inability of the NCER and the NACRE to work with each other. "It seems to me the two organizations are supplementary and are striving to attain the same ends," the Iowa State College president wrote to Keppel, urging him to call a conference between Morgan and Tyson to address the "friction and lack of unity" between the groups.[145] The upshot was, as broadcasting historian Erik Barnouw has noted, that there existed among the public and educators a "glorious confusion" about how the groups were different.[146]

To the extent that the NCER's credibility and leverage depended upon its capacity to represent the entire educational community, this confusion may have been more disastrous to it than to the NACRE. The NCER suffered numerous defections to the NACRE in the contest for educator allegiance, particularly as the prospects for broadcast reform grew dimmer. The NACRE had the advantage of being able to offer educators a tangible program for broadcasting through the major stations. Moreover, as the overseers of the U.S. educational system, the member NCER organizations were hardly comfortable in the role of political radical. Some of them worked closely with the Carnegie Corporation on other projects.[147] The director of one NCER member organization, for example, rejected the NCER's confrontational approach, arguing that "we can get more by being friendly to the big commercial broadcasters."[148] Indeed, W. W. Charters, who directed the Payne Fund's film research and also conducted a smaller program of radio audience research for the Payne Fund, agreed to serve on the NACRE's board of directors. He then repudiated the NCER's call for structural reform, much to the Payne Fund's dismay. The NCER refused to have anything more to do with Charters.[149]

The fractured appearance of the U.S. educational community was most damaging to the NCER when it attempted to cultivate the support of the BBC and its powerful director-general Sir John C. W. Reith. In a 1931 visit to the United States, Reith was shocked by the nature of U.S. commercial broadcasting. He announced his belief that the United States would soon come to its senses and adopt a nonprofit, noncommercial system along the lines of the BBC.[150] Moreover, Reith was always on the lookout for efforts to commercialize British broadcasting, and the U.S. networks were seen as likely accomplices. Perry had met with Reith during his visit and maintained regular correspondence with him and other BBC officials until 1935.

The NCER attempted to establish an alliance with Reith like it enjoyed with Spry and the Canadian Radio League. NBC and CBS also worked assiduously in the early 1930s to cultivate harmonious relations with Reith and the BBC; the last thing they wanted was for the BBC to lend its already considerable prestige to the U.S. broadcast reform movement. A critical factor in assuaging Reith's apprehension about U.S. broadcasting was the NACRE, which sponsored one Reith trip to the United States and convinced Reith that there was a legitimate noncommercial cultural component to the U.S. system. The NACRE also emphasized to Reith that the NCER was a disreputable operation and that commercial broadcasting was politically inviolable in the United States. The BBC rejected the NCER's overtures, informing Perry that "it does not wish to meddle in American affairs."[151] In 1932 the BBC commented politely that "the whole system of American broadcasting" lies "outside our comprehension" and "clearly springs from a specifically American conception of democracy."[152] Perry and the NCER were eventually regarded by the BBC as "rather a nuisance," "inclined to turn everything they can induce us to say into ammunition for their attacks on the commercial broadcasters."[153] The NCER's inability to strike a strategic alliance with Reith, the world's foremost opponent of commercial broadcasting, only highlighted the marginality of the U.S. broadcast reform movement.

Fall of the NCER and Collapse of the Broadcast Reform Movement

In January 1931 the NCER convinced Senator Simeon Fess, Republican of Ohio, to introduce legislation requiring the FRC to set aside 15 percent of the channels for educational broadcasters. The very early 1930s were the high-water mark for congressional antipathy to commercial broadcasting; despite the strength of the radio lobby, one reformer estimated that fully 70 percent of the Senate and 80 percent of the House of Representatives favored broadcast reform.[154] The NAB put the figure at closer to 90 percent for both branches of Congress.[155] Unfortunately for the reformers, however, the radio lobby had the universal backing of the relevant committee chairmen, who were able to keep reform legislation from ever getting to the floor for a vote. "If it were not for a little group of reactionary leaders in both branches of Congress," the chief labor radio lobbyist observed, reform "legislation would have been passed."[156]

The reform efforts were not helped by the political incompetence of the NCER, which eschewed working with labor, the ACLU, or even the *Ventura Free Press* radio campaign, which had been established by the Payne Fund specifically to assist it. The *Free Press* publicists and lobbyist were repeatedly exasperated in their attempts to get the NCER to do anything. "The whole educational crowd," one wrote after Tyler failed to mail him a report as he had promised, "is a bunch of theorists with no idea how to run a publicity campaign. Tell them to jump off the North end of a ferry boat going South."[157]

The NCER even took an incomprehensible position regarding its own Fess bill. Morgan informed H. O. Davis, publisher of the *Ventura Free Press,* that the only position he supported was that of the National Congress of Parents and Teachers, which resolved in 1931 for the complete nationalization and decommercialization of broadcasting, although no legislation was ever introduced to that end.[158] "Mr. Joy Elmer Morgan," Davis wrote to Crandall incredulously, "does not even approve the campaign he is conducting."[159] By the summer of 1932 it was clear that reform legislation could not get through Congress for the foreseeable future. In a biting memorandum, Crandall characterized the NCER as "making no effort to understand the entire political situation in Congress." Crandall noted that Morgan "apparently has no capacity to grasp" the political requirements of the NCER, as he was most comfortable "in the field of formal education."[160] In the autumn of 1932 the Payne Fund disbanded the *Ventura Free Press* radio campaign. At the same time it asked S. Howard Evans, the Payne Fund official who conducted the *Free Press* lobbying activities, to prepare a memorandum on whether the Payne Fund should acknowledge defeat, urge the NCER to drop the campaign for broadcast reform, and, like the NACRE, work with the commercial broadcasters.

Evans acknowledged the difficulty of reform but he argued that the "fundamental structure of broadcasting" remained "absolutely unsound" and he convinced the Payne Fund to stay the course.[161] The NCER then found a member of Congress to introduce a resolution calling for a Canadian-style federal study of broadcasting to determine a new system in the public interest. Given the situation on Capitol Hill, however, the NCER never made more than a superficial attempt to lobby on the measure's behalf. In February 1933 Crandall agreed with the NCER that its lobbying should be "abandoned for the time being," while the educators "concentrate all their forces on creating local opinion which would later be reflected in Congress."[162] The NCER pursued several courses of action along these lines, but its efforts were overwhelmed by the strength of the radio lobby and the growing public acceptance of commercial broadcasting. "I doubt if the public can be led to look to educators as administrators of a national system that includes entertainment," Perry confessed to Morgan.[163] Morgan, however, maintained his particular political perspective. "Public support is beginning to come our way," he informed Perry in April 1933. "We can afford to wait our time."[164]

A primary barrier for the NCER was its inability to get press coverage. Most Americans were unaware that it was even within their province, or that of Congress, to determine what type of broadcasting system the United States should have.[165] In a dramatic move to bring the issue before the public, the NCER used its influence to have radio adopted as the official debate topic for U.S. high schools and colleges in the 1933–34 academic year. The question of whether the United States should adopt the British system of broadcasting was debated by some fifteen hundred colleges and six thousand high schools in thirty-three states. Two and a half million Americans would be exposed to the debate.[166] "The debates will arouse an enormous amount of interest in the radio problem and will bring home the nature of this problem to millions of people who have so far given it very little thought," enthused one Payne Fund official.[167] The commercial broadcasters were terrified by the debates. The trade publication *Variety* lamented that "many, perhaps most, of these people have been unaware of the existence of the question."[168] "The Radio Industry was led into these debates through an error in judgment" by an NBC executive, "who innocently enough subscribed to the idea," Aylesworth admitted to Sarnoff.[169] The broadcasters shifted the debate, as much as possible, to a discussion of the limitations of the BBC rather than the nature of U.S. broadcasting. The NAB published a 191-page debate guide that consisted in large part of frontal assaults on the BBC.[170]

Although this industry strategy shifted the focus of the debates away from the United States, it threatened to rip asunder the truce with the BBC. Reith characterized the NAB debate guide as "a perfectly monstrous book," necessitating "that we should take action and issue a counter-blast."[171] When the debate guide was circulated in Britain in January 1934, the affair reached scandalous dimensions in the London press.[172] NBC's London representative informed Aylesworth that the BBC was considering "severing relations" with the U.S. networks.[173] The BBC responded by publishing a 12-page supplement to the *Listener,* a BBC publication, to repudiate the NAB statements regarding the BBC and distributed fifty thousand copies of the supplement in the United States.[174] Aylesworth moved quickly to defuse the situation by minimizing the significance of the debates. "We consider the whole matter of little importance in this country," he informed Reith in one of many letters on the topic. The debates were "just a lot of fun between school children who have a good time debating the subjects for which there are two good sides."[175] The issue finally blew over and the networks returned to the BBC's good graces. Moreover, the debates had little impact upon public opinion. "We were able to comply with the objective without damage," Aylesworth informed Sarnoff.[176]

The NCER's last hope was for President Franklin D. Roosevelt, inaugurated in March 1933, to come out on behalf of broadcast reform. The NCER initially was encouraged, as there were many advocates of broadcast reform in administration positions. One of Roosevelt's closest political friends, ambassador to Mexico Josephus Daniels, wrote to the president numerous times in 1933 and 1934 urging him to nationalize radio broadcasting before the system became entrenched. "There is no more reason why communications should be privately owned than the mails," a typical letter stated.[177] As one NCER member observed, "the program of protecting radio for its best public purpose would fit admirably into his entire program."[178] Nonetheless, the president elected not to take up broadcast reform and thereby engage in a potentially costly uphill battle with the radio industry. Roosevelt also did not want to jeopardize his ability to speak on the networks whenever he pleased, which the networks granted him, and thus bypass the largely Republican newspaper industry.[179] Hence the Roosevelt administration backed the agenda of the commercial broadcasters in toto. Whereas the radio lobby had not wanted Congress to consider radio legislation during 1931–32, when sentiment might have insisted upon reform, by 1933 the industry was committed to having a "thoroughly stabilized" industry. Specifically, the radio lobby wanted legislation to establish the permanent basis for telecommunications regulation, thereby removing fundamental broadcasting issues from congressional consideration thereafter and eliminating the basis for annual "attacks by unfriendly groups" in Washington.[180]

Given the support of the Roosevelt administration and the key congressional leaders, one historian notes that "all signs pointed to a quick passage" in 1934 of the industry's favored Communications Act.[181] Moreover, the NCER and the other reformers had discontinued their lobbying out of frustration. Then, most unexpectedly, the Paulist Fathers religious order of New York City, whose station WLWL had recently lost a bitter hearing before the FRC to a CBS affiliate, entered the fray. John B. Harney, superior general of the Paulists, convinced Senators Robert Wagner, Democrat of New York, and Henry Hatfield, Republican of West Virginia, to introduce an amendment requiring that the new FCC set aside 25 percent of the channels for nonprofit broadcasters. With minimal media coverage, the Paulists launched a whirlwind campaign exploiting their contacts among Roman Catholic organizations and with organized labor. By the end of April *Variety* warned that the Wagner-Hatfield amendment stood "better than a 50-50 chance of being adopted."[182] The NAB proclaimed that it "brings to a head the campaign against the present broadcasting set-up which has been smoldering in Congress for several years."[183] The radio lobby attacked the amendment as if "its passage would have destroyed the whole structure of broadcasting in America," as the NAB's chief lobbyist put it.[184]

Harney spent much of April imploring the NCER to actively support the Wagner-Hatfield amendment. If educators join Catholics and labor, Harney wrote Perry, "it is almost unthinkable" that Congress would not pass the measure. "We must not let this opportunity knock at our door in vain. A better day will hardly come in our lifetime."[185] Harney's efforts were in vain. While Perry and many of the college broadcasters were enthusiastic about the Wagner-Hatfield amendment, Tyler and Morgan, the key operatives in Washington, D.C., were uninterested, as they regarded the question of funding still unresolved in Harney's proposal. Tyler and Morgan offered only "silent sympathy," explaining to Harney that it would be possible to get even better legislation passed at a future session of Congress.[186] The Wagner-Hatfield amendment was defeated in the Senate 42-23 on May 15. A major weapon that defused support for the amendment was the late inclusion of a clause in the Communications Act requiring the new FCC to hold hearings on the Wagner-Hatfield proposal and then report back to Congress early in 1935 with its recommendations. The clause let supporters of the Wagner-Hatfield amendment vote against it in the belief that the experts on the new FCC would subject the topic of nonprofit broadcasting to comprehensive examination. The Communications Act passed on a voice vote later the same day. In June President Roosevelt signed the Communications Act of 1934 into law. "When we read it," the NAB's chief lobbyist later stated, "we found that every point we had asked for was there."[187]

Now only one opportunity remained for the reformers to advance the cause of structural reform: the FCC hearings on whether to reserve 25 percent of the channels for nonprofit organizations as mandated by the Communications Act. Harney and labor refused to participate, regarding the hearings as "a pro forma affair, designed to entrench the commercial interests in their privileged position."[188] Indeed, two of the three FCC members who would conduct the October hearings informed the NAB convention in September that they would refuse to recommend any change in the status quo, regardless of the testimony.[189] Ironically, the NCER agreed to coordinate the pro–fixed percentage side of the hearings, though, as it informed the

FCC, it "had not suggested the enactment of the specific legislation under discussion." As Tyler conceded, the FCC hearings "would be better than no study at all."[190]

Unfortunately for the NCER, the hearings were a disaster. The reform side was poorly organized, presenting numerous contradictory schemes for reorganizing U.S. broadcasting. The commercial broadcasters, on the other hand, devoted considerable resources to establish the industry's unequivocal commitment to broadcast educational and cultural programs. As NBC's chief lobbyist reported to New York headquarters, the broadcasters' case was "done to perfection" and "simply overwhelming."[191] To nobody's surprise, in January 1935 the FCC recommended against the fixed percentage proposal. When Congress reconvened it showed no interest in broadcast reform legislation. The matter was considered settled by the passage of the Communications Act of 1934 and the formation of the FCC, which regarded commercial broadcasting as the legally authorized system unless informed otherwise by Congress. The political battle for the control of U.S. broadcasting, including television as well as radio, as much as it had ever existed, was now concluded. The various elements of the broadcast reform movement unraveled and disappeared in short order.

By the end of the decade, with the demise of organized opposition, the economic and political consolidation of commercial broadcasting was followed by its ideological consolidation. "Our American system of broadcasting," Sarnoff informed an NBC audience in 1938, "is what it is because it operates in American democracy. It is a free system because this is a free country."[192] CBS president William S. Paley received little comment when he informed a meeting of educators in 1937 that "he who attacks the American system [of broadcasting], attacks democracy itself."[193] A few years earlier such a statement would have been met by derision. Now the system was not only off-limits to fundamental attack, it was elevated to the point where such criticism was becoming unthinkable.[194]

In these changing currents the Payne Fund had no interest in devoting resources to quixotic assaults upon an increasingly respectable and politically inviolable industry. In a confidential memorandum to Bolton on the NCER after the FCC hearings, Crandall noted that "the organization and administration of the committee from the beginning has been unsatisfactory."[195] The Payne Fund only decided to continue funding the NCER at a reduced rate after its initial grant expired when Morgan, Tyler, and Perry agreed to resign.[196] The fund also insisted that the revamped NCER accept the status quo and work with the commercial broadcasters. As Bolton put it upon launching the new NCER in January 1936, the NCER should "refrain from controversy or an attack" and its function "should be restricted to educational" work.[197] The NCER's headquarters were moved to New York.

For the balance of the 1930s the NCER concentrated on two tasks. First, under new chairman Arthur G. Crane, the University of Wyoming president, the NCER helped establish the Rocky Mountain Radio Council, a clearinghouse meant to assist nonprofit groups to provide noncommercial educational programming to commercial stations. In many respects this was a regional version of the NACRE with a more grassroots orientation.[198] Crane made it clear that the NCER had no interest whatsoever in creating nonprofit stations in the lucrative AM band, and that the NCER accepted the commercial broadcasters as the legitimate and rightful stewards of U.S. broadcasting, in a manner that could have made even the NACRE blush. "Private enterprise has succeeded in making exceptionally fine broadcasts available to American listeners," a typical NCER pamphlet observed.[199] Second, S. Howard Evans, whom the Payne Fund assigned to replace Tracy Tyler and run the NCER office, attempted to encourage the FCC to aggressively regulate the networks. Unlike Crane, Evans never abandoned his hatred for commercial broadcasting or his belief in the need for radical change, describing himself in 1936 as "advocating Christianity in a world that is decidedly pagan."[200] Evans eventually quit when he became frustrated with the NCER's inability to even have minor influence over policy. Crane did not fare much better with his programs. When the Payne Fund terminated the NCER in 1941, its demise went virtually unnoticed, even in the educational community.

Demise of the NACRE and Consolidation of the Status Quo

Upon leaving the NCER in December 1935, Perry concluded that the NACRE was then "well advanced in its plans to secure quasi-official standing with the United States government and place itself in a position to control, to a considerable extent, the use of the public radio channels for educational purposes."[201] This was a logical assessment in view of the praise that the NACRE and the networks routinely heaped upon each other; with the demise of the NCER and the consolidation of the status quo, the NACRE and its philosophy of cooperation with the industry appeared triumphant. Beneath the surface, however, relations between the NACRE and the networks were always tense and problematic. The NACRE wanted the networks to provide it with valuable evening time slots for noncommercial programs over which the networks had no control. The industry, on the other hand, needed to deflect public criticism of broadcasting as failing to provide adequate public service, particularly in these embryonic years before the industry was sacrosanct in public discourse. "One of the big problems facing us is the criticism we get for our so-called lack of educational programs," one NBC internal memo noted. "We are constantly being compared to the British Broadcasting Corporation."[202] The NACRE's function was to provide the legitimacy of U.S. higher education to network programming.

Tensions mounted as the networks increasingly were able to find sponsors willing to pay money for the time slots allocated to NACRE series. Tyson attempted to form strategic alliances within the networks, especially NBC, with those executives considered more sympathetic to education, though even an NBC executive for educational programming conceded that "those favoring education are in the minority."[203] Tyson's only recourse, in the end, was to emphasize the public relations benefits that the NACRE provided as he hectored network officials to keep the NACRE time slots. During one spat over a prospective cancellation of a NACRE series, Tyson reminded one NBC executive that "this lack of assurance to date" by NBC to the NACRE "has been the chief reason for the opposition and antagonism of educators to the American system of broadcasting."[204] In another similar case, Tyson warned an NBC executive that if the network failed to schedule a proposed NACRE series, "it will be perfectly apparent" to the educators associated with the NACRE "that American radio will always be relegated to the pure commercial, and that all the public service for which the medium itself gave such promise is mere bunk."[205] Despite his threatening tone, Tyson always reassured network executives that he acted with their interests in mind. "I don't want you to think for a moment that I am on the opposition side of the fence," he told one executive during the course of negotiations.[206]

The networks in turn regarded Tyson and the NACRE as nuisances. In their internal correspondence, network executives discussed NACRE programs, which were gobbling up lucrative evening time slots, in a most disparaging manner. After spelling out the attributes of good radio programs, one NBC executive noted that "none of these are found generally in NACRE programs."[207] When the BBC's Reith pressed NBC to explain why the NACRE was not accorded more program hours, Aylesworth confided to him that, unlike BBC educational fare, the NACRE programs were "dull and poorly prepared."[208]

By 1933 relations between the NACRE and NBC were so strained that their arrangement veered toward disintegration. Hutchins threatened to denounce NBC if it carried through with its planned cancellation of a NACRE series. He recanted only after Tyson implored him to remain quiet as any negative publicity might threaten the balance of the NACRE programs.[209] Tyson, for his part, agreed to serve on the ACLU's radio committee, which was formed in 1933 explicitly to determine a new structure for U.S. broadcasting that would better promote free expression. Although Tyson emerged as the most conservative member of the radio committee, this was an incomprehensible gesture to network executives.[210] In 1934, influenced perhaps by his contacts at the ACLU, Tyson asserted that the "profit motive" in broadcasting was "generally inconsistent with the public welfare."[211] NBC regarded this as an act of treason; one executive even called Tyson a "red."[212] Aylesworth finally instructed his executives to lay off Tyson and keep the issue in perspective: "Mr. Tyson is a good fellow and his motives are not to be questioned."[213]

In April 1934 the Carnegie Corporation convened a special summit of NACRE directors and educators to evaluate the NACRE's record and determine a course for the future. Hutchins argued that "educational broadcasting was unsatisfactory because of difficulties that had arisen between educators and broadcasters." Some suggested that perhaps the NACRE should dispense with its formal neutrality and support broadcast reform legislation, such as the Wagner-Hatfield amendment that was then being pushed on Capitol Hill, as the only long-range hope for noncommercial broadcasting. Owen D. Young countered that the system was entrenched and popular with listeners and that he was certain the networks still would devote time to noncommercial evening programs, despite the problems of the NACRE. The meeting resolved to stay with the original NACRE scheme of cooperation with the status quo.[214] Ironically, two months later, immediately after the passage of the Communications Act, both networks confidentially informed the Carnegie Corporation, for the first time, that the NACRE was held in low regard and there was no longer much need for such an organization. NACRE officials, commented one industry observer, seem most interested in "the keeping of their jobs and the salaries that go with them."[215]

The conflict finally became public in 1936 when NACRE released a study of its relationship with NBC between 1932 and 1936 at the first National Conference on Educational Broadcasting. The report, *Four Years of Network Broadcasting,* provided a devastating critique of NBC, concluding that "it is useless at this time to attempt systematic education by national network broadcasting at hours when it will be available to large adult audiences."[216] NBC used its influence to see that the report not be published in the conference proceedings, as had been the original plan.[217] Tyson then arranged for the report to be published by the University of Chicago Press in 1937. One NBC executive termed this "Tyson's last dying kick."[218] Tyson resigned his NACRE post shortly thereafter. "I have only one regret," he wrote to NBC on his last day at the NACRE. "It is that I was so dense that I didn't recognize six or seven years ago the futility of trying to mix oil and water."[219] The NCER's Evans argued that since the NACRE report "repudiated" the evidence at the 1934 FCC hearings, the FCC might wish to reconsider whether systemic reform was necessary.[220] By this time, however, any possibility for structural reform had long since passed. The NACRE was terminated when its grants expired at the end of 1937. Although the NACRE failed as miserably as the NCER at accomplishing its goal, it did leave a legacy of doing yeoman's service for the commercial broadcasters when the industry needed such an agency for public relations purposes.

The late 1930s were far from halcyon days for the proponents of educational and public service broadcasting in the United States. By 1936, only thirty educational stations remained, and most of these were in dire financial straits that seemingly were irreversible. Moreover, with the consolidation of the status quo, educators had almost no leverage to exact concessions from either the networks or the FCC.[221] The only recourse left to educators and proponents of public service broadcasting was to accept channels on experimental bands yet to be developed for commercial purposes. This was not a novel strategy. In early 1934, for example, just before Congress was to consider permanent broadcasting legislation, the FRC attempted to convince educators to accept slots on a newly established section of the AM band between 1500 and 1600 kilocycles, a band that few radio receivers could pick up. The NCER rejected the proposal emphatically. "The administration felt the need of shutting up every discordant element in broadcasting," Armstrong Perry explained at the time, "and is just trying to find the easy way out."[222] As Perry put it, the FRC "would let the educational stations do the experimental work," just like the college stations that had largely pioneered radio broadcasting in the early 1920s, "and then perhaps would take away the channels and allocate them for commercial use."[223]

With the consolidation of the status quo, educators were in no position to bargain. In the early 1940s, they rejoiced when the FCC granted them the exclusive right to develop the new FM band.[224] This was characterized as "educational radio's second chance," and educators were cautioned not to fumble this opportunity as they had with AM broadcasting in the 1920s.[225] This and all subsequent campaigns to reserve space for nonprofit broadcasting in the United States, however, provided pale comparisons to the lofty ambitions of the early 1930s reformers. To paraphrase Marx, if the experiences of the NCER, and even the NACRE, were tragic, the later campaigns appear mostly as farce. They could be successful or secure only to the extent that they did not interfere with the profitability, existing or potential, of commercial broadcasters; that is, to the extent that they were ineffectual.[226]

Moreover, the ante for admission for those that wished to remain active in pursuing educational and public service broadcasting in the United States was to accept the premise, as a one-time advocate of a BBC-style system put it in 1946, that commercial broadcasting "is basically sound."[227] Even those like Robert Hutchins, who could barely conceal his contempt for commercial broadcasting, accepted the capitalist basis of the industry as irreversible, adopted an elitist stance, and worked only to reserve a niche for intellectuals and dissidents on the margins.[228] The industry solidified its standing with educators by launching an aggressive program of funding academic research on broadcast communications in the late 1930s.[229] The major foundations, too, devoted their largesse to broadcasting in earnest only after the consolidation of the status quo; beginning with the Rockefeller Foundation and later with the Ford Foundation and

Carnegie Corporation, these philanthropies consciously worked with the industry, even when proposing nonprofit channel allocations.[230] All the movements for nonprofit television in the 1950s and 1960s were decidedly establishment operations; nary a word evoking the populist legacy of the NCER is anywhere to be found in their records.[231] Since these are the people and institutions responsible for most of what passes as U.S. public service broadcasting history, it is no surprise that the NCER and the NACRE play such an inconsequential role, and are often dealt with inaccurately, in the dominant histories heretofore.

Conclusion

Contemporary mainstream policy making as well as U.S. broadcasting histories, mainstream and critical, tend to regard the U.S. system as naturally dominated by profit-motivated corporations and supported by advertising. In this dominant perspective, proponents of educational and public service broadcasting were logically shunted to the margins at the outset. This can only be regarded as a half-truth at best, one that has the effect of removing the private, commercial control of media from the range of legitimate political debate. In truth, the U.S. system emerged nearly a decade after broadcasting developed in the United States, and its development was hardly the result of any sort of public referendum. A strident and principled opposition to commercial broadcasting emerged concurrent with the system itself. Based on deep-seated U.S. political traditions, these reformers argued that a commercial broadcasting system was inimical to the communication requirements of a democratic society. Although the NCER failed, to no small extent because it was never able to generate a broad-based public discussion of the issues involved, it left an important legacy of antimarket media criticism for future generations. And because the NACRE failed, the importance of structural concerns for genuinely establishing public service broadcasting is made that much more clear.

Finally, much as the NCER feared, the same forces that today advocate the thoroughgoing deregulation of broadcasting and electronic media and the elimination or neutering of public broadcasting are leading the campaign to extend market criteria and commercial principles to the education system. Although public service principles are far more deeply ingrained for U.S. education than they are for U.S. broadcasting, the democratic ideals of free, universal, public education are nonetheless under severe attack.[232] Increasingly, the debate and arguments surrounding media and education are becoming intertwined, with the stakes going directly to the future vitality of our polity and culture. If nothing else, those concerned primarily with educational policy should take one lesson from the experience of the educational broadcasters in the early 1930s: The notion that the market is innately American or democratic is exaggerated if not downright inaccurate. Until that point is made clear, the campaign to preserve and promote public service principles in education, like broadcasting and media, will be on the defensive in the United States.

CHAPTER 5

PUBLIC BROADCASTING: PAST, PRESENT, ... AND FUTURE?

One of the most striking developments of the past decade has been the decline of public service broadcasting systems everywhere in the world.[1] By *public service broadcasting,* I mean a system that is nonprofit and noncommercial, supported by public funds, ultimately accountable in some legally defined way to the citizenry, and aimed at providing a service to the entire population — one which does not apply commercial principles as the primary means to determine its programming. Within these broad parameters, public service broadcasting may be democratic or bureaucratic, benevolent or banal. Where on the spectrum any particular public broadcasting system might fall depends largely upon two things: the level of democracy in the larger society and the degree to which the system is the product of informed public debate. But today, all forms of public broadcasting — and the democratic promise that is always implicit in public broadcasting systems — are in rapid retreat. In my view, their very survival hangs in the balance.

According to mainstream policy debates in the United States, and, increasingly, elsewhere, the collapse of public service broadcasting makes perfect sense, as it really no longer has justification to exist. The main historic rationales for public broadcasting, this reasoning goes, were twofold: first, it maintained public control over scarce broadcast spectrum (the notion here is that it is better to have a public monopoly than a private monopoly over radio and television); second, public broadcasting would provide those programs that were socially beneficial but that the few commercial broadcasters would find insufficiently profitable to produce. The argument continues that with the rise of the cable, satellite, and digital broadcasting technologies that have dramatically increased the number of channels, not to mention the Internet, the notion of scarce broadcast spectrum no longer holds water. Moreover, when people can access hundreds of channels on their televisions and radios — and millions on their computers — the idea that the state need subsidize certain forms of broadcasting appears downright ludicrous. In this age of plenty, if any meaningful sector of the population wants a service, there is plenty of space in the market to provide that service. There is no justification for the "nanny state" telling people what they should be watching or listening to, or using taxpayers' money to subsidize programming that has no apparent audience.

In my view, the mainstream discourse on public broadcasting is historically inaccurate. Although there is an element of truth in the "scarcity" rationale, the rise of public broadcasting systems across the world also reflected, on more than one occasion, protracted political fights over how best to organize media in a democratic society. In this context, I believe, the rationale for public broadcasting not only remains but one can argue that it has grown. Indeed, the collapse of public broadcasting in the 1990s has less to do with technological change than it does with the worldwide neoliberal adoption of the market and its commercial values as the superior regulator of the media — and of all else. In this sense, the attack on public service broadcasting is part and parcel of the current attack on all noncommercial public service institutions and values.

In this chapter I address the rise and decline of public broadcasting, and ask under what circumstances public broadcasting has a future. To assess the validity of the scarcity rationale as the explanation for the rise of public broadcasting, I examine the original movements for public service broadcasting, especially in the United States and Canada. I believe that these experiences contradict the prevailing mainstream consensus on the origins of public broadcasting. In my discussion, the work and legacy of Graham Spry, the person who led the campaign for public broadcasting in Canada, looms large. To the extent that public broadcasting has a distinguished past and exists at all in the present, it is indebted to people like Spry who struggled and organized to bring it into being. In the second section of the chapter I outline the numerous challenges and threats to public broadcasting, leading to the current neoliberal assault. I argue that whatever "space" may have existed for public broadcasting in the past is under sustained attack as commercial values now dominate the media and political culture. I address how the established public broadcasters in Britain and the United States are attempting to cope with this hostile environment and what their prospects are for survival if they continue on their present courses. In my view, public broadcasting can only survive as a viable institution if a movement on its behalf is part of a broader democratic movement to lessen the corporate and commercial domination of society writ large.

The Historical Struggle for Public Service Broadcasting

When radio broadcasting emerged in the years immediately following World War I, it presented a distinct problem for the nations of the world. How was this revolutionary technology to be employed? Who would control radio broadcasting? Who would subsidize it? What was its fundamental purpose to be? The problem of broadcasting was especially pressing in North America and Western Europe, where the overwhelming majority of radio receivers were to be found until the 1940s and later. It was clear that national governments would play the central role in determining the manner in which broadcasting would be developed, if only because the radio spectrum was a limited resource which defied private appropriation. Beyond that, however, the matter was far from settled. In all the relevant countries, different interests made claims upon the new technology. They ranged from educators, labor, religious groups, political parties, amateur radio enthusiasts, listeners' groups, and journalists to radio manufacturers, telephone and telegraph companies, naval and military interests, advertisers, electric utilities, and the commercial entertainment industry. Each group claimed, in various ways and to varying degrees, to be the rightful steward of the nation's radio broadcasting service.

Accordingly, the outcome was different in every nation. Most strikingly, the United States and Great Britain — two nations which had so much in common culturally, economically, and politically — developed systems of broadcasting that were, in principle, diametrically opposed.[2] The British established the British Broadcasting Corporation in the 1920s to serve as a nonprofit and noncommercial broadcasting monopoly. Under John Reith, the BBC established the principles of what would become the paragon of public service broadcasting, although many other nations like Weimar Germany and the Netherlands created successful and quite different versions of public service broadcasting.[3] The United States, on the other hand, adopted a system dominated by two networks, NBC and CBS, which were supported exclusively by commercial advertising. The hallmark of this system was its emphasis upon maximizing profit by any means necessary, which meant popular entertainment programming, usually provided by advertising agencies. These two systems, the British and the American, thereafter became the archetypes employed in virtually all discussions of broadcasting policy in democratic nations.

It was also during the 1920s and 1930s that vibrant political debates took place in various nations over how best to deploy broadcasting. The decisions made then would effectively direct the course of radio and television into the 1980s and 1990s. In Britain, for example, advertisers worked diligently in the early 1930s to have the BBC accept advertising. They were unable to generate even minimal public enthusiasm for commercial broadcasting.[4] With the approval of the Ullswater Committee Report in 1936, the primacy of nonprofit and noncommercial broadcasting was established as non-negotiable for a generation. In the United States, the struggle over broadcasting was far more dramatic. By the time commercial broadcasting became established in the late 1920s, there arose a feisty movement to eliminate or markedly reduce for-profit, advertising-supported broadcasting and replace it with a nonprofit system operated on public service principles.[5] With the passage of the Communications Act of 1934 and the creation of the Federal Communications Commission, this U.S. broadcast reform movement disintegrated, and the profit-motivated basis of U.S. broadcasting was politically inviolate forever after.

If the 1920s and 1930s, specifically the years from 1926 to 1935, form a critical juncture in the formation of national broadcasting systems, it was a critical juncture with a distinct international edge quite unlike anything that had preceded it. Broadcasting was an international phenomenon that respected no political boundaries. Messages from one national broadcasting system often were audible in all surrounding nations. Broadcasting required international regulation to prevent neighboring nations from utilizing the same wavelengths and thereby jamming each others' signals.[6] Finally, shortwave broadcasting, which emerged full force in the 1930s, was suitable only for international broadcasting; technologically it was ill-suited for domestic purposes except in enormous nations such as the Soviet Union. In short, the national debates over broadcasting occurred in an international context. It is not surprising, therefore, that U.S. commercial interests worked with their British counterparts in their efforts to commercialize the British airwaves. Similarly, advocates of public broadcasting worked as closely as possible with the BBC in their efforts to promote noncommercial broadcasting in the United States. During this formative period, the protagonists in the struggles for national systems of broadcasting recognized that it was being fought on a global playing field.

Nowhere was the international dimension of broadcast policy making more apparent than in Canada. On the one hand, Canada had close political and cultural ties with both Britain and the BBC, where Gladstone Murray, a Canadian, emerged as a top executive. On the other hand, the preponderance of the Canadian population could pick up U.S. broadcasting stations on their radio receivers. This was the overwhelming fact of broadcasting as it emerged in Canada in the 1920s and 1930s, and the basis for Canada's profound political struggle to define a national broadcasting policy during these years. Not only did the United States play a critical role in the formation of Canadian policy, however; in this period Canada also played an important role in the fight for control of U.S. broadcasting.

Radio broadcasting emerged in Canada in the 1920s much as it did in the United States.[7] For most of the 1920s, nobody had a clue how to make any money at it. Broadcasting was taken up by various private groups, but it was not an engine of profit-making. In the United States at mid-decade, almost one-third of the stations were run by nonprofit groups, and those stations operated by for-profit groups were intended to shed favorable publicity on the owner's primary enterprise, not generate profit. Indeed, the hallmark of both Canadian and U.S. broadcasting was its chaotic nature, which prevented long-term planning. (It was this chaos that influenced the British to formally adopt the BBC in the early 1920s, long before other nations had formalized their broadcast systems.)[8] By 1928, however, U.S. capitalists began to sense the extraordinary commercial potential of broadcasting. With the support of the newly established Federal Radio Commission, the U.S. airwaves were effectively turned over to NBC and CBS and their advertisers.[9] This transformation was staggering—

both in scope and in the speed with which it took place. As Erik Barnouw has noted, between 1928 and 1933 U.S. commercial broadcasting sprang from nonexistence to full maturity.[10] But this stunning event did not pass unnoticed. As mentioned above, and discussed in chapter 4, the emergence of commercial broadcasting in the United States was met by a vociferous opposition that argued that commercial broadcasting was inimical to the communication requirements of a democratic society.

By the late 1920s the Canadian public wanted to see broadcasting put on a more stable basis, in order to assure that broadcasts could be received over expensive receiving sets.[11] The sudden rise of U.S. commercial broadcasting forced Canada's hand, as that country either had to determine a distinct policy or see its radio broadcasting collapse into the orbit of NBC and CBS, both of which had already established affiliations with powerful stations in Montreal and Toronto.[12] In December 1928 the Canadian government appointed a royal commission to make a thorough study of broadcasting and report to the House of Commons on the best system for Canada to adopt. The Aird Commission, named after its chairperson, held extensive public hearings across Canada. In addition, the commissioners spent four months in 1929 traveling in the United States, Britain, and other countries to examine other broadcasting systems. In New York, NBC executives candidly expressed their plans to incorporate Canada into their network.[13] But the Aird Commission was most impressed by the nonprofit and noncommercial systems in Europe, and eventually it recommended that Canada adopt a cross between the BBC and the German public service system, which (unlike the British) gave the provinces greater control over broadcasting. Commercial advertising would be severely restricted, perhaps even eliminated; the broadcasting service would be supported by license fees, as in Britain.[14] The nationalist sentiment was unmistakable; as one Canadian newspaper put it, "The question to be decided by Canada is largely whether the Canadian people are to have Canadian independence in radio broadcasting or to become dependent upon sources in the United States."[15] The BBC and the British press were delighted with the Aird Commission's report, regarding it as "a compliment to our B.B.C. system."[16]

The Aird Commission's report did not settle matters for Canada, for its recommendations did not have the force of law. First, the Supreme Court of Canada had to rule that the national government and not the provincial governments had the right to regulate broadcasting.[17] Second, the Supreme Court decision had to be upheld by the British Privy Council in London.[18] Once this was accomplished, in February 1932, the Canadian House of Commons could then act upon the Aird Commission's recommendations. In the intervening three years, however, conditions had changed dramatically in Canada. The extraordinary growth of commercial broadcasting in the United States had made a profound impression upon Canadian advertisers and important elements of the business community. In particular, the Canadian Pacific Railroad developed a plan to provide for a private, national, advertising-supported broadcasting service for Canada, to be supervised by the railroad. It began a campaign to coordinate the efforts of Canada's private broadcasters and advertisers to gain public support for the measure. Those elements supporting commercial broadcasting in Canada were allied with the U.S. commercial broadcasters and their Canadian subsidiaries. To some, it seemed that the momentum of the Aird Commission report, with its call for nonprofit, noncommercial broadcasting, had been lost amidst all the judicial haggling. Fears mounted that Canada might emulate the United States and adopt full-blown commercial broadcasting.[19]

It was in this context that the Canadian Radio League was founded in 1930 by Graham Spry and Alan Plaunt, two young Canadians determined that Canada should adopt the system recommended in the Aird report. The purpose of the Radio League was to mobilize support for public service broadcasting and to counter the campaign to bring commercial broadcasting to Canada.[20] The Canadian Radio League emphasized how commercialism would undermine the democratic potential of broadcasting for Canada. "Democracy is by definition that system of Government responsible and controlled by public opinion. Radio broadcasting is palpably the most potent and significant agent for the formation of public opinion," Spry argued. "It is no more a business than the public school system."[21] Spry detested the effect of advertising upon radio broadcasting. "To trust this weapon to advertising agents and interested corporations seems the uttermost folly."[22] With these sentiments, Spry and the Canadian Radio League were in accord with the U.S. broadcast reform movement.

Most importantly, Spry and the Radio League emphasized the threat to Canadian culture and political autonomy posed by a commercial broadcasting system. Spry argued that such a system was suitable only for those Canadians "who believe than Canada has no spirit of her own, no character and soul to express and cultivate."[23] The Radio League declared that U.S. commercial interests were working surreptitiously to undermine the consensus for public service broadcasting in Canada, and that the U.S. broadcasters were spreading lies and misinformation about both the Radio League and the BBC. "I have really come to feel," Spry wrote one Canadian editor, "that this is a struggle to control our own public opinion, and to keep it free from an American radio monopoly behind which stands General Electric, J. P. Morgan . . . Westinghouse, the motion picture and theatrical group, etc., in a word 'Capitaleesm' with a vengeance."[24] In all of its communications, the Radio League emphasized what it regarded as the asinine character of U.S. commercial broadcasting. "At present, the advertisers pay the piper and call the tune," Spry declared. "And what a tune. The tune of North America is that of the peddler boosting his wares."[25]

The Canadian Radio League was able to use this fear of U.S. commercial domination as a trump card in Canadian deliberations over broadcasting. "The fact that the Radio Corporation of America and its associates are primarily American in their outlook colours our feelings," Spry wrote to one U.S. reformer. "We fear the monopoly not only as a monopoly, but as a foreign monopoly."[26] Elements of the Canadian business community that might have opposed government broadcasting shared this concern that the United States might dominate a private Canadian system. There was the very real concern that well-heeled U.S. advertisers could afford to purchase extensive radio advertising in Canada over a commercial system, and thus gain a competitive advantage over their smaller Canadian rivals. There was also the concern that if Canada permitted commercialism to continue, capitalists might use the few Canadian frequencies to broadcast commercial programming into the heavily populated U.S. market, thereby turning their backs on Canada.[27] Still, the evidence suggests that Spry's enthusiasm for public service broadcasting was as much or more the consequence of his democratic socialism than it was the result of his Canadian nationalism. His primary concern, arguably, was that a commercial broadcasting system disenfranchised the public and empowered big business, regardless of nationality.

In this light, it did not take very long for Spry and the Canadian Radio League to establish close relations with broadcast reformers in the United States. There, the leading reformers were journalists and civil libertarians or were associated with various educational, labor, and religious groups. In fact, the reformers were a cross-section of U.S. society much like the people who made up the Canadian Radio League, though without the Radio League's business support. The U.S. reformers also lacked the Canadian Radio League's political savvy, and they could never agree upon one specific reform proposal and then coordinate their efforts to work for its passage. While the U.S. reformers never had great success generating mass support for reform, they played upon the intense dislike of American listeners for radio advertising in the early 1930s. The task for the reform movement was to convert this antipathy for radio advertising into support for reform.[28] Early in 1931 the Canadian Radio League began a continual stream of communication with their American counterparts. As Spry wrote to one U.S. reformer, "Your approach to the question of the control of radio broadcasting is precisely my own."[29]

In the summer of 1931 Spry made an extended trip to the United States to meet with U.S. reformers.[30] He was especially interested in getting information on the U.S. broadcasting industry's activities in Canada. In Columbus, Ohio, he spoke about the Canadian situation to an enthusiastic audience at the annual convention of the Institute for Education by Radio.[31] "Whatever the objective of commercial broadcasters in our country may be with reference to Canada," one U.S. activist informed Spry afterward, "I can assure you that the educators have no desire to interfere in any way with Canadian affairs. On the contrary, they are ready to cooperate in every possible way."[32] For the next two years Spry and leading U.S. reformers stayed in constant contact. As Spry wrote one American, "If Canada establishes a non-advertising system . . . your whole position in the United States will be enormously strengthened."[33] Spry repeatedly emphasized the existence of the U.S. broadcast reform movement as discrediting the notion that commercial broadcasting was popularly embraced by listeners. "Opposition to this commercial force in the United States is equally strong," he told the House of Commons.[34] And in a pamphlet he wrote: "The cry for change is coming in the United States. In Canada, it has decisively arrived."[35]

The marriage of the Canadian Radio League and the U.S. broadcast reformers was abetted by their mutual hatred for the U.S. commercial broadcasting industry. Spry was convinced that NBC and CBS were working behind the scenes with the Canadian Pacific Railway to get a private system authorized by parliament. Spry believed there was tremendous incentive for the U.S. broadcasters to support a private system; once it was in place NBC and CBS would affiliate with private broadcasters in all the other major Canadian markets besides Toronto and Montreal.[36] While he was in Washington in 1931, Spry encountered NBC president Merlin Aylesworth, for whom he had considerable distaste. Before becoming president of the network, as director of the National Electric Light Association, Aylesworth had led the fight for privately owned utilities and had intervened in a particularly bitter fight in Ontario. Spry observed dryly, "Mr. Aylesworth has always been interested in Canada — too much so from a Canadian point of view."[37] At any rate, Spry recognized that Aylesworth was a tough customer who left no doubt that U.S. commercial broadcasters wanted access to the Canadian airwaves.

That belief notwithstanding, the actual evidence of U.S. commercial broadcasters' involvement in the Canadian radio debates is thin and patchy. Spry was quick to concede that the Americans used "quiet methods," and that much of their work was to dispatch eloquent speakers to Toronto and Montreal "to praise the American system and damn the British."[38] (I can vouch for this. Having used the commercial broadcasters' records for this period extensively, this lack of a smoking gun comes as no surprise to me. Sensitive topics like these do not tend to make it into the corporate archives.)[39] But circumstantial evidence does suggest considerable involvement by U.S. commercial interests. For example, the leader of the fight for commercial broadcasting in Canada, R. W. Ashcroft, was an advertising professional who had served as NBC's representative in Canada.[40] The NBC and CBS affiliates in Toronto and Montreal sometimes carried programming highly critical of the BBC and all forms of broadcasting other than commercial.[41] By then, the threat posed by the U.S. reformers, whether real or perceived, had become an obsession among the U.S. commercial broadcasters, and they were determined to win at any cost. Hence the broadcast reformers, American and Canadian, were of no mind to grant the U.S. commercial broadcasters the benefit of the doubt. As the *New Republic* editorialized at the time: "It is bad enough that we should permit a medium which clearly should have been devoted to the finest human arts to be degraded for the distribution of soap and toothpaste. It is far worse that our radio capitalists should exert pressure, thru the air, upon the opinion of a neighboring country, in an attempt to enforce our own dull, merchandizing spirit upon it."[42]

If the U.S. commercial system served as one reference point for the Canadian debates, the BBC served as the other. By the early 1930s the BBC was widely admired the world over, in a way that had eluded NBC and CBS. The BBC was held up by the Canadian Radio League as the ideal to which Canadian broadcasting should aspire. When Canadian prime minister R. B. Bennett went to London in 1930, Spry used all his contacts to ensure that Bennett visited the BBC headquarters; he was convinced that if the conservative Bennett saw the BBC operation, he would forever oppose the move to commercial broadcasting in Canada.[43] (Although it is unclear whether Bennett's London trip turned the tide, he did indeed support the nationalization of Canadian broadcasting.) There was also an element of imperial rivalry between Britain and the United States with regard to the path of Canadian broadcasting. The explicit goal of the dominant U.S. communication firms since World War I had been to reduce, if not actually eliminate, the presence of the British in the western hemisphere. In this contest, the Canadian sympathies tended toward the British, a fact which the Radio League played upon.[44]

At any rate, in order for the proponents of commercial broadcasting in Canada to succeed, they needed to deflate the exalted image of the BBC. This they did, with relish. As Canadian reformer Brooke Claxton wrote to Gladstone Murray of the BBC, "The private companies get out the wildest kind of propaganda about the B.B.C."[45] The attack on the BBC reached its height in 1931 when John Gibbon, the publicity director of the Canadian Pacific Railway, the group leading the fight for a commercial system, published a scathing critique of the BBC in the *Canadian Forum*.[46] Gibbon wrote that the weak performance of the BBC, combined with the popularity of U.S. commercial programs, made it absurd for Canada to proceed with the recommendations of the Aird Commission. Instead, he argued, only an advertising-supported system would give Canadians the type of programming they wanted.

The Canadian Radio League immediately sent a copy of Gibbon's article to the BBC, which was so irate it threatened to take the matter to the British House of Commons. Eventually, the Canadian Pacific Railway apologized to the BBC for the factual errors contained in the article, and Gibbon was severely reprimanded by his employer.[47] In addition, the *Canadian Forum* permitted Spry to write a response to Gibbon, in which he decisively countered the attacks on both the

Radio League and the BBC.[48] In sum, this attempt to soil the BBC and the notion of public service broadcasting backfired.

In the spring of 1932 the Canadian House of Commons held extensive and widely publicized hearings on the recommendations of the Aird Commission. The U.S. broadcasting trade publication *Broadcasting* anticipated vindication for commercialism: "Most of Canada's citizens are accustomed to broadcasting by the American Plan and many will accept no substitute."[49] But Sir John Aird testified to the contrary: "The broadcasting medium in Canada should be protected from being reduced to the level of commercial exploitation as it had been reduced in a neighboring country."[50] Graham Spry coordinated the testimony of those endorsing the Aird report. "The choice before the committee is clear," he testified. "It is a choice between commercial interests and the people's interest. It is a choice between the state and the United States."[51] Spry also emphasized that unless Canada established a national public broadcasting system, it would be unable to claim its fair percentage of the world's radio frequencies at a forthcoming international radio conference to be held in Madrid.[52]

The United States loomed large in these parliamentary debates. The House of Commons requested that NBC president Merlin Aylesworth testify in Ottawa regarding NBC's plans for Canada. Aylesworth declined. Privately, he wrote RCA president David Sarnoff, saying that to testify would be a "great mistake" on his part: "it would draw the fire up there and down here."[53] U.S. reformers showed no such hesitation. U.S. radio inventor Lee De Forest submitted a statement on broadcasting to the Canadian House of Commons. De Forest's hatred of radio advertising was so intense he spent a year in the early 1930s attempting to invent a device that would automatically mute radio advertisements and then return the volume to audible levels when the programming returned.[54] (One can only speculate on the course of U.S. and global broadcasting had De Forest been successful in these experiments.) After lambasting U.S. radio for its "moronic fare," De Forest called upon "you in Canada to lead radio in North America out of the morass in which it has pitiably sunk."[55]

Most damning was the testimony of U.S. educator Joy Elmer Morgan, the only American to travel to Ottawa to testify in person. Morgan emphasized that commercial broadcasting had relegated public affairs and education to the margins and that the existence of the U.S. broadcast reform movement was "inescapable evidence of dissatisfaction" with the status quo. Morgan emphasized the importance of the Canadian hearings: "The important thing is not that a few people shall make money out of radio broadcasting, but rather that this new tool shall be used to beautify and to enrich human life. Now is the time to take a long look ahead to avoid mistakes which it would take decades or even centuries to correct."[56]

Not surprisingly, Graham Spry was ecstatic about the effect of Morgan's testimony, as discussed in chapter 4. "Until your appearance," he wrote Morgan, "the committee had regarded the American situation as largely satisfactory and . . . that educational broadcasts were eminently possible through commercial stations. . . . Your evidence gave an entirely new complexion to the situation and we are entirely grateful to you for your assistance."[57] The recommendations of the Aird Commission carried the day. Upon completion of the hearings, the Canadian parliament approved the complete nationalization of broadcasting with the elimination of direct advertising.[58]

The formal approval of nationalization elated the U.S. reformers. On one hand, those Americans living near the Canadian border — a not inconsiderable number — would now be able to hear quality noncommercial programming. Spry emphasized this point in his own testimony to the House of Commons: "A Canadian non-commercial chain . . . would seriously weaken the whole advertising basis of American broadcasting. If, for example, the Canadian chain offered two hours of the best possible jazz programs over high-powered Canadian stations, which, at night, would invariably cover a large area of the United States, would not every listener, Canadian and American, tune in on Canadian non-advertising programs, in preference to eight 15 minute American advertising programs, in which there would be 16 advertising speeches occupying from 7 to 25 per cent of the time? Would not Canadians, would not Americans, prefer programs without advertising to programs advertising corn cures, cigarettes, beauty aids, mouth washes? The answer is self evident."[59] Defenders of U.S. commercial broadcasting envisioned this same scenario, though they viewed it with alarm, not elation. "The existence and development of this Government owned system will be a challenge to American radio station owners," one U.S. senator who favored commercialism stated. "They must prove themselves more satisfactory to the people than the Canadian system, or the Government system will inevitably be established in the United States."[60]

In addition, the Canadian Radio League was seen by U.S. reformers as providing the model for how the reform effort should be organized in the United States.[61] Morgan wrote to the Canadian Radio League, "We in the United States who are working for radio reform have been greatly encouraged by your success."[62] The inability of the U.S. reformers to coalesce had been a major weakness for the Americans, especially when confronted by a powerful adversary like the commercial broadcasting lobby, which had immense power on Capitol Hill. Unfortunately, however, the Canadian model never became more than that for the U.S. reformers.

The nationalization of Canadian radio also led in the fall of 1932 to a major tactical reversal for the U.S. reform movement. Rather than lobby for specific measures — for example, reserving 15 or 25 percent of the frequencies for nonprofit broadcasting — the U.S. reformers began to lobby for Congress to authorize a full-blown investigation of broadcasting, much like the Aird Commission, which would then recommend a wholly new manner of organizing U.S. broadcasting.[63] The reformers considered it axiomatic that any neutral audit of broadcasting, conducted by people with no material link to commercial broadcasting, could only recommend nonprofit broadcasting, as in Canada. However, they never had a chance to see this belief tested. The commercial broadcasting lobby flexed its muscles to undercut the momentum for reform on Capitol Hill and all but eliminate congressional hearings on broadcast legislation. With the passage of the Communications Act of 1934, broadcast structure was no longer a legitimate political issue, and the commercial basis of the industry became politically sacrosanct.[64]

The activities of the Canadian and U.S. broadcast reformers of the early 1930s are of interest not only because of their clear historical importance in understanding the development of each nation's broadcasting system. In the work and writings of Spry, Morgan, John Dewey, and many others from the era like Charles Siepmann and James Rorty, we have the contours of a sophisticated critique of commercial broadcasting, a critique which in certain respects is every bit as valid today as it was then. It is a *political* critique which places the fight for public service broadcasting necessarily in the broader context of the fight for a more social democratic, even democratic socialist, society. These activists also recognized, from the very beginning, that theirs was a political struggle with clear global dimensions. The work of this first generation of public broadcasting activists is a continual reminder that control over broadcasting (and communication) must always be the duty of the citizenry in a democratic society; it should never, ever be entrusted to the tender mercies of corporate and commercial interests. To the extent that the aims of these activists were thwarted, or have subsequently been thwarted, it was never the result of an informed public debate of broadcasting issues. To the contrary, it was the result of powerful commercial forces getting their way, often by circumventing or undermining the possibility of such a debate.

The Present Crisis of Public Service Broadcasting

Public service broadcasting has been a cornerstone institution in the majority of developed nations and political democracies in the twentieth century. Nations would take all or most of their scarce spectrum for broadcasting and turn it over to some agency that operated under nonprofit and noncommercial auspices. The guiding principle was that broadcasting was too valuable to be consigned to private control directed by commercial motives. Of course, simply being nonprofit and not supported by advertising did not clarify how public broadcasting would be supported or managed. The crucial issues everywhere were (and are): How would public broadcasting be funded? To whom would the managers of public broadcasting be directly accountable? How could public broadcasting serve the public as citizens and not be under the thumb of politicians and political parties?

In general, the more democratic a nation, the more enlightened and viable its public broadcasting system. In nations such as the Netherlands, Britain, Germany, and Japan quite different models for how to best conduct public broadcasting evolved. At its best, public broadcasting has provided a considerable portion of the type of media that scholars such as C. Wright Mills and Jürgen Habermas regarded as mandatory for meaningful participatory democracy — that is, precisely the caliber of communication that the commercial media system tends to eschew.

Yet, despite the accomplishments of Graham Spry and countless others in establishing public service broadcasting systems in the formative years of radio (and television as well), public broadcasting has been locked in an almost continuous fight to maintain its social posi-

tion, if not its survival. At times, in view of the strength and popularity of the broadcasting systems and the general strength of social
democratic movements, in some nations public broadcasting appeared virtually unchallengeable as a social institution. But that
strength rested on a social space allocated by delicate political, economic, and technological factors — a space that barely exists today,
anywhere in the world. By the 1990s neoliberal policies have assisted in
the creation of a global commercial media market centered around
television, as described in chapter 2. It is a foreboding world for public broadcasters.

Conventional wisdom, as I explained at the outset of the chapter,
holds that the decline of public broadcasting is the result of new
technologies that offer scads of new channels and thus undermine
the leverage and appeal of the traditional national public broadcasting systems. As one writer put it in 1998, "Scandinavia's license-fee
payers are protesting, why pay for programming which is increasingly found on commercial channels?"[65] And there is an element of
truth to this scenario. Public broadcasters often respond to the rise
of numerous commercial competitors and the decline in public subsidy by turning toward advertising support. Once commercialism
begins, it is very difficult in the long run to justify receiving a public
subsidy. In New Zealand, for example, years of having public television chock full of commercials has weakened whatever resolve there
is toward keeping the system publicly owned. And once the public
subsidy goes, the public broadcaster loses its commitment to provide
a service to the entire population. It may be formally nonprofit but it
is no longer noncommercial. Inexorably, it tends to gravitate toward
the logic and behavior of the commercial media. This process varies
from nation to nation, but it generally ends up in the same place.
Even Germany, with one of the most powerful public broadcasting
systems in the world, is pressing to increase its amount of advertising on public TV.[66]

But this decline in public broadcasting is not due to technology, it
is due to politics. There is nothing intrinsic in these technologies insisting that they be used for commercial purposes; any society could
elect to simply have a multichannel public TV system if it so desired.
In addition, there is nothing that says nonprofit broadcasters cannot
compete in a noncommercial manner. Indeed, competition can have
quite beneficial effects for public broadcasters under the proper circumstances.[67] In a different political environment the new communi-

cation technologies could be employed to provide local, regional, and national nonprofit channels operating by different institutional setups — some state-run, some community-based, some by elected boards, some by the workers. There could be stations commissioned to serve the entire population and others established to serve smaller constituencies. In view of the nature of the technologies, the sky is the limit. This could be the Golden Age of public broadcasting, with the shackles of spectrum scarcity finally removed. So what the decline of public broadcasting actually reflects is the neoliberal political climate, in which the rule of profit is regarded, ipso facto, as the natural, most efficient, and democratic regulatory mechanism, regardless of the evidence.

But, to be accurate, the challenges to public broadcasting are not solely the result of the recent ascension of neoliberalism or the rise of a global commercial broadcasting system, though those are crucial to explaining the present situation. Public broadcasting has certain intrinsic problems or tensions that have existed throughout its history. Any public broadcasting system is by definition an institution that invites controversy. Providing a viable service (however defined) to the entire population is no simple matter, especially in societies marked by ethnic and cultural diversity and with adversarial social movements representing conflicting political and social agendas. How public broadcasting can reflect the informed consent of the citizenry while still exercising a degree of editorial and cultural independence from the state or some other authority is likewise an ongoing problem. Even the BBC, which is often romanticized in the United States, has wrapped its programming in an air of objectivity and neutrality that had some advantages but may well be ultimately counterproductive. As George Orwell wrote, "The more one is aware of political bias, the more one can be independent of it, and the more one claims to be impartial, the more one is biased."[68]

Regrettably, in many nations public broadcasting has never been able to escape the control of the state or dominant political forces. In some nations, public broadcasting has also done much to undermine citizen support, through its bureaucratic arrogance, or its subservience to powerful political and economic interests, or its turn to commercial mechanisms and values as a means of dealing with budget shortfalls. Yet these are all issues that can be debated, discussed, and, under the best of circumstances, resolved in some acceptable, if

not ideal, manner. On their own, these issues should not be sufficient to derail an entire public broadcasting project.

But these are not abstract problems, isolated from the balance of
society. In fact, they assume their full dimension when they are located within public broadcasting's core dilemma: how to coexist with
a capitalist political economy. To some extent this problem is similar
to the tension between participatory democracy and capitalism. Democracy works best with minimal social inequality and when people
regard the common good as important to their own well-being. But
these are two traits the market strongly discourages. As a rule, the
more egalitarian a capitalist society, the more responsive and viable
its public broadcasting system.

But there are distinct limits on how egalitarian and democratic any
capitalist society will allow itself to be. Even the best-intentioned and
best-established public broadcasting systems find navigating the waters of a class society a tricky proposition, especially as the political
system that formally controls them is unduly influenced by a wealthy
ruling class in a capitalist society. Indeed, openly antagonizing the
powers that be often produces swift and severe retribution. Hence,
many public broadcasting systems either become extremely careful
about upsetting those in economic and political power or else keep
criticism within relatively narrow boundaries. Sometimes this de facto
self-censorship becomes so pervasive that the broadcasting system
virtually abandons its commitment to a democratic system. At other
times it actually becomes antidemocratic. Moreover, public broadcasting systems build up bureaucratic "armor" to protect themselves
from interference from the powerful, and from the public at large. At
best, this is public broadcasting as a paternalistic exercise, directed by
well-meaning liberals. It is a system that tends to reveal much of the
arrogance of liberal intellectuals who regard themselves as superior to
both business and the citizenry. And it is a system that is wide open to
justifiable attack. At worst, the public system becomes thoroughly
bureaucratized and loses public support and public confidence,
thereby playing directly into the hands of those who do not oppose
public broadcasting per quo but oppose it per se.

And in capitalist societies there will always be those who oppose
public broadcasting per se. The political right and procapitalist forces
always remain skeptical of any form of noncommercial media, or
nonprofit activity for that matter. Milton Friedman, philosopher-king

of neoliberalism, argues that public broadcasting must be subject to "market discipline."[69] Sometimes they lead movements to crush public broadcasting, as we have recently seen in the United States. Through experience, promarket forces have learned that a commercial media system, especially one highly concentrated in the hands of a small number of corporations and subsidized largely by advertising, implicitly establishes boundaries on the content and nature of commercial media news, public affairs, and entertainment. It almost automatically produces programming that accepts the status quo as essentially proper and benevolent. Even a well-disciplined public broadcasting system always contains the threat of approaching and examining the sorts of antibusiness and antimarket issues that are marginalized, trivialized, or ignored by commercial systems. Whenever the journalism of the public broadcaster veers from the narrow contours of commercial journalism, therefore, the political right pounces upon the issue, with claims of bias. In Australia, for example, the conservatives were so angry at the Australian Broadcasting Corporation (ABC) for purported anticonservative bias that upon being elected to power in 1996 they broke their campaign promises and instituted deep budget cuts against the ABC.[70] This conservative charge of left-wing bias puts public broadcasters in an awkward, almost indefensible, position; if they either concede political bias or explain that it is the corporate journalism, not theirs, that is biased, they open themselves up to withering attack and endless controversy on many fronts. The easiest solution is to attempt to appease the critics. In the United States, the situation has reached its nadir, and public broadcasting faces the worst of both worlds. On the one hand, it has a small budget which requires it to solicit corporate and commercial support to survive, with all the attached strings that that entails. On the other hand, it is still politically censored by the political right in Congress, which uses its control over the subsidy to keep public broadcasting in line ideologically. Indeed, after years of conservative threats to shut it down, public broadcasting has become so tame politically that some studies found it to be more probusiness than the commercial television networks.[71]

Two other points are worth noting concerning the conservative attack on public broadcasting. First, the right crusade against public broadcasting is just one part of a broader campaign against the "liberal" media. Its aim is to reduce or eliminate the professional autonomy of journalism, with its commitment to public service over commercialism, that confers a degree of independence from the views and needs of owners and advertisers. As I discussed in chapter 1, the market has already gone a long way toward accomplishing this end in the United States, if not elsewhere, but the political right continues to encourage the process nonetheless. As Newt Gingrich informed a meeting of the Georgia Chamber of Commerce in 1997, business and advertisers ought to take more direct command of the newsroom.[72] Second, historically not *all* conservatives have opposed public broadcasting on principle. There was once a certain breed of conservative that had some skepticism toward the market, or at least toward unchecked commercialism, that had a generosity of spirit, and that had a strong belief in the importance of tradition, community, and civic values. This caliber of conservative was more prominent outside of the United States, often lending support to public broadcasting. But in the age of "damn the torpedoes, full speed ahead" free market conservatism, such a quaint view of the human condition has been relegated to the margins of the right, and in the United States banished altogether. (I leave aside the issue of the U.S. "Christian" right, an interesting subject that deserves considerable space to accurately describe.) While lip service to traditional values will be given endless play by conservatives today, their one unwavering commitment is to the market, to serving the immediate commercial needs of the wealthiest members and institutions of society, regardless of the social implications.

Even aside from organized attack from the neoliberal political right, capitalism attacks public broadcasting systematically. The spread of the market and the incessant pursuit of profit constantly put pressure on noncommercial and nonprofit institutions and values in a capitalist society. Even if public broadcasting is allotted a large budget and is seemingly immune from direct commercial influence, it is difficult to maintain standards of public service when every other aspect of the media and broader culture is subject to commercial principles. The island of public service eventually will be overwhelmed by the tidal wave of commerce. As Jürgen Habermas put it in a 1998 interview, we should not "harbour any illusions about the condition of a public sphere in which commercialized mass media set the tone."[73] But under capitalism the matter is never presented in such a manner. Public broadcasting systems always face implicit — and sometimes explicit — pressures from corporate media and advertisers who wish to exploit fully the commercial potential in public channels and systems.

This does not mean that commercial broadcasters or corporate media giants always oppose public broadcasting; on the surface, that is not the case at all. Rupert Murdoch tends to be the exception as he loudly proclaims his belief that the era of subsidized broadcasting, for the BBC and everyone else, has long since passed.[74] For the most part, the media giants have learned to exist alongside them amicably enough. Indeed, as the cases of PBS and the BBC indicate below, they often cooperate with them in commercial joint ventures. Moreover, and somewhat ironically, the commercial media firms can be allies of sorts to movements that wish to keep public broadcasting systems noncommercial — meaning free of advertising. The last thing U.S. media firms want is for PBS and NPR to begin to compete openly for their advertisers, especially in view of the public system's affluent, well-educated, upper-middle-class audience — the kind of audience many important advertisers fantasize about. When the French government reduced the amount of advertising permissible on public television in 1998, the result was an anticipated "windfall for TF1," the main French commercial broadcaster.[75] But regardless of these possible alliances, the commercial media giants (and the advertising industry) always demand and work for a broadcasting system where the commercial logic is central and public service remains on the margins, serving those audiences that the commercial interests do not find profitable enough to exploit themselves.

The commercial broadcasting, media, and advertising industries therefore direct a never-ending publicity and political lobbying campaign to promote the merits and genius of a commercial media system and, correspondingly, to deny and denigrate the supposed merits of public service broadcasting. It is well understood that the most powerful cases on behalf of public service broadcasting, from those advanced by Graham Spry and John Dewey to the present, are premised on the limitations and absurdity of a commercial system. To the extent that the two systems both depend upon public support, legislation, and government regulation, and to the extent that the logics of the two systems are in opposition, this conflict is unavoidable. The corporate media, with their great wealth and control of access to the mass of people, are notorious for the leverage they wield over politicians. A key part of this political strength is reflected in the broadcasters' expert use of public relations; indeed, the U.S. broadcast and advertising industries were arguably the first to develop the art of "spin" in its modern form during the 1930s, as a way of smashing their opponents and gaining favorable legislation and regulation.[76]

Hence, the direction is clear across the world: wherever public service principles are dominant, they eventually succumb to pressure to convert the broadcasting system to a largely commercial basis. And this always entails disastrous consequences for the nature of public broadcasting. Neoliberalism reflects a stage of capitalism where business has greater power than ever before, and nonbusiness elements of society are considerably weaker. That is why public service broadcasting is on such fragile grounds in the contemporary era.

In the United States, the marginalization of public broadcasting was settled in the mid-1930s. The defeat of the broadcast reform movement in 1934 led to a Dark Ages for U.S. public broadcasting. Prior to 1934, reformers had sought a system in which the dominant sector was nonprofit and noncommercial. From that point forward, advocates of public broadcasting had to accept that the system was established primarily to benefit commercial broadcasting, and that public stations would have to find a niche on the margins, where they would not threaten the profitability of the commercial interests.

This made public broadcasting in the U.S. fundamentally different from Britain or Canada or nearly any other nation with a comparable political economy. Whereas the BBC and the CBC regarded their mandate as providing a service to the entire nation, U.S. public broadcasters realized that they could only survive politically by not taking listeners or viewers away from the commercial networks. The function of the public or educational broadcasters, then, was to provide that programming that was unprofitable for the commercial broadcasters to produce. At the same time, however, politicians and government officials hostile to public broadcasting have long insisted that public broadcasting remain within the same ideological confines as the commercial system. This encouraged U.S. public broadcasting after 1935 to emphasize elite cultural programming at the expense of generating a large following. In the two or three decades after 1935, it seems fair to say that the vast majority of Americans did not even know that public broadcasting existed. In short, since 1935 public broadcasting in the United States has been in a no-win situation.

Even with all these limitations, however, the commercial broadcasters remained wary of public broadcasting and fought it tooth and nail well into the 1960s. It was not until 1967, after many halting starts, that Congress passed the Public Broadcasting Act, which led to the creation of the Corporation for Public Broadcasting, and soon thereafter to PBS and NPR. The commercial broadcasters finally agreed not to oppose public broadcasting, primarily because they believed the new public system could be responsible for doing the unprofitable cultural and public affairs programming that critics were constantly lambasting them for neglecting. There was a catch, however. The new public system was given a Byzantine organizational structure that made planning quite difficult. More troubling, the initial plan to have the CPB funded by a tax on receivers — similar to the BBC method — was dropped. Thus public broadcasting was deprived of a stable source of income that was vital for planning as well as editorial autonomy. From the outset, it was determined that we would have a public system, but it would be severely handicapped. Moreover, the funding mechanism meant that the public broadcasters were watched carefully to see that they did not go outside the ideological boundaries established in the commercial media. In short, public broadcasting was set up in such a way as to ensure that it was feeble, dependent, and marginal. In the 1990s, this process has reached its logical conclusion, and the proverbial bottom has fallen out of the cup.

In Canada, public service broadcasting was victorious in the early 1930s, so it started on much firmer terrain. But the eventual development of public service broadcasting in Canada did not necessarily provide the alternative to commercial broadcasting for which Graham Spry and the U.S. reformers had hoped. Although a large public network was established, which eventually became the Canadian Broadcasting Corporation, there was insufficient capital to proceed with complete nationalization. Therefore an independent group of private, advertising-supported stations remained in existence. Over time, the power of these stations vis-à-vis the CBC grew enormously.[77] Spry became a sharp critic of the manner in which the CBC developed, characterizing it as a largely undemocratic bureaucracy by 1935.[78] Spry's vision for public service broadcasting was one which provided ample entertainment along with public affairs programming, but did so with a minimum of advertising. He was innately suspicious of permitting the profit motive to play a determining role in broadcast decision-making. In the late 1950s, Spry returned to his concerns with Canadian broadcasting after twenty-five years of work in politics and business. He established the Canadian Broadcasting League to reassert the primacy of public service principles over commercialism — especially U.S. commercialism — in Canadian radio and television.[79] Although somewhat successful, the Canadian Broadcasting League was unable to stem the tide of commercialism in Canada.

This does not mean that the activities of the Canadian Radio League were a failure and that the creation of the CBC was of no lasting value. To the contrary, even by the middle 1930s the U.S. entertainment publication *Variety* acknowledged that the Canadian system was capturing (and creating) a more sophisticated audience.[80] The Canadian system was markedly different from that in the United States. It carried far less advertising and granted far more room for liberal and left-wing political ideas to circulate.[81] Over the long haul, however, commercial interests were able to circumvent the parliamentary intent of 1932 and, over time, they were able to reestablish their primacy in Canadian radio and television.[82]

In Britain, public service broadcasting had a much stronger hold. The BBC enjoyed a complete monopoly from the 1920s until the 1950s. It also enjoyed significant popular support. Even after commercial radio and television were introduced, the system managed to maintain its overriding commitment to public service for decades. This was due to no small extent to a regulatory regime that made it difficult for the commercial broadcasters to become entrenched and that required that they meet high standards for public service. In short, commercial principles were kept on a short leash and were not permitted to set the rules for the entire system. Indeed, the British experience suggests that a mixed system of public and commercial broadcasting can coexist and prosper (and even perhaps be desirable) if there is rigorous regulation to ensure public service values. But this is a difficult balance to strike; in Britain the incessant prodding of commercial interests, combined with the Thatcherite love of the market, helped turn the tide. By the 1990s British media scholar Colin Sparks announced that British broadcasting was a predominantly commercial affair, and that the BBC was taking rather than giving cues.[83]

What happened in Britain, in fact, represents an attack on whatever space has existed for public service broadcasting, even under the best of circumstances. The process is not simply a reflection of the crude neoliberal theology that guides so much policy making, so much economics, communication, and so on. It also reflects the emergence, for the first time, of a global commercial media market dominated by a handful of enormous (and enormously powerful) transnational corporations. And these firms have earmarked global television as the very special fiefdom where they can spin their wares into gold. Public service broadcasting now faces a direct challenge quite unlike anything it has known before. Moreover, the interests of these broadcast and media corporations are aggressively represented by the U.S. government (among others) in international trade and copyright acts. The entire commercialization of media into a single global market appears to be the aim of the WTO, the IMF, and the World Bank, and for very good reasons. It is difficult to imagine a viable integrated global capitalist economy without having a global commercial media (and telecommunications) market.

When one considers the myriad broadcast and media channels now available, it seems plausible to argue that scarcity is no longer a viable rationale for the existence of public service broadcasting. But when one considers the nature, logic, and trajectory of the commercial media system — both in the United States and globally — as discussed in chapters 1 and 2, the need for public broadcasting appears greater than ever before. Consider, for example, the concentrated ownership, the hypercommercialism, and the dreadful state of journalism and children's programming. More than that, consider the fragmentation of the audience. This makes considerable sense for the media giants who can now slice and dice people demographically to maximize their advertising revenues, but is it really sane policy that there be no shared media experiences across our societies? In the United States, for example, African Americans and white Americans increasingly consume an entirely different set of media products.[84] Who but public broadcasters are poised to provide a common ground where people can learn about each other? And who but the public broadcasters are prepared to offer a service to subcommunities that is not filtered by the needs of Wall Street and Madison Avenue?

So where does public service broadcasting fit into the new world order of the global commercial media system? On the surface, nowhere. With the rise of the global commercial system, there has been a corresponding decline in public service broadcasting, which only a decade ago dominated most points in Europe and many points elsewhere. In the early 1990s, the revenues of European commercial broadcasters increased at four times the rate for public broadcasters.[85] In Sweden and Germany, for example, the large public broadcasters have seen their audiences reduced by half in the 1990s — and these are among the strongest public broadcasting systems in the world. Almost everywhere, the traditional subsidies for noncommercial and nonprofit media are being cut. But, at the same time, even in decline, public service systems command large followings and possess substantial political influence. In western Europe, in particular, the combined influence of the public broadcasters has been instrumental in keeping major sport telecasts, for example, from being shifted to pay or pay-per-view television. They act, then, as the advocates for the entire population. As a result, public broadcasting remains quite popular. Even in the United States, surveys show it to be one of the most highly regarded public expenditures. The Republicans abandoned their efforts to "zero out" federal support to public broadcasting in the mid-1990s when they realized that it was a decidedly unpopular move across the political spectrum.[86]

Nevertheless, public broadcasting is on the defensive. Almost nowhere are the systems confident enough to engage in a full-scale battle with commercial media to defend their turf, and defend it on the grounds of public service principles. That is a very risky strategy requiring tremendous popular mobilization to succeed. It would also require the global cooperation of major public broadcasters to offer a powerful combined alternative to the fare provided by the corporate media giants. The preferred route — and the one that offers the best hope for survival in the short and medium term — is to accept the global commercial media system as it is, and attempt to locate a safe and lucrative niche within it.

Let's take a look first at the United States to see how public broadcasters have responded to the challenge of survival. In view of the daunting obstacles they faced, U.S. public broadcasters have done a remarkable job of establishing and maintaining a loyal, albeit small, audience. But the already compromised commitment to "public service" — meaning service to the entire population based on noncommercial determinants — has withered over the years. By the 1990s U.S. public broadcasting stations receive only some 15 percent of their revenues from federal subsidy. The balance comes from listener and viewer donations, foundations, and, increasingly, corporate grants. There is considerable pressure now from public broadcasting officials to permit full-blown advertising, as opposed to what is euphemistically termed "enhanced underwriting," so that the PBS and NPR stations can generate the revenues needed to replace the declining public subsidy.[87] Already, PBS permits corporate sponsorship of prime-time programming in a manner that is almost as explicit as anything on the commercial networks.[88] By 1996 PBS was pitching its prime-time shows to prospective corporate sponsors on Madison Avenue, just like the commercial networks. In 1998 four "flagship" PBS stations established a consortium to "provide advertisers one-stop shopping to place messages nationally in the relatively uncluttered, upscale PBS environment."[89] By 1998 PBS had over 150 corporate sponsors spending some $80 million, and PBS executives earmarked the area as a target for future growth.[90]

Moreover, PBS is engaging in the type of branding and commercial cross-promoting that mirrors the behavior of the corporate media.[91] It has launched a for-profit record label in partnership with Hollywood's Creative Artists Agency.[92] According to *Variety*, the purpose of the record label is "to create a brand name that has instant cachet among baby boomers and the intellectual set."[93] In a striking manner, PBS is capitalizing upon its children's programming to create a commercial merchandising powerhouse. It wants to rake in its share of the billions of dollars to be made selling products linked to PBS kids' show characters.[94] PBS is even establishing its own for-profit toy stores in major markets, à la Disney and Warner Bros.[95] In this spirit, Children's Television Workshop (CTW), the nonprofit group that produces PBS's award-winning *Sesame Street*, has decided to capitalize upon its work with kids by aggressively branding all of its fare for optimal commercial exploitation. As the CTW CEO stated, with no sense of irony: "one of the things that makes this brand unique is its reputation for not exploiting the kids."[96] CTW can emulate the commercial success of PBS's *Arthur*, which by 1998 was incorporated into the promotional campaigns of one of its main corporate underwriters, Nestlé's Juicy Juice beverages. "We recognize we have to live in this world and that what we do takes a lot of money," *Arthur*'s executive producer (and the development director for children's programming at Boston's public TV station, WGBH) stated. "And we have to give our corporate underwriters recognition."[97]

It was a telling sign when in 1998 the CTW and the BBC each established major joint ventures for new television channels with Viacom's Nickelodeon and Discovery Communications (owned in part by AT&T) respectively, rather than work with PBS.[98] Once public broadcasters begin to operate on commercial terms, and notions of public service are forgotten, they may well find the water is deep and they are swimming amongst sharks. If the point is simply to make money, why should CTW and the BBC team up with amateurs? "The trend in public broadcasting is clear and pronounced: more commercials, more commercial values," Bill Moyers said in December 1998. "Also, there is more corporate power and influence over what gets on the air and what doesn't, direct and indirect."[99] Legendary public broadcaster Garrison Keillor stated what many of the visionaries who worked to build a viable U.S public broadcasting service have come to believe, given the nature and direction of the current system: "I don't think there's any reason for public television to exist any more, I honestly don't."[100] That sentiment exists because for the most part public television, in the true sense, no longer exists in the United States.[101]

One could argue that the U.S. public broadcasters had no choice but to go commercial, in view of their precarious political position. So how then have the European systems handled the situation, starting from vastly stronger positions? As a result of declining public subsidies, the leading public broadcasters of the world have increasingly turned to commercial means to support their activities. The major Scandinavian public broadcasters, for example, launched a commercial cable TV channel in the U.S. in 1997.[102] By 1997, the Dutch public broadcasters had "thrown in the towel" and agreed to permit advertising during their children's programming.[103]

But nowhere has the commercialization process been more apparent than in the United Kingdom, where the BBC began in the late 1990s to make deals that "would have been inconceivable" a few years earlier.[104] The BBC has, for example, signed major coproduction deals to launch commercial channels in the United States and elsewhere with the U.S. Discovery Communications and U.K. Flextech, both owned in part by media giant AT&T-TCI.[105] It developed a children's program, *Teletubbies,* to some extent because it could capitalize on enormous merchandising sales globally through a joint venture with Hasbro, a toy manufacturer.[106] Likewise the BBC signed a deal in 1998 to coproduce programs with Berlusconi's Mediaset.[107] In 1997 the BBC launched "the beeb," a commercial website to be funded through advertising, subscriptions, and merchandising sales.[108]

The BBC defends these activities, arguing that by being a commercial enterprise (especially outside of the U.K.), it can support its public service activities domestically.[109] The BBC's commercial activities generated $125 million in 1997, and it hopes to quadruple that figure by 2006.[110] BBC officials also insist that their commitment to providing a noncommercial service to the entire British population is as strong as it has ever been.[111] Those comments notwithstanding, it is hard to see an endgame for this strategy that does not include the utter abandonment of public broadcasting. Already, British commercial media are complaining that it is unfair that they have to compete with a firm that has a public subsidy.[112] (That charge is being heard across Europe, and before the European Commission.)[113] The British press is asking the rational question about a commercialized BBC: "Is the BBC license fee justified?"[114] Even when the BBC is successful, it cannot escape attack. In the late 1990s it increased its share of the British TV audience four consecutive years, to 44.1 percent in 1997. This would seem to undermine the notion that it did not deserve the license fee because its audience was shrinking. But its main commercial competitor, ITV, charged that the BBC was only able to achieve ratings success "at the expense of its public service obligations," hence suggesting that public subsidy was no longer justified.[115] "The BBC," concluded the *Economist*, "is remodelling itself to ape the big American media companies."[116]

The nature and trajectory of PBS and the BBC can be seen in another light when one looks at their ambitious Internet strategies. The democratic and civic potential of cyberspace was discussed in chapter 3. As more than one observer has noted, the Internet would seem to be the ideal place — an extraordinary opportunity — for public service broadcasters to renew their commitment to public service and sponsor the sort of noncommercial service that the corporate media, telecommunication, and media firms have no interest in providing. It might also be the best opportunity to keep cyberspace from becoming a "virtual mall."[117] Instead, public broadcasters have made their Internet services the *most* commercialized aspects of their operations, regarding them in a manner not unlike how the media giants view their Web businesses. The BBC's beeb.com is explicitly commissioned to use the BBC brandname to generate as much money as possible; it is not a public service activity. "We feel that we are effective in putting together creative solutions for our advertisers," a beeb.com executive stated.[118] PBS's website has scads of banner ads, and even has commercial "logograms" in its special section for children.[119] The CTW website — providing Sesame Street characters to children — is advertising supported.[120]

It seems evident that while this approach may well keep these nonprofit broadcasting systems alive as institutions, there is no endgame that involves public service. As the commercial logic expands from within, it almost certainly means that what they broadcast will increasingly be indistinguishable from what is being broadcast by the commercial media giants. As Habermas concludes dourly, "Public television is now competing in a race to the bottom with the most degraded presentation and programming of commercial television."[121] And becoming, in effect, commercial broadcasters means that public broadcasters are undermining their legitimate claim to public subsidy and, eventually, their responsibility for public service to the entire population. This solution to the crisis of public service broadcasting is no solution at all. It is merely a different, if slower, form of death.

Conclusion

The notion that public broadcasting has always been a marginal affair, justified only by scarcity and incapable of meeting public needs, is untrue, although the shape of much of public broadcasting today reinforces that notion. What is more necessary than ever is to recapture the connection of public broadcasting to democratic politics that guided the early advocates of public broadcasting. The same issues that drove Graham Spry to organize for a democratic noncommercial broadcasting system in Canada in the 1930s led him to return to the battlefront in the 1960s. There is little doubt that he would be back in the trenches again today were he alive.

While the specific fate of public broadcasting can be characterized as "small potatoes" in the big scheme of things, the principle it represents goes directly to the question of what type of society will dominate in the United States and globally for the coming generations. Will it be one in which the market and profits are sacrosanct, off-limits to informed political debate? One in which the notion of citizen will be replaced by that of consumer and where we will have a society effectively based on one dollar, one vote rather than one person, one vote? Will we have a society where people are regarded primarily as fodder for corporate profitability, or will we have a society where citizens have the right to actually determine whatever economic and media systems they regard as best? This was precisely how Graham Spry and the 1930s broadcast reformers understood the long-term implications of their fight for the control of broadcasting; it remains a fundamental question before us.

CHAPTER 6

THE NEW THEOLOGY OF THE FIRST AMENDMENT: CLASS PRIVILEGE OVER DEMOCRACY

The corporate domination and hypercommercialization of the U.S. media system is encased in several myths and half-truths, such as the notion of the market "giving the people what they want" and the idea that technologies will set us free. Perhaps the most powerful new myth in the United States is that the First Amendment to the U.S. Constitution authorizes the corporate control and hypercommercialization of media and communication. Indeed, this myth, more than any of the others, is meant to shut off any possibility of informed public debate over the nature of our media system. The status quo is what the Founding Fathers and the Constitution ordained, the reasoning goes; it is unquestionably the only possible system for a democracy; and therefore any public debate over ownership and control of the media is entirely improper. The only public concern authorized by the First Amendment is to keep the government's laws and regulations off of the private media, and off of advertising as well. The topic otherwise is made off-limits by the Constitution. It is an issue that cannot be entrusted to the citizenry. End of discussion. Case closed. Period. Next item on the agenda, please!

Such is the new theology of the First Amendment. The operative word is not "theology," because that is a given, but, rather, "new." This is, in fact, a quite distinctive interpretation of the First Amendment that has only begun to gain currency since the 1970s. In core respects it goes against much of the most important First Amendment case law prior to the 1970s, and most of the great philosophical writings on the First Amendment, free speech, and democracy. It is true that plausible claims are made by proponents of this new theology that their view most closely reflects the views of the Founding Fathers and the general trajectory of First Amendment case law. My point is that radically different and, in my view, far more democratic interpretations of the First Amendment are every bit as legitimate, but they have fallen into disfavor because they contradict the corporate, commercial domination of our society. This is a battle, then, where the dominant interpretation of the First Amendment has adapted to the surrounding commercial environment, far more than being developed in any sort of exercise to determine what is best for democracy or self-government per se, or what the Founding Fathers had in mind.

But the proponents of the newfangled corporate-friendly First Amendment insist that their interpretation alone represents the true meaning of free speech and free press. This new theology extends the logic of this "laissez-faire" First Amendment to include the rights of the wealthy to virtually purchase elections and the rights of advertisers to operate without government regulation. In short, this is a First Amendment for society's owning classes. It is important to note that this view is still not accepted in toto by the U.S. Supreme Court. Currently or in the future, any number of cases are and will be working their way through the court system that would put the new theology into effect. These cases seek to prohibit any government regulation of political campaign spending, commercial broadcasting, and commercial speech (e.g., advertising or food labeling) on the grounds that such regulation would violate citizens' and corporations' First Amendment rights to free speech or free press. Each case raises quite distinct constitutional issues concerning the First Amendment, but all share the common effect of protecting the ability of the wealthy and powerful few to act in their self-interest without fear of public examination, debate, and action.

It is no surprise that the political right, the business community, and the commercial media approve of this extension of First Amendment protection to these activities. To the extent that commercial activities are given First Amendment protection, this makes the rule of capital increasingly off-limits to political debate and government regulation. And, if political campaign contributions cannot be regulated, that puts the entire political process ever more firmly under the thumbs of the wealthy. What is striking, however, is that the venerable American Civil Liberties Union (ACLU) has lined up, more often than not, as an advocate of these "extensions" of the First Amendment. In the most flowery jargon imaginable, the ACLU promotes the notion that this interpretation of the First Amendment is the truly democratic one.

I argue in this chapter that the ACLU and progressives who might be persuaded by the ACLU's logic are making a terrible mistake, one that cannot be justified if one maintains a commitment to political democracy. This error is part and parcel of a broader process whereby the First Amendment has become more a mechanism for protecting class privilege than for protecting and promoting freedom and democracy. The First Amendment has also become a barrier to informed public participation in the construction of a media system better suited to a democracy. In my view, progressives need to stake out a democratic interpretation of the First Amendment and do direct battle with the Orwellian implications of the ACLU's commercialized First Amendment. And, as should be clear, this is far more than an academic battle: the manner in which the First Amendment is interpreted has a direct bearing on our politics, media, and culture. That is why the political right and the business community have devoted so much attention to converting it into their own possession.

The Utopian Case for a Commercialized First Amendment

Beginning in the 1970s, the U.S. Supreme Court has rendered a number of decisions which have increasingly extended First Amendment protection to corporations and commercial activities. As for political contributions, the Supreme Court first considered whether the government could constitutionally regulate campaign contributions in 1976, in *Buckley v. Valeo.* It upheld that right on balance, but the Court also stated that individuals had a First Amendment right to contribute as much of their own money as they wished to their own political campaigns, à la Ross Perot. The ACLU is among those who want not only to maintain this aspect of *Buckley v. Valeo* but also to grant First Amendment protection to nearly all other forms of campaign contributions. As an ACLU counsel notes, government limitations on campaign spending "would trammel the First Amendment rights of political parties and their supporters."

The ACLU's argument, in a nutshell, goes something like this: if the First Amendment is applied to any and all forms of speech, then the net result will be a flowering marketplace of ideas. As long as the government is kept away from speech, only good things will happen for democracy. And the ability to spend money on campaigns is an inexorable aspect of speech; if it is regulated then we are on a slippery slope along which all other forms of speech may soon come under government regulation and censorship. After all, censorship is contagious. This is basically the same argument used by the ACLU to extend the First Amendment to broadcasting, advertising, cigarette marketing, and other commercial activities. If business and commercial interests lose their First Amendment rights, corporate and First Amendment lawyer Floyd Abrams wrote, liberals "stand next in line. And . . . they are much more vulnerable to attack."[1]

At its most eloquent, this liberal argument for extending the First Amendment to political spending and, with qualification, to many commercial activities promises the greatest possible democratic political culture. But we have massive firsthand experience to show how absurd this claim is. In the past thirty years the First Amendment has been extended by the courts to cover vastly more areas — generally commercial — and our media and electoral systems may be the least regulated in the developed world. According to the ACLU laissez-faire formulation this should be the golden age of participatory democracy. But, in fact, this is arguably the low point in U.S. democratic participation. In many respects we now live in a society that is only formally democratic, as the great mass of citizens have minimal say on the major public issues of the day, and such issues are scarcely debated at all in any meaningful sense in the electoral arena. This political marketplace of ideas looks a lot more like a junkyard than a flowerbed. To paraphrase a line from Woody Allen's *Hannah and Her Sisters,* if John Stuart Mill were around today, he would never stop throwing up.

There are two flaws with the ACLU vision. First is the notion that the government is the only antidemocratic force in our society. Government can be and at times is a threat to democracy — and deserves constant vigilance — but this is not a meritocratic society otherwise. Nearly all theories of democracy from Aristotle to Madison to the present have recognized that democracy was fundamentally incompatible with pronounced social inequality. In our society, corporations and the wealthy enjoy a power every bit as immense as that assumed to have been enjoyed by the lords and royalty of feudal times. This class power works through means like campaign spending to assure inequality and limit democracy. Second, markets are not value-free or neutral; not only do they tend to work to the advantage of those with the most money but they also by their very nature emphasize profit over all else. A commercial marketplace of ideas may generate the maximum returns for investors, but that does not mean it will generate the highest caliber of political exchange for citizens. In fact, contemporary evidence shows it does nothing of the kind.[2]

If income and wealth were relatively equally distributed in the United States, I would be open to an argument that equated political spending with speech.[3] But we do not live in anything remotely close to an egalitarian society. The top 1 percent of the population owns some 50 percent of the financial wealth, while the bottom 80 percent has around 6 percent. The top 1 percent of the population receives nearly 20 percent of U.S. income while the bottom 80 percent of the population divvies up around 45 percent of U.S. income.[4] Letting people spend as much money as they want is simply letting people at the top buy their way out of a genuine democracy with a level playing field. In the United States the richest one-quarter of 1 percent of Americans make 80 percent of individual campaign contributions, and corporations outspend organized labor by a margin of ten to one.[5] These contributions are really better regarded as investments, with which millionaires, billionaires, and corporations purchase the allegiance of politicians who, when in office, pass laws that work to the benefit of the wealthy few.[6] In this environment, the broader notion of civic virtue and principle — so necessary for a democratic culture to prosper — has disappeared from sight. U.S. electoral politics is basically a special interest grab bag, where the ante for admission limits the possibility for meaningful participation to a small portion of the population. Is it any surprise that voter apathy, cynicism, and abstention are so high?

An assessment of recent U.S. elections provides some indication of just how absurd our electoral system has become. It is ironic that back in the 1950s and 1960s, commentators bemoaned how commercial television had turned "political candidates into commodities."[7] By the 1960s many considered it troubling that candidates were more concerned with getting a two- or three-minute segment on a television newscast than with getting out and dealing directly with voters and constituents. Those seem like glory days in comparison to what exists today, as the Lincoln-Douglas debates evoked nostalgia in the 1950s. After three decades of devolution, the political campaign is now based largely, arguably entirely, upon the paid television advertisement. The vast majority of the money spent on political campaigns goes toward these ads. It is nearly unthinkable to be a legitimate candidate without a massive war chest to produce and run TV ads. This favors candidates who appeal to the richest one-quarter of 1 percent of Americans who give most of the money and candidates who themselves are extremely rich, since they can spend as much as they wish on their own campaigns. Hence people like Steve Forbes and Ross Perot can buy their way into the political process, while dedicated public servants like Ralph Nader who refuse big money contributions are shut out altogether. The laws also mean that vested interests like corporations can spend as much money as they want on political ads — what is called "soft money" — as longer as the ads do not formally endorse a particular candidate.[8]

What is the nature of the content of these TV ads that are the political lingua franca of our age? Except to those who have lost sight of the fact that there might be alternatives to what currently exists or to those who have a vested interest in the current electoral system, the content of these ads is uniformly understood to be, at best, troubling. It is often said that politicians' TV ads are dreadful because they have the same ambiguous interest in truth that commercial advertising has, but it is worse than that, and the stakes are higher. Political ads are protected from regulation by the First Amendment, unlike most commercial advertising, so basically any half-truth, decontextualized and misleading fact, or even outright lie is fair game. The subjects of the ads are sometimes completely irrelevant to the main policy issues the candidate would face if he or she won the election. I share the view of Robert Spero, the high-ranking ad executive at Ogilvie and Mather who spent a year analyzing the content of presidential TV ads to see how their accuracy compared to that of commercial advertisements. Spero concluded that in 1976 "[f]ew if any" of the Carter and Ford TV spots "would have been allowed on television" if they had been required to meet the standards the government then placed on commercial advertising. "They could not have met the standard that network television imposes on the most trivial product commercial."[9] Political advertising also diverges from product advertising in the widespread use of purely negative ads, generally with standards for honesty that would make

Spero cringe. It does not make sense for Coca-Cola, say, to spend a fortune merely trashing Pepsi — claiming, for example, that Pepsi workers urinate in the bottles — because it only matters to Coke ultimately if people buy Coke, not that they not buy Pepsi. It is different in politics. If candidate A can run down candidate B enough that people leaning toward candidate B opt not to vote altogether, it very much improves candidate A's chances of success. For this and other reasons, negative advertising, deployed prudently, is an indispensable weapon in the candidate's arsenal.

Political advertising and the expensive electoral system it generates, therefore, have a cause-and-effect relationship with voter cynicism, apathy, and overall depoliticization. On the one hand, in a highly aroused and informed political culture, the sort of material that gets placed in these ads would be dismissed as insults to people's intelligence and never fly. Depoliticization is due, ultimately, to deeper causes than campaign spending or political advertising. This is a subject addressed in chapter 2 and taken up again in the concluding chapter. On the other hand, this system demoralizes the body politic well beyond its state prior to the age of TV political ads. As one report on the 1998 congressional elections noted, "people are gagging on negative ads."[10] In this climate, people increasingly attempt to tune out electoral politics altogether, which makes political advertising all the more important. The only way to reach reluctant voters effectively, then, is to bombard them with ads during entertainment programs and sports events. Most voters are not seeking out the information voluntarily. This is the classic case of both a vicious cycle and a downward spiral.

This leads to the crucial role of the corporate media — especially the commercial television networks and stations — in creating and perpetuating the campaign-spending crisis. In the 1998 elections, well over $1 billion was spent on political advertising in broadcast and print media. More then $500 million was spent by candidates to buy airtime on local broadcast stations, not including national networks and cable channels, up some 40 percent from the total for 1994. As one analyst put it, political advertising "saved the quarter" for stations' earnings.[11] This biannual financial windfall is why the commercial broadcasters steadfastly oppose any viable form of campaign finance reform, or any system that would allocate broadcast time for free to candidates. They claim that it is *their* First Amendment right to do whatever they want to maximize profit. (It also points to the conclusion that if we did not have a commercial broadcasting system, we would probably not have a campaign-spending crisis.) But the complicity of the corporate media is far greater than this. Survey after survey shows that by 1998 the commercial broadcasters had reduced, almost eliminated, any meaningful coverage of electoral campaigns in their newscasts. By any calculation, TV viewers who looked to the news would have found it nearly impossible to gather enough information to assess the candidates or the issues. A survey conducted by the Annenberg School for Communication at the University of Southern California, for example, found that in the last three months of the 1998 California governor's race, local television news in that state devoted less than one-third of 1 percent of their news time to that subject. One-third of 1 percent! The percentage of local TV news coverage devoted to the California governor's race in 1974, by comparison, was nearly ten times greater.[12] Broadcasters have little incentive to cover candidates, because it is in their interest to force them to purchase time to publicize their campaigns. And as TV ads become the main form of information, broadcast news has little or no interest in examining the claims made in these ads, as that might antagonize their wealthy benefactors.[13]

Is it possible that the blackout in electoral information on television news is compensated for by the print media, especially daily newspapers? Even though an increasing number of Americans, especially younger Americans, do not use newspapers for political information on a regular basis, print journalism still is the pacesetter for what serious issues are and how they get covered. Regrettably, the trends discussed in chapter 1 tend to hold true here as well. Campaign coverage tends to provide a dissection of strategy and considerable emphasis on polling data. There is often considerable reporting on candidates' TV ad campaigns, but mostly to discuss their strategy and tactics, not to assess the ideas or the content.[14] One political reporter noted the lack of media coverage of the 1998 race for governor of California and anointed it the first truly "all-commercial political campaign."[15]

Consider the highly publicized 1998 U.S. Senate race in Wisconsin between incumbent Russell Feingold and Republican challenger Mark Neumann, for example. Neumann was able to cut Feingold's substantial lead in the polls by using soft money to marinate the airwaves with ads attacking Feingold on a number of issues. Many of these ads were dubious in character, attacking Feingold on issues like flagburning and partial birth abortion. What was striking was the lack of press coverage in the state's newspapers (and, of course, television and radio stations) investigating the allegations in Neumann's ads, or even attempting to clarify what these issues entailed. Instead, Feingold was left, in effect, to spend his limited budget (he refused to accept soft money on principle) to counter the charges. He narrowly won in a race that, had the spending been equal, most observers suspect he would have won in a rout. In short, candidates with the most money who run the most ads have the inside track to set the agendas for their races. It does not mean that they will always win, but it means a candidate without a competitive amount of cash will almost always lose. Most prospective candidates without gobs of money or ready access to those who have it, regardless of their qualifications, will rationally opt not to participate.

So the "laissez-faire" First Amendment may not generate an especially engaging political or media culture, but that still leaves the matter of the slippery slope, that government regulation of campaign contributions will open the door to the regulation of the content of books and magazines and the infringement of other freedoms. The slippery slope principle is legitimate but it simply does not apply willy-nilly. There is no evidence that anyone has ever had any trouble distinguishing the regulation of campaign contributions from the censorship of the press or speech. In a related area, for fifty some years the federal government has been regulating advertising, and to my knowledge it has never led to a single case of some zealous regulator sliding down the slope to begin censoring editorial content surrounding the ads.

The Absolutist Defense

At this point ACLU liberals change the grounds for defending the extension of the First Amendment to political spending (or commercial speech) from the claim that this is a good or necessary thing for democracy that can be verified empirically, and begin to invoke so-called principle. The argument goes that speech needs no defense to be protected by the First Amendment; it is a civil right with value to the individual that simply cannot be abridged. This is sometimes characterized as the "absolutist" position, and, in the end, this principle provides the strongest case for protecting spending and perhaps even extending the First Amendment to new commercial activities. But it still does not fly, because absolutism is anything but absolute. Modern free speech absolutism and civil libertarian groups like the ACLU were born in the tumultuous first decades of the twentieth century, with strident commitments to the protection of dissident political opinion and labor activism from government harassment. As one historian wrote, during its early years the ACLU "focused on protecting political speech" exclusively.[16] Absolutism was inspired by the promise of democracy but, then, after defining what speech was necessary for democracy, it was absolutist in its rejection of any government regulation, regardless of the justification.

Hence absolutism, and arguably any theory of the First Amendment for that matter, has two components. The theory first determines what constitutes "speech," or, put another way, what speech is protected. Then, once that determination has been made, what speech is protected is protected absolutely. But even the most strident "absolutist" cannot avoid determining what speech qualifies, or what constitutes speech. Hence today the debate is over whether advertising, or food labeling, or campaign contributions are speech. I have no qualms about extending the First Amendment net to include areas that may not have any clear connection to politics, but I think principle is necessary to guide the debate. And a good start is this: if the rights to be protected by the First Amendment can only be effectively employed by a fraction of the citizenry, and their exercise of these rights gives them undue political power and undermines the ability of the balance of the citizenry to exercise the same rights and/or other constitutional rights, then it is not necessarily legitimately protected by the First Amendment.

The first great wave of twentieth-century absolutists, including people like Alexander Meiklejohn, argued that the First Amendment protected any and all political speech under any and all circumstances. "The primary purpose of the First Amendment," Meiklejohn wrote in 1948, "is, then, that all the citizens shall, so far as possible, understand the issues which bear upon our common life. That is why no idea, no opinion, no belief, no counterbelief, no relevant information, may be kept from them." The First Amendment "is protecting the common needs of all members of the body politic."[17] But Meiklejohn also argued that commercial speech (e.g., advertising) was not protected by the First Amendment, but rather by the

Fifth Amendment and its "freedom to contract" clause. Indeed, he argued that if commercial speech were given the same weight under the First Amendment as political speech, the First Amendment would lose its integrity and soon become primarily a tool for commercial interests who had no particular interest whatsoever in politics and public life per se.[18] And I would argue that that is exactly what is happening today. Meiklejohnian absolutism, like all other theories of the First Amendment, presents several problems in determining what exactly is protected speech, but it has the core strength of keeping its eyes on the prize: democracy.

Since campaign spending was not a particularly pressing issue in the first two-thirds of the twentieth century — due largely to the lack of paid TV political advertising — it does not get discussed much by the first and second generations of absolutists, people like Meiklejohn, Hugo Black, and Thomas Emerson.[19] But there is reason to assume that it would have been considered a form of speech had it ever been tested in the courts before *Buckley v. Valeo* in 1976. Commercial speech, on the other hand, was never considered fair game for First Amendment protection by the first great generation of absolutists, nor by their most principled academic heirs today. When the Supreme Court considered whether advertising should be protected by the First Amendment from government regulation — in 1942 — the Supreme Court, including absolutist Black, voted 9-0 against that proposition. "We are equally clear," the Supreme Court's opinion on the case stated, "that the Constitution places no such restraint on government as respects purely commercial advertising."[20] "The idea that commercial advertising," University of Chicago law professor Cass Sunstein wrote in 1997, "is always protected by the First Amendment is a bizarre rereading of history."[21] Even with regard to the press, the First Amendment was not traditionally regarded as being trade legislation to protect media owners from government regulation. Justice Black, universally recognized as the ultimate First Amendment absolutist, invariably lionized to this day by the ACLU, was no friend of what would become the ACLU's newfangled absolutism late in the twentieth century. "It would be strange indeed," Black wrote in 1945, "if the grave concern for freedom of the press . . . should be read as a command that the government was without power to protect that freedom. . . . Surely a command that the government itself shall not impede the free flow of ideas does not afford non-governmental combinations a refuge if they impose restraints upon that constitutionally guaranteed freedom."[22]

The Opening to a Corporate, Commercial First Amendment

The extension of the First Amendment to cover corporate and commercial activity is a recent phenomenon, taking place over the past twenty-five or thirty years.[23] This was not due to any profound philosophical debates or discussions over the meaning of freedom and democracy. To the contrary, this "extension" of the First Amendment was basically a conservative response by the court system to the sheer commercialization of the culture and corporate domination of society, as the market began its spread into every nook and cranny of social life. Even the advertising industry, ever on the lookout for ways to eliminate government regulation, did not begin taking the idea that commercial speech was protected by the First Amendment seriously until the late 1970s.[24] When commercialism penetrates everything, and when noncommercial public life diminishes or merges with commercialism, the capacity to distinguish between the two is compromised. This position was fueled to some extent by aggressive media, advertising, and corporate lobbies ever eager to eliminate government regulation of their activities and always quick to invoke high-minded principle to justify their self-interest. If not on the law faculties, then at least in the popular mind these corporate interests and their think-tank ideologues have been among the leading definers of this newfangled "absolutism." And, regrettably, the ACLU has increasingly accepted this Philip Morris interpretation of the First Amendment.

But this alone only begins to explain this striking shift in interpretation of the First Amendment. The critical factor that accentuated the problem with maintaining a strict line between political and commercial speech was the commercialization of the press or the media. The commercialization and corporate ownership of media have also been the primary reasons for the explosion in political campaign costs that underlies the concerns about unregulated political spending. In this way the issue of whether campaign contributions are protected from government regulation by the First Amendment is indelibly linked to the commercialization of the culture and of the First Amendment.

Although discussions of the First Amendment protection of a "free press" often simply take arguments about individual speech and apply them to the press without qualification, there are important differences. It is one thing to assure individuals the right to say whatever they please without fear of government regulation or worse. This is a right that can be enjoyed by everyone on a relatively equal basis. Anyone can find a street corner to stand on to pontificate. It is another thing to say that any individual has the right to establish a free press to disseminate free speech industrially to a broader audience than could be reached by the spoken word. Here, to the extent that the effective capacity to engage in a free press is quite low for a significant portion of the population, the free speech analogy weakens. Moreover, those with the capacity to engage in free press are in a position to determine who is empowered to disseminate speech to the great mass of citizens and who is not. This accords special privileges to some citizens who can then dominate public debate. (Proponents of the newfangled First Amendment tend to conflate the two issues, and accuse those who disapprove of the commercialized First Amendment of also being in favor of measures such as regulating so-called hate speech. In fact, the Meiklejohnian tradition is opposed to any such regulation.)

The core issue for First Amendment theorists, then, is whether the First Amendment protects the rights of press owners absolutely regardless of the implications for democracy much as it protects individual speech regardless of the content of that speech. The alternative is to view the First Amendment protection of a free press as a social right to a diverse and uncensored press. In this view the right to a free press is a right enjoyed by all citizens equally, not just by press owners. Here the explanation for constitutional protection is implicitly linked to the need for a free press in order to have a functioning democracy. Otherwise there is no more need for its inclusion in the First Amendment than there would be for a guarantee of the right to establish a bread-baking business or a shoe-repair service. As Meiklejohn points out, those commercial rights are explicitly covered in the Constitution by the Fifth Amendment.

Indeed, there is little dissent to the argument that the free press clause was inserted in the First Amendment to protect democracy. The First Amendment's "historic purpose," Sunstein writes, has been to assure "the construction of a well-functioning system of democratic deliberation."[25] As the press system of that era was explicitly connected to political parties and factions, such protection was necessary to protect out-of-power political opinion from direct harassment by the dominant political party that controlled Congress and the government. Moreover, as Akhil Reed Amar argues persuasively, the First Amendment when drafted was not so much a protection of dissident views from the tyranny of the majority as it was a populist document mostly concerned with protecting popular majorities from a Congress that had been set up by the Constitution in such a way as to have the potential of being more aristocratic than democratic. Were these legitimate concerns? Absolutely. Only a few years after the adoption of the First Amendment, the crisis surrounding the Alien and Sedition Acts emerged, during which the dominant Federalist Party attempted to use the law to muzzle the voices of Republican newspaper editors.[26]

The conflict between the antidemocratic potential of a private press system and the needs of democracy has not been an important debate for much of U.S. history. During the Republic's early days, the press system was highly partisan, often subsidized by government printing contracts or partisan contributions, politically motivated, and relatively noncommercial. In this period even small political factions found it relatively easy to publish and support all shades of political organs. One need only consider the broad array of abolitionist and feminist newspapers in the first half of the nineteenth century to appreciate the capacity of the press system to accommodate a wide range of political opinion. During much of the later nineteenth century, the partisan press system was replaced by a highly competitive, yet still fairly political, commercial press system. In this system there was still relative ease of entry to the market and a cursory glance at any city of moderate or large size would tend to find a diverse press representing nearly every segment of the population. The press systems of the Republic's first century were far from perfect, but they were also not by any means a primary barrier to political democracy.

All this began to change toward the end of the nineteenth century, when the press (and, later, media) became an important capitalist industry, following the explicit logic of the commercial marketplace. Over time the media system became vastly less competitive in the economic sense. Not only were most media industries concentrated in the hands of a small number of large firms, barriers to entry made new competitive challenges almost impossible. Hence the "ease of entry" to make the free press protection in the First Amendment a near universal right for citizens was effectively eliminated. Along these lines, virtually no new daily newspapers have been successfully launched in existing markets in the United States since World War I, despite their immense profitability and growth. And, likewise, no new major Hollywood film studios have been established in sixty years either. Moreover, the logic of the marketplace has led to the conglomeration of media giants so that the largest firms like Time Warner and Disney have dominant holdings across many major media sectors.

And that's not all. The media have become increasingly dependent upon advertising revenue for support, which has distinct implications for the nature of media content. Modern advertising only emerged with the arrival of corporate capitalism in the past century and is conducted disproportionately by the very largest corporations. In the business press, the media are often referred to in exactly the way they present themselves in their candid moments: as a branch of the advertising industry. This corporate media system has none of the intrinsic interest in politics or journalism that existed in the press of earlier times. Its commercialized newsfare, if anything, tends to promote depoliticization, and all evidence suggests that its fundamental political positions, such as they are, are closely linked to political and business elites. In view of the ownership and subsidy, anything else would be astonishing. To be fair, the formal right to establish free press is exercised by dissidents on the margins, but the commercial system is such that these voices have no hope to expand beyond their metaphorical house arrest.

The rise of this corporate media system augurs a moment of truth for the First Amendment and its protection of a free press. Are corporations the same as people? Do shareholders and executives of corporations — clearly driven by law and the market to maximize profit regardless of the social implications — have the unconditional right to censor media content? Should investors be granted the First Amendment right to select and censor journalists when they have no more concern for the press per se than they have for any other potentially profitable investment? Is it right that this capacity to censor be restricted to the very wealthiest Americans, or those they hire to explicitly represent their interests? How does one distinguish what speech is necessary for politics — and thereby absolutely protected by the First Amendment — when it seems that all speech is increasingly concerned only with commercial gain, and political democracy is not even a prerequisite for its existence? Being an absolutist for a commercial media system then appears to have precious little to do with democracy and a great deal to do with protecting a powerful industry (and the class that owns it) from the same legal potential for public accountability that other similar industries face. And if the First Amendment covers corporate media, by what logic should it not cover corporate advertisers, or food manufacturers, or commerce in general? So it was that newspaper publisher and one-time president of NBC News Michael G. Gartner became a leading advocate of extending the First Amendment to commercial speech. "Restrictions on commercial speech," he wrote, are "dangerous to democracy."[27]

For media owners there is no doubt about what the First Amendment is about: it is *their* First Amendment and, as one trade publication put it in 1998, "the public's primary interest in relation to the government and the media is to keep the former as far removed as possible from the editorial decisions of the latter."[28] When the government had the audacity to suggest that commercial broadcasters might have to provide some public service programming to merit receiving at no charge scarce spectrum for digital broadcasting valued in the tens of billions of dollars, one trade publication characterized it as an "attempt to turn the First Amendment into digital road kill."[29]

This conflict over what the First Amendment means in an age of corporate commercial media operating in oligopolistic markets first emerged in the Progressive Era, when chain newspaper ownership, one-newspaper towns, and advertising had converted much of the U.S. press into blatant advocates for the status quo, while the formal right to launch newspapers meant little to dissidents who could not survive commercially in a semimonopolistic market.[30] The extent of this crisis regrettably has received far too little attention in media and journalism histories. An incident in Wisconsin in 1922 provides some inkling of the problem facing newspapers at the time. William Evjue, the editor of the progressive Madison daily newspaper, the *Capital Times,* founded by supporters of U.S. Senator Robert M. La Follette, threw down the gauntlet to his fellow newspaper editors. Evjue noted that newspaper editors were no longer "free to tell the truth," due to "advertising pressure, economic considerations and social influence." "The plight of the American editor today is the direct result of an economic system that has been builded up in this country over the past 25 years," Evjue wrote, referring to the concentration of wealth and the rise to dominance of "trusts and monopolies." According to Evjue, these "big financial interests" realized that control over the press — through ownership, advertising, and a variety of social mechanisms — made their political and economic power virtually incontrovertible. As a result, "the great mass of people have been losing confidence in newspapers in state and nation for 25 years." Evjue concluded: "The future of America is safe as long as the American people have the ballot and can obtain information and facts on which to base an intelligent opinion. When, however, the steel trust, the railroads, the packers, the coal barons and the industrial plutocrats can pervert public opinion to suit their purposes then we are treading on dangerous ground."[31]

Had Evjue's contribution merely been to make the above points, his name could be added to a list of like-minded luminaries from that period including Will Irwin, Upton Sinclair, and John Dewey, among others. But Evjue went a step further. At the annual meeting of Wisconsin newspaper editors then taking place in Madison, he offered to give $100 to the favorite charity of any newspaper editor in the state who could establish that their newspaper was not "affected by the pressure of organized wealth." Evjue stated that if a paper accepted his challenge, he would go to the town for a public hearing where each side could state its case and the audience would vote for the winner. Evjue asked for nothing if, by chance, his side should win.[32] While most editors ignored the Evjue challenge, the Merrill *Daily Herald* took him up on it. Evjue gathered his information for the Merrill debate by spending an afternoon conversing with Merrill residents and studying the public records in the county clerk's office. At the evening debate, before a standing room only crowd of twelve hundred, Evjue chronicled the *Daily Herald*'s service to the area's dominant industrial concerns and answered questions for three and one-half hours, before winning a landslide victory.[33] After that debacle, few other editors or publishers wished to tangle with Evjue or take him up on his challenge. Evjue noted with delight that the newspapers "seem to be squirming as a result of these charges."[34] In general, however, genuine public forums on media performance along the lines of the Evjue challenge (as opposed to the occasional public relations exercise) have been all but nonexistent in modern U.S. history. Editors who thought like Evjue were very few and far between; even posing the question as Evjue did would have been unthinkable to most other editors then and in subsequent years.

The Evjue incident pointed to the fundamental problem facing media owners at the time: how could people trust the journalism being produced? The material response to this crisis for journalism would not be structural reform where the power was taken away from the owners and advertisers but, rather, the introduction of "professional" and "objective" journalism, as I discussed in chapter 1. It was during this period that newspaper publishers led the campaign for the establishment of formal university-level schools of journalism to train the new breed of editor and reporter. By the logic of professionalism, the journalists would produce a neutral product that did not reflect the biases of the owners, the advertisers, or themselves. Hence, while the owners maintained control of the industry and First Amendment protection, they would informally and voluntarily recognize the need for autonomous journalism with integrity that the public could trust. How successful or viable professionalism has been as a counterbalance to corporate commercial media control has been the subject of considerable debate over the years.[35] In recent years, however, many observers concede that journalistic autonomy has been shrunk or eliminated under commercial pressures from corporate owners.

Some Meiklejohnians — most notably Jerome Barron — would eventually argue that a commitment to the spirit of the First Amendment required the government to intervene to assure that semimonopolistic newspapers provide a diverse range of views.[36] But for the most part those in the Meiklejohnian tradition have shied away from this response to the antidemocratic implications of the corporate media market: the prospect of government intervention in the press is identified *by definition* as constituting censorship and is therefore not acceptable under any circumstances. The experience with fascist and authoritarian media systems justifiably gave everyone trepidation about government-regulated media. And when the Supreme Court heard Barron's argument in *Miami Herald v. Tornillo* in 1974, it voted 9-0 against his position. Justice William O. Douglas is reputed to have displayed his utter contempt for Barron's position by reading a newspaper during his argument.

It is worth noting, however, that the Supreme Court did not directly state that the right of the First Amendment belonged to the owners. The government cannot regulate "the exercise of editorial control and judgment," Chief Justice Warren Burger's opinion stated. Justice Byron White's concurring opinion noted that the government cannot "insinuate itself into the editorial rooms of this nation's press."[37] Clearly, the Court accepted the traditional presupposition that there was no important distinction between owners and editors, and its concern was to protect editors, not investors. In fact, editors and journalists have no First Amendment protection unless ceded by the owners. As a News Corp. executive put it in 1998, when two News Corp. TV reporters were fired for doing a critical investigative report on Monsanto, "We paid $3 billion for these TV stations. We will decide what the news is. The news is what we tell you it is."[38] Wallowing in the nineteenth-century mythology preferred by the corporate media lawyers and ideologues, the Supreme Court has never directly addressed what the First Amendment means for a free press in the modern corporate commercial system.

There are two other Meiklejohnian solutions to the crisis for democracy generated by a corporate-dominated, commercially marinated media system. The most radical is to eliminate commercial media for the most part and create a large nonprofit, noncommercial media system accountable to the public. In the Progressive Era, for example, John Dewey and others proposed that newspapers be established as nonprofit and noncommercial enterprises, supported by endowments like universities and managed through direct public election (or election by the workers) of their officers. Even press magnate Joseph Pulitzer broached the idea of converting his newspapers into nonprofit trusts to be run like universities, but he backed down, one suspects, when his heirs got wind of the idea.

The less radical solution is to accept the existence of the corporate media giants, seek to regulate at least the broadcasters, and then tax the media giants or use public monies to establish a viable nonprofit and noncommercial media system that can service the needs of those citizens unable to own media corporations. But proposals like these have met with significant corporate opposition and concerns that they would let the government control media to an unacceptable extent, no matter how the nonprofit media system might be structured. From the Progressive Era to the present day, the corporate media giants have fanned the flames of this sentiment, using their immense resources to popularize the notion that a gulag-style, darkness at noon, media system was the only possible alternative to the corporate, commercial status quo. Hence any challenge to their power was a challenge to democracy. It may well be that the various commercial media industries — from newspaper publishers to broadcasters to film studios to advertisers — have been the foremost practitioners of public relations in this century. Anything more than marginal structural media reform, it is clear, cannot be successfully implemented unless it is part of a broader political challenge to the business domination of U.S. society.

Broadcasting, on balance, offered the most hope for those who wished to see a First Amendment committed to democratic media, as the limited number of possible channels meant that there was no escaping that the government would determine who would broadcast and who would not, and the terms under which they would broadcast. All Supreme Court decisions have affirmed the right of the government to regulate broadcasting in a manner that would be unconstitutional with the print media. In broadcasting, at least, the First Amendment has formally been acknowledged to be the property of viewers and listeners more than that of the licensed broadcasters. In his opinion in the seminal 1969 Red Lion case, Justice Byron White wrote that "It is the right of the listening and viewing public, and not the right of the broadcaster, that is paramount."[39] (The commercial broadcasters have devoted the past thirty years to overturning the Red Lion decision, as that would provide them with virtual ownership of the airwaves, and no possibility of government regulation.)

Broadcasting provided the Waterloo as such for Meiklejohnian absolutism. In the late 1920s and early 1930s the government in effect turned over the very best slots to a handful of private commercial operations including NBC and CBS, with virtually no public or congressional debate on the matter. Meiklejohn was appalled by commercial broadcasting and became one of its sharpest critics. After outlining the great promise of the technology, he wrote in 1948: "But never was a human hope more bitterly disappointed. The radio as it now operates among us is not free. Nor is it entitled to the protection of the First Amendment. It is not engaged in the task of enlarging and enriching human communication. It is engaged in making money. And the First Amendment does not intend to guarantee men freedom to say what some private interest pays them to say for its own advantage. It intends only to make men free to say what, as citizens, they think, what they believe, about the general welfare." Commercial radio "is not cultivating those qualities of taste, of reasoned judgment, of integrity, of loyalty, of mutual understanding upon which the enterprise of self-government depends. On the contrary, it is a mighty force for breaking them down."[40]

As I chronicled in chapters 4 and 5, in the early 1930s sections of the U.S. population were appalled by this giveaway and the resulting commercial carpetbombing of the publicly owned airwaves. In the 1930s the ACLU, inspired by its mentor Meiklejohn and with the active encouragement of Dewey, was so alarmed by the explicit and implicit censorship in corporate and advertiser control of radio — especially against labor and the Left — that it argued that the very system of commercial broadcasting was a violation of the First Amendment. For most of the 1930s the ACLU worked to have the government establish a nonprofit and noncommercial radio system that would foster more coverage of social issues and public affairs, greater exchange of ideas, and diversity of opinion. The ACLU only backed off from this position when it became clear that the corporate power was entrenched and unchallengeable, not through any principled debate. After abandoning its commitment to structural reform, the ACLU went from being a proponent of an aggressive regulation of commercial broadcasters in the public interest to being the ambiguous defender of the commercial broadcasters to do whatever they pleased to maximize profits without government interference. Eventually many liberals connected with the ACLU and elsewhere began to concentrate on defending the First Amendment rights of commercial broadcasters to censor material as they saw fit.

The 1930s experience with radio also sheds fresh light on the commercial broadcasters who so valiantly claim they deserve full First Amendment protection from government regulation. In the late 1920s and early 1930s, while the government was aggressively reordering the airwaves for profitable exploitation, the leading commercial broadcasting attorneys argued emphatically that the government needed to have absolute power over broadcasting, without even providing much in the way of due process for those nonprofit and noncommercial broadcasters who felt they were getting mistreated by the Federal Radio Commission. Once the commercial system became entrenched and Congress passed the 1934 Communications Act, however, commercial broadcasting attorneys took a 180-degree turn and began to argue that any government regulation of broadcasting was now a violation of the First Amendment.[41] It is difficult to study this period and not regard the commitment to "principle" of commercial broadcasters with a degree of skepticism.

Since the 1970s, the ACLU and the liberal community in general have warmed to the arguments of the corporate media, and have shown increased willingness to include commercial activities under the rubric of the First Amendment, even if their relationship to political democracy is weak or nonexistent. Liberal Supreme Court Justice William Brennan, for example, was the unabashed champion of extending full First Amendment protection to advertising in the 1970s and 1980s.[42] Brennan, too, is reputed to be the anonymous author of the Court's majority opinion in *Buckley v. Valeo* that equated money with speech. But Brennan was not necessarily a newfangled First Amendment absolutist of the Floyd Abrams/ACLU variety. His defense of extending the First Amendment to commercial speech was that it protected the marketplace of ideas for the public, not that it was some innate right of advertisers. And in his final years on the Court he opened the door to regulation of campaign spending to protect the integrity and viability of the electoral process. In short, Brennan's motion of the First Amendment may well have been bathed in the same commitment to democracy as Hugo Black's, and perhaps even Meiklejohn's. That he went the direction he did highlights the dilemma facing the First Amendment in recent times, and the difficulty of maintaining a link between the First Amendment and democratic governance. If the line between what is commercial and what is political is muddled, as has happened over the course of the twentieth century, absolutists and civil libertarians have two options. One is to extend the First Amendment to include more commercial fare and the other is to narrow the First Amendment so that it only covers noncommercial and perhaps even nonprofit speech. The former course offends no one in power and comports to the existing social structure, hence requiring no social change. The latter course goes directly counter to the trajectory of the political economy, hence demanding an explicit commitment to sweeping institutional change in the media industries and placing one in direct conflict with dominant media and corporate power. Proponents of the latter course regard the First Amendment as a fundamentally radical statement, not a fundamentally conservative one. This was also the logical trajectory of Meiklejohnian absolutism and its decline mirrors the general decline of the democratic left in the United States.

It should be mentioned, too, that the ACLU's turn to a corporate-friendly interpretation of the First Amendment also has some material benefits. Between 1988 and 1996 the ACLU and its branches received over $1 million in donations from Philip Morris, RJR Nabisco, and other tobacco companies. This money was used to spearhead ACLU committees to protect "smokers' rights" and to battle to see that the First Amendment be extended to protect the right of to-bacco companies to advertise their wares. Curiously, the ACLU kept these donations secret and avoided sharing this information with its members during its fundraising drives.[43]

Conclusion

As impractical as Meiklejohnian absolutism seems today, its analysis hit the bull's-eye. As Meiklejohn feared, we are losing our capacity to distinguish public life from the commercial realm, with public life suffering as a consequence. This loss is a primary factor in the raging depoliticization and atomization of social life. Indeed this is a theme that resounds in some of the most penetrating social criticism ranging from that of C. Wright Mills and Jürgen Habermas to Noam Chomsky and Robert Putnam. It is a crisis that the proponents of extending the First Amendment to all campaign contributions and to commercial speech are incapable of addressing, so it is one they dismiss as irrelevant. As one legal scholar has noted, in the nineteenth century the image of the market was used to expand the boundaries of free speech, whereas in the twentieth century the image of free speech has been used to expand the power and terrain of the market.[44]

In the hands of the wealthy, the advertisers, and the corporate media, the newfangled First Amendment takes on an almost Orwellian cast. On the one hand, it defends the right of the wealthy few to effectively control our electoral system, thereby taking the risk out of democracy for the rich and making a farce of it for most everyone else. And these semimonopolistic corporations that brandish the Constitution as their personal property eschew any public service obligations and claim that public efforts to demand them violate their First Amendment rights, which in their view means their unimpeded ability to maximize profit regardless of the social consequences. Indeed, the media giants use their First Amendment protection not to battle for open information but to battle to protect their corporate privileges and subsidies.[45]

This points to the extraordinarily unprincipled nature of the ACLU's present position on the First Amendment. The tragedy of this interpretation is not that it regards government as the sole enemy of democracy. It is that it spends all its time jousting with government when regulation might possibly challenge the prerogatives of the wealthy but steadfastly ignores the widespread activities of the government to shape the marketplace of ideas on behalf of corporate and commercial interests. Hence the fact that the federal government has turned over valuable radio and television channels to a small number of commercial firms at no charge and with virtually no public debate is not considered a violation of the First Amendment, or a matter of concern to civil libertarians. Yet this activity has put distinct limits on the range of ideas that could emanate from the resulting broadcasting system.

And the fact that the U.S. government subsidizes a top secret national security apparatus to the tune of at least $30 billion per year — with a significant aspect of its work going to the dissemination of propaganda and harassment of political dissidents — is also not apparently a First Amendment concern. Indeed, recent evidence suggests that the ACLU's Washington office effectively cooperated with the CIA in its efforts to censor the writings of its former employees and to restrict journalists' coverage of CIA operations in the 1980s.[46] How ironic that the modern-day corporate-friendly absolutists at the ACLU cut deals in back rooms with groups like the CIA, while publicly evoking a self-righteous commitment to principle as they advance the rights of advertisers, media corporations, and cigarette companies. In Meiklejohn's perspective, the very existence of the CIA signified that this was not a democratic society, because the rulers had a weapon of immense power unaccountable to the citizenry.

It would be comforting to think that we could depend on the Supreme Court to do the right thing in all these areas and reclaim the First Amendment for democracy, but we cannot. This Court was put in office by the politicians who benefit by the status quo, and it has already shown a lack of backbone on related issues. And the courts tend to be conservative institutions, more often than not only willing to reverse earlier decisions when they see significant changes in social attitudes on an issue. In the end, we will probably only get changes in the courts when we have built up a significant social movement to challenge the corporate control over our society. In the meantime, we need to continue to expose the phony basis for the corporate-friendly, commercialized First Amendment. We need to reclaim the First Amendment and aim it for the stars, rather then let it continue to mindlessly point at the ground. And in the process of doing so we need to pressure the ACLU to return to its roots as a force for justice and democracy, or expose it as a fig leaf for plutocracy.

THE
U.S. LEFT
AND
MEDIA
POLITICS

The main argument of the book to this point has been that U.S. democracy is in a decrepit state — exemplified by a depoliticization that would make a tyrant envious — and that the corporate commercial media system is an important factor, though not the only or even the most important factor, in understanding how this sorry state came to be. The corporate media cement a system whereby the wealthy and powerful few make the most important decisions with virtually no informed public participation.[1] Crucial political issues are barely covered by the corporate media, or else are warped to fit the confines of elite debate, stripping ordinary citizens of the tools they need to be informed, active participants in a democracy. Moreover, the media system is not only closely linked to the *ideological* dictates of the business-run society, it is also an integral element of the economy. Hence, for those who regard inequality and untrammeled commercialism as undermining the requirements of a democratic society, media reform must be on the political agenda.

At present, however, and for generations, the control and structure of the media industries has been decidedly off-limits as a subject in U.S. political debate. So long as that holds true, it is difficult to imagine any permanent qualitative change for the better in the U.S. media system. And without media reform, the prospects for making the United States a more egalitarian, self-governing, and humane society seem dim to the point of nonexistence.

I argue in this chapter that the only hope for significant media reform in the United States (and elsewhere) will be the emergence of a strong left political movement that puts media reform on the political agenda. Hence this is an argument aimed at those concerned with the antidemocratic tendencies of the U.S. media system, urging them to see media reform as part of a broader political project. And it is an argument aimed at those on the political left, stressing that it is imperative that the left incorporate media reform into its platform. This has been, and remains, a weak spot in much U.S. left organizing. In my view, the left needs to do this because the vast, unbridled power of the media is central to the antidemocratic nature of U.S. society and to the dominant role of corporations and combinations of wealth. In addition, I believe that there exists considerable dissatisfaction with the U.S. media system, and that this could become an organizing tool for an aggressive left. I believe this dissatisfaction cuts across many of the left constituencies that are sometimes at odds with each other and reaches many people who would not regard themselves as being anywhere near the political left. In short, media reform is an issue with the potential to help galvanize a movement to democratize U.S. society.

In this chapter I first elaborate on what I mean by "the left" and why the left must play this decisive role with regard to media reform. I then discuss traditional left activities with regard to media and the still prevalent apathy on the left toward media issues. (I consider the left and labor to be distinct enterprises at one level, but to have such overlapping long-term interests that at times I refer to them interchangeably.) I conclude by discussing what is being done — and what should be done — on behalf of media reform by activists, whether of the left or otherwise. My purpose in this chapter is not to spell out in detail the blueprints for a more democratic media system; rather, I only hope to convince people that we need to encourage debate and analysis to that end, and to present some of the principles that may gird a democratic media structure. I then describe some of the nascent efforts at democratic media activism outside of the United States, as these might provide a model or vision of sorts for U.S. activists. The good news is that there has been an upsurge in U.S. media activism in the 1990s. The bad news is that this only highlights how very, very far we have to go.

Democracy, the Left, and the Media

To some it may not seem politically astute to connect the movement for democratic media to the fortunes of the political left. In the United States, the term "left" is now largely in disrepute, deemed the failed ideology of inefficient and arrogant state bureaucracies, even political dictatorships. For many who propose democratic reform, the wisest move is to seek new terminology, avoiding terms like "the left" with its undesirable baggage altogether. In my view, the only course that makes sense in the long run is to reclaim "left" and recharge it with its historic meaning. "If 'left' means anything anymore," Joel Rogers writes, "it means 'democracy.' As applied to organizing our lives together, it means greater popular control over the terms and conditions of that life, and greater social justice inscribed in those terms."[2] The purpose of the left, then, is to struggle for conditions that make genuine democracy, genuine self-government, possible. Because democracy works best with as much political equality as possible, it works best when there is as little social inequality as possible. The political left has been and is the primary social agency against social inequality, and it has acted thus through popular mobilization that gives meaning to the term democracy. The left's "singular contribution" to history, Frances Fox Piven and Richard A. Cloward observe, "has been to bring working-class people fully into history, not simply as victims but as actors."[3]

Being on the left does not necessarily make one a proponent of socialism as much as it makes one a proponent of the principle that it is proper that a society determine the type of economy it prefers through informed debate in which everyone has a legitimate opportunity to participate. The core principle is that the economy should be subservient to democracy, to the will of the people. In this sense, the "left" position is the organic product of the best elements of the liberal democratic tradition. The point of the left, then, is to struggle to establish the conditions under which such democratic debate can take place, and then the organization of the economy should result from that debate. In my view, the evidence points strongly to the conclusion that when the conditions of democracy are fruitful, there will be considerable pressure to reduce economic inequality and insecurity and to rein in the market, if not necessarily to establish a flat-out socialist economy where private investment and the profit motive are drastically curtailed. (If we have the conditions for genuine self-government and the majority of people opt for neoliberal market economics, I will sleep at peace with that decision, and then work to move people to my antimarket point of view. But the move toward neoliberalism has taken place with minimal popular advice and consent.) Wealthy interests in the United States have little interest in testing my hypothesis; that is why they work resolutely to limit the capacity for informed self-government, through, among other things, maintaining corrupt campaign finance and lobbying systems, elite-dominated economic policy making, distorted electoral systems, weakened educational systems, and commercial media.

This tension between the democratic interests of the many and antidemocratic interests of the wealthy few has existed since the dawn of civilization. There has always been conflict between class societies and democracy. Prior to the late eighteenth century, in Europe and North America, democracy often was considered synonymous with classless or one-class societies, because it was assumed that if there were universal adult suffrage, no people would agree to their continued economic subjugation. James Madison wrote that if British elections "were open to all classes of people, the property of landed proprietors would be insecure."[4] Even in ancient Greece this was a central concern. In his *Politics,* Aristotle not only characterized democracy as "rule of the poor" but also added that would always be democracy's nature and raison d'être even if the poor comprised a minority of the citizenry.[5] It was also widely accepted that if a person had to work for another person, that person could never be a political equal. This was a primary justification for limiting suffrage to property owners and the middle and upper classes prior to the nineteenth century. Liberal democracy, as C. B. Macpherson so eloquently put it, is the modern and unprecedented marriage of the most sophisticated form of class society — capitalism — with some semblance of formal democracy; it is the combination of egalitarian politics with inegalitarian economics.[6] This idea that democratic polities would invariably dispense with class societies persisted into the twentieth century. When Edgar Snow traveled with the Chinese communists in the 1930s, he recounted the Chinese peasants' shock that much of the United States had universal adult suffrage yet somehow the nation was not socialist. We know well now that universal suffrage does not guarantee the rule of the many in capitalist societies; control over the economy is a significant, often the dominant, source of power generally outside of parliamentary or direct popular control.[7]

So capitalism and democracy are not synonymous, nor have they ever been. Capitalism requires that commercial activities be granted considerable freedom, and this has at times opened the door to broader civil liberties; but even under the best of circumstances, capitalism is innately in conflict with the core tenets of democracy. The core reason is that capitalism is invariably a class society where a very small percentage of the population has most of the society's wealth and a disproportionate share of its income. This permits the wealthy few a distinct advantage in pursuing their own political interests, and it also permits them to undermine the efforts of the many to strive for a more egalitarian society. Hence, the logical type of democracy that accords to a capitalist society is one where the poorer one is, the less possible it is to influence political outcomes and the more rational it is to become apathetic and depoliticized. Accordingly, for those who believe in democracy, it is imperative to reduce social and economic inequality. Democracy also works best when there exists a democratic spirit, a notion that an individual's welfare is directly and closely attached to the welfare of the community, however broadly community may be defined. Capitalism, with its incessant pressure to think only of Number One regardless of the implications for the balance of the community, is hardly conducive to building a caring, democratic culture.[8]

This does not mean that capitalism cannot coexist with some version of democracy, merely that the two are in unavoidable tension. One need not be a socialist to be a democrat, but I think it fair to say that to be a democrat one must possess an awareness of the problems of class inequality and a strong skepticism toward the unfettered market. "A moral condemnation of great wealth must inform any defense of the free market" in a democracy, Christopher Lasch observed, "and that moral condemnation must be backed up by effective political action."[9] In these neoliberal times, this critical notion of the market — once not uncommon among a certain breed of liberal and conservative — has become heretical. It is worth noting that capitalist societies have been made vastly more democratic and humane when left movements and parties have been able to organize significant economic and political power. Democracy has never been handed down from elites to those beneath them in the social pecking order. Democracy must be proclaimed, organized around, fought for, and won.[10] The most striking examples of how an organized socialist movement could ameliorate the worst elements in capitalism came with the social democracies of Scandinavia. But it is a never-ending struggle, as the right-wing assault on social democracy in Scandinavia and elsewhere in the past twenty years testifies.

Since the rise of capitalism, the upper classes have revealed a deep contempt for and a fear of democracy, just like their predecessors in precapitalist societies.[11] They fought tooth and nail against popular movements to limit suffrage, and universal adult suffrage only became the norm in the twentieth century. Business's conception of democracy has always tended to be one where the rights to buy, sell, and invest for private gain in the marketplace are the only nonnegotiable freedoms: all other freedoms are acceptable only to the extent they do not interfere with these commercial rights.[12] (A similar attitude toward democracy could be found in the Communist model that dominated Eastern Europe for much of the twentieth century. Elections are permissible, in the view of the leaders, as long as the power of the commissars and the dominance of the Communist Party is unchallengeable. So it was that Lenin stated that his ultimate plan for the Soviet Union — after it became "long-established and secure" — was to "have a two-party system such as the British have — a left party and a right party — but two Bolshevik parties, of course.")[13]

Even some of the great architects of liberal democratic theory have had reservations about popular rule. For example John Stuart Mill, the great liberal, advocated plural voting, whereby intellectuals, professionals, and the well-to-do would be entitled to more votes in elections than the balance of the population.[14] Although it was not necessarily his intention to do so, arguably Mill staked out the modern liberal position: if conservatives have wanted to preserve the rule of capital with minimal popular interference, liberals have wanted to see the rule of capital complemented by the rule of the professionals and the self-professed do-gooder intelligentsia. This is to some extent the range of elite debate in capitalist society. In either scenario, the bulk of the population is more or less akin to a mob, who would be best off taking orders or cues from those above them. The only question is from whom.

Prior to the twentieth century the class basis of societies was dealt with candidly, and the need to "keep the rabble in line" was understood to be a major concern of politics. By the late nineteenth century, with the rise of mass mobilization, such candor disappeared. As Eric Hobsbawm notes regarding the European upper class's concerns about popular sovereignty, "the growing democratization made it impossible to debate them publicly with any degree of frankness."[15] In the United States, too, in the twentieth century such open contempt for the ability of the mass of humanity to govern itself remained — as in the seminal books and essays of Edward Bernays, Walter Lippmann, and Harold Lasswell — but it assumed new forms, subtle and less overt.[16] The rise of near universal adult suffrage made such outward displays of antidemocratic sentiment potentially counterproductive. What is important to note is that this strain of thinking, far from having disappeared, remains in the bedrock of U.S. political thinking: the liberal "pluralist" theories of U.S. democracy that have dominated in the second half of the twentieth century rest on arguably elitist foundations and posit a low level of popular political participation that is at odds with democratic theory.[17]

In the era of universal adult suffrage, however, the cold fist of class arrogance, hubris, and power was replaced by many new ideological developments, not the least of which was the art and science of "public relations." Public relations, Alex Carey observed, is all about protecting the wealthy and their corporations from the wrath of universal suffrage. It was and is about using surreptitious ideological warfare to discredit antibusiness ideas, to disrupt the possibility of informed public debate, and to glorify the market and the status quo. As Carey so aptly put it, PR is about helping to "tak[e] the risk out of democracy" for the wealthy few in societies with universal adult suffrage.[18] "Our society has grossly overbuilt its expectations of what can be achieved and provided," Philip Lesly, a leading U.S. PR figure wrote in 1974. "This is a consequence of the extremism of 'democracy' — never foreseen by the most visionary founders of our democratic society — that seeks to give a voice and power to everyone on every issue, regardless of his merit in serving society or ability."[19] As PR historian Stuart Ewen observed, Lesly argued "the task of public relations must be to curtail Americans' democratic expectations."[20] In fact, the idea of using disinformation techniques to undermine the ability of the great mass of people to effectively govern their lives first occurred to upper-class French thinkers in 1793, the very year that France became the first nation in history to grant — albeit briefly — universal adult male suffrage. As the notorious conservative Joseph de Maistre put it then, "Man's cradle must be surrounded by dogmas, and when his reason awakens, he must find all his opinions already made, at least those concerning his social behavior."[21]

Unlike their predecessors, contemporary upper classes and business loudly swear their allegiance to democracy — even to the idea of popular sovereignty — but in private do whatever they can to limit its actual viability. As Noam Chomsky has noted with considerable irony, when the mass of people became politically active in the 1960s in the United States and worldwide, some among the governing elite solemnly characterized this as posing a "crisis of democracy."[22]

So where do media fit into this struggle over what constitutes democracy, and to the relationship of social inequality to self-government? Smack dab in the middle. If democracy is genuinely committed to letting citizens have equal influence over political affairs, it is crucial that all citizens have access to a wide range of well-formulated political positions on the core issues of the day, as well as a rigorous accounting of the activities of the political and economic powers that be and the powers that want to be. Unless communication and information are biased toward equality, they tend to enhance social inequality, whether the society happens to be democratic or otherwise. In densely populated and complex societies, this means — if the governing process is predicated upon having an informed citizenry — that the media perform a crucial function. While growing from the merest of existences in democratic Athens to a vital role in the era of democratic revolutions in the late eighteenth and nineteenth centuries, it is only in the twentieth century that media have assumed an absolutely central role in the political and cultural realms. Whereas the media were rightly understood as a "dependent" variable in classical political theory and analysis in the past, today the media seem a force to be reckoned with in their own right. Moreover, if the emergence of universal adult suffrage has demanded more subtle forms of public opinion management, the media are also the central institutions in that regard. In sum, the media have become an increasingly important battleground for political debate and culture.

The political left, as I noted above, has been the historic agency which has worked to advance the cause of democracy and democratic values against the needs of property and the wealthy. It was the left that has always led in the struggle for universal suffrage. Indeed, the commitment to popular rule is its defining characteristic. Without a left political movement, there is nobody else organized or commissioned to engage in such a struggle. That explains why the political left is feared by the powerful everywhere, and why U.S. history is chock full of organized campaigns by the government to crush the left.[23] This is one reason that the left has never been especially strong in the United States — and it is arguably weaker today than at any other time in the century. To some extent the weakness of the left both explains and is explained by the near complete domination of U.S. life by corporate and commercial interests.

Although the left is ultimately committed to establishing a full and vibrant political democracy with liberty and justice for all, that does not mean that all who are on the left or all left movements are without flaws or are even democratic. The left is a heterogeneous mass of variant ideas and people, ranging from social democrats to Marxists to anarchists. For a good portion of the twentieth century some — perhaps not much, but still too much — of the U.S. left was captivated by the one-party state model of the communist "people's democracies," where there was little or no democracy for most people. Conservatives argue that all left movements by definition must lead to totalitarian outcomes; hence any efforts to challenge capitalism are inherently antidemocratic. I believe this reduces complex historical phenomena to little more than self-serving public relations slogans meant to close off debate and study rather than to encourage it. But it is true that there has been a troubling antidemocratic tendency in too much of the left — a tendency which principled people on the left are devoted to examining, reducing, and eliminating. In the larger scheme of things, we have to hope that the Stalinist era will no more represent the full range or logical trajectory of socialism than the Spanish Inquisition represents the essence of Christianity. And the history of the left is replete with principled democrats leading campaigns and struggles on behalf of the working class, the oppressed, the dispossessed, and indeed the interests of all who favor social justice and democracy.

I would even go so far as to say that if we abandon the hope for a democratic left, we are to some extent abandoning our hopes for democracy. In the final analysis, for democracy to be viable, it must extend to cover the most important economic decisions: socialism may be the logical full development of democratic principle. Even if one is skeptical of the possibility of socialism — a thoroughly understandable position — it must be conceded that capitalism is at its most humane and democratic when there is a socialist left challenging corporate dominance.[24] We can see all around us what the caliber of capitalist democracy entails when business and the upper classes are left to their own devices. It is a formal democracy at best where the vast majority of important decisions are made by the few for the few, both in the corporate world and in the state sector. It is a dead-end street for humanity.

For more than two hundred years, the left has been (and still is) closely interlinked with the labor movement. Labor and the left are not synonymous, and on certain issues there are sometimes conflicts between the two; but in most important respects the two are joined at the hip. Labor without a strong political left will invariably founder, just as it is impossible to conceive of a strong left without labor's playing a cornerstone role. Labor is the only institution that deals directly with corporate power as an adversary on a daily basis. It is the only institution with the resources to coordinate a serious challenge to corporate power. But labor, no matter how well organized, has never been sufficient to comprise the left in the past, nor is it sufficient today. The U.S. left can and must include feminist, environmental, civil rights, religious, and similar dissenting groups that may or may not be linked to labor. A successful left requires a broad democratic vision that is appealing to the great bulk of the population as well as to the social organizations and movements that represent the interests of all of the left's constituencies. If one defines the left as being primarily about democracy, as I do, then it is a movement that should have appeal across broad sections of what is called the middle class, and perhaps even the upper middle class. It is worth noting that in the Progressive Era, for example, some elements of the U.S. middle class were drawn to left ideas because they saw them as addressing the problem of maintaining viable participatory democracy in the face of highly concentrated and unaccountable corporate power.[25]

One might argue that never has the need for an organized left been more pressing in the United States than it is today. "Nowhere else in the world," Philip Green writes, "is there to be found such a gap, an immense gap, between the rhetoric of equality on one hand and the actual substance of inequality on the other."[26] There exists some encouraging left political activity, especially on the local level, at the end of the twentieth century, but it is too early to see if this will amount to anything of substance. Perhaps most exciting, that element of the organized left that had become enthralled with one-party states and repressive "people's democracies" has all but disappeared. The left is returning to its historic mission of being the avatar of genuine democracy in the teeth of a class-dominated, business-oriented society. It is the dedicated opponent of inequality, democracy's invariable cancer. This means working for electoral laws like proportional representation that encourage an informed, participating citizenry and for publicly subsidized electoral campaigns that take the overt stench of wealth out of the political process. But this struggle to reduce inequality and to strengthen democracy will be incomplete for any prospective U.S. left without a vision of a more democratic media system, a program for media reform, and a strategic plan to organize around the issue.

The Left and Media Heretofore

Historically, labor and the left have understood the importance of having their own media to communicate with members and potential members. There was not a great deal written on the role of media, nor were there major debates on the matter; it was generally taken for granted as a key area of development for labor and the left. Indeed, one can almost date the origins of any specific organized left party or labor organization to when it developed the wherewithal to produce its own media. Some of the more successful and aggressive unions and political parties had extensive media outlets. In the early 1900s, Socialist party members and supporters published some 325 English and foreign language daily, weekly, and monthly newspapers and magazines. Most of these were privately owned or were the publications of one or another of the five thousand Socialist party locals. They reached a total of more than two million subscribers. Similarly, from the late nineteenth century on, just about every labor union had its own newspaper. (Even as recently as the 1940s, there were eight hundred U.S. labor newspapers reaching twenty to thirty million people per week.)[27] It was the aim of many of these movements to provide a near complete working-class civil society, replete with media, a political platform, and cultural and educational services. This sentiment continued into the twentieth century, to varying degrees around the world, but of late it has diminished as a result of an increasingly powerful, pervasive, and commercialized media and culture. Today, working-class people get the lion's share of their news and entertainment from the commercial media, and labor and left media are generally at the margins.

So it was in the twentieth century that issues of media control and ownership became truly political matters in the fullest sense. The response from labor and the left to the commercialization of media and the marginalization of labor or pro-working-class media has taken many forms. In the first two decades of this century, progressives and socialists worked to establish municipally owned newspapers and telephone systems.[28] In Hollywood, there was a strong socialist and pro-working-class component prior to the 1920s that only fell after a drawn-out fight with the emerging studio system.[29] Labor and the left were also active in the unsuccessful campaign in the 1930s to establish a public service broadcasting system, and to keep radio and television from falling into unaccountable corporate hands with support generated through advertising.[30] And aside from organized political activism, at an intellectual level, left critics have tended to regard the rise of the corporate media system as quite detrimental to the interests of the dispossessed and the prospects for participatory democracy. But with the demise of organized reform campaigns, this criticism has declined.

Some of the most aggressive left and labor movements have had aggressive media platforms, especially in the first half of the twentieth century. The Congress of Industrial Organizations (CIO) highlighted an explicit hostility to capitalist media in the 1930s and 1940s. It made the creation of labor and public service media a high priority, explaining that the labor movement could not thrive if the press remained in the hands of capital.[31] Even the more conservative American Federation of Labor's (AFL) Chicago chapter established a radio station explicitly to have a radical pro-working-class broadcasting network.[32] In a broader sense, media organizing was part and parcel of establishing a viable popular "cultural front," as Michael Denning terms the surge in pro-working-class and democratic culture in the 1930s and 1940s.[33] What is crucial to understand is that labor and the left did not abandon organizing around structural media issues because they became newly satisfied with the status quo and came to regard the matter as unimportant. To the contrary, labor and the left media activities were crushed in the 1930s by corporate interests, making the notion of challenging them any further seem politically untenable. And then, with the smashing of the militant left in the 1940s, organized labor's interest in battling commercial and corporate media interests collapsed altogether, and the corporate media power became ever more entrenched. The "cultural front" was crushed as well, together with a left alternative vision for democratizing the United States.

In sum, the decline of labor's interest in media activism in the postwar years can be traced to the following: the conservatism of labor; the decline of the left with a broad social democratic notion of democracy; and the sheer economic, political, and ideological power of the corporate media, which made their dominance seemingly unchallengeable and acceptance of the commercial media system seem politically neutral, relatively benign, and not a necessary hindrance to labor. (The latter is predicated on the idea that "professionalism" would protect the public from the class bias of owners and advertisers.) Finally, labor has dismissed the media as unimportant in any meaningful sense — meaning that the "real action" for labor and social change in general lay elsewhere. By this reasoning, if labor got its act together elsewhere, media would fall in line; if it did not, that would be no big deal. As a result, in the United States at least, media reform became the province of do-gooder middle-class liberals who lacked any popular support and had no ambition to generate it. Accordingly, it has gone nowhere and accomplished next to nothing. I discussed the severe limitations of this recent "inside-the-beltway" media reform movement in chapter 1.

There are signs that organized labor's fifty-year-old iceberg concerning media reform is beginning to thaw. Under John Sweeney, the AFL-CIO has placed greater emphasis on public outreach and political organizing, so dealing with the corporate media system becomes an explicit concern. There is an increasing recognition that the existing corporate commercial media system is a huge barrier to labor's advance, and even a factor in labor's long-term decline. Yet this sentiment remains largely inchoate. At the 1997 AFL-CIO annual convention, perhaps the most political and vibrant meeting in that organization's history, the issue of media was not even mentioned in passing. The AFL-CIO's initial foray into media activism under Sweeney has been the half-baked idea of spending a small fortune on TV ads to be aired on commercial stations and to hire PR firms to attempt to massage the press.[34] The most encouraging developments have come from the United Auto Workers (UAW), which recently made a major investment in the United Broadcasting Network, a 100-station radio operation. This is a page out of the UAW's (failed) 1940s strategy to establish a network of labor radio stations across the U.S. to combat the antilabor bias of the commercial radio broadcasters of that era. Yet aside from the UAW, the structural barriers to a democratic or prolabor media remain unaddressed by labor. And, aside from establishing a labor radio network, nobody in labor is aggressively organizing on media policy issues, either in Washington or at the local level.

There remains considerable disinterest in (or opposition to) the idea of organizing for structural media reform across the democratic left in the United States. Two of the three new left electoral parties — the Labor Party, and the New Party — avoid any mention of media in their core platforms.[35] Some chapters of the Green Party have made an issue of media ownership and control, perhaps influenced by Ralph Nader's persistent call for stricter control over the publicly owned airwaves; but these are token gestures at best. The Progressive caucus of the U.S. Congress has shown slight interest in the matter; its most outspoken advocate seems to be Representative Bernie Sanders (Ind., Vt.).[36] "This is an issue that is absolutely vital to democracy, and that only the left can address. The New Party, the Green Party, the Labor Party, progressive Democrats should be all over this issue," says Sanders. "But, for most of the left, it's not even on the agenda." Sanders, arguably the U.S. socialist with the greatest success at winning statewide elections in fifty years, is unequivocal about the importance of media reform: "The challenge of our time is to make media relevant for a vibrant democracy. This issue is absolutely vital to rebuilding democracy in America and to reasserting the voice of democracy on a global scale."[37]

To a large extent, this absence of informed radical media politics reflects the power of the U.S. media corporations to control and dominate not only mainstream debate of media issues but also debate on the left. After all, why pick a fight with these guys when the chances for success seem so slim, and when there seems to be little vocal public recognition of structural media issues and/or opposition to the status quo? The corporate media may well be the most powerful adversary in the ranks of capital. They are in the enviable position of owning the very media that would provide any coverage of media politics to the general public. In general, that means that the news media avoid any discussion of media structure, leaving analysis of media ownership and advertising to the business pages and the trade press, where they are covered as issues that concern investors, not workers, consumers, or citizens. If it is not a "no lose" situation, it is certainly one where the corporate media enjoy a favorably sloped playing field.[38]

This may explain why so many of the most insightful media critics have spent little of their time working on media reform: it seemed so remote a possibility that it simply did not appear on the radar. And this is not only the case in the United States. Jürgen Habermas, one of the most influential critics of commercial media of the twentieth century, provided a devastating critique of the limitations of the corporate media for democracy in a 1998 interview. When asked how the role of the media might be redefined, he replied: "That is a very good question, for which I have no immediate answer. I have not thought enough about the issue."[39]

But the dominant position of the U.S. left toward media reform — to the extent one can generalize — is unsympathetic, to the point that it states that organizing around media reform is a waste of time. This position is advanced, I regret to say, not by cliché-spouting chowderheads but rather by some of the U.S. left's most perceptive social critics. But it is also clearly not an issue that has received much sustained thought, and dismissals range from blanket condemnations of the corporate media system as irreformable to assertions that the media system is not that bad or that its influence is exaggerated. Along these lines, Doug Henwood stated, "the left whines too much about the big media. They're tools of capital — and capitalist enterprises in themselves — what else do you expect? We should support our own institutions instead."[40] In addition to suggesting that the system is immune to reform, Henwood also argues that the current corporate media scene is no worse than it was in years past, implying that if it was not a viable issue then it should not be one now. Media reform struggles, therefore, are dismissed as the logical province of middle-class liberals and single-issue knuckleheads with no broader political vision or platform, and therefore should be avoided by those on the left as a distraction from the real battles with the ruling class.[41]

This left position is correct on a couple of key points: media reform is no substitute for building a democratic left social movement or for building a strong labor movement. But the options are not simply to put all efforts and resources into building a media reform movement or to put no effort and resources into that area. It is not an either/or proposition. Virtually all the leading left media critics and activists incorporate media criticism and activism within a broader left political platform. Indeed, as the middle-class experience has shown, media reform independent of a broader political vision has zero chance of success, if one were even to ponder such a route. And it is also correct to argue that if we ever built a solid left or labor movement, we would have less reason to be concerned about how the corporate media system operates. But that begs the question of why we have been incapable of building even a tiny left in the United States for the past thirty years. The corporate media system is not the sole or even the primary reason for the lack of a left or a strong labor movement, but it is one of the significant reasons, and it contributes mightily to the ideological and political power of business.

The political "free market" neoliberal right understands the importance of media far better than the left and has devoted considerable resources to its campaigns to push the media to an explicitly procorporate, antilabor position. Billionaire right-wingers establish political media primarily to propagate probusiness politics and to push the range of political debate ever rightward.[42] Since the 1970s the political right has worked mightily and with considerable success to establish right-wing journalism and to push the mainstream to the right. As award-winning journalist Robert Parry concludes, after this two-decade assault, "the mainstream press is more acquiescent in following the conservative lead."[43] Indeed, the conservative jeremiad that journalists tended to be on the left or, at least, political liberals has been all but repudiated. A 1998 study showed that while leading Washington editors and reporters tend to be more "liberal" than most adult Americans on social issues, they tend to be more conservative and probusiness than the balance of the population on issues of taxation, trade policy, corporate power, and government spending priorities. In short, journalists' political views are similar to those of others of the same social class.[44] And, as discussed in chapter 1, whatever autonomy journalists had in the first place from owners, advertisers, and commercial pressures has been truncated in the past generation, to the hearty approval of conservative media critics.

The leading U.S. right-wing foundations have devoted nearly all their resources to pushing the media and educational systems to provide more explicitly probusiness positions.[45] These same "free market" foundations have also highlighted the need to reduce or eliminate the role of organized labor in society. It is also worth noting that the political right leads the fight against any and all forms of noncommercial and nonprofit media; and, failing that, leads the battle to see that public broadcasting stays within the same narrow ideological boundaries as the commercial media. As a result of this pressure, the Public Broadcasting Service refuses to permit labor to sponsor programs about workers but permits business to lavishly subsidize programs extolling free enterprise.[46]

In the United States, at least, the response of the progressive and mainstream foundations to this right-wing ideological assault has been tepid at best. These groups are uncomfortable about being "political," and most of their funds are reserved for examining disasters produced by the market, especially in an era of reduced public spending for the poor and working class.[47] Regrettably, organized labor, too, has been snoozing for the most part, providing little counter to this right-wing ideological class war. Liberal and progressive foundations play by the rules of the Marquis of Queensbury; the political right plays to win; labor and the left are hardly playing at all.

This uncontested war is all the more debilitating because the greatest single casualty of a concentrated corporate media system may well be coverage of the labor movement and political views that fall outside the range of debate countenanced by the business class. To some extent, this reflects the logical workings of a commercial marketplace that gives affluent consumers the material they want. The entire corporate media system is all about selling audiences to advertisers or media products to consumers; the logic is drenched in a commercialism that is scarcely compatible with a labor skepticism of the market and corporate power. And to some extent it also reflects the antilabor attitudes and activities of the largest media firms and their chief executives. Rupert Murdoch, for example, is a notorious proponent of neoliberalism whose antilabor record is part of his business credo. But Murdoch is no exception: he is merely more publicized than his peers. All the corporate media giants are the direct beneficiaries of probusiness policies, and all are going to be hostile to anything that stands in their way — left governments, organized labor, environmentalists, whatever. Disney is not alone in manufacturing much of its lucrative merchandise in the sweatshops of Haiti and other Third World locales.

At any rate, when one sees how labor and progressive social movements have fared in the U.S. media over the past fifty years, the importance of media reform becomes less abstract. In the 1930s and

1940s, for example, nearly every medium-to-large circulation daily newspaper had at least one full-time labor editor or beat reporter. When the Flint sitdown strikes established the UAW as a major trade union in the late 1930s, it was a front-page story across the nation. The coverage often was unsympathetic, but at least it was there. At the outer limits of what mainstream journalism could produce, consider the New York 1940s daily newspaper *PM,* which ran extensive coverage of strike activities (and civil rights activities) with careful presentations of the workers' positions. But then, *PM* did not accept advertising, which explains its content and, regrettably, perhaps its demise.[48] In the 1990s there are fewer than ten labor reporters on daily newspapers in the entire nation. (Conversely, there are seemingly thousands and thousands of business writers who daily fill the nation's papers with their stories.) In 1989, when the largest sitdown strike since Flint took place in Pittston, Virginia, the episode went virtually unreported in the U.S. media. When several leading U.S. trade unions formed a new Labor political party in 1996, that, too, was likewise almost completely unreported in the commercial media. Labor coverage has been reduced to rare coverage of strikes — usually in the context of how the strikers are threatening violence or creating a burden for the people in their communities. If one read only the commercial media, it would be difficult to determine what on earth good was served by having labor unions at all.

I do not mean to suggest that corporate media hostility to labor is swallowed hook, line, and sinker by the populace. The 1997 Teamster strike against UPS elicited the usual right-wing hysteria about labor, and the press was far from sympathetic to the strikers; yet overall there was a remarkable amount of public support for the strikers. The antilabor propaganda must at some point bump up against reality: a world where corporate power has run amuck and the exploitation of working-class people is on the rise. But imagine: what if there were an informed labor or left presence in the media to develop these sentiments and this line of analysis? The corporate media system has a strong internal bias toward reflecting elite opinion; hence the so-called dominant "liberal" voices in the United States — the *New York Times* and the *Washington Post* — are stridently procapitalist and were among the leading media to favor passage of GATT and NAFTA. When, in 1997, labor led the fight to defeat the law before Congress that would permit the "fast-tracking" of trade agreements, thereby making them largely unaccountable to popular deliberation, the *Times* and the *Post* — along with virtually the entirety of the corporate media — barely concealed their contempt for labor's intrusion into the policy-making process.[49] And these are the media that, in mainstream mythology, are supposed to be the most sympathetic to the interests of working people.

This does not mean that corporate media are incapable of improving their labor coverage and their coverage of progressive politics. If and when a viable left and labor movement emerges in the United States, it will likely create space within the mainstream for some dissident views to exist, perhaps to prosper and multiply. And in other nations, where the left and labor are more strongly entrenched, the corporate media may give them more credence. But the historical and international track record are also clear: when push comes to shove, the commercial media will support the system in which they prosper from political attack, regardless of the "facts."[50] And the overarching trajectory of the corporate media system is decidedly antilabor. It produces a market journalism in which the fact that 350 billionaires have as much wealth as one-half the world's population is accepted as a given, and no particular problem, whereas even modest efforts to interfere with business control of society are regarded with the greatest possible skepticism, if not outright hostility.

In short, any effort to reform the balance of class power in the United States, or any other effort for that matter, has to deal directly with corporate media power. Nor is this merely an ideological issue, as may have been the case in generations past. Today the largest communication firms rank among the most important firms in the global capitalist economy; media, advertising, and communication increasingly are at the very center of the capital accumulation process and the global market economy. To leave the communication sector untouched, while elsewhere labor and the left challenge the prerogatives of capital — as any left or labor movement invariably must do — is absurd. There can and should be plenty of left debate over the proper strategy and tactics for media politics, and there should be plenty of debate concerning media reform proposals. But the left needs to accept the necessity of media reform and move forward.

Moreover, making media reform a component of the left agenda has many positive benefits. It is an area that can generate much popular support, and from people who are not necessarily identified with the left. Social conservatives are concerned about the commercial carpetbombing of our culture, and some free market conservatives may see media as an area where the market is producing disastrous "externalities." Although the issue receives scant attention in the media, there is evidence of growing public dissatisfaction with the hypercommercialized media system. In few areas are the conflicts between corporate rule and the needs of a democracy more apparent. The left can use media as an educational tool to explain the flaws in the existing social order and to present its vision of what a more democratic society would look like. And labor and the left can use media reform as an issue that can unite elements of the citizenry, like labor, environmentalists, feminists, civil rights activists, journalists, artists, educators, librarians, parents, and many others who would benefit from major media reform. Nor is this really much of an option. If labor and the left do not step forward with a vision and program for media reform, the dissident critique of media will be provided solely by the far right, with its bogus analysis and censorial solutions. Under no circumstances is that an acceptable situation.

The Struggle for Democratic Media

So what should the left do to address the commercial media system? First and foremost, it has to put media reform on its agenda, devote resources to the matter, and work to get media reform on the broader political agenda. The core principle is that control over communication has to be taken away from Wall Street and Madison Avenue and put in the hands of citizens, journalists, and others whose concerns are not limited to the bottom line. There are numerous ways to accomplish this goal, and it is a subject we need to devote energy toward exploring.

Although the U.S. left and organized labor have been slow to take on media reform, there is no shortage of non-right-wing media activism. Some of the surging 1990s media activism is ill-conceived and suffers from the lack of an overarching democratic critique and vision. Hence, among some foundations, academics, and journalists there is a movement for "civic" or "public" journalism. This is a well-intentioned attempt to reduce the sensationalism and blatant political manipulation of mainstream journalism.[51] Unfortunately the movement completely ignores the structural factors of ownership and advertising that have led to the attack on journalism, working hand in hand with the very corporate chieftains who benefit by the status quo. Public journalism, not surprisingly, is averse to "ideological" approaches to the news — that is, understanding and presenting political conflict in class terms — and it therefore works toward the sort of boringly "balanced" and antiseptic newsfare that could put the entire nation into a deep slumber. By claiming they want to give readers news they think is important to their lives, advocates of public journalism may in fact be assisting in the process of converting journalism into the type of consumer news and information that delights the advertising community. Such is the logic of a commercialized and depoliticized society. The real course of action for those who wish to increase the integrity of commercial journalism is to increase the power to journalists to control the news — and that is accomplished by establishing strong, progressive unions. It is also something that foundations and corporate media executives have shown little interest in pursuing.

Another burgeoning area of interest is the media literacy movement. The idea here is to educate people to be skeptical and knowledgeable users of the media. It is fueled by the large public discontent with the hypercommercialism, banality, and asininity of corporate media fare, as well as the commercialization of education and every possible facet of social life. Media literacy has considerable potential so long as it involves explaining how the media system actually works and does not posit that the existing system is by definition good, democratic, and immutable. But the media literacy movement has a highly visible wing that accepts money from corporate media and advertisers. This version of media literacy implicitly buys into the corporate line that the commercial media "give the people what they want."[52] So the media literacy crowd's job is to train people to demand better fare from willing and obedient corporate media servants. Like public journalism, this attracts foundation support because it is noncontroversial. But unless media literacy takes a more structural approach to analysis and solutions, it may simply help to prop up the existing system.[53] "Hey, don't blame *us* for the lousy stuff we provide," the corporate media giants will say. "We even bankrolled media literacy to train people to demand higher quality fare. The morons simply demanded more of what we are already doing."

But some of the other new elements of media activism are more promising. Fairness and Accuracy in Reporting (FAIR), a media watchdog group launched in the 1980s, provides outstanding analysis of media trends through published reports and its magazine *Extra!* FAIR's work helps both those who wish to improve the quality of existing journalism and those who seek structural change. The Cultural Environment Movement (CEM), founded in the middle 1990s, attempts to draw all sorts of nonprofit and public-interest groups into the campaign for media reform. Like FAIR, it works for improvement within the status quo as well as for broader structural reform. (In a related development, Ralph Nader organized a group called Consumer Alert in 1998, with the aim of starting "a national debate on excessive consumerism.")[54] In 1998 the Rainbow/PUSH Coalition formally made media reform one of its two main organizing issues, publishing a twelve-point plan to democratize the U.S. system.[55] Local media alliances have been established in numerous North American cities in the middle and late 1990s, to set up alternative media and to watchdog the local commercial media. These local groups have shown some potential to draw ordinary citizens into media politics by targeting issues like violence-obsessed local TV news, the newspaper "redlining" of poor neighborhoods, the proliferation of alcohol and cigarette billboards in poor and working-class neighborhoods, and the commercialization of education. Even culture "jamming" has caught on, as activists deface, with pointed and often hilarious messages, the advertising on billboards that mushroom across the urban landscape.[56] Likewise, microradio broadcasting — unlicensed low-power noncommercial broadcasting conducted on open slots in the radio spectrum — has become a notable enterprise nationally in the late 1990s. It offers poor, dispossessed, and marginalized voices an unprecedented opportunity to be heard.[57]

That all of this activity has blossomed in the current political environment suggests there may be a wellspring for further media organizing. One thing it lacks to succeed are the resources to fully exploit this opportunity. This is the province of organized labor and the philanthropic community. It also lacks an overarching vision of where media reform fits into a broader movement for social justice and democracy. Without such a contextualization, the prospects for exacting fundamental media reform in the United States are next to nil. This is the province of the political left.

There are two general areas — and they sometimes overlap — for media activism. In each, a nascent left, organized labor, and the progressive foundations must become active. First, labor (and the left) can use its own efforts to create better noncommercial media and to generate better results from commercial media independent of changes in government policies and the corporate media system. Some labor unions and federations, for example, have begun to encourage the production of labor video documentaries.[58] Now all of labor needs not only to support aggressively newspapers, magazines, broadcast stations, and websites; it also needs to give money and resources to community and nonprofit media without direct labor affiliation. This is a crucial point: labor needs to be willing to grant considerable editorial leeway to the media it subsidizes. Unless it does so, the media will tend to be timid, overly concerned with pleasing labor's political hierarchy, and unlikely to produce a medium with vitality and broad appeal. The same holds true for progressive philanthropies: alternative media cannot be micromanaged by funders and at the same time develop an audience. (This is something funders on the right understand, and it has contributed to the success of their media program.)

Unlike the right, labor and the left can never consider funding alternatives or independent media a satisfactory media program in and of itself. The agenda and activities of the right mesh well with the corporate control of the media, and right media figures move comfortably at all echelons of the corporate media system. A well-established left independent media can and will influence mainstream media in a positive manner, but there can never be a marriage. The upper limit of this approach is to establish a strong left niche on the margins — but it will always be on the margins. This point holds true for the Internet as well. Merely establishing left websites only dresses up the left's marginality; it does not change it. As I discuss in chapter 3, the Internet has been incorporated for the most part into the corporate media and communication systems. Technology alone cannot undermine the media system.

In addition, labor and the left need to take another page from the political right, which manipulates traditional U.S. journalism practices as masterfully as a surgeon does a scalpel. Like the right, labor and the progressive philanthropic community need to support think tanks of experts who can provide labor and left perspectives on social issues for commercial and noncommercial journalists alike. These think tanks can also monitor the massive right-wing campaigns to shape news coverage. The recently formed Institute for Public Accuracy, under the direction of Norman Solomon, is beginning to provide this service. These activities will never suffice, if only because the corporate sector and the media giants have greater resources. But they can help vitalize a noncommercial media sector on the margins and guarantee the best possible performance by the commercial system. In addition — to follow up on a point made regarding civic journalism — tremendous effort must go into strengthening and expanding media workers' unions. The assault on journalists' unions in the United States has been an important factor in the decline of the quality of journalism. Ideally, journalists' and media workers' unions should negotiate for as much control as possible of the editorial and creative process. We need to work to detach the control of capital over our journalism and culture, without substituting a deadening bureaucratic control.

Structural Media Reform

But the most important area of political activity ultimately is to organize to change government media policies. The core problem with the U.S. media system relates to how it is owned, its profit motivation, and its reliance upon advertising. Moreover, as chapters 1–3 discuss, the media system is the direct result of explicit government subsidies and policies, though that point is rarely acknowledged. Any attempt to affect U.S. media that does not address structural issues directly through government policies will prove inconsequential in the long run. Corporate media power must be confronted directly, and reduced.

That the key to understanding how the media system works is looking at its structure is not a radical notion per se. Mainstream assessments of media often acknowledge that the nature of ownership and subsidy are crucial to understanding the way media perform. And mainstream observers will even concede that the current system of concentrated, conglomerated ownership is generating dubious results. But mainstream observers, wed to the rule of business as the best of all possible worlds, are incapable of addressing the problem in any meaningful way whatsoever. The *New York Times,* for example, says any change in the system is virtually impossible, despite its many flaws: "The road away from conglomeration will be a hard one to find."[59] And *Business Week,* after a long piece detailing how closely knit through joint ventures the six largest media firms are, and how they dominate the U.S. media landscape, concluded that there was no reason to worry: the six CEOs are all such competitive people and dislike each other so much that their antipathy will protect the public interest.[60]

This is the great advantage of the left: it can provide real solutions to the problem of the media. But providing real solutions is no simple matter. There are many ways to reach the objective of a more diverse and competitive commercial system with a significant — preferably a dominant — nonprofit and noncommercial sector. Many left media critics present superb analyses of the weaknesses of the status quo but are reticent about providing concrete solutions; these will develop, they argue, over the course of political struggle and debate. But by the end of the 1990s we have reached the point where, in order to proceed, media reformers have to provide concrete examples of an alternative; otherwise, many people will not have any idea of what, exactly, they are fighting for. I therefore offer forthwith four general proposals for media reform. These are by no means explicit blueprints; they are meant to open discussion in a fruitful manner, not close it off. If and when a significant element of U.S. society began to engage with the idea of recasting the media system, these ideas probably would be readily improved upon.

1. *Building nonprofit and noncommercial media.* The starting point for media reform is to build up a viable nonprofit, noncommercial media sector. Such a sector currently exists in the United States, and produces much of value, but it is woefully small and underfunded. As I mentioned above, it can be developed independent of changes in laws and regulations. For example, foundations and organized labor could and should contribute far more to nonprofit media. Sympathetic government policies could also help foster a nonprofit media sector, and media reform must work to this end. Government subsidies and policies have played a key role in establishing lucrative commercial media. Since the nineteenth century, for example, the United States has permitted publications to have quality, high-speed mailing at relatively low rates. We could extend this principle to lower mailing costs for a wider range of nonprofit media, and/or for media that have little or no advertising. Likewise we could permit all sorts of tax deductions or write-offs for contributions to nonprofit media. Dean Baker of the Economic Policy Institute has developed a plan for permitting taxpayers to take up to $150 off of their federal tax bill, if they donate the money to a nonprofit news medium. This would per-

mit almost all Americans to contribute to nonprofit media — not just those with significant disposable incomes — and help create an alternative to the dominant Wall Street/Madison Avenue system.

2. *Public broadcasting.* Establishing a strong nonprofit sector to complement the commercial giants is not enough. The costs of creating a more democratic media system simply are too high. Therefore, it is important to establish and maintain a noncommercial, nonprofit, public radio and television system. The system should include national networks, local stations, public access television, and independent community radio stations. Every community should also have a stratum of low-power television and micropower radio stations.

In chapter 5 I discuss the marked limitations of U.S. public broadcasting, historically and to this day. It is really a system of nonprofit commercial broadcasting, serving a sliver of the population. What we need is a system of real public broadcasting, with no advertising, that accepts no grants from corporations or private bodies and that serves the entire population, not merely those who are disaffected from the dominant commercial system and have disposable income to contribute during pledge drives. Two hurdles stand in the way of such a system. The first is organizational: How can public broadcasting be structured to make the system accountable and prevent a bureaucracy impervious to popular tastes and wishes, but to give the public broadcasters enough institutional strength to prevent implicit and explicit attempts at censorship by political authorities? The second is fiscal: Where will the funds come from to pay for a viable public broadcasting service? At present, the federal government provides $260 million annually. The public system I envision — which would put per capita U.S. spending in a league with, for example, Britain and Japan — may well cost $5–10 billion annually.

There is no one way to resolve the organizational problem, and perhaps an ideal solution can never be found. But there are better ways, as any comparative survey indicates. One key element in preventing bureaucratic ossification or government meddling will be to establish a pluralistic system, with national networks, local stations, community and public access stations, all controlled independently. In some cases direct election of officers by the public and also by public broadcasting employees may be appropriate, whereas in other cases appointment by elected political bodies may be preferable.

As for funding, I have no qualms about drawing the funds for fully public radio and television from general revenues. We subsidize education, but the government now subsidizes media only on behalf of owners. Bona fide nonprofit and noncommercial broadcasting should be a cornerstone of a modern democracy. This is a crucial point: all current discussion of U.S. public broadcasting is premised on the notion that any proposal must come up with the explicit source of any additional public funds that go to the public system. Such a demand is politically loaded to derail the possibility of real public broadcasting; why is this demand never made when federal moneys go to military spending, corporate bailouts, or to the IMF? We should seek to have a stable source of funding that cannot be subject to political manipulation by politicians with little direct interest in the integrity of the system.

A powerful public radio and television system could have a profound effect on our entire media culture. It could lead the way in providing the type of public service journalism that commercialism is now killing off. This might in turn give commercial journalists the impetus they need to pursue the hard stories they now avoid. It could have a similar effect upon our entertainment culture. A viable public TV system could support a legion of small independent filmmakers. It could do wonders for reducing the reliance of our political campaigns upon expensive commercial advertising. It is essential to ensuring the diversity and deliberation that lie at the heart of a democratic public sphere.

3. *Regulation.* A third main plank is to increase regulation of commercial broadcasting in the public interest. Media reformers have long been active in this arena, if only because the public ownership of the airwaves gives the public, through the FCC, a clear legal right to negotiate terms with the chosen few who get broadcast licenses. Still, even this form of media activism has been negligible, and broadcast regulation has been largely toothless, with the desires of powerful corporations and advertisers rarely challenged.

Experience in the United States and abroad indicates that if commercial broadcasters are not held to high public service standards, they will generate the easiest profits by resorting to the crassest commercialism and overwhelm the balance of the media culture. Moreover, standard-setting will not work if commercial broadcasters are permitted to "buy" their way out of public service obligations; the record shows that they will eventually find a way to reduce or eliminate these payments. (It is worth noting that most current proposals to maintain federal funding for public broadcasting — usually not much above the current ridiculously low amounts — include provisions to let the commercial broadcasters buy their way out of public service programming, passing these duties on to the public broadcasters.)[61] Hence the most successful mixed system of commercial and public broadcasting in the world was found in Britain from the 1950s to the 1980s. It was successful because the commercial broadcasters were held to public service standards comparable to those employed by the BBC; some scholars even argue that the commercial system sometimes outperformed the BBC as a public service broadcaster. The British scheme worked because commercial broadcasters were threatened with loss of their licenses if they did not meet public service standards. (Regrettably, Thatcherism, with its mantra that the market can do no wrong, has undermined the integrity of the British broadcasting system.)

The U.S. experience also makes clear one other point: the commercial broadcasters will do everything in their power to avoid public interest obligations if they in any way detract from the bottom line; that is, if they in any way might be effective. To make the commercial broadcasters comply with public service obligations would require little short of a permanent war with one of the strongest lobbies in Washington, D.C., hardly a desirable proposition. The solution is clear: commercial broadcasters should receive their licenses for only eighteen to twenty hours per day. The remaining four to six hours should be taken out of their control and dedicated to public service. Some might complain that it would be unfair to reduce the time of the commercial broadcasters in such a manner, as they have purchased these stations thinking that they would get access to the full day. In my view, that reasoning is wrong. This is public property, and the public has the right to set the terms of its use. Firms that purchased TV and radio stations were assuming that the broadcast lobby would be able to continue to run roughshod over Congress and the FCC. That was the risk they were taking when they made these investments; there was never any formal agreement that these broadcast licenses were to be theirs permanently on terms of their choosing.

The four to six hours of "liberated" time on the broadcast stations should be applied to two specific areas: children's programming and news/public affairs shows. In each case, we must devise systems so that control over these time blocks is in the hands of artists and educators for children's programs, and in the hands of journalists for news and public affairs. This will not be an easy task, but if we study the matter we can certainly devise adequate systems. At any rate, the result would have to be far superior to the commercial carpet-bombing of children and the junk news that currently dominates the airwaves. A core problem with this recommendation is that it only applies to over-the-air broadcasters and not to cable channels. Insofar as cable television increasingly provides much of what is aimed at children and an increasing portion of the national news, regulating commercial broadcasting in these areas might not have the full effect desired. We will need to think creatively about ways to get public service commitments from the cable channels. But short of that, there will still be value in having a solid block of ad-free children's and news programming in the heart of the schedule. In particular, local TV news remains almost entirely on over-the-air channels, so putting this on noncommercial terms would definitely improve news coverage in local communities. In view of the pathetic state of local commercial television news at present, that, alone, makes this a worthwhile proposition.

As for funding this public service programming, I subscribe to the principle that it should be subsidized by the beneficiaries of commercialized communication. This principle might be applied in several ways. We could charge commercial broadcasters rent on the electromagnetic spectrum they use to broadcast. Or we could charge them a tax whenever they sell the stations for a profit. In combination these mechanisms could generate well over a billion dollars annually. Or we could tax advertising. Some $212 billion will be spent to advertise in the United States in 1999. A very small sales tax on this or even only on that portion that goes to radio and television could generate several billion dollars. It might also have the salutary effect of slowing down the commercial onslaught on American social life. And it does not seem like too much to ask of advertisers who are permitted otherwise to marinate most of the publicly owned spectrum in commercialism.

In November 1998 the FCC provided a creative idea for solving this problem fairly, albeit unwittingly. It decided to levy a 5 percent fee on all commercial revenues broadcasters generate from the use of their licensed frequencies aside from traditional broadcasting. (In the digital era, broadcasters have located many new revenue-generating uses of their spectrum.) Such charges are justified by the FCC because these are purely commercial activities, unlike traditional broadcasting, and therefore the public has a right to expect cash compensation. As I explained in chapters 1 and 3, the thinking goes that broadcasters do not have to pay for the spectrum they use for broadcasting because they compensate the public by doing all sorts of public interest broadcasting, that is, broadcasting material that would make no sense if they were strictly out to maximize profit. The absurdity of this rationale for broadcasters getting the spectrum for free is self-evident. In view of complete and utter lack of any semblance of public interest programming on commercial stations, it seems logical to extend this fee to all commercial broadcasting revenues. If we were to raise it to the 10 percent level recommended by the public advocacy group the Media Access Project, this would provide billions of dollars to subsidize noncommercial children's and news programming.[62]

What would be fair compensation for commercial broadcasters to pay for their use of the public spectrum? At a 1998 Gore Commission meeting, the National Association of Broadcasters asserted that commercial broadcasters provided $6.85 billion in public service annually. As I mentioned in chapter 3, the NAB claimed that this amount was sufficient to satisfy the broadcasters' public service obligations. Being conciliatory by nature, I am willing to accept the NAB's benchmark for public service. I think it is clear, however, that the NAB, if its figures are to be trusted, is not getting much bang for its public service dollar, based on the state of U.S. broadcasting in 1999. (Let's hope they use their money with greater effect in their other ventures.) Henceforth, let us set a fee structure on commercial broadcasters (through any of the ideas mentioned above) that will generate $6.85 billion annually in revenues in 1998 dollars. Then, in addition to four to six hours daily of ad-free time set aside for children's and news programming, this amount of money would provide, without question, resources to have the most extraordinary children's and news programming imaginable. This would be real public service, the likes of which Americans have never seen. And with this public interest program in place, the commercial broadcasters could cut out any pretense of caring about the public interest and use the other eighteen to twenty hours every day to do what they do best: make money.

Even if these changes cannot be made in U.S. broadcasting, there are two other measures that could be taken that would provide immediate value: require free time set aside for all candidates to discuss issues and prohibit all paid television political advertising. As I discussed in chapter 6, the exorbitant cost of these ads (not to mention their lame content) has virtually destroyed the integrity of electoral democracy here. Short of banning them, then perhaps a provision should be made that if a candidate purchases a TV ad, his or her opponents will all be entitled to free ads of the same length on the same station immediately following the paid ad. This would prevent rich candidates from buying elections. I suspect it would pretty much eliminate the practice altogether.

4. *Antitrust.* The fourth strategy for creating a more democratic media system is to break up the largest firms and establish more competitive markets, thus shifting some control from corporate suppliers to citizen consumers. Antitrust action was once applied with some frequency by the government, even enjoying a "golden age" of sorts from 1945 to the early 1970s. But the Reagan-Bush era targeted antitrust as something to be reduced, as part of its campaign to "get government off our backs." As a result, one expert observed in 1998 that "antitrust is sick and has been in retreat for over two decades."[63] Antitrust has enjoyed a very minor resurgence in the late 1990s, but even the best that antitrust enforcement can hope for today is to make monopolies into duopolies, or make duopolies into oligopolies of three or four firms. And that is quite rare indeed.[64] And, it is important to note, antitrust has yet to be employed to stop a major media deal. Indeed, the government has basically stood by as radio has concentrated almost overnight, as described in chapter 1.[65] To some extent, intervention on specific deals at this point would be impossible, even unfair. Why prevent current dealmakers from doing that which their competitors have already done?

It is ironic that applying antitrust effectively to media and communications would not require that we abandon the spirit and principles that led to its rise a century ago. On the contrary, it would mean that we *return* to them. Antitrust, as Eben Moglen has brilliantly written, grew out of a Jacksonian concern that concentrated wealth would lead to private power destroying democratic government. "The connection between antitrust and the defense of democracy is intimate and long-standing, but largely ignored. Our failure to remember the history has been convenient for magnates and multinationals," Moglen writes. "Contemporary academic writing about antitrust tends to ignore this aspect of our history, pretending that 'consumer welfare' — defined almost exclusively in terms of product price and quality — is the primary goal competition serves. The effect is to make antitrust law an administrative system for dealing with minor market failures, by preventing supermarket chains, toy megastores or office-supply retailers from gaining local leverage over prices. Thus reined in, antitrust is a subject for technicians. The public loses interest" in antitrust as a policy, quite unlike earlier years when it was a populist rallying issue. Moglen observes that the newfangled, technocratic notion of antitrust leads clearly to the conclusion that "antitrust has no appropriate application to the question of who owns our media of broadcast communication." In fact, as Moglen concludes, the corporate media system richly deserves antitrust attention if we hold to the spirit in which antitrust statutes were drafted and passed into law in the late nineteenth and early twentieth centuries.[66] The political power implied in the consolidation of media into a handful of corporate behemoths rivals that of the great trusts of the Gilded Age.

What is needed, then, is a new media antitrust statute, similar in tone to the seminal Clayton and Sherman Acts, that lays out the general values to be enforced by the Justice Department and the Federal Trade Commission. It would put an emphasis on valuing the importance of ideological diversity and noncommercial editorial content. The objective should be to break up such media conglomerates as Time Warner, News Corporation, and Disney, so that their book publishing, magazine publishing, TV show production, movie production, TV stations, TV networks, amusement parks, retail store chains, cable TV channels, cable TV systems, and so on all become independent firms. With reduced barriers to entry in these specific markets, new firms could join in. It could lead to the radical reconfiguration, for example, of radio broadcasting, to the point where stations might be locally owned and not part of massive chains.

The media giants claim that their market power and conglomeration make them more efficient and therefore able to provide a better product at lower prices to the consumer. There is not much evidence for these claims, though it is clear that market power and conglomeration make these firms vastly more profitable. Moreover, even if one accepts that antitrust would lead to a less efficient economic model, perhaps we should pay that price to establish a more open and competitive marketplace. In view of media's importance for democratic politics and culture, they should not be judged by purely commercial criteria.

Antitrust is the wild card in the media reform platform. It has tremendous appeal across the population and is usually the first idea citizens suggest when they are confronted with the current media scene. But it is unclear how antitrust legislation could be effectively implemented. What is necessary are genuine congressional hearings on the matter, fueled by the democratic impulse that spawned antitrust one hundred years ago. But even if antitrust can be made to work, the system would remain commercial, albeit more competitive. Such legislation would not, in other words, reduce the need for the first three proposals.

So how does the rise of the Internet alter my proposals for structural media reform? Very little. There are, of course, some specific policy reforms we should seek for the Internet: for example, guaranteeing universal public access at low rates, perhaps for free. But in general terms, we might do better to regard the Internet as the corporate media giants regard it: as part of the emerging media landscape, not its entirety. So when we create more and smaller media firms, when we create public and community radio and television networks and stations, when we create a strong public service component to commercial news and children's programming, when we use government policies to spawn a nonprofit media sector, all these efforts will have a tremendous effect on the Internet's development as a mass medium. Why? Because websites will not be worth much if they do not have the resources to provide a quality product. And all the new media that result from media reform will have websites as a mandatory aspect of their operations, much like the commercial media. By creating a vibrant and more democratic "traditional" media culture, we will go a long way toward creating a democratic cyberspace.

In addition, media activists and the left need to press for the repeal of the Telecommunications Act of 1996 and its replacement with a law that reflects not just the interests of Washington's corporate lobbying superstars but the informed consent of the bulk of the citizenry. We need to press for full and open public hearings on the future of electronic communication and the Internet. Digital communication presents many new and complex issues of unimaginable magnitude; society is best off if these decisions are made by as many people as possible in the light of day, not by commercial interests "self-regulating" themselves in near complete secrecy with a wink and a nod from the politicians they bankroll.

The aim of these combined measures is not to produce a media system that propagandizes for the left in the manner that the corporate media is biased toward capital and commercialism. The aim is to produce a media system that is fair and accurate, that scrupulously examines the activities of the powerful — including the left and the labor movement — and that provides a legitimate accounting of the diverse views and interests of society. It will be a system that will limit the capacity of the wealthy and powerful few to have high-quality information so they may rule the world while the bulk of the population is fed a diet of schlock. It will provide a culture based on artists' interactions with people and ideas, not based on their obeying orders from Madison Avenue. The only stated bias is a fervent commitment to democracy. There is no evidence that a corporate commercial system, even at its best, is capable of such a journalism and culture. And, it is worth noting, that even if all four of these proposals were enacted, the vast majority of media and entertainment would be provided by private firms in pursuit of profit with no more regulation of their editorial activities than they currently experience.

Lessons from Abroad

Some sense of how an emerging democratic left can employ media reform can be seen by looking abroad. As mentioned in chapter 2, many of the world's nations have seen their media systems reconfigured in the past decade, with the pronounced tendency toward integration into the global commercial media market. In many such nations, as in the United States, there are nascent grassroots media activist organizations struggling to promote noncommercial and nonprofit media. These are usually movements self-identified as being on the democratic left.[67] Media workers, too, are organizing for media reform. A strike of BBC workers in 1998, for example, listed "no privatization of resources" and "public service instead of commercialism" as two of its six demands.[68] But, most important, democratic left electoral parties are increasingly making the breakup of the corporate commercial media system and the establishment of a viable nonprofit media sector a main part of their platforms. The key is to present media reform as part of a broader package of democratic reforms addressing electoral systems, taxation, employment, education, health care, civil rights, and the environment. As important as media reform may seem, it is not a strong enough issue to build a mass movement around. But it has a necessary and fruitful role as part of a broad left agenda. And without a broad base of support, media reform cannot succeed.

In Canada, for example, labor has drawn together consumers and other citizens groups to oppose the plans of the corporate telecommunication giants.[69] Perhaps more striking, the New Democratic party more than doubled its number of parliamentary seats in that country's May 1997, elections. The NDP platform included calls for breaking up the Canadian corporate media chains and for expanding the Canadian Broadcasting Corporation, Canada's public service broadcaster. NDP managers considered the message so vital to the party's efforts to distinguish itself from other parties that, on the eve of a key debate, party leader Alexa McDonough took time from her preparations to participate in a demonstration protesting cutbacks at the CBC. In the words of NDP member of parliament Svend Robinson, who has made media issues a prime focus in his campaigns, "This is an issue that's emerging all over the world. It's a huge concern. People are genuinely alarmed that at the same time we're witnessing growing concentration of ownership of media we're also seeing massive cuts in publicly owned media. It's a double whammy," Robinson stated in a 1997 interview. "This neoliberal, right-wing takeover of the media is something that people are aware of, and they don't like it. But the old-line parties aren't willing to address the issue. This is what is going to distinguish new-line parties all over the world — a willingness to talk frankly about issues of media control and to propose an alternative to what's happening. It's inevitable. After you've had somebody say to you for the thousandth time, 'How come we never hear about these issues in the media,' you start to realize that the media itself is an issue."[70]

In Sweden, the national labor federation has led a national boycott of a TV station that refused to honor Swedish law and not air commercials to children.[71] In Sweden, also, the Left party, a socialist grouping that has filled the void created by the Swedish Social Democrats' move to the right, is sounding even more radical themes. The platform on which the Left party has emerged as one of Scandinavia's fastest growing political movements calls for abolishing all advertising on radio and television and for an aggressive program of subsidies to maintain a diverse range of viewpoints in the print media. Media reform is at the heart of the party's program, characterized in its preamble as being necessary to "strengthen and intensify democracy." In Sweden's 1998 national elections, the Left party doubled its vote from the preceding election, to 12 percent of the total.[72]

In New Zealand, Pam Corkery left her job as one of that nation's top broadcast journalists and won election to the parliament in 1996 on the ticket of the Alliance, a newly formed left-wing grouping that surprised observers with the strength of its showing. Corkery's issue, and a central theme in the Alliance's platform, was a call to roll back corporate control of the media and to beef up nonprofit, noncommercial broadcasting. After her election, she declared that the battle to reassert popular control over the media is, "at the very least, a human rights issue." The Alliance party has focused national attention on the demise of journalistic competition that followed the sale in 1995 of a publicly owned network of commercial radio stations to Tony O'Reilly, a former Heinz soup company executive who is rapidly building an international media conglomerate. O'Reilly already owns the largest newspaper in New Zealand, the *Auckland Herald,* and after he purchased the privatized stations he quickly moved to buy up the remaining major radio stations in key New Zealand markets. That move was followed by decisions to lay off staff, weaken competition between media outlets, and give notice that the O'Reilly stations were unlikely to continue purchasing news from Radio New Zealand. The Alliance has used its parliamentary position to spark a national debate about O'Reilly's actions in particular and about the wisdom of privatization in general. Working inside of parliament, the Alliance has raised fundamental questions about the danger of one man's controlling so much of a nation's media, and it has dogged O'Reilly's every move with calls for hearings, debates, and investigations. Outside parliament, the coalition has turned anger at O'Reilly's actions and at cuts in public broadcasting expenditures into an organizing tool, working with labor unions, native groups, environmentalists, and community activists to build a broad coalition of media-conscious activists.

In so doing, the coalition has raised profound questions about the wisdom of privatization of Television New Zealand, which remains publicly owned. So successful has the Alliance's campaign been, in fact, that the New Zealand Labour party, which for years had supported privatization, has indicated that it will oppose any further media privatization. But the Alliance is not satisfied; according to John Pagani, its media director, the Labour party "appears very reluctant to move on regulation of media organizations — particularly the issue of limiting foreign ownership or imposing cross-media ownership restrictions." The Alliance has no such reluctance. And, Pagani expects, the willingness of the coalition to raise issues of media monopoly and battle for a reversal of privatizations will continue to distinguish it from more cautious players — a distinction that, some political observers in New Zealand say, could eventually win it a defining role in the governance of the nation. As Pagani says, "Media issues, privatization issues, this is where you start to see real distinctions between the Alliance and other parties, and that distinction is what people are looking for."

These are not isolated developments. Although the new parties of the left are not reading off the same page as regards issues of media control and direction, there are remarkable parallels from country to country. In general, the key issues most everywhere for the left are similar to the proposals made above. They include:

- To protect and expand traditional public-service broadcasting, making it fully noncommercial and democratically accountable;
- To develop a distinct community and public access radio and television system that is thoroughly decentralized;
- To strengthen journalists' and media workers' trade unions, giving the members of these trade unions a greater role in determining editorial content;
- To hold commercial broadcasters to strict standards, such as prohibiting advertising directed at children;
- To limit the concentration of media ownership as much as possible;
- To reduce the sheer amount of advertising, through regulation and taxation;
- To subsidize film and cultural production eschewed by the market;
- To subsidize the existence of multiple newspapers and magazines to provide a diversity of opinion.

The focus varies from nation to nation. The Australian Democratic party has worked closely with media unions in that country in mounting a massive grass-roots campaign against cuts in government funding for the Australian Broadcasting Corporation; the Brazilian Workers party has organized mass protests outside the headquarters of broadcast companies that fail to devote serious attention to the political process; the Canadian NDP is developing legislation that would limit the percentage of newspapers in any region that can be controlled by a single company.

When put together in this manner, these global activities give the appearance of a stunning movement with tremendous momentum. In fact, this is misleading. Were one to visit any of these nations the overall mood on the democratic left is mostly one of despair; neoliberalism remains in the driver's seat. What is important — and unprecedented — is that media reform has emerged as a core political issue in so many places, and that these parties are thinking along similar lines. What is missing at present, and may be critical for ultimate success, is for these parties to work together across national lines. This is especially true with regard to media policy. In the end, the goal should be not merely to have a series of national media systems with dominant public service components but to have a global public sphere as well, where people can communicate with each other without having the communication filtered and censored by corporate and commercial interests.[73]

Conclusion

Media reform will not, cannot, be won in isolation from broader democratic reform. The only way to wrestle some control over media and communication from the giant firms that presently dominate the field will be to mobilize some semblance of a popular movement. As Saul Alinsky noted, the only way to beat organized money is with organized people. And while media reform is a necessary component — even a cornerstone — for any democratic movement, it is not enough. Although it can attract the enthusiastic support of many people — including many people not formerly politically active — it is insufficient on its own to capture the imagination of enough people to establish a mass movement. But when combined with electoral reform, workers' rights, civil rights, environmental protection, health care, tax reform, and education, it can be part of a movement that can reshape our society, putting power in the hands of the many. Put another way, the crisis in communication facing the United

States and, to varying degrees, the entire world, is one aspect of the broader crisis emanating from the tension of combining a highly concentrated corporate-driven economy that generates significant social inequality and insecurity with an ostensibly free and democratic society. Regrettably our existing institutions — governmental, educational, and commercial — are ill-equipped to address these crises with solutions that point toward democracy. They are either dominated by powerful interests that oppose reform or they are weighed down by dubious ideologies that assume the beneficence and dominance of the market. In short, we are handcuffed by these myths as we attempt to reform our institutions to resolve the problems before us. And we are blindfolded by a media system that suits, first and foremost, those who benefit not by reform but by the preservation of the status quo.

The truth is, media reform will not be an easy area in which to gain victories. The media giants are unusually canny and powerful political adversaries; few mainstream politicians wish to tangle with them. But it is also an area with unusual promise for the left as it can draw together people who might otherwise work independently of each other. And there is little evidence that people are captivated by commercial media fare to the extent the media giants' PR declares. Unless the left does something significant concerning media, it is difficult to imagine the labor movement and the left in general escaping their long-term downward trajectory. The fate of media reform and the U.S. left are inexorably intertwined, and in their fortunes reside perhaps the last, best hope of the United States to become a democracy ruled by the many rather than the few.

NOTES

In these notes I use the following abbreviations frequently:

BBC British Broadcasting Corporation Papers, BBC Written Archive
Centre, Reading, England

CC Carnegie Corporation of New York Papers, Butler Library,
Columbia University, New York, N.Y.

GS Graham Spry Papers, Manuscript Group 30, D297, National
Archives of Canada, Ottawa, Canada

NBC National Broadcasting Company Papers, State Historical Society
of Wisconsin, Madison, Wis.

OE Office of Education Papers, Record Group 12, National Archives,
Washington, D.C.

PF Payne Fund, Inc. Papers, Western Reserve Historical Society,
Cleveland, Ohio

SHSW State Historical Society of Wisconsin, Madison, Wis.

Introduction

1. Martin Peers, "Can Congloms Cope with Cash Cache?" *Variety,* July 20–
26, 1998, pp. 1, 62.
2. John Consoli, "The 11.8-Hour Daily Diet," *Mediaweek,* Apr. 20, 1998, pp.
8, 12.
3. John Merli, "Internet Users Not Forsaking Radio," *Broadcasting and Cable,*
Oct. 19, 1998, p. 59.
4. Eben Shapiro, "Surfers of the Web Still Love TV and, in Fact, Often
Watch Both," *Wall Street Journal,* June 12, 1998, p. B9.
5. John Harwood, "Are You Apathetic about Fall's Election? You're Written
Off," *Wall Street Journal,* July 13, 1998, pp. A1, A7.

6. Robert M. Entman, *Democracy without Citizens: Media and the Decay of American Politics* (New York: Oxford University Press, 1989).

7. Ellen Meiksins Wood, *Democracy against Capitalism* (Cambridge: Cambridge University Press, 1995), chap. 7.

8. Richard N. Rosenfeld, *American Aurora* (New York: St. Martin's Press, 1997), p. 3.

9. Quoted in Anna Couey and Joshua Karliner, "Interview with Noam Chomsky," *Z Magazine,* June 1998, p. 9.

10. Robert W. McChesney, *Telecommunications, Mass Media, and Democracy: The Battle for the Control of U.S. Broadcasting, 1928–1935* (New York: Oxford University Press, 1993); Robert W. McChesney, *Corporate Media and the Threat to Democracy* (New York: Seven Stories Press, 1997); Edward S. Herman and Robert W. McChesney, *The Global Media: The New Missionaries of Corporate Capitalism* (London: Cassell, 1997).

11. Bruce Cumings, *War and Television* (London: Verso, 1992), p. 267.

12. Nat Hentoff, "Fair-Weather Friends of the First Amendment," *Progressive,* Jan. 1999, p. 29.

Chapter 1: U.S. Media at the Dawn of the Twenty-first Century

1. Marc Gunther, "The Rules according to Rupert," *Fortune,* Oct. 26, 1998, p. 104.

2. Diane Mermigas, "Seagram Co. to Shed Parts of PolyGram," *Electronic Media,* May 25, 1998, p. 32.

3. "Bertelsmann Purchase Set to Open a Whole New Chapter," *Financial Times,* Mar. 25, 1998, p. 18.

4. Martin Arnold, "Nervous Twitch in the Wallet," *New York Times,* July 2, 1998, p. B3.

5. From the 1940s see, for example, Morris Ernst, *The First Freedom* (New York: Macmillan Company, 1946); Commission on Freedom of the Press, *A Free and Responsible Press* (Chicago: University of Chicago Press, 1947).

6. For one of the few moments it did, see McChesney, *Telecommunications, Mass Media, and Democracy.*

7. See Robert A. Hackett and Yeuzhi Zhao, *Sustaining Democracy: Journalism and the Politics of Objectivity* (Toronto: Garamond Press, 1998).

8. "How the Studios Stack Up in '97," *Variety,* Jan. 5–11, 1998, p. 96.

9. "Basic Movie Statistics," *Cowen Perspectives,* May 14, 1998, p. 1.

10. For a clear discussion of chain newspapers and one-newspaper towns, see Ben H. Bagdikian, *The Media Monopoly,* 5th ed. (Boston: Beacon Press, 1997).

11. Iver Peterson, "California Draws Newspaper Chains Eager to Cluster," *New York Times,* Sept. 1, 1997, pp. B1, B4.

12. Dorianne Perrucci, "Papering the Town," *Adweek,* Apr. 20, 1998, p. 8.

13. I. Jeanne Dugan, "Boldly Going Where Others Are Bailing Out," *Business Week,* Apr. 6, 1998, p. 46.

14. Alice Rawsthorn, "The Perils of Artistic Growth," *Financial Times,* May 26, 1998, p. 15; "Birth of a Giant," *Variety,* June 22–28, 1998, p. 22; "Sony Music Spins the Hits," *Wall Street Journal,* Feb. 23, 1998, p. B4.

15. Les Brown, "Market Forces Killed the Media Dream," *Television Business International,* Apr. 1998, p. 10.

16. "All Together Now," *Electronic Media,* Dec. 15, 1997, p. 14.

17. John Dempsey, "Cable Ops Caught in the Nets," *Variety,* Feb. 17–23, 1997, p. 1.

18. Matthew Schifrin, "Radio-active Men," *Forbes,* June 1, 1998, p. 131.

19. Eric Bates, "Chaining the Alternatives: What Started as a Movement Has Become an Industry," *Nation,* June 29, 1998, pp. 11–18.

20. "Kohlberg Kravis Said to Seek Deal for Regal Cinemas Chain," *New York Times,* Jan. 17, 1998, p. B4.

21. Steven Lipin and Bruce Orwall, "KKR, Hicks Muse to Buy Regal Cinemas," *Wall Street Journal,* Jan. 20, 1998, pp. A3, A8; Allen R. Myerson and Geraldine Fabrikant, "2 Buyout Firms Make Deal to Acquire Regal Cinemas," *New York Times,* Jan. 21, 1998, p. C2.

22. Hardy Green, "Superstores, Megabooks — and Humongous Headaches," *Business Week,* Apr. 14, 1997, p. 93.

23. "Random Thoughts," *Economist,* Mar. 28, 1998, p. 58.

24. Bagdikian, *Media Monopoly.*

25. Eben Shapiro, "John Malone Prepares for a New Life as Pa Bell," *Wall Street Journal,* June 25, 1998, p. B1.

26. Robert La Franco, "Rupert's on a Roll," *Forbes,* July 6, 1998, p. 186; Frank Rose, "There's No Business like Show Business," *Fortune,* June 22, 1998, pp. 86–104, esp. p. 88.

27. Jim McConville, "Liberty Has Money to Spend," *Electronic Media,* June 29, 1998, p. 1A.

28. Martin Peers, "Liberty Ends Up Home Malone," *Variety,* June 29–July 12, 1998, pp. 1, 52; Diane Mermigas, "Malone's New Fun House," *Electronic Media,* July 6, 1998, p. 10.

29. Diane Mermigas, "TCI Headed in the Right Direction," *Electronic Media,* Sept. 1, 1997, p. 20.

30. Bruce Orwall, "Cineplex Odeon–Loews Merger Is Backed by Regulators, with Sales of Theaters," *Wall Street Journal,* Apr. 17, 1998, p. B3.

31. "Series for Sale," *Variety,* May 25–31, 1998, p. 40.

32. Dominic Schreiber, "Murdoch Re-Groups Businesses," *Television Business*

International, July/Aug. 1998, p. 11; Michael Stroud, "Programmers Clash over Ownership," *Broadcasting and Cable,* Sept. 28, 1998, p. 34.

33. Michael Schneider, "Studios Feel Networks' Strong-arm," *Electronic Media,* May 25, 1998, p. 26.

34. John Gapper, "Star of His Own Show," *Financial Times,* June 22, 1998, p. 8.

35. Michael Schneider, "Independent Producers Left Out," *Electronic Media,* Apr. 6, 1998, p. 20.

36. Richard Morgan, "Radio Biz Stirs in Cross-Promo Fizz," *Variety,* June 22–28, 1998, p. 25.

37. Henry Goldblatt, "Viacom's Itty-Bitty, Synergistic, Billion-Dollar Franchise," *Fortune,* Nov. 23, 1998, p. 223.

38. Diane Mermigas, "Surf and Groove," *Electronic Media,* May 4, 1998, pp. 16, 20.

39. "Size Does Matter," *Economist,* May 23, 1998, p. 57.

40. Frank Rich, "Tina and Disney Elope," *New York Times,* July 11, 1998, p. A19.

41. Tim Carvell, "How Sony Created a Monster," *Fortune,* June 8, 1998, p. 162.

42. Bruce Orwall, "'Armageddon,' Missing Disney Targets, Draws Less Than Astronomical Numbers," *Wall Street Journal,* July 6, 1998, p. A20.

43. Bruce Orwall and John Lippmann, "Lawsuit Casts Tim Allen TV Series as Victim of Synergy," *Wall Street Journal,* Mar. 17, 1997, p. B1.

44. Mira Schwirtz, "ESPN Expands Push in Radio," *Mediaweek,* Aug. 29, 1998, p. 8.

45. Robin Pogrebin, "ESPN Rivals Set for Fight as Magazine Debut Nears," *New York Times,* Jan. 19, 1998, pp. C1, C6; "Promo Muscle of Cable Net Will Back 'ESPN Magazine,'" *Advertising Age,* Oct. 13, 1997, p. 6.

46. Lisa Granatstein, "*ESPN* Shoots, Scores," *Mediaweek,* June 15, 1998, p. 23.

47. Bruce Orwall, "Disney to Enter Restaurant Business, and Chain Will Sport an ESPN Theme," *Wall Street Journal,* Oct. 15, 1997, p. B6.

48. Henry Goldblatt, "TV's Most Lucrative Franchise: It's a Mystery," *Fortune,* Jan. 12, 1998, p. 114.

49. Jeff Jensen, "Fox Lands Intrigue for Big 'X-Files' Push," *Advertising Age,* Jan. 12, 1998, p. 8.

50. Adam Sandler, "WB to Promote Its Music on Vids," *Variety,* June 1–7, 1998, p. 11.

51. Jeff Jensen, "Nickelodeon Channels into Retail with 3 Stores," *Advertising Age,* Nov. 24, 1997, p. 45.

52. Ann Marie Kerwin, "Branding Is the Buzzword at Murdoch's Print Group," *Advertising Age,* Jan. 12, 1998, pp. 6, 39.

53. Dominic Schreiber, "Tie-ins That Bind," *Television Business International*, Sept. 1997, pp. 29–30.

54. *Economist*, May 23, 1998, p. 57.

55. Dagmar Mussey, "Disney Sniffs Out Profit," *Advertising Age International*, July 13, 1998, p. 8.

56. Jeff Jensen, "New Fox Unit to Revitalize 'Simpsons' Merchandise," *Advertising Age*, May 11, 1998, p. 65.

57. Eben Shapiro, "Can the Rugrats Take on Mickey Mouse?" *Wall Street Journal*, May 22, 1997, pp. B1, B5; De'Ann Weimer, "Hardly a Household Name," *Business Week*, Dec. 22, 1997, p. 42.

58. Diane Mermigas, "Comparing Survival Strategies," *Electronic Media*, Oct. 12, 1998, p. 22.

59. Rawsthorn, "Perils of Artistic Growth."

60. Jennifer Nix, "Indies Make Big Book Mark," *Variety*, May 18–24, 1998, pp. 1, 89.

61. Monica Roman and Benedict Carver, "Ya Gotta Have Art," *Variety*, May 4–10, 1998, pp. 1, 103.

62. Dan Cox, "Studios Woo New Indies," *Variety*, Jan. 19–25, 1998, p. 1.

63. Geraldine Fabrikant, "'Prince of Egypt' Is No King at the Box Office," *New York Times*, Dec. 28, 1998, pp. C1, C4.

64. Geraldine Fabrikant, "Dreamworks' Lackluster Start Is Putting Pressure on the Company to Perform," *New York Times*, Mar. 2, 1998, p. C7. DreamWorks is a bit of an anomaly, however, as its founders, including Steven Spielberg and David Geffen, have unusual market power. Without the likes of a Spielberg or a Geffen the idea of establishing an independent major Hollywood studio would seem farfetched, to say the least. It has not been done since the 1930s.

65. See Peter Burrows and Ronald Grover, "Steve Jobs, Movie Mogul: Can He Build Pixar into a Major Studio?" *Business Week*, Nov. 23, 1998, pp. 140–54.

66. Christopher Parkes, "Chancellor to Acquire Martin Media," *Financial Times*, June 23, 1998, p. 22.

67. Schifrin, "Radio-active Men," p. 132.

68. John M. Higgins, "Capital Research's Gordon Crawford," *Broadcasting and Cable*, Aug. 17, 1998, p. 30.

69. *Business Week*, Feb. 16, 1998, p. 95.

70. Elizabeth Lesly Stevens and Ronald Grover, "The Entertainment Glut," *Business Week*, Feb. 15, 1998, p. 95.

71. Alan Deutschmann, "The Ted and Jerry Show," *Gentleman's Quarterly*, Dec. 1997, pp. 131–32; Eben Shapiro, "Viacom Considers Selling All or Part of Its Simon & Schuster Publishing Unit," *Wall Street Journal*, Dec. 30, 1997, p. A2.

72. Mark Landler, "From Gurus to Sitting Ducks," *New York Times,* Jan. 11, 1998, sec. 3, pp. 1, 9.

73. Geraldine Fabrikant, "Cooperation Counts," *New York Times,* Dec. 15, 1997, p. C12.

74. Frank Rose, "There's No Business like Show Business," pp. 90–91.

75. Peter Phillips, with the research assistance of Bob Klose, Nikki Mazumdar, and Alix Jestron, "Self Censorship and the Homogeneity of the Media Elite," in *Censored 1998,* ed. Peter Phillips (New York: Seven Stories Press, 1998), chap. 5.

76. "The Forbes 400," *Forbes,* Oct. 12, 1998, pp. 414–28.

77. "Salary Survey," *Advertising Age,* Dec. 7, 1998, pp. s18, s20.

78. See, for example, Ken Auletta, *The Highwaymen: Warriors of the Information Highway* (New York: Random House, 1997).

79. "Elbow Power," *Economist,* Nov. 21, 1998, "Technology and Entertainment Survey," p. 5.

80. Ronald Grover, "Michael Eisner Defends the Kingdom," *Business Week,* Aug. 4, 1997, pp. 73–75.

81. John Leonard, "Of Love and Bile," *Nation,* June 8, 1998, p. 7.

82. Donna Petrozzello, "'Awful Truth' and Moore on Bravo," *Broadcasting and Cable,* Nov. 16, 1998, p. 59.

83. I critique the "give the people what they want" notion in detail in McChesney, *Corporate Media and the Threat to Democracy.*

84. Christopher Hitchens, "Free to Choose," *Nation,* July 13, 1998, p. 9.

85. Christopher Parkes, "US Radio Gets an Earful as Melody Marketers Tune into the Internet," *Financial Times,* June 16, 1998, p. 4.

86. Paul D. Colford, "Scott Muni: A Radio Classic," *Mediaweek,* Nov. 30, 1998, p. 17.

87. David Schiff, "Classical Radio Plays Only to Sweet Tooths," *New York Times,* May 31, 1998, sec. 2, p. 1.

88. "Shall We Go, Yawn, to a Film?" *Economist,* Feb. 1, 1997, pp. 85–86.

89. Christopher Stern, "Researchers Shocked to Find — TV Violence," *Variety,* Apr. 20–26, 1998, p. 24.

90. James T. Hamilton, *Channeling Violence: The Economic Market for Violent Television Programming* (Princeton: Princeton University Press, 1998).

91. Lawrie Mifflin, "TV Stretches Limits of Taste, to Little Outcry," *New York Times,* Apr. 6, 1998, p. A1.

92. Cynthia Littleton, "Just How Low Will Howard Stern Go? *Variety,* Oct. 26–Nov. 1, 1998, p. 9.

93. George Lipsitz, *Rainbow at Midnight: Labor and Culture in the 1940s* (Urbana: University of Illinois Press, 1994), chap. 13.

94. Sidney Finkelstein, *Jazz: A People's Music* (New York: Citadel Press, 1948), pp. 157–58.

95. Keith Negus, "Cultural Production and the Corporation: Musical Genres

and the Strategic Management of Creativity in the US Recording Industry," *Media, Culture and Society* 20, no. 3 (1998): 377.

96. See Fred Goodman, *The Mansion on the Hill: Dylan, Young, Geffen, Springsteen, and the Head-on Collision of Rock and Commerce* (New York: Times Books, 1997).

97. Neil Strauss, "A Culture of Reruns, and Pollsters at the Mall," *New York Times,* Sept. 14, 1998, p. B1.

98. See Michael Jacobson and Laurie Ann Mazur, *Marketing Madness* (Boulder, Colo.: Westview Press, 1995).

99. Robert La Franco, "Salsa, Inc.," *Forbes,* Sept. 22, 1997, p. 155.

100. Alice Rawsthorn, "Spice Girls Tune Up for Merchandising Push," *Financial Times,* Oct. 7, 1997, p. 9; Richard C. Morais and Katherine Bruce, "What I Wanna, Wanna, Really Wannabe," *Forbes,* Sept. 22, 1997, pp. 186–90.

101. Michael Wilke, "Polaroid Hikes Budget to Stay Relevant," *Advertising Age,* Feb. 23, 1998, p. 41.

102. Patrick M. Reilly, "Rich Marketing Alliances Keep Music Stars Glowing," *Wall Street Journal,* Jan. 22, 1998, pp. B1, B1, B12.

103. Alice Rawsthorn, "Nike Deal Sweetens a British Band's Fortunes in the US," *Financial Times,* Apr. 6, 1998, p. 6.

104. Patrick M. Reilly, "TV Commercials Turn Obscure Songs into Radio Hits," *Wall Street Journal,* Oct. 9, 1998, p. B1.

105. John Nichols, "Patti Smith," *Progressive,* Dec. 1997, pp. 36–37.

106. Tom Engelhardt, "Gutenberg Unbound," *Nation,* Mar. 17, 1997, pp. 18–28; Mark Crispin Miller, "The Crushing Power of Big Publishing," *Nation,* Mar. 17, 1997, pp. 11–18.

107. Chris Petrikin, "Book Biz: Read It and Weep," *Variety,* May 12–18, 1997, pp. 1, 77; Doreen Carvajal, "Middling (and Unloved) in Publishing Land," *New York Times,* Aug. 18, 1997, pp. C1, C6.

108. Doreen Carvajal, "The More the Books, the Fewer the Editors," *New York Times,* June 29, 1998, pp. B1, B3.

109. G. Bruce Knecht, "Book Superstores Bring Hollywood-like Risks to the Publishing Business," *Wall Street Journal,* May 29, 1997, pp. A1, A6.

110. I. Jeanne Dugan, "The Baron of Books," *Business Week,* June 29, 1998, p. 115.

111. Doreen Carvajal, "Book Chains' New Role: Soothsayers for Publishers," *New York Times,* Aug. 12, 1997, pp. A1, C5.

112. Knecht, "How Magazines Arrive on Shelves."

113. Diane Mermigas, "BCFM Gets Net, Digital Alert," *Electronic Media,* May 25, 1998, p. 14.

114. Bill Carter, "In About-Face, NBC Is Marketing Its Wares with Toll-free Number," *New York Times,* May 1, 1998, p. A1.

115. Diane Mermigas, "Infomercials Were News to Karmazin," *Electronic*

Media, Dec. 21–28, 1998, p. 2; Dan Trigoboff and Joe Schlosser, "'Not the End of the World'?" *Broadcasting and Cable,* Dec. 14, 1998, p. 15.

116. Paul A. Eisenstein, "Vehicles That Really Perform," *WorldTraveler,* Jan. 1997, pp. 18–23.

117. Jensen, "New Fox Unit to Revitalize 'Simpsons' Merchandise," p. 65.

118. Judith Pollack and Jeff Jensen, "Warner Bros., Frito-Lay Join in Global Promo Pact," *Advertising Age,* June 23, 1997, p. 2.

119. Bruce Orwall, "Miramax and Tommy Hilfiger Join Forces," *Wall Street Journal,* May 7, 1998, p. B10.

120. James B. Arndorfer, "007's Sponsor Blitz," *Advertising Age,* Dec. 1997, p. 24.

121. Stuart Elliott, "Advertising," *New York Times,* June 10, 1998, p. C7; Jeff Jensen, "'Godzilla' Effort Looms over '98 Movie Marketing," *Advertising Age,* May 4, 1998, p. 12.

122. Bruce Orwall, "Here Is How Disney Tries to Put the 'Event' into the Event Film," *Wall Street Journal,* June 30, 1998, pp. A1, A6.

123. "Why Baseball Is in Trouble, How GE Makes Money, and Other Insights into the True Origin of Corporate Profits," *Fortune,* May 11, 1998, p. 183.

124. John Conselli, "A Crescendo of Clutter," *Mediaweek,* Mar. 16, 1998, p. 4.

125. Mercedes M. Cardona, "Coen: Ad Spending in '98 Will Outpace Overall Economy," *Advertising Age,* Dec. 15, 1997, p. 6.

126. Ron Aldridge, "Old Problem Making New Appearance on Television," *Electronic Media,* Nov. 24, 1997, p. 27.

127. "This Ad Sucks," *Mediaweek,* Jan. 12, 1998, p. 28.

128. Stuart Elliott, "A Vivid-Livid Divide," *New York Times,* June 19, 1998, pp. C1, C4.

129. Yumiko Ono, "Wal-Mart Uses TV-Set Displays for Ad Network," *Wall Street Journal,* Oct. 7, 1997, pp. B1, B10.

130. Lisa Bannon, "Commercial Appeal: Jim Carrey Is Coming to a Fruit Bin near You," *Wall Street Journal,* Aug. 21, 1997, p. B1.

131. Jeff Jensen, "Disney, Gillette Sign for Adsticks," *Advertising Age,* June 8, 1998, p. 48.

132. Richard Tomkins, "Sold to the Person on Hold," *Financial Times,* Sept. 22, 1997, p. 12.

133. Ellen Neuborne, "This Call Brought to You By," *Business Week,* June 29, 1998, p. 8.

134. Ellen Neuborne and De'Ann Weimer, "Saturday Night at the Ads," *Business Week,* Sept. 15, 1997, pp. 63–64.

135. Robyn Meredith, "G.M. and Sony Join Forces to Market Cars to Moviegoers at a Michigan Theater Complex," *New York Times,* June 23, 1997, p. C7.

136. Joshua Levine, "Zap-proof Advertising," *Forbes,* Sept. 22, 1997, pp. 146–50.

137. "A Breath of Fresh Air," *Economist,* Apr. 11, 1998, pp. 49–50.

138. Robert Nyland, "Billings Rise — with No End in Sight," *Advertising Age,* July 20, 1998, p. A4.

139. Ellen Neuborne, "Great Ad! What's It For?" *Business Week,* July 20, 1998, pp. 118, 120.

140. Sally Beatty, "Interpublic Buys Event Firm Jack Morton," *Wall Street Journal,* Apr. 14, 1998, p. B8.

141. Carol Marie Cooper, "Fruit to Walls to Floor, Ads Are on the March," *New York Times,* Feb. 26, 1998, pp. A1, C8.

142. Chuck Ross, "NBC Mulls Fewer, Longer Ad Breaks," *Advertising Age,* Apr. 13, 1998, p. 4.

143. Jere Longman, "Smiling Hosts and Splendid Performances," *New York Times,* Feb. 23, 1998, pp. A1, C13.

144. Joe Flint and Gary Levin, "P&G, Sony Polish Pact for Programs," *Variety,* Mar. 17–23, 1997, pp. 25, 29.

145. Michael Schneider, "Now, a Show from Our Sponsors," *Electronic Media,* May 19, 1997, p. 28.

146. Michael Schneider, "P&G Raises No Dander," *Electronic Media,* Dec. 21–28, 1998, p. 8.

147. Jim McConville, "Cable Tinkers with Ad-time Setups," *Advertising Age,* Oct. 20, 1997, p. 62.

148. Sally Goll Beatty, "Interpublic Agrees to Buy Control of a Talent-Management Firm," *Wall Street Journal,* Aug. 7, 1997, p. B2.

149. Ronald Grover, "'Barry Owns the Whole Shooting Match,'" *Business Week,* June 15, 1998, pp. 120–22.

150. "Leo-san," *Economist,* Apr. 25, 1998, p. 85.

151. Rawsthorn, "Nike Deal Sweetens a British Band's Fortunes in the US," p. 6.

152. Eben Shapiro, "On MTV, Studios Find No Such Thing as a Free Plug," *Wall Street Journal,* May 29, 1998, pp. B1.

153. Jeff Jensen, "E! Blurs Ad-programming Divider in Sponsorship Pact with Miller," *Advertising Age,* Aug. 17, 1998, p. 4.

154. Sara Brown, "Payola Plagues Spanish-language Stations," *Broadcasting and Cable,* June 8, 1998, p. 11; Patrick M. Reilly, "Radio's New Spin on an Oldie: Pay-for-Play," *Wall Street Journal,* Mar. 16, 1998, pp. B1, B8; Neil Strauss, "Pay-for-Play Back on the Air but This Rendition Is Legal," *New York Times,* Mar. 31, 1998, pp. A1, A21.

155. Parkes, "US Radio Gets an Earful as Melody Marketers Tune into the Internet," p. 4.

156. Chuck Philips and Michael A. Hiltzik, "Radio Conglomerates Skirt Pay-

ola Laws, Critics Say," *Los Angeles Times,* Dec. 16, 1998, p. A1; Jim Abbott, "Radio Deal Puts Spin on Airplay," *Orlando Sentinel,* Dec. 19, 1998, p. C1.

157. Susan G. Davis, *Spectacular Nature: Corporate Culture and the Sea World Experience* (Berkeley: University of California Press, 1997).

158. Bruce Orwall, "Disney Smells Profits in Animal Park," *Wall Street Journal,* Apr. 24, 1998, pp. B1, B4.

159. Dennis Blank, "Another Mouse Hunt from the Right," *Business Week,* Jan. 26, 1998, p. 8.

160. For an overview of the historical relationship of sport and media in the United States, see Robert W. McChesney, "Media Made Sport: A History of Sports Coverage in the United States," in *Media, Sports, and Society: Research on the Communication of Sport,* ed. Lawrence A. Wenner, pp. 49–69 (Beverly Hills, Calif.: Sage, 1989).

161. Regarding collegiate sport, see Langdon Brockington, "Packaging the Pac-10," *Mediaweek,* Mar. 30, 1998, p. 16.

162. Leslie Cauley and Stefan Fatsis, "Cablevision's Talks over an Acquisition of New York Yankees Are Broken Off," *Wall Street Journal,* Nov. 25, 1998, p. B15.

163. Steve Donohue, "Turner, NBC Want a League of Their Own," *Electronic Media,* June 1, 1998, pp. 1, 28; Joe Schlosser, "A League of Their Own?" *Broadcasting and Cable,* June 1, 1998, p. 8.

164. Jon Lafayette, "CBS, Fox Float Ideas for New Hoops League," *Electronic Media,* July 6, 1998, pp. 2, 27.

165. Mir Maqbool Alam Khan, "X Marks the Spot in Thailand for ESPN Competition Debut," *Advertising Age International,* Apr. 13, 1998, n.p.; Jeff Jensen, "Vans to Broker Board-sports Sponsorships," *Advertising Age,* Apr. 6, 1998, p. 44.

166. Joe Schlosser, "In Hot Pursuit," *Broadcasting and Cable,* June 22, 1998, pp. 26–32.

167. Barry Singer, "The New Musical: Will Corporate Money Call the Tune?" *New York Times,* Aug. 30, 1998, pp. 5, 25; Kate Fitzgerald, "Casting for Sponsor," *Advertising Age,* Sept. 28, 1998, pp. 28, 32.

168. Bernard Weinraub, "Three Hollywood Egos Could Turn Broadway into Their Battleground," *New York Times,* Apr. 15, 1998, pp. B1, B10; Lisa Gubernick, "Hollywood Prospects for Gold on Broadway," *Wall Street Journal,* Apr. 14, 1998, pp. B1, B4; "Disney's High Kicks on Broadway," *Economist,* May 23, 1998, pp. 77–78.

169. Jim McConville, "Coming at Kids Market, Full Steam Ahead," *Electronic Media,* Jan. 19, 1998, p. 78.

170. "Hey Kids! Marketers Want You!" *Wall Street Journal,* May 6, 1997, p. B8.

171. Lisa Bannon, "As Children Become More Sophisticated, Marketers Think Older," *Wall Street Journal,* Oct. 13, 1998, p. A1.

172. David Leonhardt and Kathleen Kerwin, "Hey Kid, Buy This," *Business Week,* June 30, 1997, pp. 62–67.

173. Jim McConville, "Higher Stakes in Kids Cable Battle," *Electronic Media,* Nov. 17, 1997, pp. 3, 63.

174. Ronald Grover, "Crowded in Toon Town," *Business Week,* May 11, 1998, p. 35.

175. Andrea Adelson, "Children's Radio Pioneer Is Challenged by Disney," *New York Times,* July 21, 1997, p. C10.

176. David Barboza, "Television Commercials for Video Games Aimed at Youths and Adults Take a Violent Turn," *New York Times,* Dec. 26, 1997, p. C5.

177. Jon Lafayette, "Are 1-year-olds Ready for Britain's 'Teletubbies?'" *Electronic Media,* Feb. 2, 1998, p. 31.

178. Noreen O'Leary, "The Boom Tube," *Adweek,* May 18, 1998, p. 50.

179. Pete Egoscue, "Children Are Dying for Some Exercise," *New York Times,* May 10, 1998, sports section, p. 29.

180. See Alex Molnar, *Giving Kids the Business* (Boulder, Colo.: Westview Press, 1996).

181. Helen Jones, "Brands Enter the Classroom," *Financial Times,* Sept. 1, 1997, p. 12.

182. Louise Lee, "School's Back, and So Are the Marketers," *Wall Street Journal,* Sept. 15, 1997, pp. B1, B6.

183. Constance L. Hays, "Be True to Your Cola, Rah! Rah!" *New York Times,* Mar. 10, 1998, pp. C1, C4.

184. Constance L. Hays, "Advertising," *New York Times,* Mar. 26, 1998, p. C5.

185. Pat Wechsler, "This Lesson Is Brought to You By," *Business Week,* June 30, 1997, pp. 68–69.

186. Channel One Network advertisement, *Electronic Media,* Feb. 9, 1999, p. 36.

187. William Bulkeley, "Channel One Taps Principals as Promoters," *Wall Street Journal,* Sept. 15, 1997, pp. B1, B6.

188. Lawrie Mifflin, "Nielsen to Research Channel One's Audience," *New York Times,* Dec. 28, 1998, p. C6.

189. Amity Shlaes, "The Next Big Free-Market Thing," *Wall Street Journal,* July 9, 1998, p. A18.

190. Michael Winerip, "Schools for Sale," *New York Times Sunday Magazine,* June 14, 1998, pp. 42–48.

191. Ralph Reed, speech at Dartmouth College, broadcast on C-SPAN, June 1998.

192. "The Next Big Thing?" *Fortune,* June 23, 1997, p. 114; see also Clinton E. Boutwell, *Shell Game: Corporate America's Agenda for Schools* (Bloomington, Ind.: Phi Delta Kappa Educational Foundation, 1997).

193. Antony Thorncroft, "Blockbuster in a Frame," *Financial Times,* Feb. 21–22, 1998, weekend section, p. I.

194. Chin-tao Wu, "Embracing the Enterprise Culture: Art Institutions since the 1980s," *New Left Review,* no. 230 (July-Aug. 1998): 29.

195. Constance L. Hays, "No More Brand X," *New York Times,* June 12, 1998, pp. C1, C4.

196. Kyle Pope, "'Must See TV' Folks Sell 'Must Buy' Dog Dishes," *Wall Street Journal,* June 9, 1998, pp. B1, B12.

197. See Bagdikian, *Media Monopoly.*

198. William Greider, *Fortress America: The American Military and the Consequences of Peace* (New York: Public Affairs, 1998).

199. Steven Lee Myers, "Clinton Proposes a Budget Increase for the Military," *New York Times,* Jan. 2, 1999, pp. A1, A9.

200. For classic treatments of these hypotheses, which to my knowledge have never been disproven, see Edward S. Herman and Noam Chomsky, *Manufacturing Consent: The Political Economy of the Mass Media* (New York: Pantheon, 1988); Noam Chomsky, *Necessary Illusions: Thought Control in Democratic Societies* (Boston: South End Press, 1989).

201. Sadly, some communication scholarship manages not only to ignore this trend but to use research sloppily to conclude that there is a greater emphasis on quality instead of profits among large newspapers. The flaw in this research is that it accepts editors' and publishers' claims that they are attempting to "improve" the news product at face value, as meaning that journalism is being improved. In fact, the corporate notion of "improving" journalism generally means to turn it into a more commercially viable entity. See David Demers, "Large Dailies Focus More on Quality, but Small Dailies Eying Bottom Line, Survey Finds," unpublished paper, Washington State University, 1997.

202. Jon LaFayette, "The Most Powerful Person in Television News," *Electronic Media,* Sept. 15, 1997, p. 21.

203. Diane Mermigas, "GE Brings Quality Control to NBC," *Electronic Media,* Oct. 13, 1997, p. 15.

204. Arthur Kent, "'Breaking Down the Barriers,'" *Nation,* June 8, 1998, p. 29. His book is *Risk and Redemption: Surviving the Network News Wars* (Tortola, British Virgin Islands: Interstellar, 1997).

205. Bill Carter, "ABC Shelves Report on Parent Disney," *New York Times,* Oct. 15, 1998, p. A16; Lawrie Mifflin, "An ABC News Reporter Tests the Boundaries of Investigating Disney and Finds Them," *New York Times,* Oct. 19, 1998, p. C8; Jon Lafayette, "Critical ABC News Story on Disney Dies," *Electronic Media,* Oct. 19, 1998, pp. 1A, 28.

206. Jon LaFayette, "Journalists Hash Out Trust Issue," *Electronic Media,* Sept. 22, 1997, p. 35.

207. David Broder, "Whose Values Rule Journalism Today?" *Wisconsin State Journal* (Madison), May 11, 1998, p. 7A.

208. Richard Reeves, *What the People Know: Freedom and the Press* (Cambridge, Mass.: Harvard University Press, 1998), pp. 98, 118, 61.

209. James Fallows, *Breaking the News* (New York: Pantheon, 1996).

210. Stuart Elliott, "CNN Orders Its News Staff to Avoid Ads," *New York Times,* June 16, 1997, p. C3.

211. Bill Carter, "David Brinkley, Now an Archer Daniels Spokesman, Returns to Network Television," *New York Times,* Jan. 6, 1998, p. C5.

212. Jennifer Nix, "After ABC Blinks, CNN Winks at Brinkley Ads," *Variety,* Jan. 19–25, 1998, p. 3.

213. Maureen Dowd, "Good Night, David," *New York Times,* Jan. 7, 1998, p. A21.

214. Rance Crain, "What I Don't Understand: Huizenga, Huff over Brinkley," *Advertising Age,* Jan. 19, 1998, p. 25.

215. *Tyndall Report,* Dec. 31, 1996.

216. James Sterngold, "Journalism Goes Hollywood, and Hollywood Is Reading," *New York Times,* July 10, 1998, p. C5.

217. Danny Schechter, "The News Biz Goes Showbiz," *In These Times,* Dec. 27, 1998, p. 7.

218. Kyle Pope, "How Many TV News Magazines Are Too Many?" *Wall Street Journal,* May 30, 1997, p. B1.

219. Edward Seaton, keynote speech to IPI World Congress, Moscow, May 26, 1998, p. 1.

220. Jon LaFayette, "Crime Wave Hits Network News: Study," *Electronic Media,* Aug. 18, 1997, p. 6.

221. Mark Landler, "CNN Ratings Head South. Calling O. J., Calling O. J.," *New York Times,* July 14, 1997, pp. C1, C7.

222. Paul Kite, Robert A. Bardwell, and Jason Salzman, *Baaad News: Local TV News in America,* 2/26/97 (Denver: Rocky Mountain Media Watch, 1997); see also Lisa Bannon, "In TV Chopper War, News Is Sometimes a Trivial Pursuit," *Wall Street Journal,* June 4, 1997, pp. A1, A10.

223. Jon Lafayette, "News Study: Violence Still Dominates," *Electronic Media,* Aug. 10, 1998, pp. 24, 22.

224. Christopher Parkes, "Felons Provide Freeway Freak Show," *Financial Times,* Feb. 17, 1998, p. 24.

225. Michael Winerip, "Looking for an 11 O'Clock Fix," *New York Times Magazine,* Jan. 11, 1998, p. 33.

226. Mark Crispin Miller, "Crime-Time News in Baltimore: The Economic Cost of Local TV's Bodybag Journalism," study released to public June 1998; Dan Trigoboff, "Study Blasts Baltimore News," *Broadcasting and Cable,* July 8, 1998, p. 33.

227. Seaton, keynote speech to IPI World Congress, p. 1.

228. Richard Gibson, "Minneapolis Publisher Awaits Suitors, Looks in Mirror," *Wall Street Journal,* Sept. 12, 1997, p. B4.

229. Sheila P. Calamba, "At Big Dailies, More News Jobs Are Temporary," *Wall Street Journal,* Aug. 26, 1997, pp. B1, B6.

230. Iver Peterson, "Newspaper Owners Proselytize Business Sense to Their Reporters and Editors," *New York Times,* June 9, 1997, p. C23.

231. Iver Peterson, "Rethinking the News: Papers Seek More Personal Connection with Readers," *New York Times,* May 19, 1997, pp. C1, C8.

232. Iver Peterson, "Editors Discuss Their Frustrations in the Age of Refrigerator-Magnet Journalism," *New York Times,* Apr. 14, 1997, p. C9.

233. John Lippert, "War Wounds in Detroit," *Columbia Journalism Review,* May–June 1998, p. 17.

234. Iver Peterson, "New Issue for Journalists: Corporate Writing Duties," *New York Times,* Jan. 12, 1998, p. C13.

235. James Sterngold, "Editor of Los Angeles Times Quits amid News Shake-Up," *New York Times,* Oct. 10, 1997, p. C5; Iver Peterson, "At Los Angeles Times, a Debate on News-Ad Interaction," *New York Times,* Nov. 17, 1997, pp. C1, C11.

236. "PR Day at the *L.A. Times,*" *Extra! Update,* Aug. 1998, p. 4.

237. Felicity Barringer, "Publisher of *Los Angeles Times* Apologizes for Gaffe on Women," *New York Times,* June 3, 1998, p. A19.

238. Ann Marsh, "Rewriting the Book of Journalism," *Forbes,* June 15, 1998, pp. 47, 48.

239. Rance Crain, "Conservative Editors Need to Heed Radicals like 'L.A. Times' Willes," *Advertising Age,* May 4, 1998, p. 30.

240. Ann Marie Kerwin, "New Doors Cut in Wall between Business, Edit," *Advertising Age,* Apr. 27, 1998, p. 62.

241. G. Bruce Knecht, "Magazine Advertisers Demand Prior Notice of 'Offensive' Articles," *Wall Street Journal,* Apr. 30, 1997, pp. A1, A8.

242. Alicia Mundy, "The Church-State Dodge," *Mediaweek,* May 12, 1997, pp. 24–25; Constance L. Hays, "Titleist Withdraws Advertising in Dispute with *Sports Illustrated,*" *New York Times,* Apr. 28, 1997, p. C10.

243. Robin Pogrebin, "Magazine Publishers Circling Wagons against Advertisers," *New York Times,* Sept. 29, 1997, pp. C1, C6; G. Bruce Knecht, "Magazine Groups Reject Early Disclosure," *Wall Street Journal,* Sept. 24, 1997, p. B12; Constance L. Hays, "Editors Urge Limits on Input by Advertisers," *New York Times,* June 23, 1997, p. C7.

244. Robin Pogrebin, "Magazine Marketing Raises Question of Editorial Independence," *New York Times,* May 4, 1998, p. C9.

245. Alex Kuczynski, "Time Magazine's One-Advertiser Issues Become an Issue for Debate," *New York Times,* Nov. 16, 1998, pp. C1–C2; Alex

Kuczynski, "Advice about Clothing and a Snug Fit for the Ads," *New York Times*, Oct. 19, 1998, p. C4.

246. Lisa Granatstein and Betsy Sharkey, "The Talk of the Town," *Mediaweek*, July 13, 1998, pp. 4–5.

247. Felicity Barringer and Geraldine Fabrikant, "Tina Brown Edits Her Career to Match the Zeitgeist," *New York Times*, July 13, 1998, pp. C1, C7.

248. Peter Phillips, "Corporate Media Sells Out Journalists for Profits," *Censored Alert*, Summer 1998, p. 2.

249. Jennifer Nix, "Hard-Hitting News Harder to Air," *Variety*, Apr. 20–26, 1998, p. 5.

250. "Two Fired for Trying to Tell the Truth," *Journalist*, June 1998, p. 24; Steve Wilson, "Fox in the Cow Barn," *Nation*, June 8, 1998, p. 20.

251. Dirk Smillie, "Backlash at Black Rock," *Nation*, Nov. 30, 1998, p. 10.

252. See Gary Webb, *Dark Alliance* (New York: Seven Stories Press, 1998); Alexander Cockburn and Jeffrey St. Clair, *Whiteout: The CIA, Drugs and the Press* (London: Verso, 1998).

253. James Risen, "C.I.A. Reportedly Ignored Charges of Contra Drug Dealing in '80s," *New York Times*, Oct. 10, 1998.

254. April Oliver and Jack Smith, "Smoke Screen," *In These Times*, Sept. 6, 1998, pp. 10–13.

255. Siddarth Varadarajan, "CNN's Capitulation: No Freedom to Accuse U.S. of War Crimes," *The Times of India*, July 11, 1998.

256. Barbara Bliss Osborn, "'Are You Sure You Want to Ruin Your Career?'" *Extra!* Mar.–Apr. 1998, pp. 20–21.

257. Varadarajan, "CNN's Capitulation."

258. Victoria Calkins, "CNN Reporters Casualty of Corporate and Military Fire," *Censored Alert*, Summer 1998, p. 3.

259. Norman Mintz, "Where Is the Outrage?" *Nation*, Oct. 26, 1998, p. 10.

260. Alexander Cockburn, "The Press Devours Its Own," *Nation*, Aug. 24–31, 1998, pp. 10, 24.

261. See, for example, David Croteau and William Hoynes, *By Invitation Only: How the Media Limit Political Debate* (Monroe, Maine: Common Courage Press, 1994).

262. Christopher Parkes, "Murdoch Rails against Regulators," *Financial Times*, June 28–29, 1997, p. 2.

263. Chuck Ross, "From the Top of TCI," *Electronic Media*, Sept. 29, 1997, p. 50.

264. Norman Solomon, "Media Moguls on Board," *Extra!* Jan.–Feb. 1997, pp. 19–22.

265. Milton Glaser, "Censoring Advertising," *Nation*, Sept. 22, 1997, p. 7.

266. Thomas I. Emerson, *Toward a General Theory of the First Amendment* (New York: Random House, 1963).

267. See McChesney, *Telecommunications, Mass Media, and Democracy.*

268. Arthur E. Rowse, "A Lobby the Media Won't Touch," *Washington Monthly,* May 1998, pp. 8–13, esp. p. 12.

269. Alan Murray, "Broadcasters Get a Pass on Campaign Reform," *Wall Street Journal,* Sept. 29, 1997, p. A1; Leslie Wayne, "Broadcast Lobby's Formula: Airtime + Money = Influence," *New York Times,* May 5, 1997, pp. C1, C9; Jeffrey H. Birnbaum, "Washington's Power 25," *Fortune,* Dec. 8, 1997, pp. 144–58.

270. See, for example, Charles Lewis, *The Buying of the Congress* (New York: Avon Books, 1998); Jeffrey H. Birnbaum, "The Influence Merchants," *Fortune,* Dec. 7, 1998, pp. 134–52.

271. Ken Silverstein, "His Biggest Takeover — How Murdoch Bought Washington," *Nation,* June 8, 1988, pp. 18–32.

272. Bill Mesler, "Field Guide to Lobbyists," *Nation,* June 8, 1998, p. 27; "The Washington Buddy System," *Washington Monthly,* May 1998, pp. 12–13.

273. See McChesney, *Corporate Media and the Threat to Democracy.*

274. "Behind Your Soaring Cable Rates," *New York Times,* Dec. 29, 1997, p. A16.

275. Paige Albiniak, "Cable Dodges Rate Regs," *Broadcasting and Cable,* July 27, 1998, p. 4.

276. Christopher Stern, "Pols Threaten to Sack Cable over Rate Hikes," *Variety,* Jan. 19–25, 1998, pp. 63–64.

277. Chris McConnell, "Minority Ownership: Fox's 45% Solution," *Broadcasting and Cable,* July 8, 1998, p. 6.

278. Silverstein, "His Biggest Takeover," p. 31.

279. Steve McClellen, "Spot Walks a Tightrope," *Broadcasting and Cable,* June 22, 1998, p. 4; Louise McElvogue, "When News Becomes Fiction," *Television Business International,* Mar. 1988, p. 64.

280. Lawrie Mifflin, "F.C.C. Chief Backs Off on Rules for Free Air Time for Candidates," *New York Times,* Mar. 26, 1998, p. A13.

281. Alicia Mundy, "FCC LMA Plan Irks McCain," *Mediaweek,* Nov. 30, 1998, p. 6.

282. Chris McConnell, "FCC Rejects Denver License Challenge," *Broadcasting and Cable,* May 4, 1998, p. 20.

283. See Susan Smulyan, *Selling Radio: The Commercialization of American Broadcasting, 1920–1934* (Washington, D.C.: Smithsonian Institution Press, 1994).

284. Ira Teinowitz, "NAB Defends Using Marketer Promos as PSAs," *Advertising Age,* May 12, 1997, pp. 3, 87.

285. Sally Goll Beatty, "Brawl Erupts over Do-Good Advertising," *Wall Street Journal,* Sept. 29, 1997, pp. B1, B8; Ira Teinowitz, "Ad Council Pact with Networks Ends PSA Feud," *Advertising Age,* Sept. 29, 1997, pp. 3, 60.

286. Rance Crain, "Ruth Wooden Wheels and Deals to Lure Ad Council Sponsors," *Advertising Age,* Mar. 9, 1998, p. 34.

287. David Hatch, "V-chip Makes Its Debut," *Electronic Media*, June 22, 1998, pp. 3, 27.

288. George Gerbner, "TV Ratings Deadly Choice: Violence or Alcohol," May 31, 1998, distributed online over CEMnet; see also Testimony of George Gerbner before the Senate Commerce Committee, June 16, 1998.

289. Sally Goll Beatty, "White House Pact on TV for Kids May Prove a Marketing Bonanza," *Wall Street Journal*, Aug. 2, 1996, p. B2.

290. Lawrie Mifflin, "TV Complies, Barely, with New Rules on Shows for Children," *New York Times*, Sept. 11, 1997, p. B4.

291. Greg Spring, "Educational Shows Chart New Course to Success," *Electronic Media*, Feb. 9, 1998, pp. 27, 34.

292. "Broadcasters Must Have Educational Programs for Children by Today," *New York Times*, Sept. 1, 1997, p. B7; Greg Spring, "Home Depot Building Kids How-to Show," *Electronic Media*, Dec. 15, 1997, pp. 1A, 46.

293. Lawrie Mifflin, "PBS Series on Science Departs for the World of 'X-Men,'" *New York Times*, Nov. 29, 1997, p. A23.

294. Jon Lafayette, "CTW Raising Kids TV Profile," *Electronic Media*, Mar. 2, 1998, pp. 8, 34.

295. Chris McConnell, "Low Marks for Kids TV," *Broadcasting and Cable*, June 29, 1998, p. 26.

296. This episode is discussed in detail in McChesney, *Telecommunications, Mass Media, and Democracy*, chap. 8.

297. See, for example, Roger O. Crockett and Dee Gill, "Scary Signals on Pagers," *Business Week*, Dec. 29, 1997, p. 50E2.

298. Paula Dwyer, "Can Rupert Conquer Europe?" *Business Week*, Mar. 25, 1996, p. 129.

299. Bryan Gruley, John Simons, and John R. Wilke, "Is This Really What Congress Had in Mind with the Telecom Act?" *Wall Street Journal*, May 12, 1998, p. A1.

300. "Cable's Hold on America," *Economist*, Jan. 24, 1998, p. 61.

301. Jon Lafayette, "Ownership Ranks Rapidly Thinned by Consolidation," *Electronic Media*, May 18, 1998, pp. 1A, 12.

302. David Johnston, "U.S. Acts to Bar Chancellor Media's L.I. Radio Deal," *New York Times*, Nov. 7, 1997, p. C10.

303. Charles V. Bagli, "As SFX Deal Is Announced, Analysts Expect More Radio Mergers," *New York Times*, Aug. 26, 1997, pp. C1, C8; Mira Schwirtz, "Ganging Up, and Gaining," *Mediaweek*, May 11, 1998, p. 6.

304. Ira Teinowitz, "Westinghouse Deal Fuels Consolidation in Radio," *Advertising Age*, Sept. 29, 1997, p. 61.

305. Goldman Sachs report on broadcasting, May 15, 1998, p. 7. Available to prospective customers upon request.

306. Schifrin, "Radio-active Men," p. 131.

307. Timothy Aepel and William M. Bulkeley, "Westinghouse to Buy American Radio," *Wall Street Journal,* Sept. 22, 1997, p. A3.

308. Eben Shapiro, "A Wave of Buyouts Has Radio Industry Beaming with Success," *Wall Street Journal,* Sept. 18, 1997, p. A1.

309. Elizabeth A. Rathbun, "Wall Street Tuned to Radio," *Broadcasting and Cable,* Apr. 8, 1998, p. 58.

310. Shapiro, "Wave of Buyouts Has Radio Industry Beaming with Success," p. A1.

311. Diane Mermigas, "Kagan Sees a Consolidated Happy New Year for Media in '98," *Electronic Media,* Jan. 5, 1998, p. 15.

312. Robert La Franco, "Tough Customers," *Forbes,* June 1, 1998, pp. 78–79.

313. Lafayette, "Ownership Ranks Rapidly Thinned by Consolidation," p. 1A.

Chapter 2: The Media System Goes Global

1. Emma Duncan, "Wheel of Fortune," *Economist,* Nov. 21, 1998, "Technology and Entertainment Survey," p. 4.

2. Michael J. Mandel, "The New Business Cycle," *Business Week,* Mar. 31, 1997, pp. 58–68.

3. Brushan Bahree, "U.S. Will Ask WTO to Keep Internet Free," *Wall Street Journal,* Feb. 19, 1998, p. B20.

4. Martin Peers, "Movie Biz Enjoys Global Warming," *Variety,* Apr. 7–13, 1997, pp. 1, 32.

5. Henry Goldblatt, "The Universal Appeal of Schlock," *Fortune,* May 12, 1997, p. 32.

6. Alice Rawsthorn, "Film Industry Focuses on Distribution Scene," *Financial Times,* Oct. 4–5, 1997, p. 5.

7. Alice Rawsthorn, "Put to the Screen Test," *Financial Times,* Aug. 30–31, 1997, p. 7; Adam Dawtrey, "Polygram Sets Sail for American Market," *Variety,* Dec. 15–21, 1997, pp. 11, 40.

8. Adam Sandler, "BMG's Potent Portfolio Boosts Market Share," *Variety,* Dec. 15–21, 1997, pp. 38, 78.

9. Adam Sandler, "Seagram Making a Music Monolith," *Variety,* May 25–31, 1998, p. 10.

10. Alice Rawsthorn, "Film Rights Revenue Set for Growth," *Financial Times,* Apr. 30, 1998, p. 5.

11. Michael Williams, "NBC Europe Enters Spain, Eyes France," *Variety,* Sept. 8–14, 1997, p. 33.

12. Robert Frank and Matthew Rose, "A Massive Investment in British Cable TV Sours for U.S. Firms," *Wall Street Journal,* Dec. 17, 1997, p. A1.

13. Gail DeGeorge and Elisabeth Malkin, "Satellite TV: Still a Fuzzy Picture," *Business Week,* Dec. 29, 1997, p. 50E4; Louise McElvogue, "Dig-

ging for Gold in Latin America," *Television Business International,* Sept. 1997, p. 92.

14. Miriam Hils, "Tube Time on the Rise in Europe," *Variety,* Jan. 5–11, 1998, pp. 41, 48.

15. Marie-Agnes Bruneau, "Report Reveals French Kids Spend More Time Watching Television," *European Television Analyst,* Apr. 23, 1998, p. 14.

16. See Ted Magder, "Franchising the Candy Store: Split-run Magazines and a New International Regime for Trade in Culture," *Canadian-American Public Policy,* no. 34 (Apr. 1998), esp. pp. 15–22, 35–51.

17. John Urquhart and Brushan Bahree, "WTO Body Orders Canada to Change Magazine Role," *Wall Street Journal,* July 1, 1997, p. B8; Joseph Weber, "Does Canadian Culture Need This Much Protection?" *Business Week,* June 8, 1998, p. 37.

18. Liz Fell, "Trade Treaty Override Quotas," *Television Business International,* June 1998, p. 14.

19. Mary Sutter, "At Last, Mexican Film Industry Finds Coin," *Variety,* Mar. 23–29, 1998, p. 50; Hanna Lee, "Samsung Ups Local Pic Coin," *Variety,* May 4–10, 1998, p. 27; Mary Sutter, "Mexico Fires Up Film Fund," *Variety,* Mar. 23–29, 1998, p. 16; John Hopewell, "Spain Eyes TV for $100 Mil Film Fund," *Variety,* May 11–17, 1998, p. 41; James Ulmer, "Norwegian Cinema Rides New Wave," *Variety,* May 18–24, 1998, p. 26; Marlene Edmunds, "Danes Tap into Double Subsidy," *Variety,* Apr. 20–26, 1998, p. 17; Bryan Pearson, "South African Gov't Grant Boosts Local Filmmakers," *Variety,* June 29–July 12, 1998, p. 11.

20. Craig Turner, "19 Nations Join to Counter Spread of U.S. Culture," *Capital Times* (Madison, Wis.), July 1, 1998, p. 1A.

21. "Culture Wars," *Economist,* Sept. 12, 1998, p. 97.

22. John Lippmann, "'Big Bad Mama,' 'Stripped to Kill' Spell Trouble for Murdoch in India," *Wall Street Journal,* July 7, 1998, p. B1.

23. "Home Alone in Europe," *Economist,* Mar. 22, 1998, p. 74.

24. Adam Dawtrey, "Brit Pic Policy Goosed by Report's Proposals," *Variety,* Mar. 30–Apr. 5, 1998, p. 20.

25. Adam Dawtrey, "U.K. Gov't Scotches Proposal for Pix Tax," *Variety,* Nov. 30–Dec. 6, 1998, p. 10.

26. David Rooney, "Italy Moves Closer to Euro Primetime," *Variety,* Jan. 26–Feb. 1, 1998, p. 16.

27. Alice Rawsthorn, "More Support for Music Industry Urged," *Financial Times,* Jan. 14, 1998, p. 8.

28. Edmund L. Andrews, "European Commission May Revoke Exemption for U.S. Movie Studios," *New York Times,* Feb. 18, 1998, p. C7; Alice Rawsthorn and Emma Tucker, "Movie Studios May Have to Scrap Joint Distributor," *Financial Times,* Feb. 6, 1998, p. 1.

29. Emma Tucker, "EU Tells Telecoms Groups to Isolate Cable TV," *Finan-*

cial Times, Dec. 17, 1997, p. 3; Neil Buckley and John Gapper, "Publishing Merger Plan Probed by Brussels," *Financial Times,* Dec. 12, 1997, p. 15; Emma Tucker, "German Groups to Halt Digital TV Promotion," *Financial Times,* Dec. 16, 1997, p. 3.

30. Martin DuBois, "Reed Elsevier and Wolters Kluwer End Merger Plans after Concerns at EU," *Wall Street Journal,* Mar. 10, 1998, p. A19.

31. John Gapper and Emma Tucker, "Bad Reception in Brussels," *Financial Times,* Apr. 28, 1998, p. 14.

32. Samer Iskander, "New Campaign on Pay-TV Deal," *Financial Times,* May 5, 1998, p. 3; Frederick Studemann, "Murdoch Set to Lift German TV Interests," *Financial Times,* June 15, 1998, p. 20.

33. Wilfried Ahrens, "Van Miert Ban Opens Way to a Monopoly," *Television Business International,* June 1998, p. 16.

34. Emma Tucker, "EU Media Initiative Bogged Down," *Financial Times,* Mar. 13, 1997, p. 3; Emma Tucker, "TV Law Finds the Off-switch," *Financial Times,* Apr. 17, 1997, p. 3.

35. "Broadcasting across Borders," *Financial Times,* July 15, 1997, p. 11; "TV Restrictions Unlawful," *Financial Times,* June 3, 1997, p. 25.

36. Michael Smith, "New Defeat for Tobacco Advertising," *Financial Times,* Apr. 23, 1998, p. 2; Suzanne Bidlake, "Europe to Halt Tobacco Ads, Sponsorships," *Advertising Age,* May 18, 1998, p. 56.

37. Andy Stern, "EC Faces Static on Pubcast Funding Cuts," *Variety,* Oct. 26–Nov. 1, 1998, p. 77; Andy Stern, "Coalition Fights EU on Pub Subsidies," *Variety,* Nov. 16–22, 1998, p. 29.

38. Thierry Leclercq, "Europeans Give Blessing to Public Service," *Television Business International,* July–Aug. 1997, p. 13.

39. "Top 100 Global Marketers by Ad Spending outside the U.S.," *Advertising Age International,* Nov. 9, 1998, p. 16.

40. Richard Tomkins, "P&G to Get Ahead by Marketing," *Financial Times,* June 5, 1997, p. 21; Sally Goll Beatty, "Bad-Boy Nike Is Playing the Diplomat in China," *Wall Street Journal,* Nov. 10, 1997, pp. B1, B10.

41. Cardona, "Coen: Ad Spending in '98 Will Outpace Overall Economy."

42. Laurel Wentz and Jon Herskovitz, "Asian Economic Turmoil Douses Torrid Ad Growth," *Advertising Age,* Dec. 8, 1997, p. 18; Laurel Wentz, "Happy New Year? Asia Drops Long Shadow over Forecast," *Advertising Age International,* Jan. 1998, pp. 3, 6.

43. Janine Stein and Mansha Daswani, "Counting China," *Television Business International,* Dec. 1997, pp. 30–31.

44. Louis Lucas, "Business Television in Asia Receiving Mixed Signals," *Financial Times,* Dec. 11, 1997, p. 14.

45. Vanessa O'Connell, "Ad-Spending Forecast for Next Year Is Cut Slightly, but Growth of 5.5% Is Still Seen," *Wall Street Journal,* Dec. 8, 1998, p. B9.

46. Juliana Koranteng, "Top Global Ad Markets," *Advertising Age International,* May 11, 1998, pp. 15–19.

47. Stuart Elliott, "Billion Here, Billion There, and Soon Your Estimate on 1998 U.S. Ad Spending Reaches $200.3 Billion," *New York Times,* June 24, 1998, p. C8.

48. Diane Mermigas, "Scandinavia's SBS Has Eye on Prize," *Electronic Media,* Oct. 12, 1998, p. 50.

49. "Omnicom Group," *Advertising Age,* Apr. 27, 1998, p. s22.

50. "World's Top 50 Advertising Organizations," *Advertising Age,* Apr. 27, 1998, p. s10.

51. Sally Beatty, "Merger Boom Is Expected in Ad Industry," *Wall Street Journal,* May 21, 1998, p. B10.

52. Sally Goll Beatty, "Interpublic Plans Acquisitions, Starting Off with Hill Holliday," *Wall Street Journal,* Feb. 25, 1998, p. B9.

53. Helen Jones, "The Search Is On for a Global Message," *Financial Times,* Nov. 11, 1998, p. viii; Rekha Balu, "Heinz Places Ketchup in Global Account," *Wall Street Journal,* Sept. 9, 1998, p. B8.

54. Mercedes M. Cardona and James B. Arndorfer, "Citibank's Global Plum Lands at Y&R," *Advertising Age,* Aug. 11, 1997, p. 4.

55. Stuart Elliott, "The Consolidation Trend Reaches the Industry's Second Tier as Lois/USA Acquires a Smaller Rival," *New York Times,* May 21, 1998, p. C6.

56. Alison Smith, "Strength through Unity," *Financial Times,* Nov. 10, 1997, p. 15.

57. Alice Z. Cuneo and Bruce Crumlet, "Publicis' Levy Views Riney Buy as a Start," *Advertising Age,* May 18, 1998, pp. 3, 60.

58. See, for example, Mercedes M. Cardona, "Agency Groups Scramble for Top Tier," *Advertising Age,* Feb. 2, 1998, p. 44; Stuart Elliott, "In a Further Push into Latin America, DDB Needham Is Buying a Stake in a Brazilian Agency," *New York Times,* June 16, 1997, p. C12; Rebecca A. Fannin, "DDB Needham Takes Majority Interest in Brazil Hot Shop DM9," *Advertising Age,* June 16, 1997, p. 12.

59. Norihiko Shirouzu, "Madison Avenue Looks to Japanese Market," *Wall Street Journal,* July 6, 1998, p. A20.

60. Alexandra Harney, "Omnicom Arm Buys Stake in Japan's Nippo," *Financial Times,* Aug. 20, 1998, p. 20; John William and Alexandra Harney, "WPP Takes 20% Stake in Japanese Ad Agency," *Financial Times,* July 31, 1998, p. 17.

61. Doreen Carvajal, "Book Publishers Seek Global Reach and Grand Scale," *New York Times,* Oct. 19, 1998, p. C1.

62. "The Top 100 Companies," *Business Week,* July 13, 1998, p. 53.

63. "FT 500," *Financial Times,* special section, Jan. 22, 1998, p. 3.

64. Martin Peers, "Showbiz Bullish on the Future," *Variety,* Apr. 6–12, 1998, p. 7.

65. Frank Rose, "There's No Business like Show Business," p. 98.

66. James Brooke, "American Publishers Add Readers in Booming Latin America," *New York Times,* May 11, 1998, p. C1.

67. Eben Shapiro, "Sony Says It's Weighing Digital Moves and Hires Blackstone Group to Assist," *Wall Street Journal,* Nov. 21, 1997, p. B6.

68. Patrick M. Reilly and Greg Steinmetz, "Bertelsmann to Buy Random House," *Wall Street Journal,* Mar. 24, 1998, p. B1.

69. Cynthia Littleton and Martin Peers, "All American Raises Brit Flag," *Variety,* Oct. 6–12, 1997, p. 36.

70. Alice Rawsthorn, "Playing in a Minor Key," *Financial Times,* Nov. 22–23, 1997, p. 22.

71. Kyle Pope, "NBC Is Expected to Sharply Scale Back Its TV Programming in Europe and Asia," *Wall Street Journal,* Apr. 16, 1998, p. B14; Steve McClellen, "NBC Gets Help from Geographic," *Broadcasting and Cable,* Apr. 27, 1998, p. 31.

72. This second tier is presented in detail in Herman and McChesney, *Global Media,* chap. 3.

73. Debra Johnson, "Solid Foundation," *Television Business International,* June 1988, pp. 28–36.

74. "Hot Wires," *Economist,* June 20, 1998, p. 78.

75. Joseph Weber, "The Murdoch of the North," *Business Week,* Aug. 3, 1998, p. 64.

76. Anthony DePalma, "Merger Would Create Canada's 2nd-Largest Newspaper Group," *New York Times,* Dec. 10, 1998, p. C5.

77. Paul Smith, "Murdoch Eye on Cash Cow TV2," *Variety,* May 11–17, 1998, p. 170; Paul Smith, "Study Favors Sale of TVNZ," *Variety,* June 15–21, 1998, p. 29.

78. Don Groves and Mark Woods, "Expand or Die," *Variety,* May 4–10, 1998, p. A1.

79. Elena Cappuccio and Lucy Hillier, "Mediaset Develops Its International Strategy," *European Television Analyst,* May 8, 1998, p. 1.

80. Alejandro Bodipo-Memba and Jonathan Friedland, "Chancellor Sets Pact for Purchase of Radio Centro," *Wall Street Journal,* July 13, 1998, p. B6; Carlos Tejada, "Hicks Muse to Pay $700 Million for 30% of Argentine Media Firm CEI Citicorp," *Wall Street Journal,* May 28, 1998, p. B9; Allen R. Myerson, "Polishing His Game," *New York Times,* May 25, 1998, pp. C1, C2; Ken Warn and William Lewis, "Hicks Muse in Argentine Telecoms Purchase," *Financial Times,* May 28, 1998, p. 15; Pamela Druckerman, "Hicks Muse, GE to Invest in Brazil," *Wall Street Journal,* Nov. 24, 1998, p. A14.

81. This is covered in detail in Herman and McChesney, *Global Media.*

82. Martin Peers, "The Global 50," *Variety,* Aug. 25–31, 1997, p. 31.

83. John Hopewell, "Running with the Big Dogs," *Variety,* Mar. 23–29, 1998, p. 40.

84. Al Goodman, "Spanish Digital TV Services To Merge After Costly Fight," *New York Times,* July 23, 1998, p. C5.

85. Don Groves, "Heir Power," *Variety,* Sept. 8–14, 1997, p. 8.

86. Lee Hall and Jim McConville, "Time Warner, News Corp.: Make Profits, Not War," *Electronic Media,* July 28, 1997, pp. 3, 38.

87. "Ted Turner's Management Consultant," *Economist,* Mar. 22, 1997, p. 86.

88. Karen Anderson, "CNNI's Money Makers," *Cable and Satellite Express,* May 8, 1997, p. 6.

89. Thea Klapwald, "Int'l Division Gobbles Up New Countries," *Variety,* Nov. 3–9, 1997, p. 56; see also Don Groves, "Hooks and 'Faith' Helped Delivery," *Variety,* June 9–15, 1997, p. 63; John Nadler, "HBO Gets Sat Hookup," *Variety,* Apr. 7–13, 1997, p. 66; Cathy Meils, "HBO Goes Sat for Slovak Launch," *Variety,* Mar. 17–23, 1997, p. 35; Vladimir Dutz, "HBO Takes First Steps with Romanian Service," *TV East Europe,* Jan. 1998, p. 1.

90. "Nippon, Time Warner Join Toshiba to Produce Movies," *Wall Street Journal,* July 13, 1998, p. B6; Adam Dawtrey, "Warners Intl. Favors Local Flavor," *Variety,* May 26–June 1, 1997, p. 19; Paul Karon, "WB, Village Ink Prod'n Pact," *Variety,* Dec. 15–21, 1997, p. 20; Rex Weiner, "H'Wood's Euro Fever," *Variety,* May 19–25, 1997, pp. 1, 70.

91. "Warner Bros. Develops Co-production Deals," *Television Business International,* May 1998, p. 10.

92. Rebecca A. Fannin, "Every Title a Pearl," *Advertising Age International,* May 1997, p. 116; Maggie Brown, "A Whiff of the Exotic," *Financial Times,* Sept. 8, 1997, p. 11.

93. See Nicole Vulser, "Time Warner to Buy 10% Stake in Canalsatellite," *Cable and Satellite Express,* Nov. 20, 1997, pp. 1, 2; Andrew Jack, "Warner to Purchase 10% of Canal Satellite," *Financial Times,* Nov. 18, 1997, p. 20; John Hopewell, "WB Creates Spanish Axis," *Variety,* Jan. 5–11, 1998, p. 28; John Hopewell and Elizabeth Guider, "Sogecable, WB in Pact," *Variety,* July 14–20, 1997, p. 33.

94. Diane Mermigas, "Strong Profit Picture for Animation," *Electronic Media,* Dec. 22–29, 1997, p. 14.

95. Don Groves, "Tough Going: Sino the Times," *Variety,* Dec. 1–7, 1997, pp. 1, 86.

96. John Voland, "Disney Sets Sites on New Game," *Variety,* Aug. 11–17, 1997, pp. 7, 8.

97. Michiyo Nakamoto, "Walt Disney Presents: A Japanese Story," *Financial Times,* July 17, 1997, p. 5; Bruce Orwall, "Disney's Miramax Signs Pay-TV Pact with Canal Plus," *Wall Street Journal,* May 16, 1997, p. B6; Andrew

Paxman, "It's a Smaller World Already for Disney in Mexico," *Variety,* Mar. 17–23, 1997, p. 32.

98. Christopher Parkes, "Disney Hires Once More, to Keep the Brits A'Coming," *Financial Times,* Nov. 4, 1997, p. 5.

99. Andy Fry, "On Top of Their Game," *Variety,* Jan. 19–25, 1998, special section, "ESPN Intl. at 15," p. A1.

100. "Let Battle Commence," *Economist,* Apr. 26, 1997, pp. 60, 63.

101. Don Groves, "Fox Oz Studios Eye Int'l Biz," *Variety,* Aug. 25–31, 1997, p. 18; Don Groves, "Bowing Complex Courts New Strategies," *Variety,* Sept. 15–21, 1997, pp. 21, 27.

102. John Lippmann, "News Corp.'s Murdoch Is Shopping to Expand Empire," *Wall Street Journal,* Apr. 16, 1997, p. B10.

103. John Gapper, "News Corporation Raises Coverage," *Financial Times,* Sept. 15, 1997, p. 23.

104. Julian Clover, "Sky Launches Nordic Package," *European Television Analyst,* Mar. 12, 1997, p. 5; Erich Boehm, "BSkyB Eyes Move into U.K. Film Market," *Variety,* Apr. 21–27, 1997, p. 8.

105. Gary Davey, "Star TV," *Asia Research* (a Goldman Sachs publication), Oct. 24, 1997, pp. 5–13.

106. Robert Frank, "Prince Waleed Invests $850 Million in News Corp., Netscape, Motorola," *Wall Street Journal,* Nov. 25, 1997, p. B4.

107. Jonathan Karp, "India May Pull Plug on News Corp.'s TV," *Wall Street Journal,* Sept. 2, 1997, p. A15; Anil Wanravi, "Star in a Storm," *Television Business International,* Oct. 1997, pp. 82–83.

108. Tony Walker and Raymond Snoddy, "Murdoch Woos China on Satellite TV," *Financial Times,* May 16, 1997, p. 1.

109. John Gapper, "Murdoch Eyes Media in an Integrated Europe," *Financial Times,* Apr. 7, 1998, p. 8; Hilary Clarke and Dawn Hayes, "Murdoch Eyes Kirch Stake," *Independent,* June 7, 1998; *Financial Times,* June 15, 1998, p. 20; Beatriz Goyoaga, "Murdoch, Cisneros Eyeing CEI," *Variety,* May 4–10, 1998, p. 41.

110. "News Corp. Plants Flag in Europe, Kick-starts Italian DTH," *TV International,* Nov. 30, 1998, p. 1.; John Gapper and Paul Betts, "Murdoch Gains Some Ground in Continental Europe," *Financial Times,* Nov. 24, 1998, p. 25.

111. Robert Preston and James Blitz, "Magnate Finds Premier He 'Could Do Business With,'" *Financial Times,* Mar. 25, 1998, p. 9.

112. Nick Cohen, "The Death of News," *New Statesman,* May 22, 1998, p. 20.

113. Mike Galetto, "How to Protect Local Content in a Global Era?" *Electronic Media,* Dec. 1, 1997, p. 22.

114. Kathy Chen, "China's Reforms Reach Culture Sector," *Wall Street Journal,* Dec. 16, 1997, p. A14.

115. For thoughtful discussions of the issue of cultural and media imperial-

ism see the contributions to the following two excellent books: Peter Golding and Phil Harris, eds., *Beyond Cultural Imperialism: Globalization, Communication and the New International Order* (London: Sage, 1997); Daya Kishan Thussu, ed., *Electronic Empires: Global Media and Local Resistance* (London: Arnold, 1998).

116. Frank Rose, "There's No Business like Show Business," p. 90.

117. "Movers and Shakers," *Economist,* May 9, 1998, p. 86.

118. "Culture Wars," p. 98.

119. Christopher Stern, "U.S. Ideas Top Export Biz," *Variety,* May 11–17, 1998, p. 50.

120. Paul Fahri and Megan Rosenfeld, "American Pop Penetrates Worldwide," Oct. 25, 1998, p. A1.

121. James Wilson, "Film Piracy Move on Honduras," *Financial Times,* Jan. 23, 1998, p. 6.

122. Alice Rawsthorn and James Harding, "Clinton Will Lobby China to Let Hollywood Show Its Wares," *Financial Times,* June 18, 1998, p. 4.

123. Rosanna Tamburri, "Canada Considers New Stand against American Culture," *Wall Street Journal,* Feb. 4, 1998, p. A18.

124. Bahree, "U.S. Will Ask WTO to Keep Internet Free," p. B20.

125. Rance Crain, "Cozy Doesn't Cut It for Marketers Playing the Game on Global Scale," *Advertising Age,* Jan. 26, 1998, p. 24.

126. David Hatch, "Program Teaches American Way of Life," *Electronic Media,* Jan. 19, 1998, pp. 83, 90.

127. The writer is the dean of the Yale School of Management, a former investment banker, and a former official for international trade in the U.S. Department of Commerce. See Jeffrey E. Garten, "'Cultural Imperialism' Is No Joke," *Business Week,* Nov. 30, 1998, p. 26.

128. Michael Williams, "Sacre Bleu! Gallic Pix Speak English," *Variety,* Dec. 14–20, 1998, p. 9.

129. "A World View," *Economist,* Nov. 29, 1997, pp. 71–72.

130. Andrew Paxman, "Latins Hot for U.S. TV," *Variety,* Mar. 31–Apr. 6, 1997, p. 62; Laurel Wentz, "Pan-Asian TV Survey Represents Baby Step for Regional Research," *Advertising Age International,* Oct. 1997, p. 13.

131. Alice Rawsthorn, "From Bit Part to Star Billing," *Financial Times,* Jan. 31–Feb. 1, 1998, p. 7.

132. Cynthia Littleton, "Is It Global Village of the Suburbs?" *Variety,* June 15–21, 1998, p. 6.

133. *Forbes,* July 27, 1998, pp. 167–70.

134. Dugan, "Boldly Going Where Others Are Bailing Out," p. 46.

135. Marc Gunther, "Bertelsmann's New Media Man," *Fortune,* Nov. 23, 1998, p. 176.

136. Thane Peterson and Richard Siklos, "Cautious Company, Risk-Taking CEO," *Business Week,* Nov. 9, 1998, p. 147.

137. Patrick M. Reilly, "Bertelsmann Picks Zelnick, 41, to Head BMG Entertainment Music, Video Unit," *Wall Street Journal,* July 28, 1998, p. B5.

138. "Home Alone in Europe," p. 74.

139. "Culture Wars," p. 97.

140. "Why Rupert Murdoch Is Polite," *Economist,* Apr. 11, 1998, p. 39.

141. "Box Office Winners," *Variety,* June 8–14, 1998, p. 10.

142. Ibid., p. 14.

143. Peter Bart, "Can H'wood Afford Superstars?" *Variety,* Apr. 20–26, 1998, p. 4.

144. Stuart Elliott, "Research Finds Consumers Worldwide Belong to Six Basic Groups That Cross National Lines," *New York Times,* June 25, 1998, p. C8.

145. Adam Dawtrey, Michael Williams, Miriam Hils, David Rooney, and John Hopewell, "Euro Pix Revel in Plextasy," *Variety,* Apr. 27–May 3, 1998, pp. 1, 70–72.

146. Andrea Campbell, "Telefonica Alliance Hunts for Argentine Media Bargains," *Financial Times,* Mar. 12, 1998, p. 16.

147. David Rooney, "Mediaset Stays Home," *Variety,* Sept. 22–28, 1997, p. 103.

148. Benedict Carver, "Hollywood Going Native," *Variety,* Feb. 23–Mar. 1, 1998, pp. 9, 57.

149. Constance L. Hays, "Even Titles Are Flexible as U.S. Magazines Adapt to Foreign Ways," *New York Times,* Aug. 4, 1997, p. C7.

150. Cacilie Rohwedder, "Ein Popcorn, Bitte: Hollywood Studios Invade Europe," *Wall Street Journal,* Nov. 5, 1997, pp. B1, B11; Alice Rawsthorn, "Hollywood Turns Focus on Europe," *Financial Times,* Feb. 16, 1998, p. 19; Alice Rawsthorn, "PolyGram's Uncertain Future Threatens Europe's Rising Star," *Financial Times,* May 13, 1998, p. 14; John Hopewell and Benedict Carver, "Reuther Taps Euro Partners for WB Co.," *Variety,* Mar. 16–22, 1998, p. 5; Eric Boehm, "British Sky B'casting Bows Pic Production Arm," *Variety,* May 25–31, 1998, p. 21; Jon Hersovitz, "Japanese Pic Gets Disney Coin," *Variety,* Apr. 27–May 3, 1998, p. 18; Sarah Walker, "The Localisation of Hollywood," *Television Business International,* Oct. 1998, pp. 30–46; Cathy Meils, "WB Poland Boosts Local Pic Prod'n," *Variety,* Nov. 16–22, 1998, p. 19; Benedict Carver, "Sony Launches Hong Kong Unit," *Variety,* Oct. 5–11, 1998, p. 19.

151. Don Groves, "U Locks in the Locals," *Variety,* Jan. 19–25, 1998, p. 22.

152. Louise Lee, "To Sell Movies in Asia, Sing a Local Tune," *Wall Street Journal,* Sept. 22, 1998, pp. B1, B4.

153. Julian Clover, "Cartoon Network Expands Nordic Feed," *Cable and Satellite Express,* Jan. 15, 1998, p. 7.

154. Julian Clover, "Fox Kids Breaks Language Barrier," *Cable and Satellite Express,* Feb. 12, 1998, p. 7.

155. Steve Donohue, "Nickelodeon Bound for Asia," *Variety,* July 20, 1998, pp. 10, 42.

156. Cited in Herman and McChesney, *Global Media,* p. 43.

157. In Galetto, "How to Protect Local Content in a Global Era?" p. 22.

158. Felicia Levine and Cheryl Kane Heimlich, "Latin Cable Arms Flex Miami's Post Edge," *Variety,* May 19–25, 1997, pp. 52–53.

159. Herman and McChesney, *Global Media,* p. 53.

160. Andrew Paxman, "Trimming for the 21st Century," *Variety,* Dec. 9–14, 1997, pp. 51, 58, 70.

161. See, for example, Raymond Colitt, "Fund Aims at LatAm Media," *Financial Times,* Dec. 17, 1997, p. 24; Jonathan Friedland, "Citicorp Group Makes Move in Argentina," *Wall Street Journal,* Oct. 20, 1997, p. A17; Nuno Cintra Torres, "SIC, Globo, TV Cabo Form Pay-TV Alliance," *Cable and Satellite Express,* Sept. 11, 1997, pp. 1, 2.

162. Tim Westcott, "Cisneros Jumps Ahead," *Television Business International,* Jan./Feb. 1998, pp. 85–86. This is true across the world, not just in the Third World. See, for example, Marlene Edmunds, "Mergers Make Sense," *Variety,* Feb. 9–15, 1998, pp. 61, 64.

163. Mary Sutter, "They Might Be Moguls," *Advertising Age International,* Feb. 9, 1998, p. 9.

164. Raymond Colitt, "Venezuela's Unfolding Television Drama," *Financial Times,* Mar. 24, 1998, p. 22; Michael Kepp, "Globo Signs Portugal Pay-TV Pact," *Television Business International,* Mar. 1998, p. 14; Jonathan Friedland and Joel Millman, "Led by a Young Heir, Mexico's Televisa Puts New Stress on Profits," *Wall Street Journal,* July 10, 1998, pp. A1, A8.

165. Andrea Mandel-Campbell, "Clarin Faces Argentine Media War," *Financial Times,* Jan. 20, 1998, p. 19.

166. Adam Sandler, "U.S. Sounds Lost in Translation," *Variety,* Mar. 23–29, 1998, pp. 27, 102.

167. Jonathan Wheatley, "Brazil Keeps Watch for Music Pirates," *Financial Times,* Dec. 4, 1997, p. 5.

168. Alice Rawsthorn, "Records Sold All around the World," *Financial Times,* Mar. 12, 1998, p. 19.

169. Paul Raeborn, "The World Beat Goes On," *Business Week,* June 23, 1997, pp. 166E2, 166E4; Alice Rawsthorn, "Music Groups Dream of Capturing Global Market," Aug. 23–24, 1997, p. 2; Mark Nicholson, "India Spices Up Its Youth Music Market," *Financial Times,* Nov. 10, 1997, p. 15.

170. See Thomas Frank, *The Conquest of Cool: Business Culture, Counterculture, and the Rise of Hip Consumerism* (Chicago: University of Chicago Press, 1997).

171. See Fred Goodman, *Mansion on the Hill.*

172. Mermigas, "Surf and Groove," p. 20.

173. "On-Air Opportunities," *Television Business International,* Jan./Feb. 1998, p. 49.

174. Andrea Adelson, "The Battle of Summer Blockbusters Extends from Theaters to Fast-food Chains to Grocery Aisles," *New York Times,* June 9, 1997, p. C25.

175. Richard Gibson and Bruce Orwall, "New Mission for Mickey Mouse, Mickey D," *Wall Street Journal,* Mar. 5, 1998, pp. B1, B5; Louise Kramer, "McD's, Disney: Year-old Pact Is a Happy Deal," *Advertising Age,* May 11, 1998, p. 24.

176. Soren Baker, "A Beat Becomes a Profitable Fashion," *New York Times,* Aug. 18, 1997, p. C7.

177. Jeffrey D. Zbar, "Kids' Networks Mature into Global Programming Force," *Advertising Age International,* Mar. 1997, p. i6; Dominic Schreiber, "A Global Battle," *Television Business International,* Sept. 1997, pp. 36–37.

178. Mike Galetto, "Univision, HSN Venture May Be a Gem," *Electronic Media,* Nov. 17, 1997, pp. 10, 52.

179. Tim Carvell, "A Star Is Born in the Wee Hours," *Fortune,* May 26, 1997, pp. 36–38.

180. John Blau, "$ell It like It Is," *Communications Week International,* Apr. 7, 1997, pp. 12–16; Bernhard Weaver, "Ads in the Ether on PCS Phones, Pagers," *Mediaweek,* Mar. 31, 1997, pp. 34–36.

181. Julie Wolf and Ernest Beck, "Gorbachev Plugs Pizza Hut," *Wall Street Journal,* Dec. 3, 1997, p. B13.

182. Bethan Hutton, "Winning Word-of-Mouth Approval," *Financial Times,* Sept. 8, 1997, p. 10.

183. Bernard Wysocki, Jr., "In the Emerging World, Many Youths Splurge, Mainly on U.S. Goods," *Wall Street Journal,* June 26, 1997, pp. A1, A11; Erik Eckholm, "Delectable Materialism Catching On in China," *New York Times,* Jan. 10, 1998, pp. A1, A4.

184. For an argument that global market concerns have influenced Hollywood film content since the 1920s, see Ruth Vasey, *The World according to Hollywood* (Madison: University of Wisconsin Press, 1997).

185. Annette Insdorf, "Like the World, Casting Is Going Multinational," *New York Times,* Nov. 8, 1998, arts and entertainment section, p. 13.

186. Mark Woods, "Action Shows Pack a Punch in Asia," *Variety,* May 26–June 1, 1997, p. 48.

187. Les Brown, "TV Violence Leaves Striking Impression," *Television Business International,* Nov. 1997, p. 4.

188. Louise McElvogue, "Making a Killing out of Nature," *Television Business International,* Nov. 1997, p. 52.

189. "HMOs, the New Nasties," *Economist,* July 11, 1998, p. 34.

190. Quoted in John Pilger, *Hidden Agendas* (London: Vintage, 1998), p. 486.

191. Milton Friedman, *Capitalism and Freedom* (Chicago: University of Chicago Press, 1962), pp. 7–36; see also David Kelley and Roger Donway, "Liberalism and Free Speech," in *Democracy and the Mass Media,* ed. Judith Lichtenberg (New York: Cambridge University Press, 1990), pp. 95–96.

192. Jaime Guzmán, "El Camino Político," *Estudios Públicos* 42 (Autumn 1991): 375–78. The article originally appeared in *Realidad* 1 (Dec. 1979): 13–23, and is translated in Patrick Barrett, "Forging Compromise: Business, Parties, and Regime Change in Chile (Ph.D. dissertation, University of Wisconsin–Madison, 1997), esp. pp. 314–15.

193. All the material in this paragraph comes from Marc Cooper, "Chile: Twenty-Five Years after Allende," *Nation,* Mar. 23, 1998, pp. 11–23.

194. Cited in Serge Halimi, "When Market Journalism Invades the World," presented at "Is Globalisation Inevitable and Desirable?" conference sponsored by London School of Economics, London, May 7, 1997.

195. John Thornhill, "Russia's Unfinished Revolution," *Financial Times,* May 30, 1996, p. 13.

196. Cited in *Multinational Monitor,* Oct. 1996, p. 13.

197. Robert L. Pollock, "A Socialist 'Third Way' Turns Out to Be a Dead End," *Wall Street Journal,* June 17, 1998, p. A16.

198. Jane Birch, "Package Deal," *Television Business International,* Nov. 1997, pp. 31–32.

199. Louise McElvogue, "Not in My Back Yard," *Television Business International,* Nov. 1997, pp. 16–22.

200. CNN International advertisement, *Advertising Age International,* June 29, 1998, p. 6.

201. "Here Is the News," *Economist,* July 4, 1998, p. 13.

202. Nick Cohen, "Death of News," p. 20.

203. John Keane, *The Media and Democracy* (Cambridge, Mass.: Polity Press, 1991), pp. 91–92.

204. James Harding, "Gang of Four Found on Mars," *Financial Times,* Dec. 6–7, 1997, p. 7; Robert S. Greenberger, "Interim Pact with China Is Reached on Access for Financial-News Providers," *Wall Street Journal,* Oct. 27, 1997, p. B10.

205. Elisabeth Rosenthal, "A Muckraking Program Draws 300 Million Daily," *New York Times,* July 2, 1998, p. A8.

206. Alan Riding, "Why 'Titanic' Conquered the World," *New York Times,* Apr. 26, 1998, section 2, pp. 1, 28.

207. Joyce Barnathan, Matt Miller, and Dexter Roberts, "Has Disney Become the Forbidden Studio?" *Business Week,* Aug. 4, 1997, p. 51.

208. Bernard Weinraub, "Disney Hires Kissinger," *New York Times,* Oct. 10, 1997.

209. Dan Cox, "Disney Trumps Sony with China Card," *Variety,* Dec. 8–14, 1997, p. 3.

210. "Disney's Appointment of a China Executive Signals a New Thrust," *Wall Street Journal,* June 8, 1998, p. B2.

211. Christopher Parkes, "Disney Hints at Better Ties with Beijing," *Financial Times,* Dec. 14, 1998, p. 6.

212. Eric Alterman, "Murdoch Kills Again," *Nation,* Mar. 23, 1998, p. 7; Silverstein, "His Biggest Takeover," p. 29.

213. "HarperCollins Settles Row with Patten and Apologizes," *Wall Street Journal,* Mar. 10, 1998, p. A13.

214. "Murdoch Hunt," *Financial Times,* Mar. 2, 1998, p. 19.

215. Maureen Sullivan, "Murdoch, Welch on Advisory Board," *Variety,* Oct. 12–18, 1998, p. 36.

216. Craig S. Smith, "China Television Appeals to Beijing as Broadcaster Nears End of Its Funds," *Wall Street Journal,* Feb. 27, 1998, p. B6.

217. John Gapper, "News Corp Joins Hong Kong Book Row," *Financial Times,* Feb. 28/Mar. 1, 1998, p. 5.

218. Louise Lucas, "Hong Kong's ATV Won by Pro-Beijing Interests," *Financial Times,* May 27, 1998, p. 4.

219. Janine Stein, "ATV Sale Prompts Censorship Fears," *Television Business International,* June 1998, p. 11.

220. James Kynge and John Gapper, "Murdoch Mends Fences with Beijing," *Financial Times,* Dec. 12–13, 1998, p. 1.

221. Don Groves, "Star Shines Bright in East," *Variety,* Dec. 21, 1998–Jan. 3, 1999, p. 37.

222. Erik Eckholm, "Beijing, Toughening Crackdown, Gives 2 Activists Long Sentences," *New York Times,* Dec. 22, 1998, pp. A1, A6; James Kynge, "Third China Dissident Gets Jail Sentence," *Financial Times,* Dec. 23, 1998, p. 4.

223. Andrew Paxman, "TV Mogul Out to Retake Peru Broadcast Empire," *Variety,* Mar. 23–29, 1998, p. 68.

224. Sam Dillon, "After a Murder Attempt, an Editor Is Unbowed," *New York Times,* Mar. 7, 1998, p. A4.

225. Celestine Bohlen, "Slain Editor Makes Moscow Take Notice," *New York Times,* June 12, 1998, p. A11.

226. "Killing the Messengers," *Economist,* July 4, 1998, p. 41.

227. Committee to Protect Journalists, *Attacks on the Press in 1997* (New York: Committee to Protect Journalists, 1998).

228. Felicity Barringer, "In a Country Run by the Military, a Station Manager Sees Talk Radio as a Democratic Duty," *New York Times,* Nov. 30, 1998, p. C9.

229. Sally Bowen, "Peruvian TV at Centre of Legal Drama," *Financial Times,* Sept. 23, 1997, p. 8; Calvin Sims, "Crusading TV Station Is the City's Daytime Drama," *New York Times,* July 22, 1997, p. A4.

230. Paul Lewis, "Call to Arms: A Free Media Can Do Battle with Graft," *New York Times,* Oct. 11, 1998, p. 11.

231. Tor Wennerberg to Edward S. Herman, private correspondence, Aug. 18, 1997.

232. Raymond Colitt, "Latin America Reforms 'Fail to Cut Income Disparities,'" *Financial Times,* Nov. 13, 1997, p. 7.

233. Robert Brenner, "From Neoliberalism to Depression," *Against the Current,* Dec. 1998, p. 22.

Chapter 3: Will the Internet Set Us Free?

1. I also address these arguments in some detail in *Corporate Media and the Threat to Democracy,* and in Herman and McChesney, *Global Media.*

2. Thomas Friedman, "The Internet Wars," *New York Times,* Apr. 11, 1998, p. 25.

3. The classic statement is Nicholas Negroponte, *Being Digital* (New York: Alfred A. Knopf, 1995).

4. William M. Bulkeley, "Peering Ahead," *Wall Street Journal,* Nov. 16, 1998, p. R4.

5. Nick Wingfield, "Let Us Entertain You," *Wall Street Journal,* Nov. 16, 1998, pp. R27, R29.

6. Steve Lohr, "Media Convergence," *New York Times,* June 29, 1998, p. A11.

7. Cited in Herman and McChesney, *Global Media,* p. 107.

8. Landler, "From Gurus to Sitting Ducks," p. 9.

9. For a discussion of the new "wired" house, see Erick Schonfeld, "The Network in Your House," *Fortune,* Aug. 3, 1998, pp. 125–28.

10. Quoted in Norman Solomon, "Motherhood, Apple Pie, Computers," syndicated newspaper column, June 1998.

11. "All Together Now," p. 14.

12. See James W. Carey, "The Internet and the End of the National Communications System: Uncertain Predictions of an Uncertain Future," *Journalism and Mass Communication Quarterly,* Spring 1998, pp. 28–34.

13. See, for example, Wilson Dizard, Jr., *Meganet: How the Global Communications Network Will Connect Everyone on Earth* (Boulder, Colo.: Westview Press, 1997).

14. Leslie Browne and Heather Green, "Welcoming Spanish Speakers to the Web," *Business Week,* Dec. 29, 1997, p. 50E8.

15. See Neil Postman, *Amusing Ourselves to Death* (New York: Penguin, 1995).

16. See Robert Avery, ed., *Public Service Broadcasting in a Multichannel Environment* (New York: Longman, 1993).

17. See Mary Vipond, *Listening In: The First Decade of Canadian Broadcasting, 1922–1932* (Montreal: McGill-Queens University Press, 1992).

18. W. Russell Neuman, Lee McKnight, and Richard Jay Solomon, *The Gordian Knot: Political Gridlock on the Information Highway* (Cambridge, Mass.: MIT Press, 1997).

19. Leslie Eaton, "The Silicon Valley Gang," *New York Times,* June 11, 1998, pp. C1, C3.

20. Rebecca Quick, "On-Line Groups Are Offering Up Privacy Plans," *Wall Street Journal,* June 22, 1998, pp. B1, B3; Amy Harmon, "U.S., in Shift, Drops Its Effort to Manage Internet Addresses," *New York Times,* June 6, 1998, p. B2.

21. John Simons, "How a Vice President Fills a Cyber-Cabinet: With Gore-Techs," *Wall Street Journal,* Mar. 13, 1998, pp. A1, A6.

22. Amy Borrus and Linda Himelstein, "Seeking Geeks Bearing Gifts, the GOP Courts Silicon Valley," *Business Week,* July 27, 1998, p. 39.

23. Denise Caruso, "Digital Commerce: A Commercial Code Revision Tries to Take on the Task of Legislating the Internet," *New York Times,* June 22, 1998, p. C3.

24. "Helping to Groom the Net," *Communications Week International,* Feb. 16, 1998, p. 9.

25. Rebecca Quick, "U.S. Sidesteps Thorny Issue of Internet Names," *Wall Street Journal,* June 4, 1998, p. B4.

26. Michael Hauben and Ronda Hauben, *Netizens: On the History and Impact of Usenet and the Internet* (Los Alamitos, Calif.: IEEE Computer Society Press, 1997).

27. "The Death of an Icon," *Economist,* Oct. 24, 1998, p. 91.

28. Hauben and Hauben, *Netizens,* chap. 12.

29. Quick, "U.S. Sidesteps Thorny Issue of Internet Names," p. B4.

30. Mitchell Kapor, "Where Is the Digital Highway Really Heading? The Case for a Jeffersonian Information Policy," *Wired* 1, no. 3 (1993).

31. Hauben and Hauben, *Netizens,* chap. 11.

32. Adrienne Ward Fawcett, "Interactive Awareness Growing," *Advertising Age,* Oct. 16, 1995, p. 20.

33. Bruce Ingersoll, "Internet Spurs U.S. Growth, Cuts Inflation," *Wall Street Journal,* Apr. 16, 1998, pp. A3, A6.

34. Harmon, "U.S., in Shift, Drops Its Effort to Manage Internet Addresses," p. B2.

35. Jeri Clausing, "Critics Contend U.S. Policy on the Internet Has 2 Big Flaws," *New York Times,* June 15, 1998, p. C1.

36. Jeri Clausing, "U.S. Report on Net Commerce Set for Release," *New York Times,* Nov. 30, 1998, pp. C1, C6.

37. Jeri Clausing, "Group Proposes Voluntary Guidelines for Internet Policy," *New York Times,* July 21, 1998, p. C4.

38. Louise Kehoe, "Lords of the Internet," *Financial Times,* Feb. 7–8, 1998, p. 6.

39. "Untangling the Web," *Economist,* Apr. 25, 1998, p. 80.

40. Louise Kehoe, "The End of the Free Ride," *Financial Times,* July 1, 1998, p. 14.

41. Harmon, "U.S., in Shift, Drops Its Effort to Manage Internet Addresses," pp. A1, B2.

42. Catherine Yang, "How the Internet Works: All You Need to Know," *Business Week,* July 20, 1998, p. 60.

43. Christopher Stern, "Congress Steers H'w'd Wish List," *Variety,* Oct. 19–25, 1998, p. 6; Kenneth Cukier, "U.S. Passes Legal Framework for Net Commerce," *Communications Week International,* Nov. 23, 1998, p. 10.

44. Denise Caruso, "The Clinton Administration Is Taking a Tough Stance on Cyberspace Copyrights," *New York Times,* Jan. 19, 1998, p. C3; Jeri Clausing, "Legislation on On-Line Copyrights Advances," *New York Times,* May 4, 1998, p. C12.

45. John Simons, "White House to Unveil Plans to Expand Internet Projects to Developing Nations," *Wall Street Journal,* Nov. 30, 1998, p. B6.

46. Vanessa Houlder, "Surfing in the Wake of the Americans," *Financial Times,* June 17, 1998, p. 22.

47. Alan Cane, "Operators Race to Surf 'Data Wave,'" *Financial Times,* June 10, 1998, FT telecoms section, p. 1; John Ridding, "Pacific Century Goes Online in Asia," *Financial Times,* Mar. 13, 1998, p. 27.

48. Houlder, "Surfing in the Wake of the Americans," p. 22.

49. John Markoff, "Difference over Privacy on the Internet," *New York Times,* July 1, 1998, pp. C1, C7.

50. Kenneth Cukier, "Time to Break U.S. Grip on Internet Says OECD," *Communications Week International,* Apr. 20, 1998, p. 1.

51. Louise Kehoe, "Battles Still Rage as the Control of Key Internet Function Remains Unresolved," *Financial Times,* Sept. 28, 1998, p. 5; "Rifts Remain on Internet Rules," *Financial Times,* Oct. 12, 1998, p. 4.

52. Louise Kehoe, "Private Sector Moves Closer to Web Venture," *Financial Times,* Oct. 28, 1998, p. 8.

53. Rebecca Quick, "Internet Giants Plan Campaign to Teach Consumers Their Online Rights," *Wall Street Journal,* Oct. 7, 1998, p. B9; John Authers, "Media and Telecoms Chiefs Aim for Self-Regulation of Internet," *Financial Times,* Jan. 15, 1999, p. 12.

54. Stephen N. Brown, "The United States Exports Telecommunications Act," *Lightwave,* Jan. 1997, p. 22.

55. Guy de Jonquieres, "The Changing of the Guards," *Financial Times,* July 10, 1998, p. 13.

56. Guy de Jonquieres, "Pact on Electronic Commerce," *Financial Times,* May 20, 1998, p. 8.

57. Jennifer Schenker, "European Union Considers Methods to Safeguard Consumers on the Web," *Wall Street Journal,* Oct. 19, 1998, p. B15I.

58. "Modernizing the ITU," *Communications Week International,* Nov. 2, 1998, p. 9.

59. David Molony and Kenneth Cukier, "Industry Pushes ITU into Truce with Net Task Force," *Communications Week International,* Oct. 5, 1998, pp. 1, 33.

60. David Molony and Vineeta Shetty, "Utsumi Pledges to Usher in More Business-Friendly ITU," *Communications Week International,* Nov. 2, 1998, p. 1.

61. Clausing, "Critics Contend U.S. Policy on the Internet Has 2 Big Flaws," pp. C1, C5.

62. David Bank and Leslie Cauley, "TCI Set-Top-Box Pacts Pits Microsoft against Sun," *Wall Street Journal,* Jan. 12, 1998, p. A3; Richard Wolffe, "Court Backs Microsoft in Landmark Antitrust Battle," *Financial Times,* June 24, 1998, p. 1.

63. Richard Wolffe and Nancy Dunne, "Internet Access 'Must Be Equal,'" *Financial Times,* Apr. 28, 1998, p. 7.

64. Seth Schiesel, "Cuts Are Urged in Internet Fund Clinton Praises," *New York Times,* June 6, 1998, pp. B1, B3.

65. John Simons, "FCC Is Scaling Back Effort to Connect Nation's Schools, Libraries to Internet," *Wall Street Journal,* June 15, 1998, p. B7.

66. Dan Schiller, *Digital Capitalism* (Cambridge, Mass.: MIT Press, 1999), pp. 199–200.

67. Kathryn C. Montgomery, "Gov't Must Take Lead in Protecting Children," *Advertising Age,* June 22, 1998, p. 40.

68. John McHugh, "Politics for the Really Cool," *Forbes,* Sept. 8, 1997, pp. 172–92.

69. See George Gilder, *Life after Television,* rev. ed. (New York: W. W. Norton, 1994).

70. See, for example, Milton Friedman, *Capitalism and Freedom.*

71. See Allan Engler, *Apostles of Greed: Capitalism and the Myth of the Individual in the Market* (London: Pluto Press, 1995); Paul M. Sweezy, *Four Lectures on Marxism* (New York: Monthly Review Press, 1981), esp. chap. 2, appendix B, "Competition and Monopoly."

72. Peter Martin, "The Merger Police," *Financial Times,* Mar. 12, 1998, p. 10.

73. Stephanie N. Mehta, "US West Is Set to Offer TV Programming and Internet Access over Phone Lines," *Wall Street Journal,* Apr. 20, 1998, p. B6.

74. Diane Mermigas, "Strong Media Forecast for '98," *Electronic Media,* Nov. 3, 1997, p. 31; Mercedes M. Cardona, "Media Industry Grows Faster than GDP: Veronis," *Advertising Age,* Nov. 3, 1997, p. 16.

75. Jerry Colonna, "For Internet Stocks, the Fall of Overvalued Companies Can Hurt Strong Companies as Well," *New York Times,* June 1, 1998, p. C5.

76. Kenneth N. Gilpin, "Thinking Rationally as the Web Goes Wild," *New York Times,* July 12, 1998, p. 7.

77. Donald L. Bartlett and James B. Steele, "Corporate Welfare," *Time,* Nov. 9, 1998, pp. 36–54.

78. Cited in Noam Chomsky, *World Orders Old and New* (New York: Columbia University Press, 1994).

79. Mark Zepezauer and Arthur Naiman, *Take the Rich Off Welfare* (Tucson, Ariz.: Odonian Press, 1996), pp. 75–80.

80. Amy Harmon, "Technology to Let Engineers Filter the Web and Judge Content," *New York Times,* Jan. 19, 1998, pp. C1, C4.

81. See, for example, Michael R. Gordon, "Soviet Mindset Defeating Rural Capitalism," *New York Times,* Nov. 30, 1998, pp. A1, A6.

82. See, for example, Robert Kuttner, *Everything for Sale: The Virtues and Limits of Markets* (New York: Alfred A. Knopf, 1997).

83. James Sterngold, "A Racial Divide Widens on Network TV," *New York Times,* Dec. 29, 1998, pp. A1, A12.

84. T. Charbeneau, "Dangerous Assumptions," *Toward Freedom,* 43, no. 7 (1995): 28–29.

85. Amy Harmon, "Sad, Lonely World Discovered in Cyberspace," *New York Times,* Aug. 30, 1998, pp. A1, A22; Richard Waters, "Net Address May Be Home to Depression," *Financial Times,* Aug. 31, 1998, p. 1; Denise Caruso, "Critics Are Picking Apart a Professor's Study That Linked Internet Use to Loneliness and Depression," *New York Times,* Sept. 14, 1998, p. C5.

86. Price Coleman, "Digital Cable: When, Not If," *Broadcasting and Cable,* May 4, 1998, pp. 42, 46.

87. Don Clark and David Bank, "Microsoft, Sony to Cooperate on PCs, Devices," *Wall Street Journal,* Apr. 8, 1998, p. B8.

88. Stephen H. Wildstrom, "Weaving the Web into Your TV," *Business Week,* June 1, 1998, p. 27; Diane Mermigas, "A Passage to Digital," *Electronic Media,* Mar. 30, 1998, pp. 1, 14.

89. Frederick Rose, "Broadcom Set to Unveil TV-Internet Chip," *Wall Street Journal,* Nov. 9, 1998, p. B3.

90. Diane Mermigas, "Windows 98 Can Also Turn on TV," *Electronic Media,* May 18, 1998. pp. 10, 28; Evan Ramstad, "Matsushita, Philips to Sell DTV Aid for Computers," *Wall Street Journal,* Nov. 10, 1998, p. B4.

91. Jim McConville, "AMC Has No Room for Its Pop," *Electronic Media,* Apr. 6, 1998, pp. 60–61; Lee Hall, "TNN Skips Digital, Heads Right to Web," *Electronic Media,* Mar. 16, 1998, pp. 1A, 42.

92. Marc Graser, "WWW.Crossover.Net," *Variety,* Oct. 19–25, 1998, p. 58.

93. Walter S. Mossberg, "To Be a Mass Medium, the Web Must Be Freed from the PC," *Wall Street Journal,* Nov. 5, 1998, p. B1.

94. Dianne Mermigas, "Searching for a Network Foothold on the Web," *Electronic Media,* June 8, 1998, p. 36.

95. Andrew Pollack, "Hughes to Buy a Satellite TV Competitor," *New York Times,* Dec. 15, 1998, p. C12.

96. Lee Hall, "Cable Hails Open Digital Set-Top Deal," *Electronic Media,* Dec. 22–29, 1997, p. 1.

97. Peter H. Lewis, "Silicon Valley Courts Cable TV," *New York Times,* Dec. 22, 1997, p. C2; Chuck Ross, "Next Generation Cable: Interactivity," *Advertising Age,* Dec. 22, 1997, p. 12.

98. Martin Peers, "Giants Chow Down Indies," *Variety,* Sept. 15–21, 1997, p. 31.

99. John Dempsey, "Cablers Fight for Shelf Life," *Variety,* May 4–10, 1998, pp. 33, 35; John Dempsey, "Cablenets Place Digital Bets," *Variety,* Dec. 8–14, 1997, pp. 37–38; Christopher Parkes, "US Cable Achieves End-of-Term High," *Financial Times,* Dec. 13–14, 1997, p. 23; Michael Burgi, "Channel Change," *Mediaweek,* Dec. 1, 1997, p. 1.

100. Ray Richmond, "Showtime Takes Action with Extreme Plan," *Variety,* Dec. 22, 1997–Jan. 4, 1998, p. 28.

101. Steve McClellen, "CTW, Nick Team Up in 'Suite' Deal," *Broadcasting and Cable,* May 4, 1998, p. 97; John M. Higgins, "HBO Sets New Digital Networks," *Broadcasting and Cable,* Apr. 13, 1998, p. 10; Jim McConville, "HBO's Branching Out," *Electronic Media,* Apr. 13, 1998, p. 4.

102. Geraldine Fabrikant, "New Cable Services Are Everywhere, but They All Seem to Be Owned by the Same Big Companies," *New York Times,* May 11, 1998, p. C10; see also Jim McConville, "Boyz and Girlz, This Is How Fox Grows," *Electronic Media,* Nov. 2, 1998, pp. 1A, 37; Donna Petrozzello, "A&E Unveils Digital Networks," *Broadcasting and Cable,* Nov. 16, 1998, p. 56.

103. "'Ma and Pa Days' of TV Recede as Digital Advances," *Electronic Media,* Nov. 3, 1997, p. 28.

104. Leslie Cauley, "Yes, It's Possible: An Outsider Launches a Cable-TV Network," *Wall Street Journal,* Nov. 13, 1998, p. A1.

105. Betsy Sharkey, "Master of His Domain," *Adweek,* June 1, 1998, p. 37.

106. Leslie Cauley, "TCI Group Tallies Digital Subscribers at 1 Million and Posts $52 Million Net," *Wall Street Journal,* Nov. 16, 1998, p. B6.

107. Ross, "Next Generation Cable," p. 12.

108. Judann Polack, "Kraft Takes Target-Marketing to Ground Zero via TCI Test," *Advertising Age,* Apr. 13, 1998, p. s2.

109. Chuck Ross, "TCI's Malone Seeks Summit with Agencies," *Advertising Age,* May 18, 1998, pp. 11–12.

110. Chuck Ross, "New Century Readies Test of Addressable Advertising," *Advertising Age,* Aug. 3, 1998, p. 10.

111. Chuck Ross, "TCI Hosts Interactive 'Brainstorm,'" *Advertising Age,* Nov. 9, 1998, p. 92.

112. Mark Vernon, "Sporting Chance of a Sale," *Financial Times,* June 3, 1998, IT supplement, p. 13.

113. Steve Donohue, "An Open Window to Convergence," *Electronic Media,* June 29, 1998, p. 20.

114. Brian Seth Hurst, "Are You Ready for Convergence?" *Electronic Media,* June 15, 1998, p. 24.

115. Diane Mermigas, "Dawn Approaches for Cable's E-Commerce," *Electronic Media,* Nov. 16, 1998, p. 20.

116. Diane Mermigas, "The Lure of Interactivity," *Electronic Media,* Apr. 6, 1998, p. 48.

117. Chuck Ross, "Media Giants Near Pact for Interactive TV Rules," *Advertising Age,* Jan. 26, 1998, p. 2.

118. Kyle Pope and Evan Ramstad, "HDTV Sets: Too Pricey, Too Late?" *Wall Street Journal,* Jan. 7, 1998. pp. B1, B11.

119. Much of the discussion that follows comes from Robert W. McChesney, "The Digital TV Scandal: How a Powerful Lobby Stole Billions in Public Property," *Public Citizen News,* Fall 1997, pp. 8–9.

120. Silverstein, "His Biggest Takeover," p. 31.

121. Rowse, "Lobby the Media Won't Touch."

122. This quote from Robert W. McChesney, "The Digital TV Heist," *In These Times,* May 12–25, 1997, pp. 20–24.

123. Rowse, "Lobby the Media Won't Touch," p. 9.

124. Christopher Stern, "High Def Doesn't Stand Up to Scrutiny," *Variety,* July 13–19, 1998, p. 29.

125. Diane Mermigas, "New Study Has Some Good News for DTV," *Electronic Media,* Nov. 23, 1998, p. 4.

126. Christopher Stern, "B'cast 'Loan' Has Xmas Wrapping," *Variety,* Apr. 4, 1997, p. 24.

127. Jim McConville, "A&E's Davatzes Talks Digital, Rates, History," *Electronic Media,* Dec. 8, 1997, p. 36.

128. Mermigas, "BCFM Gets Net, Digital Alert," p. 14.

129. Joel Brinkley, "A Gulf Develops among Broadcasters on Programming Pledge," *New York Times,* Aug. 18, 1997, p. C1.

130. Claude Brodesser and Jim Cooper, "NBC May Air Cable Nets," *Mediaweek,* Jan. 26, 1998, p. 3.

131. La Franco, "Tough Customers," pp. 78, 80.

132. Michael Freeman, "Strength in Numbers," *Mediaweek,* Apr. 6, 1998, p. 42.

133. Jim McConville, "Digital Blast from TCI's Hindery," *Electronic Media,* Sept. 1, 1997, pp. 1, 18.

134. Christopher Stern, "Gore Dishes up Digital Split with Free-Ad Fudge," *Variety,* Oct. 27–Nov. 2, 1997, p. 24.

135. Alicia Mundy, "HDTV Sends Shock Waves over the Political Spectrum," *Mediaweek,* Apr. 13, 1998, p. 16.

136. John Dempsey, "B'casters, Cable Cook Digital Pie," *Variety,* Aug. 18–24, 1997, pp. 21, 24.

137. Jon Lafayette, "Sinclair Chief Has a Simple, and Radical, Plan," *Electronic Media,* Jan. 19, 1998, p. 100.

138. Christopher Stern, "Network Nettle over Digital Date," *Variety,* Dec. 1–7, 1997, p. 39.

139. Bill McConnell, "Easing the Digital Path," *Broadcasting and Cable,* Nov. 23, 1998, p. 48; Doug Halonen, "FCC Tackling Consistency," *Electronic Media,* Nov. 23, 1998, p. 42.

140. Alicia Mundy, Michael Freeman, and Jim Cooper, "The Digital Dilemma," *Mediaweek,* Oct. 12, 1998, p. 7.

141. Jon Lafayette, "The Vision for Digital Still Blurry," *Electronic Media,* Aug. 17, 1998, p. 3; Catherine Yang, Neil Gross, Richard Siklos, and Stephen V. Brull, "Digital D-Day," *Business Week,* Oct. 26, 1998, pp. 144–58.

142. Alicia Mundy, "Nets Shift Gears on HDTV," *Mediaweek,* Sept. 29, 1997, p. 5.

143. Lawrie Mifflin, "Voluntary Political TV Advertising Urged," *New York Times,* Dec. 18, 1998, p. A18.

144. Alicia Mundy, "TV That's Good for You," *Mediaweek,* Oct. 5, 1998, p. 26.

145. David Hatch, "Final Gore Report Has Few Surprises, Many Dissents," *Electronic Media,* Dec. 21–28, 1998, p. 4.

146. "Airwave Avarice," *Los Angeles Times,* Dec. 7, 1998.

147. Bill McConnell and Paige Albiniak, "'Bigwigs' Weigh In on Ownership," *Broadcasting and Cable,* Dec. 14, 1998, p. 22.

148. Steve Behrens, "Soft Gore Report Will Be Price of Consensus with Commercial TV," *Current,* Nov. 23, 1998.

149. Chris McConnell, "Service with a $6.85 Billion Smile," *Broadcasting and Cable,* Apr. 8, 1998, p. 18.

150. "To Air Is Human," *Broadcasting and Cable,* Sept. 29, 1998, p. 78.

151. Christopher Stern, "Free Air Trendy, but Full of Holes," *Variety,* Mar. 23–29, 1998, p. 33.

152. Doug Halonen, "Battle over Free Airtime Looms," *Electronic Media,* Feb. 2, 1998, pp. 1, 44; John R. Wilke, "FCC Chief to Push for Free Air Time in Political Races," *Wall Street Journal,* Jan. 28, 1998, p. A6.

153. Alicia Mundy, "In Whose Interest?" *Mediaweek,* Dec. 8, 1997, pp. 4–5; for a discussion of why the advertising industry will also battle against free TV ads for political candidates, see Ira Teinowitz, "Push for Free Political Ads Worries Paid Advertisers," *Advertising Age,* Feb. 2, 1998, p. 49.

154. David Hatch and Noel Holston, "Panel Drafting Conduct Code," *Electronic Media,* June 15, 1998, p. 3.

155. Mifflin, "Voluntary Political TV Advertising Urged," p. A18.

156. A transcript is available online at www.ntia.doc.gov/pubintadvcom/decmtg/transcript.html.

157. "What's Ahead for the New FCC," *Electronic Media*, Nov. 3, 1997, p. 10.

158. Lake Snell Perry and Associates, *Television in the Digital Age: A Report to the Project on Media Ownership and the Benton Foundation* (Washington, D.C., 1998).

159. Mifflin, "Voluntary Political TV Advertising Urged," p. A18.

160. Newton Minow, "Minow Dissents on Digital Report," *Electronic Media*, Dec. 7, 1998, p. 13.

161. Tim Westcott, "Boxing Clever," *Television Business International*, Jan.–Feb. 1998, p. 53.

162. Raymond Snoddy, "Chronicle of a Death Foretold," *Financial Times*, Aug. 18, 1997, p. 7; Jared Sandberg, "It Isn't Entertainment That Makes the Web Shine; It's Dull Data," *Wall Street Journal*, July 20, 1998, pp. A1, A6.

163. Rich Karlgaard, "The Web Is Recession-Proof," *Wall Street Journal*, July 14, 1998, p. A18.

164. Nicholas Denton, "mainstream.com," *Financial Times*, Jan. 3–4, 1998, p. 6.

165. John M. Higgins, "IP Telephony: Does AT&T Have Its Number?" *Broadcasting and Cable*, July 8, 1998, pp. 36–38; "Growing Up," *Economist*, May 2, 1998, pp. 56–58; Paul Taylor, "Big Shake-up for Telecom Suppliers," *Financial Times*, May 6, 1998, IT supplement, p. 1.

166. Richard Waters, "Sprint Remodels Network to Adapt to Internet Age," *Financial Times*, June 3, 1998, p. 15; Richard Waters, "Sprint Leap Needs Firm Landing," *Financial Times*, June 3, 1998, p. 18.

167. Yang, "How the Internet Works," pp. 58–60.

168. Bernhard Warner, "Dialing for ISP Dollars," *Mediaweek*, June 1, 1998, pp. 30, 32.

169. Richard Poynder, "Internet Small Fry on the Road to Oblivion," *Financial Times*, Apr. 29, 1998, p. 12.

170. Jared Sandberg and Steven Lipin, "Bell Atlantic and GTE Agree on a Merger," *Wall Street Journal*, July 28, 1998, p. A3.

171. Guttam Naik, "Phone Firms Jump to Buy Rich Markets," *Wall Street Journal*, Dec. 10, 1998, p. A18.

172. Seth Schiesel, "AT&T and British Telecom Merge Overseas Operations," *New York Times*, July 27, 1998, pp. A1, A6; Gautum Naik and Stephanie N. Mehta, "AT&T, BT Form World-Wide Alliance," *Wall Street Journal*, July 27, 1998, p. A3.

173. See Herman and McChesney, *Global Media*, chap. 4.

174. Seth Schiesel, "F.C.C. May Act to Aid Home Internet Access," *New York Times*, July 17, 1998, pp. C1, C3.

175. Price Coleman, "Malone Proposes In-tier-net," *Broadcasting and Cable*, June 15, 1998, p. 53.

176. Thomas E. Webber, "Who, What, Where: Putting the Internet in Perspective," *Wall Street Journal,* Apr. 16, 1998, p. B12.

177. Saul Hansell, "Hooking Up the Nation," *New York Times,* June 25, 1998, p. C5.

178. Rebecca Quick, "Internet Contains a Racial Divide on Access and Use, Study Shows," *Wall Street Journal,* Apr. 17, 1998, p. B6.

179. Diane Mermigas, "TCI Goes Digital with Microsoft," *Electronic Media,* Jan. 19, 1998, pp. 3, 119.

180. Roger O. Crockett, Gary McWilliams, Susan Jackson, and Peter Elstrom, "Warp Speed Ahead," *Business Week,* Feb. 16, 1998, pp. 80–83.

181. Dean Takahashi and Stephanie N. Mehta, "Bells Push a Modem Standard to Rival Cable's," *Wall Street Journal,* Jan. 21, 1998, p. B6; Seth Schiesel, "Venture Promises Far Faster Speeds for Internet Data," *New York Times,* Jan. 20, 1998, pp. A1, C7.

182. David Bank and Leslie Cauley, "Microsoft, Compaq Make Net-Access Bet," *Wall Street Journal,* June 16, 1998, p. A3.

183. "Microsoft Buys into Thomson," *Electronic Media,* Dec. 7, 1998, p. 44; "Microsoft Invests $200 Million in Qwest," *Wall Street Journal,* Dec. 15, 1998, p. B12.

184. Steve Hamm, Amy Cortese, and Susan B. Garland, "Microsoft's Future," *Business Week,* Jan. 19, 1998, pp. 58–68.

185. Steve Lohr and John Markoff, "How Software Giant Played Hardball Game," *New York Times,* Oct. 8, 1998, pp. A1, C8; David Bank, "Microsoft's Digital-TV Efforts Are Stymied," *Wall Street Journal,* Dec. 3, 1998, p. B7.

186. Steve Lohr, "If Microsoft Loses Case, Remedies Are Thorny," *New York Times,* Dec. 14, 1998, pp. C1, C5.

187. Diane Mermigas, "Avoiding the Web's Pitfalls," *Electronic Media,* May 18, 1998, p. 18.

188. Diane Mermigas, "Change Is the Key to Survival," *Electronic Media,* Dec. 7, 1998, p. 26.

189. Steven Abraham, "Internet Proving Itself a Good Test Market for Digital TV," *Electronic Media,* Nov. 30, 1998, p. 68.

190. Louise Kehoe, "Internet Plumber Needed," *Financial Times,* June 17, 1998, p. 12.

191. See Herman and McChesney, *Global Media,* chaps. 3 and 4; Nick Flaherty, "Diving In at the Deep End," *Cable and Satellite Europe,* Mar. 1997, pp. 61, 63.

192. Diane Mermigas, "Analysts Adding Up AT&T-TCI Deal," *Electronic Media,* July 6, 1998, pp. 3, 25; Henry Goldblatt, "AT&T's Costly Game of Catch-up," *Fortune,* July 20, 1998, pp. 25–26.

193. Kyle Pope, "Telecom World Is Wondering: 'Who's Next?'" *Wall Street Journal,* June 25, 1998, p. B1.

194. Diane Mermigas, "Telephony Will Transform Cable," *Electronic Media,* Nov. 23, 1998, p. 10.

195. Mark Suzman, "AT&T Chief Sees Further Industry Tie-ups," *Financial Times,* July 8, 1998, p. 21.

196. Stephen Labaton, "Three Proposed Telecommunications Mergers Draw Challenges at an F.C.C. Hearing," *New York Times,* Dec. 15, 1998, p. C8.

197. Quick, "On-Line Groups Are Offering Up Privacy Plans," p. B3.

198. Peggy Hollinger, "Internet Shopping Set to Soar in Next Four Years," *Financial Times,* Jan. 27, 1998, p. 5.

199. Heather Green, Amy Cortese, Paul Judge, and Robert D. Hof, "Click Here for Wacky Valuations," *Business Week,* July 20, 1998, pp. 32–34; "The 'Click Here' Economy," *Business Week,* June 22, 1998, p. 124.

200. Ingersoll, "Internet Spurs U.S. Growth, Cuts Inflation," p. A3.

201. Kate Maddox, "Forrester Study Says Users Ready for E-Commerce," *Advertising Age,* Mar. 23, 1998, p. 34.

202. Eric Nee, "Welcome to My Store," *Forbes,* Oct. 19, 1998, p. 140.

203. Heather Green, "The Skinny on Niche Portals," *Business Week,* Oct. 26, 1998, p. 66.

204. Christopher Parkes and Louise Kehoe, "Mickey Wants Us All Online," *Financial Times,* June 20–21, 1998, p. 7.

205. Marc Gunther, "The Internet Is Mr. Case's Neighborhood," *Fortune,* Mar. 30, 1998, pp. 69–80.

206. "Ma Bell Convenience Store," *Economist,* June 27, 1998, pp. 61–62.

207. Heather Green, Robert D. Hof, and Paul Judge, "Vying to Be More Than a Site for More Eyes," *Business Week,* May 18, 1998, p. 162.

208. Beth Snyder, "AOL's Partners Put Up Millions, Wait for Payoff," *Advertising Age,* Apr. 20, 1998, p. 30.

209. William Lewis, Richard Waters, Louise Kehoe, "AOL Shares Leap as Group Rebuffs AT&T," *Financial Times,* June 18, 1998, p. 20.

210. Diane Mermigas, AOL Aims to Be Anywhere, Everywhere," *Electronic Media,* Nov. 9, 1998, pp. 1A, 33.

211. Steve Lohr and John Markoff, "Deal Is Concluded on Netscape Sale to America Online," *New York Times,* Nov. 25, 1998, p. A1; Thomas E. Webber, "A Merger That Would Rock the Web," *Wall Street Journal,* Nov. 24, 1998, p. B1.

212. Amy Harmon, "Culture Clash Seen in Merger of Companies," *New York Times,* Nov. 24, 1998, pp. C1, C4.

213. Diane Mermigas, "AOL Getting Ready to Leap into Television," *Electronic Media,* Nov. 2, 1998, pp. 1, 25.

214. Green, Hof, and Judge, "Vying to Be More Than a Site for More Eyes," p. 162.

215. John Labate, "Internet Shares Boosted by Alliances," *Financial Times,* Sept. 24, 1998, p. 17.

216. Roger Taylor, "Compaq to Promote AltaVista Portal," *Financial Times,* Nov. 16, 1998, p. 20.

217. George Anders, "Yahoo! to Expand Shopping Channel amid Online Boom," *Wall Street Journal,* Nov. 18, 1998, p. B6.

218. Steve Lohr, "Microsoft Will Soon Offer Peek at New-Media Strategy," *New York Times,* Feb. 2, 1998, p. C5; Kara Swisher, "Microsoft Readies New Home Page for the Internet," *Wall Street Journal,* Feb. 3, 1998, p. B5; Anya Sacharow, "Wolf at the Portal?" *Mediaweek,* Feb. 9, 1998, p. 47.

219. Amy Harmon, "Microsoft and Barnes & Noble Join Forces," *New York Times,* Dec. 8, 1998, p. C6.

220. J. William Gurley, "The Soaring Cost of E-Commerce," *Fortune,* Aug. 3, 1998, p. 226.

221. Thomas E. Weber, "Inside the Race to Grab High-Speed Connections," *Wall Street Journal,* Oct. 22, 1998, pp. B1, B8.

222. Gunther, "Internet Is Mr. Case's Neighborhood," p. 80.

223. Bernhard Warner, "Online Sprawl," *IQ,* May 25, 1998, p. 21.

224. Saul Hansell, "The Battle for Internet Supremacy Is Shifting to the Companies That Sell Connections to Users," *New York Times,* June 29, 1998, p. C4.

225. Bill McConnell, "TCI/AT&T Likely to Dodge Unbundling," *Broadcasting and Cable,* Dec. 21, 1998, p. 16; Doug Halonen, "AOL Wants Fair Access," *Electronic Media,* Nov. 9, 1998, p. 42; Seth Schiesel, "The F.C.C. Faces Internet Regulation," *New York Times,* Nov. 2, 1998, p. C5; Catherine Yang, Ronald Grover, and Andy Reinhardt, "Filling the Need for Speed," *Business Week,* Dec. 28, 1998, pp. 50–52.

226. Diane Mermigas, "Convergence Takes Next Step," *Electronic Media,* Sept. 14, 1998, p. 38; Diane Mermigas, "AOL Sets Battle Plan for DTV," *Electronic Media,* Oct. 26, 1998, pp. 3, 51.

227. Roger Taylor, "Dell Deal Boosts America Online," *Financial Times,* Dec. 22, 1998, p. 17.

228. Saul Hansell, "Disney Will Invest in a Web Gateway," *New York Times,* June 19, 1998, p. C3.

229. Olya Evanitsky, "Evolution of the Internet Portal," *Goldman Sachs Investment Research,* Aug. 18, 1998, p. 7; John Markoff, "A $6 Billion Deal for Internet Site," *New York Times,* Jan. 19, 1999, pp. A1, C6.

230. Landler, "From Gurus to Sitting Ducks," p. 1.

231. Emma Duncan, "Wheel of Fortune," *Economist,* "Technology and Entertainment Survey," Nov. 21, 1998, p. 17.

232. Landler, "From Gurus to Sitting Ducks," p. 9.

233. Matt Richtel, "Survey Finds TV Is Major Casualty of New Surfing," *New York Times,* July 16, 1998, p. D3.

234. Linda Himelstein, Heather Green, Richard Siklos, and Catherine Yang, "Yahoo! The Company, the Strategy, the Stock," *Business Week,* Sept. 7, 1998, p. 68.

235. Diane Mermigas, "Why Big 3 Need to Change," *Electronic Media*, Dec. 21–28, 1998, p. 16.

236. Michael Wolff, "Burn Rate," *Advertising Age*, June 8, 1998, pp. 1, 16, 18.

237. I. Jeanne Dugan, "New-Media Meltdown," *Business Week*, Mar. 23, 1998, pp. 70–71.

238. Wolff, "Burn Rate," p. 18.

239. "Times Web Site Ends Fee for Foreign Users," *New York Times*, July 15, 1998, p. C6.

240. Geof Wheelwright, "Tap into the Sound of the Superhighway," *Financial Times*, June 2, 1998, p. 11; Richard Tedesco, "N2K Links with Disney, ABC Radio," *Broadcasting and Cable*, July 8, 1998, p. 46.

241. Kelly Barron, "Bill Gates Wants Our Business," *Forbes*, Apr. 6, 1998, p. 46–47; Anya Sacharow, "After Divorce, Online Newspapers Regroup," *Mediaweek*, Mar. 16, 1998, p. 31; Katrina Brooker, "Papers Lose Tweedy 'Tude, Find Black Ink," *Fortune*, June 8, 1998, pp. 36–37.

242. "MTV Emphasizes Online Synergy," *Broadcasting and Cable*, June 22, 1998, p. 59; Jim McConville, "New Nick Web Site Not Just for Kids," *Electronic Media*, Mar. 16, 1998, p. 18.

243. Jeff Jensen, "Columbia Tristar Teen TV Show Adds Interactive," *Advertising Age*, July 13, 1998, p. 27.

244. Beth Snyder, "Web Publishers Morph into Online Retailers," *Advertising Age*, Feb. 9, 1998, p. 30.

245. Chuck Ross, "Hachette Looks for Online Profits with Outside Help," *Advertising Age*, June 29, 1998, p. 50.

246. Nicholas Denton, "Online Media Face Heavy Job Losses," *Financial Times*, Mar. 12, 1998, p. 6.

247. "Brands Bite Back," *Economist*, Mar. 21, 1998, p. 78.

248. Paul Karon, "Online Entertainment Crashes," *Variety*, May 4–10, 1998, p. 3.

249. "AOL Tops Website Ratings," *Broadcasting and Cable*, June 22, 1998, p. 63.

250. Himelstein, Green, Siklos, and Yang, "Yahoo!" p. 70.

251. Joel Brown, "MSNBC on the Net Ready to Play Ball," *Electronic Media*, Jan. 19, 1998, p. 96.

252. Patricia Riedman, "Cyber Brands Spread the Word with Offline Ads," *Advertising Age*, July 6, 1998, p. 18.

253. Paul Taylor, "Publishers to Charge Web Users," *Financial Times*, Dec. 29, 1997, p. 11; Robin Pogrebin, "For $19.95, Slate Sees Who Its Friends Are," *New York Times*, Mar. 30, 1998, pp. C1, C7.

254. Bruce Orwall, "On-Line Service by Disney's ABC Unit Will Be Promoted by AOL, Netscape," *Wall Street Journal*, Apr. 4, 1997, p. A5.

255. David Bank, "Microsoft May Face Battle over 'Content,'" *Wall Street Journal*, Feb. 13, 1999, p. B6.

256. "Microsoft to Feature 250 Content Channels in New Web Browser," *Wall Street Journal*, July 15, 1997, p. B3.

257. Himelstein, Green, Siklos, and Yang, "Yahoo!" p. 72.

258. Richard Tedesco, "Net Players Making Music in Web Deals," *Broadcasting and Cable,* Nov. 8, 1998, p. 71.

259. This is drawn from Herman and McChesney, *Global Media,* chap. 4.

260. "Tribune Company," *Goldman Sachs Investment Research,* May 14, 1998, p. 27.

261. Diane Mermigas, "NBC Pieces Together Internet Strategy," *Electronic Media,* Aug. 10, 1998, p. 10.

262. Kate Maddox, "Rapid Growth Online," *Electronic Media,* Apr. 6, 1998, p. 10; Lee Hall, "Web Ads Changing Online Business," *Electronic Media,* Mar. 23, 1998, p. 16; Green, Hof, and Judge, "Vying to Be More Than a Site for More Eyes," p. 183.

263. Chuck Ross, "Broadband Kicks Open Internet Door for Cable," *Advertising Age,* Apr. 13, 1998, pp. s6, s23; Adrienne Mand, "Beyond Hits and Clicks," *Mediaweek,* Mar. 30, 1998, pp. 48, 52; Patricia Riedman, "P&G Plans Pivotal Ad Forum about Net," *Advertising Age,* May 11, 1998, p. 4; Adrienne Mand, "P&G to Hold Marketer Confab about Online Ads," *Mediaweek,* May 11, 1998, p. 41.

264. Teresa Riordan, "Combing the Web for Data on Consumers That Will Let Companies Aim Ads More Effectively," *New York Times,* Dec. 7, 1998, p. C9.

265. Saul Hansell, "Big Web Sites to Track Steps of Their Users," *New York Times,* Aug. 16, 1998, pp. A1, A16.

266. J. William Gurley, "How the Web Will Wart Advertising," *Fortune,* Nov. 9, 1998, p. 120.

267. Sally Beatty, "P&G Brainstorms to Improve Internet Ads," *Wall Street Journal,* Aug. 13, 1998, p. B9.

268. Saul Hansell, "Selling Soap without the Soap Operas," *New York Times,* Aug. 24, 1998, pp. C1, C7.

269. Kate Maddox, "P&G's Plan: Jump-Start Web as Viable Ad Medium," *Advertising Age,* Aug. 17, 1998, p. 14.

270. Stuart Elliot, "Procter & Gamble Calls Internet Marketing Executives to Cincinnati for a Summit Meeting," *New York Times,* Aug. 19, 1998, p. C3.

271. Susan Kuchinskas, "Addicted to Advertising," *Mediaweek,* Oct. 19, 1998, p. 80.

272. Sally Beatty, "Companies Push for Bigger On-Line Ads," *Wall Street Journal,* Aug. 20, 1998, p. B10.

273. "Web Becomes a Viable Channel," *Advertising Age,* Dec. 22, 1997, p. 21.

274. George Anders, "Internet Advertising, Just like Its Medium, Is Pushing Boundaries," *Wall Street Journal,* Nov. 30, 1998, p. A6.

275. Vanessa O'Connell, "Soap and Diaper Makers Pitch to Masses of Web Women," *Wall Street Journal,* July 20, 1998, pp. B1, B6.

276. "Media and Technology Strategies," *Forrester Reports* 2, no. 6 (Feb. 1998): 9–10.

277. Les Brown, "Market Forces Killed the Media Dream."

278. Denise Caruso, "If It Embraces Everything from CD's to Films, It Must Be the New Synergy," *New York Times,* July 20, 1998, p. C3.

279. Patrick M. Reilly, "Web Publishers Wage War for Music Scoops," *Wall Street Journal,* Apr. 15, 1998, p. B1.

280. Ronald Grover, "Online Sports: Cyber Fans Are Roaring," *Business Week,* June 1, 1998, p. 155.

281. Beth Snyder, "Sport Web Sites Rely on Strength of TV Networks," *Advertising Age,* May 11, 1998, pp. 46, 50.

282. Beth Snyder, "AT&T Inks $120 Mil Package at Disney," *Advertising Age,* June 29, 1998, pp. 1, 52.

283. Richard Tedesco, "NFL Keeps ESPN Game Plan," *Broadcasting and Cable,* June 1, 1998, p. 37.

284. Andrew Gellatly, "Online Crowd-Pleasers," *Financial Times,* June 10, 1998, p. 24.

285. Timothy Hanrahan, "What's News?" *Wall Street Journal,* Nov. 16, 1998, p. R36.

286. Norman Solomon, "Motherhood, Apple Pie, Computers."

287. M. L. Stein, "Are Basic Rules Crumbling on Web?" at http://www.mediainfo.com/e.

288. Rebecca Quick, "The Crusaders," *Wall Street Journal,* Dec. 8, 1997, p. R6.

289. Noam Chomsky, "'Hordes of Vigilantes,'" *Z Magazine,* July–Aug. 1998, pp. 51–54.

290. Patrick Barkham, "Dissidents and Defiants Slipping through the Net," *Guardian,* Dec. 4, 1998.

291. See, for example, Christopher Harper, *And That's the Way It Will Be* (New York: New York University Press, 1998).

292. "The Press in Spin Cycle," *Economist,* June 20, 1998, p. 35.

293. Landler, "From Gurus to Sitting Ducks," p. 9; Laurie Freeman, "Led by Warner, Animation Leads Syndicators to Web," *Advertising Age,* Jan. 19, 1998, p. S10.

294. Lars Jakobsen, "CNN Interactive in Swedish," *Cable and Satellite Express,* Mar. 20, 1997, p. 8; Mike Galetto, "CNN Spots Online Gold and Starts Speaking Swedish," *Electronic Media,* Mar. 17, 1997, p. 28.

295. Victoria Griffith, "Get Them While They're Young," *Financial Times,* Jan. 5, 1998, p. 19; Russell Shaw, "CNN/SI Challenges ESPN Site," *Electronic Media,* July 21, 1997, pp. 20, 32.

296. Stuart Elliott, "A Big World Wide Web Site by Time Inc. New Media Is Devoted to the 1998 Soccer World Cup," *New York Times,* June 4, 1998, p. C12.

297. Juliana Koranteng, "Time Inc. New Media Explores outside U.S.," *Advertising Age International,* June 29, 1998, p. 20.

298. Kate Maddox, "Warner Bros. Develops New Web Content Model," *Advertising Age,* June 22, 1998, p. 8.

299. Betsy Sharkey, "Warner's Web," *IQ,* Aug. 18, 1997, pp. 10–14.

300. Patricia Riedman, "ParentTime 1st Channel for PointCast," *Advertising Age,* Aug. 18, 1997, p. 19.

301. Kyle Pope, "High Definition TV Is Dealt a Setback," *Wall Street Journal,* Aug. 13, 1997, p. B5.

302. Bruce Orwall, "Disney Blitzes Cyberspace with 'Daily Blast' Service," *Wall Street Journal,* July 28, 1997, p. B4.

303. Anya Sacharow, "Disney-B&N Deal Signals Shift in Online Sales Business," *Mediaweek,* Feb. 2, 1998, p. 22.

304. Anya Sacharow, "Star Power," *Adweek,* May 5, 1997, p. 48.

305. Freeman, "Led by Warner, Animation Leads Syndicators to Web," p. s10.

306. "The Electronic Mall," *Wall Street Journal,* Dec. 7, 1998, p. R4.

307. Karlgaard, "Web Is Recession-Proof," p. A18.

308. Alice Rawsthorn, "US Online Bookshop Eyes Video Market," *Financial Times,* Nov. 11, 1998, p. 20; Alice Rawsthorn, "Amazon to Open UK and German Sites," *Financial Times,* Oct. 12, 1998, p. 19.

309. Robert D. Hof, "A New Chapter for Amazon.com," *Business Week,* Aug. 17, 1998, p. 39.

310. Jody Mardesich and Marc Gunther, "Is the Competition Closing In on Amazon.com?" *Fortune,* Nov. 9, 1998, p. 234.

311. Saul Hansell, "Amazon Ponders Effects of Rivals' Planned Mergers," *New York Times,* Oct. 8, 1998, p. C3; Saul Hansell, "2 Big On-Line Music Stores Said to Be Discussing Merger," *New York Times,* Oct. 7, 1998, p. C4.

312. Alice Rawsthorn, "Internet Sales Could Become Key to the Music Industry," *Financial Times,* June 2, 1998, p. 18.

313. Alice Rawsthorn, "Discord over Online Music Royalties," *Financial Times,* Jan. 21, 1998, p. 8.

314. Neil Strauss, "2 Giant Forces Are Converging to Change the Sale of Music," *New York Times,* Dec. 10, 1998, pp. B1, B11; Nikhil Hutheesing, "The Web Plays On," *Forbes,* Nov. 16, 1996, pp. 51–53.

315. Jason Chervokas, "Internet CD Copying Tests Music Industry," *New York Times,* Apr. 6, 1998, p. C3; William M. Bulkeley, "Sound Off," *Wall Street Journal,* June 15, 1998, p. R24.

316. Neil Crossley, "Rougher Times Ahead for the Music Pirates," *Financial Times,* Oct. 6, 1998, p. 17.

317. Alice Rawsthorn, "IBM to Test Internet Music Delivery," *Financial Times,* Nov. 26, 1998, p. 17; Eben Shapiro, "Record Industry Makes a Bold Deadline to Protect Music Sold via the Internet," *Wall Street Journal,* Dec.

16, 1998, p. B12; Eben Shapiro, "Record Firms Combat Piracy via the Web," *Wall Street Journal,* Dec. 15, 1998, p. B6; Jon Pareles, "Industry Plan Is Aimed at Selling Music over the Internet," *New York Times,* Dec. 16, 1998, p. C4.

318. Jon Pareles, "Records and CD's? How Quaint," *New York Times,* July 16, 1998, pp. B1, B6.

319. Alice Rawsthorn, "Sound of the Digital Jukebox Is Sweet Music to the Ears of New Groups on the Internet," *Financial Times,* Nov. 19, 1998, p. 7.

320. Alice Rawsthorn, "Digital Music On-line for Cable TV Customers," *Financial Times,* Jan. 20, 1998, p. 2.

321. Richard Siklos, "Can Record Labels Get Back Their Rhythm?" *Business Week,* July 27, 1998, pp. 52–53.

322. Alice Rawsthorn, "Record Companies See Their Stars Fly Away to the Net," *Financial Times,* Nov. 27, 1998, p. 6; Jon Pareles, "With a Click, a New Era of Music Dawns," *New York Times,* Nov. 15, 1998, sect. 2, pp. 1, 22; Eben Shapiro, "The Beastie Boys Get into an Internet Groove and Their Label Frets," *Wall Street Journal,* Dec. 18, 1998, pp. A1, A6.

323. Eben Shapiro, "Time Warner Builds Internet Superstore," *Wall Street Journal,* Sept. 14, 1998, pp. B1, B4.

324. Anya Sacharow, "Rhapsody in BMG: Music Service Expands Online," *Mediaweek,* Apr. 13, 1998, p. 34.

325. Jennifer Nix, "Bertelsmann to Sell Books on the Internet," *Variety,* Mar. 2–8, 1998, p. 7.

326. "Bertelsmann in Deals with Internet Firms over Online Bookstore," *Wall Street Journal,* Nov. 17, 1998, p. B8.

327. "Making a Mark," *Economist,* Oct. 10, 1998, pp. 69, 72.

328. Adrienne Mand, "Euro E-Comm: Giant Bertelsmann Tests Site," *Mediaweek,* Nov. 30, 1999, p. 37.

329. Chuck Ross, "NBC Opens Online Revenue Stream," *Advertising Age,* June 1, 1998, p. 2.

330. Chris Peacock, "Yes, but What about the Website Itself?" *Fortune,* Aug. 17, 1998, p. 192.

331. Mermigas, "Why the Big 3 Need to Change," p. 16.

332. Lee Hall, "Chancellor Will Be Radio's Biggest Giant," *Electronic Media,* Aug. 31, 1998, p. 24.

333. Gunther, "Internet Is Mr. Case's Neighborhood," pp. 79–80.

334. Saul Hansell, "NBC Buying a Portal to the Internet," *New York Times,* June 10, 1998, pp. C1, C8.

335. Richard Tedesco, "NBC Snaps Up iVillage Stake," *Broadcasting and Cable,* Dec. 7, 1998, p. 72; Steve Lohr, "New Service for High-Speed New Users," *New York Times,* Jan. 19, 1999, p. C6.

336. Parkes and Kehoe, "Mickey Wants Us All Online," p. 7.

337. Richard Tedesco, "Disney Stakes Big 'Net Claim with Infoseek," *Broadcasting and Cable,* June 15, 1998, p. 15.

338. Saul Hansell, "With Go Network, Disney Steps into the Portal Wars," *New York Times,* Dec. 13, 1998, sect. 3, p. 1.

339. Patricia Riedman, "Infoseek, Disney Prepare to Give Go the Green Light," *Advertising Age,* Dec. 14, 1998, p. 34.

340. Frank Rose, "Mickey Online," *Fortune,* Sept. 28, 1998, p. 274.

341. Diane Mermigas, "New Media Takes On the Old," *Electronic Media,* May 11, 1998, pp. 28–29; Leslie Scism and Kara Swisher, "Internet Firms Heat Up on News of Interest by Media Companies," *Wall Street Journal,* June 19, 1998, pp. C1, C2.

342. Lohr, "Media Convergence," p. A11.

343. Anya Sacharow, "NBC Opens Door to Its Portal Strategy with CNET's Snap," *Mediaweek,* June 15, 1998, p. 33.

344. Tedesco, "Disney Stakes Big 'Net Claim with Infoseek," p. 15.

345. Raymond Snoddy, "Programmer Turned Publisher," *Financial Times,* June 9, 1997, p. 7.

346. Saul Hansell, "A Quiet Year in the Internet Industry. Right? Right," *New York Times,* Dec. 28, 1998, pp. C1, C7.

347. William M. Bulkeley, "Radio Stations Make Waves on the Web," *Wall Street Journal,* July 23, 1998, pp. B1, B5.

348. From the back cover of John Keane, *Tom Paine: A Political Life* (Boston: Little, Brown and Company, 1995).

349. See Joseph Turow, *Breaking Up America* (Chicago: University of Chicago Press, 1997); Christopher Parkes, "The Birth of Enclave Man," *Financial Times,* Sept. 20–21, 1997, p. 7.

350. See Robert A. Dahl, *Democracy and Its Critics* (New Haven: Yale University Press, 1989); Thomas Christiano, *The Rule of the Many* (Boulder, Colo.: Westview Press, 1996).

351. C. Wright Mills, *The Power Elite* (Oxford: Oxford University Press, 1956).

Chapter 4: Educators and the Battle for Control of U.S. Broadcasting, 1928–35

1. Eugene E. Leach, *Tuning Out Education: The Cooperation Doctrine in Radio, 1922–39* (Washington D.C.: Current, 1983), p. 2.

2. For these reasons, I use the terms *educational* and *public service* interchangeably in this chapter. I realize that in other contexts one can draw useful distinctions between the terms.

3. See Werner J. Severin, "Commercial vs. Non-Commercial Radio during Broadcasting's Early Years," *Journal of Broadcasting* 20 (Fall 1978): 491–

504; S. E. Frost, Jr., *Education's Own Stations* (Chicago: University of Chicago Press, 1937).

4. "Report of the Committee on Radio," *American Newspaper Publishers Association Bulletin,* no. 5374, May 5, 1927, p. 285; see also John W. Spalding, "1928: Radio Becomes a Mass Advertising Medium," *Journal of Broadcasting* 8 (Winter 1963–64): 31–44.

5. Broadcasting Station Survey, Jan. 1, 1926, 07 01 02, box 77, Edwin H. Colpitts Papers, American Telephone and Telegraph Archives, Warren, N.J.

6. This period is discussed in detail in McChesney, *Telecommunications, Mass Media, and Democracy,* chap. 3.

7. See Donald G. Godfrey, "The 1927 Radio Act: People and Politics," *Journalism History* 4 (Autumn 1977): 78; Erik Barnouw, *A Tower in Babel: A History of Broadcasting in the United States to 1933* (New York: Oxford University Press, 1966), p. 281.

8. "The Menace of Radio Monopoly," *Education by Radio,* Mar. 26, 1931, p. 27; "The Power Trust and the Public Schools," *Education by Radio,* Dec. 10, 1931, p. 150; "Radio Censorship and the Federal Communications Commission," *Columbia Law Review* 39 (Mar. 1939): 447; 97 percent figure cited in William Boddy, *Fifties Television: The Industry and Its Critics* (Urbana: University of Illinois Press, 1990), p. 36.

9. Martin Codel, "Networks Reveal Impressive Gains," undated, sometime in Jan. 1931, entry in scrapbook for North American Newspaper Alliance, a news service that covered radio among other topics for approximately sixty U.S. daily newspapers in the early 1930s. In vol. 61, Martin Codel Papers, SHSW (hereafter cited as Codel Papers). Codel was radio editor for the North American Newspaper Alliance and a co-founder of Broadcasting magazine.

10. See Robert W. McChesney, "Press-Radio Relations and the Emergence of Network, Commercial Broadcasting in the United States, 1930–1935," *Historical Journal of Film, Radio and Television* 11 (1991): 41–57; McChesney, *Telecommunications, Mass Media, and Democracy,* chap. 7.

11. Cited in Michele Hilmes, *Hollywood and Broadcasting: From Radio to Cable* (Urbana: University of Illinois Press, 1990), p. 52.

12. S. Howard Evans to Walter V. Woehlke, Feb. 29, 1932, folder 1138, container 69, PF.

13. Henry Volkening, "Abuses of Radio Broadcasting," *Current History* 33 (Dec. 1930): 396–400; see also Barnouw, *Tower in Babel,* p. 270; Philip T. Rosen, *The Modern Stentors: Radio Broadcasting and the Federal Government 1920–1934* (Westport, Conn.: Greenwood Press, 1980), p. 12.

14. See *Digest of Hearings. Federal Communications Commission Broadcast Division, under Sec. 307(c) of the "Communications Act of 1934"* October 1–20, November 7–

12, 1934 (Washington, D.C.: Federal Communications Commission, 1935), pp. 180–249.

15. This is a common theme among educational and nonprofit broadcasters during this period. See, for example, John Henry McCracken, "The Fess Bill for Education by Radio," *Education by Radio,* Mar. 19, 1931, p. 21; George H. Gibson, *Public Broadcasting: The Role of the Federal Government, 1919–1976* (New York: Praeger Publishers, 1976), p. 8; Armstrong Perry, "The College Station and the Federal Radio Commission," in *Education on the Air: Second Yearbook of the Institute for Education by Radio,* ed. Josephine H. MacLatchy (Columbus: Ohio State University, 1931), p. 33.

16. Federal Radio Commission, *Third Annual Report of the Federal Radio Commission to the Congress of the United States Covering the Period from October 1, 1928 to November 1, 1929* (Washington, D.C.: United States Government Printing Office, 1929), pp. 32–36.

17. Jos. F. Wright to Sam Pickard, Oct. 25, 1928, Substance of Telegram to Congressman, May 29, 1928, file 001, box 1, series 2–4, WHA Papers, University of Wisconsin Archives, Madison, Wis.

18. W. S. Gregson to B. B. Brackett, Feb. 25, 1932, box 1a, general correspondence, National Association of Educational Broadcasters Papers, SHSW.

19. Walter V. Woehlke to S. Howard Evans, Dec. 22, 1932, folder 1147, container 60, PF.

20. "Neither Sponsors nor Stations Heed Listeners' Grumbling," *Business Week,* Feb. 10, 1932, pp. 18–19.

21. Tracy Tyler to Roger Baldwin, Oct. 26, 1933, vol. 599, American Civil Liberties Union Papers, Princeton University, Princeton, N.J.

22. For a discussion of the radio lobby, see McChesney, *Telecommunications, Mass Media, and Democracy,* chap. 5; for two examples of commercial broadcasters' promotional material, see National Association of Broadcasters, *Broadcasting in the United States* (Washington, D.C.: National Association of Broadcasters, 1933); National Broadcasting Company, *Broadcasting,* vols. 1–4 (New York: National Broadcasting Company, 1935).

23. For a discussion of the relationship of the radio lobby to the newspaper industry see n. 10. For a discussion of the relationship of commercial broadcasters to the legal community, see Robert W. McChesney, "Free Speech and Democracy! Louis G. Caldwell, the American Bar Association, and the Debate over the Free Speech Implications of Broadcast Regulation, 1928–1938," *American Journal of Legal History* 35 (Oct. 1991): 351–92; McChesney, *Telecommunications, Mass Media, and Democracy,* chap. 6.

24. Paul F. Peter, NBC chief statistician, "Appearances by U.S. Federal Officials over National Broadcasting Company Networks, 1931–1933," Nov. 1933, folder 26, box 16, NBC.

25. Joy Elmer Morgan to John Henry McCracken, Aug. 2, 1932, folder 801, container 43, PF.

26. See Robert W. McChesney, "The Payne Fund and Radio Broadcasting, 1928–1935," in *Media, Power and Social Control: The Payne Fund Studies, 1928–1933,* ed. Garth Jowett et al. (New York: Cambridge University Press, 1996), pp. 303–35. The other essays in this volume concentrate upon the Payne Fund's work with motion pictures and mass communication research.

27. Report of B. H. Darrow, Mar. 7, 1928, folder 1368, container 70, PF; Armstrong Perry, "The Ohio School of the Air and Other Experiments in the Use of Radio in Education," May 29, 1929, folder 1353, container 69, PF.

28. Armstrong Perry to H. M. Clymer, Apr. 6, 1929, folder 1067, container 56, PF.

29. Ibid.

30. Leach, *Tuning Out Education,* p. 5; Ray Lyman Wilbur, "The Radio in Our Republic," in *Radio and Education: Proceedings of the First Assembly of the National Advisory Council on Radio in Education, 1931,* ed. Levering Tyson (Chicago: University of Chicago Press, 1931), pp. 85–89 (hereafter *Proceedings, NACRE, 1931*).

31. Armstrong Perry to Ella Phillips Crandall, July 9, 1929, folder 1068, container 56, PF.

32. Armstrong Perry to J. L. Clifton, Aug. 21, 1929, folder 1068, container 56, PF.

33. Armstrong Perry to H. M. Clymer, June 14, 1929, folder 1353, container 69, PF.

34. Advisory Committee on Education by Radio, *Report of the Advisory Committee on Education by Radio Appointed by the Secretary of the Interior* (Columbus, Ohio: F. J. Heer Printing Company, 1930), pp. 35–37, 76.

35. W. John Cooper to H. Robinson Shipherd, Mar. 31, 1930, box 31, OE; Armstrong Perry to Ella Phillips Crandall, Mar. 17, 1930, folder 1069, container 56, PF.

36. Armstrong Perry memo, July 26, 1930, folder 1070, container 56, PF; William John Cooper to Ray Lyman Wilbur, Dec. 8, 1930, box 148, Commerce series, Herbert Hoover Papers, Herbert Hoover Presidential Library, West Branch, Iowa; W. John Cooper to Land Grant Institutions having Broadcasting Stations, undated, summer 1930, box 32, OE; Armstrong Perry, "The Status of Education by Radio in the United States," in *Education on the Air: First Yearbook of the Institute for Education by Radio,* ed. Josephine H. MacLatchy (Columbus: Ohio State University, 1930), pp. 80–81.

37. Ella Phillips Crandall to Armstrong Perry, July 9, 1930, folder 1070, container 56, PF.

38. Ella Phillips Crandall to Armstrong Perry, July 17, 1930, folder 1070, container 56, PF; Ella Phillips Crandall, "Memorandum of Conference with Mr. Perry," July 23, 1930, folder 1352, container 69, PF.

39. Armstrong Perry to Ella Phillips Crandall, Mar. 17, 1930, folder 1069, container 56, PF.

40. Memorandum for Interview with Dr. Charters, Mar. 14, 1931, folder 1352, container 69, PF.

41. Armstrong Perry to Ella Phillips Crandall, Oct. 14, 1930, folder 1070, container 56, PF; "Proposed Plan of Action," Oct. 2, 1930, folder 1352, container 69, PF.

42. The other six groups were the National University Extension Association, the Association of Land Grant Colleges and Universities, the Association of College and University Broadcasting Stations (which renamed itself the National Association of Educational Broadcasters by the mid-1930s), the National Council of State Superintendents, the Jesuit Education Association, and the National Catholic Education Association.

43. Minutes of the Conference on Educational Radio Problems, Stevens Hotel, Chicago, Oct. 13, 1930, At the Invitation of the U.S. Commissioner of Education, box 31, OE.

44. Memorandum re: General Situation of Radio in Education, Dec. 29, 1930, folder 1352, container 69, PF.

45. Frances Payne Bolton to Joy Elmer Morgan, June 17, 1932, folder 1071, container 42, PF.

46. Ella Phillips Crandall to Armstrong Perry, Dec. 23, 1930, folder 1071, container 56, PF.

47. Armstrong Perry to H. M. Clymer, Jan. 7, 1931, folder 1343, container 68, PF.

48. Armstrong Perry to Edward Klauber, Mar. 9, 1931, folder 1052, container 55, PF.

49. Ella Phillips Crandall to H. O. Davis, Apr. 15, 1931, folder 1142, container 59, PF.

50. Walter Woehlke memorandum, undated, summer 1931, folder 945, container 49, PF.

51. See McChesney, *Telecommunications, Mass Media, and Democracy,* chaps. 3, 7.

52. "Congress Is Asked for Radio Freedom," *New York Times,* Dec. 6, 1931, sec. 2, p. 8.

53. Cited in *Education by Radio,* Oct. 29, 1931, 123.

54. See Joy Elmer Morgan and E. D. Bullock, *Selected Articles on Municipal Ownership* (Minneapolis: Wilson, 1911); see also Joy Elmer Morgan, "The Corporation in America," *Journal of the National Education Association* 23 (Dec. 1934): 227–29.

55. "Intelligence Tests Called a Crime," *New York Times,* June 22, 1930, sec. 2, p. 3.

56. Joy Elmer Morgan, "Education's Rights on the Air," in *Proceedings, NACRE, 1931,* p. 122.

57. Ibid., p. 128.

58. Cited in *Education by Radio,* Feb. 2, 1933, p. 11.

59. Morgan, "Education's Rights on the Air," pp. 120–21.

60. Ibid., p. 128.

61. Joy Elmer Morgan to Dr. William McAndrew, Sept. 20, 1932, drawer 3, FCB 2, Joy Elmer Morgan Papers, National Education Association, Washington, D.C.

62. "The Fittest Survive," *Broadcasting,* Jan. 15, 1933, p. 16; "Listeners Society," *Broadcasting,* Apr. 1, 1933, p. 14.

63. "Mass Action Is Imperative," *Broadcasters' News Bulletin,* Feb. 14, 1931.

64. "Exit Mr. Morgan," *Broadcasting,* Sept. 15, 1935, p. 30.

65. See Robert W. McChesney, "Labor and the Marketplace of Ideas: WCFL and the Battle for Labor Radio Broadcasting, 1927–1934," *Journalism Monographs* 134 (Aug. 1992): 1–40; Robert W. McChesney, "Crusade against Mammon: Father Harney, WLWL and the Debate over Radio in the 1930s," *Journalism History* 14 (Winter 1987): 118–30; Robert W. McChesney, "Constant Retreat: The American Civil Liberties Union and the Debate over the Meaning of Free Speech for Radio Broadcasting in the 1930s," in *Free Speech Yearbook,* vol. 26: *1987,* ed. Stephen A. Smith (Carbondale: Southern Illinois University Press, 1988), pp. 40–59; McChesney, *Telecommunications, Mass Media, and Democracy,* chap. 4.

66. McChesney, *Telecommunications, Mass Media, and Democracy,* chaps. 4 and 5; Robert W. McChesney, "An Almost Incredible Absurdity for a Democracy," *Journal of Communication Inquiry* 15 (Winter 1991): 89–114.

67. Joy Elmer Morgan, "The New American Plan for Radio," in *A Debate Handbook on Radio Control and Operation,* ed. Bower Aly and Gerald D. Shively (Columbia, Mo.: Staples Publishing Co., 1933), p. 82.

68. Cited in *Education by Radio,* Dec. 24, 1931, p. 156; see also *School and Society,* Dec. 15, 1934, p. 805.

69. John Dewey, "Our Un-Free Press," *Common Sense* 4 (Nov. 1935): 6–7; see also Robert B. Westbrook, *John Dewey and American Democracy* (Ithaca, N.Y.: Cornell University Press, 1991), pp. 429–62.

70. "Public Interest, Convenience, and Necessity in a Nutshell," *Education by Radio,* Apr. 28, 1932, p. 61. The industry countered this criticism by asserting its complete neutrality on political and social issues and its willingness to broadcast the entire range of legitimate opinion. See the material cited in n. 22.

71. See J. Fred MacDonald, *Don't Touch That Dial: Radio Programming in American Life, 1920–1960* (Chicago: Nelson-Hall, 1979), pp. 29–34.

72. "Improve Radio Programs," *Education by Radio,* June 22, 1933, p. 29.

73. "Report of the Committee on Radio Broadcasting," in *Transactions and Proceedings of the National Association of State Universities in the United States of America 1931,* vol. 29, ed. A. H. Upham (n.p.: National Association of State Universities, 1931), p. 150.

74. Morgan, "New American Plan," p. 88.

75. *Education by Radio,* June 23, 1932, p. 73.

76. *Education by Radio,* Feb. 4, 1932, p. 18.

77. Morgan, "New American Plan," p. 95.

78. "Advertising Invades the Schools," *Education by Radio,* Sept. 10, 1931, p. 103.

79. See McChesney, "Labor and the Marketplace of Ideas"; Lizabeth Cohen, *Making a New Deal: Industrial Workers in Chicago, 1919–1939* (Cambridge: Cambridge University Press, 1990), pp. 136–42.

80. Morgan, "New American Plan," p. 81.

81. Morgan, "Education's Rights on the Air," p. 130.

82. Arthur G. Crane, "Safeguarding Educational Radio," in *Education on the Air . . . and Radio and Education 1935,* ed. Levering Tyson and Josephine H. MacLatchy (Chicago: University of Chicago Press, 1935), pp. 118–19.

83. Armstrong Perry, Comments following talk by C. M. Jansky, Jr., in *Radio and Education: Proceedings of the Second Annual Assembly of the National Advisory Council on Radio in Education, Inc., 1932,* ed. Levering Tyson (Chicago: University of Chicago Press, 1932), p. 223.

84. Eugene J. Coltrane, "A System of Radio Broadcasting Suited to American Purposes," in *Radio Control and Operation,* ed. E. R. Rankin (Chapel Hill: University of North Carolina Extension Bulletin, 1933), p. 36.

85. Gross W. Alexander to Graham Spry, Sept. 2, 1931, folder 7, vol. 95, GS.

86. Joy Elmer Morgan to H. O. Davis, Mar. 8, 1932, folder 901, container 47, PF.

87. Armstrong Perry to Ella Phillips Crandall, Mar. 8, 1932, folder 1144, container 59, PF.

88. See, for example, Joy Elmer Morgan, "The Radio in Education," in *Proceedings of the Seventeenth Annual Convention of the National University Extension Association 1932,* vol. 15 (Bloomington: Indiana University Press, 1932), p. 83.

89. Armstrong Perry to British Broadcasting Company, Dec. 17, 1935, folder 1110, container 58, PF.

90. S. Howard Evans to Walter V. Woehlke, Feb. 15, 1932, folder 1165, container 60, PF.

91. Joy Elmer Morgan to Alan B. Plaunt, June 9, 1932, drawer 3, fcb 2, Joy Elmer Morgan Papers, National Education Association, Washington, D.C.

92. Graham Spry to J. King Gordon, Apr. 11, 1931, folder 2, vol. 95, GS.

93. Graham Spry to Gross W. Alexander, May 12, 1931, folder 4, vol. 95, GS.

94. Graham Spry to Gladstone Murray, May 28, 1931, folder 4, vol. 95, GS.

95. Graham Spry to F. D. L. Smith, Aug. 21, 1931, folder 7, vol. 95, GS.

96. Testimony of Graham Spry, in *House of Commons Special Committee on Ra-*

dio Broadcasting, Minutes of Proceedings and Evidence (Ottawa: F. A. Acland, 1932), p. 555.

97. Testimony of Joy Elmer Morgan, in ibid., pp. 469–89.

98. Testimony of Spry, in ibid., p. 564.

99. "A Congressional Investigation of Radio," *Education by Radio,* Dec. 8, 1932, p. 105.

100. See Ellen Condliffe Lagemann, *The Politics of Knowledge: The Carnegie Corporation, Philanthropy, and Public Policy* (Middletown, Conn.: Wesleyan University Press, 1989).

101. Levering Tyson, discussion at 1935 Conference on Canadian-American Affairs, St. Lawrence University, Canton, N.Y., in 121, folder 32, vol. 108, GS.

102. Josephine Young Case and Everett Needham Case, *Owen D. Young and American Enterprise* (Boston: David R. Godine, 1982), esp. p. 561; Owen D. Young to Harry F. Ward, Dec. 3, 1929, 11-14-101, Owen D. Young to Karl A. Bickel, July 19, 1932, 11-14-116, Owen D. Young Papers, St. Lawrence University, Canton, N.Y.

103. R. M. Lester to F. P. Keppel, Memorandum on Studies and Experiments in Radio Education, Dec. 27, 1928, NACRE 1929, NACRE box 1, CC.

104. Minutes of Conference between Mr. Cooper, Mr. Cartwright and Mr. Tyson, Sept. 20, 1929, general correspondence, box 2, OE; Levering Tyson, *Education Tunes In* (New York: American Association for Adult Education, 1930), p. 9.

105. Memorandum of telephone conversation MAC had with Mr. Case, Dec. 14, 1929, NACRE 1929, NACRE box 1, CC.

106. Leach, *Tuning Out Education,* p. 7; Tracy F. Tyler, "The Joint Survey of Radio in Land-Grant Colleges and Separate State Universities," in *Education on the Air: Third Yearbook of the Institute for Education by Radio,* ed. Josephine H. MacLatchy (Columbus: Ohio State University, 1932), p. 16; Minutes of the Meeting of the Executive Board of the National Advisory Council on Radio in Education, Dec. 17, 1930, NACRE 1930, NACRE box 1, CC (hereafter NACRE minutes).

107. Tyson, *Education Tunes In,* p. 58.

108. Resolutions of Radio Conference, Nov. 18, 1929, NACRE 1929, NACRE box 1, CC.

109. Armstrong Perry, "National Broadcasting Company," Dec. 1935, folder 986, container 52, PF.

110. Merlin H. Aylesworth, "Broadcasting Today," *Dun's Review,* Mar. 5, 1932, p. 3.

111. "When Educators Differ," *Broadcasting,* June 1, 1933, p. 20.

112. See Harry S. Ashmore, *Unseasonable Truths: The Life of Robert Maynard Hutchins* (Boston: Little, Brown and Company, 1989).

113. R. M. Hutchins to Harris Randall, May 6, 1931, folder 9, box 7, The Presidents' Papers, ca. 1925–45, University of Chicago Library, Chicago, Ill. (hereafter PP).

114. Allen Miller to Robert M. Hutchins, Apr. 18, 1934, folder 20, box 66, PP; see also William H. McNeill, *Hutchins' University: A Memoir of the University of Chicago, 1929–1950* (Chicago: University of Chicago Press, 1991), pp. 57–58.

115. Allen Miller to Robert M. Hutchins, Aug. 13, 1934; Allen Miller, "The Progress of Broadcasting at the University," Apr. 1934, folder 20, box 66, PP.

116. M. H. Aylesworth to David Sarnoff, Oct. 10, 1934, folder 6, box 32, NBC.

117. Robert M. Hutchins, "Radio and Public Policy," *Education by Radio*, Dec. 6, 1934, p. 58.

118. Levering Tyson to Armstrong Perry, Sept. 25, 1929, folder 1069, container 56, PF.

119. Memorandum from Levering Tyson to Dr. H. Robinson Shipherd, Sept. 25, 1929, folder 1069, container 56, PF.

120. Levering Tyson, Foreword to *Some Public Service Broadcasting,* comp. Cline M. Koon (Chicago: University of Chicago Press, 1934), p. iii; Levering Tyson to Harold W. Dodds, Sept. 11, 1934, NACRE 1934, NACRE box 1, CC.

121. Levering Tyson to J. O. Keller, Mar. 22, 1932, folder 797, container 41, PF; Levering Tyson, "Where Is American Radio Heading?" in *Education on the Air: Fifth Yearbook of the Institute for Education by Radio,* ed. Josephine H. MacLatchy (Columbus: Ohio State University, 1934), p. 15.

122. NACRE minutes; Levering Tyson, "The Work of the National Advisory Council on Radio in Education," Jan. 1936, pp. 5, 6, NACRE 1936, NACRE box 2, CC.

123. Levering Tyson, "Report of the Director to the Board of Directors," in *Radio and Education: Proceedings of the Third Annual Assembly of National Advisory Council on Radio in Education, Inc., 1933,* ed. Levering Tyson (Chicago: University of Chicago Press, 1933), pp. 18–19.

124. Levering Tyson to F. P. Keppel, Dec. 22, 1933, NACRE 1933, NACRE box 1, CC.

125. Levering Tyson to F. P. Keppel, Dec. 4, 1929, NACRE 1929, NACRE box 1, CC.

126. F. P. Keppel Memorandum on N.A.C.R.E., May 5, 1931, NACRE 1931, NACRE box 1, CC.

127. Levering Tyson to Richard C. Patterson, Nov. 29, 1932, folder 15, box 12, NBC.

128. See Peter Dubkin Hall, *Inventing the Nonprofit Sector and Other Essays on Phi-*

lanthropy, Voluntarism, and Nonprofit Organizations (Baltimore: Johns Hopkins University Press, 1992), p. 66.

129. Henry Suzzallo to F. P. Keppel, Jan. 15, 1932, NACRE 1932, NACRE box 1, CC.

130. S. Howard Evans to Walter V. Woehlke, Oct. 18, 1932, folder 1167, container 60, PF.

131. Memorandum Re Conference, Dr. Joy Elmer Morgan and Miss Crandall, Oct. 1, 1932, folder 812, container 42, PF.

132. Armstrong Perry, "National Education Association," Dec. 1935, folder 986, container 52, PF.

133. Levering Tyson to F. P. Keppel, Jan. 2, 1934, NACRE 1934, NACRE box 1, CC.

134. Armstrong Perry, "National Advisory Council on Radio in Education," Dec. 1935, folder 986, container 52, PF.

135. NCER memorandum on the National Advisory Council on Radio in Education, Nov. 1931, folder 744, container 39, PF.

136. "The Magnitude of Education by Radio," *Education by Radio,* Jan. 7, 1932, p. 4.

137. Comments of I. Keith Tyler, Tracy's brother. Cited in Calvin Fredrick Ruskaup, "The Other Side of Broadcasting: A History of Challengers to the Use of the Airwaves" (Ph.D. diss., Ohio State University, 1979), p. 60.

138. S. Howard Evans to E. H. Harris, Oct. 8, 1934, folder 1350, container 69, PF.

139. Memorandum to Mr. Perry Re General Situation of Radio in Education, Dec. 29, 1930, folder 1352, container 69, PF.

140. "A Winning Issue," *Education by Radio,* June 9, 1932, p. 76.

141. "Shall Foundations Control Educational Radio?" *Education by Radio,* May 25, 1933, p. 27.

142. Ella Phillips Crandall to Dr. W. W. Charters, Nov. 26, 1930, folder 1352, container 69, PF.

143. Levering Tyson to F. P. Keppel, Oct. 28, 1930, NACRE 1930, NACRE box 1, CC.

144. Levering Tyson to F. P. Keppel, Jan. 2, 1934, NACRE 1934, NACRE box 1, CC.

145. R. M. Hughes to Frederick P. Keppel, Feb. 9, 1934, NACRE 1934, NACRE box 1, CC.

146. Barnouw, *Tower in Babel,* p. 57. Since both the NACRE and the NCER professed their devotion to educational broadcasting and they rarely criticized each other in public, this confusion remains in much of the historical literature. See Robert K. Avery and Robert Pepper, "An Institutional History of Public Broadcasting," *Journal of Communication* 30 (Summer 1980): 127.

147. Hugh Hawkins, *Banding Together: The Rise of the National Associations in American Higher Education, 1887–1950* (Baltimore: Johns Hopkins University Press, 1992), pp. 104–17.

148. Cited in B. B. Brackett to T. M. Beaird, Dec. 15, 1931, general correspondence 1932, box 1a, National Association of Educational Broadcasters Papers, SHSW.

149. The relationship of Charters to the NCER is discussed in McChesney, "Payne Fund and Radio Broadcasting."

150. Dean Collins, "U.S. Monopoly of Radios Is Suggested," *Pittsburgh Press*, June 12, 1931; "Freeing Radio from Its Bondage," *Brockton Enterprise*, May 21, 1931. Both in S60/6/6, 1931–32, Reith Scrapbooks, BBC; Armstrong Perry to Sir John C. W. Reith, Aug. 28, 1935, folder 1110, container 58, PF.

151. Cited in Armstrong Perry to W. W. Charters, undated, summer 1930, folder 1069, container 56, PF.

152. "American Broadcasting," *The B. B. C. Year-book 1932* (London: British Broadcasting Corporation, 1932), p. 47.

153. Memorandum from Miss Quigley, July 8, 1936, memorandum from Miss Quigley, Jan. 7, 1936, National Committee on Education by Radio, E1/197, BBC.

154. Edward N. Nockels, "Labor's Rights on the Air," *Federation News*, Feb. 7, 1931, p. 2.

155. "Labor Resolution Presented," *Broadcasters' News Bulletin*, Jan. 12, 1931.

156. Nockels, "Labor's Rights," p. 2.

157. Walter Woehlke to S. Howard Evans, Nov. 25, 1931, folder 1164, container 60, PF.

158. Telegram, Joy Elmer Morgan to H. O. Davis, Mar. 8, 1932, folder 901, container 47, PF.

159. H. O. Davis to Ella Phillips Crandall, Mar. 8, 1932, folder 1144, container 59.

160. Memorandum on discussion between Miss Crandall and Mr. Perry on Radio, Aug. 11, 1932, folder 1075, container 56, PF.

161. Memorandum concerning Payne Fund cooperation with commercial radio stations, Nov. 15, 1932, folder 783, container 41, PF.

162. Ella Phillips Crandall to William John Cooper, Feb. 19, 1933, folder 1337, container 68, PF.

163. Armstrong Perry to Joy Elmer Morgan, Apr. 15, 1933, folder 1077, container 56, PF.

164. Joy Elmer Morgan to Armstrong Perry, Apr. 18, 1933, folder 1062, container 55, PF.

165. For a discussion of this topic see the sources cited in n. 10.

166. Tracy M. Tyler to T. M. Beaird, Apr. 14, 1933, folder 916, container 47, PF; "Radio Question Popular," *Education by Radio*, June 22, 1933, p. 24.

167. H. O. Davis to Cranston Williams, July 27, 1933, folder 1147, container 59, PF.

168. "British vs. American Radio Slant, Debate Theme in 40,000 Schools," *Variety*, Aug. 29, 1933, p. 1. Cited in Joel Spring, *Images of American Life: A History of Ideological Management in Schools, Movies, Radio, and Television* (Albany: State University of New York Press, 1992), p. 97.

169. Merlin H. Aylesworth to David Sarnoff, Aug. 20, 1934, folder 7, box 32, NBC.

170. See n. 22 for citation to NAB debate guide.

171. Reith diaries, part 1, vol. 4, 1934–36, BBC.

172. Response of the London press collected in Press Cuttings 1934, Policy, P12, BBC.

173. Fred Bate to Merlin Aylesworth, Jan. 10, 1934, folder 25, box 24, NBC.

174. "British Broadcasting," *Listener*, Jan. 31, 1934, pp. i–xii.

175. M. H. Aylesworth to Sir John C. W. Reith, Jan. 27, 1934, folder 27, box 24, NBC.

176. Aylesworth to Sarnoff, Aug. 20, 1934, folder 7, box 32, NBC.

177. Josephus Daniels to Franklin D. Roosevelt, July 12, 1933, reel 59, container 95, A,C, 18416, Josephus Daniels Papers, Library of Congress, Washington, D.C. See also Robert W. McChesney, "Franklin Roosevelt, His Administration, and the Communications Act of 1934," in *Media Voices: An Historical Perpective*, ed. Jean Folkerts (New York: Macmillan, 1992): 334–52; McChesney, *Telecommunications, Mass Media, and Democracy*, chap. 8.

178. A. G. Crane to Tracy F. Tyler, Mar. 19, 1934, folder 785, container 41, PF.

179. Martin Codel, "President Aided by Chains," undated, Mar. 1933, North American Newspaper Alliance dispatch (see n. 9). In vol. 61, Codel Papers, SHSW; "F.D.R.'s Radio Record," *Broadcasting*, Mar. 15, 1934, p. 8.

180. Sol Taishoff, "'War Plans' Laid to Protect Broadcasting," *Broadcasting*, Mar. 1, 1933, p. 5.

181. Rosen, *Modern Stentors*, p. 177.

182. "Air Enemies Unite Forces," *Variety*, May 8, 1934, pp. 37, 45.

183. "Wagner Amendment Up Next Week," *NAB Reports*, May 5, 1934, 375.

184. Henry A. Bellows, "Report of the Legislative Committee," *NAB Reports*, Nov. 15, 1934, p. 618.

185. John Harney to Armstrong Perry, Apr. 3, 1934, folder 1132, container 59, PF.

186. John Harney to Tracy F. Tyler, Apr. 3, 1934, folder 850, container 44, PF.

187. Bellows, "Report," p. 618.

188. "Commercial Control of the Air," *Christian Century*, Sept. 26, 1934, pp. 1196–97.

189. "Government Interference Fears Groundless, Say Commissioners," *Broadcasting*, Oct. 1, 1934, p. 18.

190. Tracy F. Tyler to Clarence C. Dill, June 5, 1934, folder 824, container 43, PF.

191. Frank Russell to William Hard, Oct. 23, 1934, folder 28, box 26, NBC.

192. Cited in "In Their Own Behalf," *Education by Radio,* June–July 1938, p. 21.

193. William S. Paley, "The Viewpoint of the Radio Industry," in *Educational Broadcasting 1937,* ed. C. S. Marsh (Chicago: University of Chicago Press, 1937), p. 6.

194. For a discussion of the broader implications of this process, see Robert W. McChesney, "Off-Limits: An Inquiry into the Lack of Debate over the Ownership, Structure and Control of the Mass Media in U.S. Political Life," *Communication* 13 (1992): 1–19.

195. Miss Crandall memorandum to Mrs. Bolton, Mr. Maxfield, Nov. 5, 1934, folder 1352, container 69, PF.

196. Memorandum for Mrs. Bolton from Miss Crandall, Oct. 24, 1935, folder 945, container 49, PF; Memorandum by S. H. Evans, Nov. 1, 1935, folder 1152, container 69, PF.

197. Excerpt from Minutes of Executive Committee Meeting on National Committee on Education by Radio, Jan. 18–19, 1936, folder 1147, container 69, PF.

198. "The Rocky Mountain Radio Council," *Education by Radio,* second quarter 1940, pp. 7–14.

199. Arthur G. Crane, *A Plan for an American Broadcasting Service and Proposals for the Immediate Establishment of Two Regional Units* (Laramie, Wy.: National Committee on Education by Radio, 1937), p. 1.

200. S. Howard Evans to A. G. Crane, June 19, 1936, folder 1147, container 69, PF.

201. Armstrong Perry, "National Advisory Council on Radio in Education," Dec. 1935, folder 986, container 52, PF.

202. John F. Royal to Richard C. Patterson, Jr., May 21, 1935, folder 52, box 34, NBC.

203. "Meeting of the Radio Committee," Feb. 1932, small envelope, Allen Miller Papers, SHSW.

204. Levering Tyson to Richard C. Patterson, Dec. 9, 1932, folder 15, box 12, NBC.

205. Tyson to Patterson, Nov. 29, 1932, folder 15, box 12, NBC.

206. Levering Tyson to Richard C. Patterson, Dec. 1, 1932, folder 15, box 12, NBC.

207. Franklin Dunham to R. C. Patterson, Jr., May 12, 1934, folder 16, box 30, NBC.

208. Merlin H. Aylesworth to John W. Reith, Oct. 8, 1934, folder 27, box 24, NBC.

209. Levering Tyson to Robert M. Hutchins, Oct. 24, 1933, folder 7, box 99, R. M. Hutchins Papers Addenda, University of Chicago Library, Chicago, Ill.

210. See McChesney, "Constant Retreat."

211. Tyson, "Where Is American Radio Heading?" p. 53.

212. Frank E. Mason to E. W. Harden, July 25, 1934, folder 16, box 30, NBC.

213. Aylesworth to Sarnoff, Aug. 20, 1934, folder 7, box 32, NBC.

214. Notes of Discussion at a Conference on Educational Broadcasting called by Dr. F. P. Keppel of the Carnegie Corporation of New York, Apr. 14, 1934, NACRE box 1, CC, pp. 17, 23.

215. Confidential memorandum for Frederick P. Keppel, July 13, 1934, NACRE 1934, NACRE box 1, CC.

216. Committee on Civic Education by Radio of the National Advisory Council on Radio in Education and the American Political Science Association, *Four Years of Network Broadcasting* (Chicago: University of Chicago Press, 1937), pp. 49, 73.

217. David Sarnoff to George Zook, Mar. 18, 1937, folder 48, box 55, NBC.

218. John F. Royal to David Sarnoff, Oct. 21, 1937, folder 48, box 55, NBC.

219. Levering Tyson to John Royal, July 31, 1937, folder 48, box 55, NBC.

220. "Dr. Tyson Retires from the Radio Field," *Education by Radio*, Feb. 1937, p. 8; *Education by Radio*, Dec. 1937, p. 61.

221. See Willard D. Rowland, Jr., "Continuing Crisis in Public Broadcasting: A History of Disenfranchisement," *Journal of Broadcasting and Electronic Media* 30 (Summer 1986): 251–74.

222. Round Table Discussion, "The Problems of College and University Stations," in *Education on the Air: Fifth Yearbook,* p. 201.

223. Ibid., p. 200.

224. *Education by Radio,* second quarter 1940, p. 12.

225. C. M. Jansky, Jr., "FM — Educational Radio's Second Chance — Will Educators Grasp It," Aug. 5, 1946, folder on educational FM, box 59, Edwin H. Armstrong Papers, Butler Library, Columbia University, New York, N.Y.

226. Karl Marx, "The Eighteenth Brumaire of Louis Bonaparte," in *The Marx-Engels Reader,* ed. Robert C. Tucker (New York: W. W. Norton and Company, 1972), p. 436.

227. Charles A. Siepmann, *Radio's Second Chance* (Boston: Little, Brown and Company, 1946), p. x.

228. Robert M. Hutchins, "The State of American Radio," *B.B.C. Quarterly* 4 (Winter 1949–50): 193–97; see also Commission on Freedom of the Press, *Free and Responsible Press,* pp. 97–98.

229. See, for example, Paul F. Lazarsfeld, *The People Look at Radio* (Chapel Hill: University of North Carolina Press, 1946), pp. vii–ix.

230. William Buxton, "The Rockefeller Foundation, Communications Research/Policy, and the American State: 1930–1937," paper presented to Annual Meeting of the Canadian Political Science Association, June 2, 1991, Kingston, Ontario.

231. For a discussion of the futility of those who continued to lobby to generate a commitment to public service in the regulated commercial system after World War II, see Willard D. Rowland, Jr., "The Illusion of Fulfillment: The Broadcast Reform Movement," *Journalism Monographs* 79 (Dec. 1932): 36.

232. See Joel Spring, *Images of American Life,* pp. 1–10.

Chapter 5: Public Broadcasting

1. This chapter was inspired by a series of lectures I gave in Canada in December 1997 at the invitation of the Graham Spry Fund for Public Broadcasting.

2. For the best treatment of the development of broadcasting in Britain, see Asa Briggs, *The Birth of Broadcasting,* vol. 1 of *The History of Broadcasting in the United Kingdom* (London: Oxford University Press, 1961). Two books that chronicle the development of broadcasting in the United States in the 1920s are Smulyan, *Selling Radio,* and Rosen, *Modern Stentors.* The classic work is Barnouw, *Tower in Babel.*

3. See, for example, John L. Hiemstra, *Worldviews on the Air: The Struggle to Create a Pluralistic Broadcasting System in the Netherlands* (Lanham, Md.: University Press of America, 1997).

4. I hope to pursue this topic in my present research. For a sense of the issues involved, see Donald R. Browne, "Radio Normandie and the IBC Challenge to the BBC Monopoly," *Historical Journal of Film, Radio and Television* 5, no. 1 (1985): 3–18.

5. I discuss this period in detail in *Telecommunications, Mass Media, and Democracy.* See also chap. 4 above.

6. A subplot in the broadcasting relationship between Canada and the United States between 1925 and 1935 was the constant negotiation concerning how to allocate the medium wave frequencies (550–1500 kilocycles) between the two nations. I will not examine these negotiations in this chapter, although I will in the future.

7. See Vipond, *Listening In.*

8. For a discussion of this point, see R. H. Coase, *British Broadcasting: A Study in Monopoly* (London: Longman, Green and Co., 1950).

9. See McChesney, *Telecommunications, Mass Media, and Democracy,* chap. 2. See also chap. 4 above.

10. See Barnouw, *Tower in Babel,* p. 270.

11. See John Egli O'Brien, "A History of the Canadian Radio League: 1930–1936" (Ph.D. diss., University of Southern California, 1964), pp. 40–47.

12. By 1928 NBC was working with Canadian General Electric to establish a

network of affiliates in Canada. See H. L. Sheen to George F. McClelland, Mar. 22, 1928, container 2, folder 86, NBC.

13. John O'Brien, "History of the Canadian Radio League," p. 46.

14. Royal Commission on Radio Broadcasting, *Report* (Ottawa: F. A. Acland, 1929).

15. Cited in John O'Brien, "History of the Canadian Radio League," p. 64.

16. "Canada Pays a Compliment to Our B.B.C. System," *Public Opinion,* Oct. 4, 1929. This and many similar British press clippings on the Aird Commission's report can be found in Press Cuttings P415, Overseas Transmissions 1928–30, BBC.

17. "Provincial Control of Radio Denied," *Editor and Publisher,* July 11, 1931, p. 14.

18. Martin Codel, "Canadian Control of Radio Upheld," Feb. 16, 1932. Clipping found in vol. 61, Codel Papers, SHSW.

19. See Marc Raboy, *Missed Opportunities: The Story of Canada's Broadcasting Policy* (Montreal: McGill-Queen's University Press, 1990), chap. 1.

20. The most comprehensive account of the Canadian Radio League can be found in John O'Brien, "History of the Canadian Radio League," which unfortunately has never been revised for publication. For Spry's account, see Graham Spry, "Public Policy and Private Pressures: The Canadian Radio League 1930–36 and Countervailing Power," in *On Canada: Essays in Honour of Frank H. Underhill,* ed. Norman Penlington (Toronto: University of Toronto Press, 1971), pp. 24–36. See also Margaret Prang, "The Origins of Public Broadcasting in Canada," *Canadian Historical Review* 46 (Mar. 1965): 1–31. For Spry's response to Prang, see Graham Spry, "The Origins of Public Broadcasting in Canada: A Comment," *Canadian Historical Review* 46 (June 1965): 134–41.

21. House of Commons of Canada, Session 1932, *Special Committee on Radio Broadcasting: Minutes and Proceedings of Evidence* (Ottawa: F. A. Acland, 1932), testimony of Graham Spry, pp. 546–47 (hereafter cited as HOC 1932).

22. Graham Spry to Gross W. Alexander, May 12, 1931, folder 1136, container 59, PF.

23. HOC 1932, p. 546.

24. Graham Spry to George Ferguson, Mar. 2, 1931, folder 11, vol. 94, GS.

25. Graham Spry, "A Canadian Radio Broadcasting Company," no date, approx. Mar. 1931, folder 11, vol. 97, GS.

26. Graham Spry to Armstrong Perry, May 12, 1931, folder 873, container 45, PF.

27. This was what happened in Mexico, where the domestic market for commercial broadcasting was much weaker than that of Canada. A number of Americans, often times religious figures or patent medicine hucksters,

purchased Mexican stations in the 1930s and proceeded to broadcast exclusively in English to the United States. For discussions of this phenomenon, see Gene Fowler and Bill Crawford, *Border Radio* (Austin, Tex.: Texas Monthly Press, 1987); Gerald Carson, *The Roguish World of Dr. Brinkley* (New York: Holt, Rinehart and Winston, 1960); Ansel Harlan Resler, "The Impact of John R. Brinkley on Broadcasting in the United States" (Ph.D. diss., Northwestern University, 1958).

28. I develop the themes in this paragraph throughout *Telecommunications, Mass Media, and Democracy.*

29. Spry to Alexander, May 12, 1931, folder 1136, container 59, PF.

30. Graham Spry to Gladstone Murray, May 28, 1931, folder 4, vol. 95, GS.

31. Graham Spry, "The Canadian Radio Situation," in *Education on the Air: Second Yearbook of the Institute for Education by Radio,* ed. Josephine H. Mac-Latchy (Columbus: Ohio State University, 1931), pp. 47–60.

32. Armstrong Perry to Graham Spry, Apr. 24, 1931, folder 1122, container 58, PF.

33. Graham Spry to Joy Elmer Morgan, Apr. 7, 1932, Joy Elmer Morgan Papers, National Education Association, Washington, D.C., 1932 correspondence, FCB 2, drawer 3 (hereafter cited as Morgan Papers).

34. HOC 1932, testimony of Graham Spry, p. 555.

35. Spry, "A Canadian Radio Broadcasting Company," folder 11, vol. 97, GS.

36. Spry to Morgan, Apr. 7, 1932, 1932 correspondence, FCB 2, drawer 3, Morgan Papers.

37. Graham Spry, "Visit to Washington and Federal Radio Commission 1931," dictated July 21, 1976, folder 13, vol. 84, GS.

38. Graham Spry to George Ferguson, Mar. 2, 1931, folder 11, vol. 94, GS.

39. Perhaps it is only coincidental but, to my knowledge, the only two folders missing from the Owen D. Young collection at St. Lawrence University are the ones dealing with Canadian and Mexican broadcasting in the 1930s. Young, president of General Electric and founder of RCA, also had a strong interest in Canada.

40. HOC 1932, testimony of R. W. Ashcroft, p. 329; Graham Spry to Mac, Mar. 2, 1931, folder 11, vol. 94, GS.

41. I discuss this in *Telecommunications, Mass Media, and Democracy,* chap. 7. Spry makes reference to an NBC attack on the BBC carried over its Toronto affiliate in Jan. 1931 in Graham Spry to Henry Roberts, Feb. 17, 1931, folder 10, vol. 94, GS.

42. From *New Republic,* Aug. 12, 1931. Cited in "Propaganda Pipelines," *Education by Radio,* Sept. 24, 1931, p. 110.

43. Graham Spry to W. D. Herridge, Oct. 15, 1930, folder 6, vol. 94, GS.

44. Graham Spry, "Empire Broadcast," July 27, 1976, folder 13, vol. 84, GS.

45. Brooke Claxton to Gladstone Murray, Jan. 26, 1932, Brooke Claxton pa-

pers, National Archives of Canada, Ottawa, Canada, manuscript group 32 B 5, vol. 5.

46. John Murray Gibbon, "Radio as a Fine Art," *Canadian Forum* 11 (Mar. 1931): 212–14.

47. This episode is discussed in John O'Brien, "History of the Canadian Radio League," pp. 202–13.

48. Graham Spry, "The Canadian Broadcasting Issue," *Canadian Forum* 11 (Apr. 1931): 246–49.

49. "Watch Canada," *Broadcasting*, Mar. 1, 1932, p. 16.

50. Cited in *Education by Radio*, Oct. 13, 1932, p. 98.

51. HOC 1932, testimony of Graham Spry, p. 46.

52. Ibid., p. 42.

53. Merlin H. Aylesworth to David Sarnoff, Apr. 30, 1932, container 14, folder 1, NBC.

54. Arthur Kittredge, "De Forest Devises Radio Ad Quietus," no date, approx. Oct. 1930, in vol. 60, Codel Papers.

55. HOC 1932, statement of Lee De Forest, p. 491.

56. HOC 1932, testimony of Joy Elmer Morgan, p. 470.

57. Graham Spry to Joy Elmer Morgan, May 2, 1932, folder 822, container 42, PF.

58. Martin Codel, "Canadian Broadcasting to Be Nationalized," *Broadcasting*, May 15, 1932, p. 7.

59. HOC 1932, testimony of Graham Spry, p. 564.

60. Statement of Senator C. C. Dill, Democrat of Washington. Cited in "Dill Sees U.S. Radio in Danger," *Broadcasters' News Bulletin*, May 14, 1932. Dill was the crucial figure who steered the cause of commercial broadcasting through turbulent congressional waters in the early 1930s. See McChesney, *Telecommunications, Mass Media, and Democracy*, esp. chaps. 6 and 8.

61. S. Howard Evans to Walter V. Woehlke, Jan. 4, 1933, folder 1168, container 60, PF.

62. Joy Elmer Morgan to Alan Plaunt, June 9, 1932, 1932 correspondence, FCB 2, drawer 3, Morgan Papers.

63. "A Congressional Investigation of Radio," *Education by Radio*, Dec. 8, 1932, p. 105.

64. I realize these are sweeping statements. I hope I back them up in *Telecommunications, Mass Media, and Democracy*, chap. 9. See also chap. 4 above.

65. Thomas Dodd, "Public Service or Populist Choice?" *Television Business International*, May 1998, p. 18.

66. Frederick Studemann, "Call to Lift Curb on German TV Advertising," *Financial Times*, Mar. 18, 1998, p. 3; Miriam Hils, "Airing Grievances," *Variety*, June 8–14, 1998, pp. 17, 20.

67. "Stop Press," *Economist,* July 4, 1998, p. 18.

68. Quoted in Pilger, *Hidden Agendas,* p. 525.

69. Friedman quote found on back cover of Laurence Jarvik, *PBS: Behind the Screen* (Rocklin, Calif.: Forum, 1997).

70. Mark Woods, "Australian Pubcaster, Conservatives at Odds," *Variety,* Nov. 23–29, 1998, p. 46; see also Robyn Williams, *Normal Service Won't Be Resumed: The Future of Public Broadcasting* (Sydney: Allen & Unwin, 1996).

71. William Hoynes, *Public Television for Sale: Media, the Market, and the Public Sphere* (Boulder, Colo.: Westview, 1994).

72. Kevin Sack, "Gingrich Attacks the Media as Out of Touch," *New York Times,* Apr. 23, 1997, p. A16.

73. Jürgen Habermas, "There Are Alternatives," *New Left Review,* no. 231 (Sept.–Oct. 1998): 8.

74. Adam Dawtrey, "Rupert Rips Pubcasters," *Variety,* Apr. 13–19, 1998, p. 25; Gapper, "Murdoch Eyes Media in an Integrated Europe," p. 8; "Why Rupert Murdoch Is Polite," p. 39.

75. Robert Graham, "Reduced Role for Adverts on State TV," *Financial Times,* Nov. 11, 1998, p. 3.

76. See McChesney, *Telecommunications, Mass Media, and Democracy;* see also Inger L. Stole, "Selling Advertising: A History of the U.S. Advertising Industry, 1933–1945" (Ph.D. diss., University of Wisconsin–Madison, 1998).

77. Marc Raboy chronicles the long unfolding relationship in detail in *Missed Opportunities.*

78. Spry's first public denunciation of the Canadian broadcasting situation was at a conference on Canadian-American relations in 1935. See Graham Spry, "Radio Broadcasting and Aspects of Canadian-American Relations," in *Proceedings of the Conference on Canadian-American Affairs Held at the St. Lawrence University, Canton, New York, June 17–22, 1935,* ed. W. W. McLaren (n.p., n.d.), pp. 106–27.

79. See Graham Spry, "The Canadian Broadcasting Corporation, 1936–1961," *Canadian Communications* 2 (Autumn 1961): 1–13; Graham Spry, "The Costs of Canadian Broadcasting," *Queen's Quarterly* 67 (Winter 1960–61): 503–13; Graham Spry, "The Decline and Fall of Canadian Broadcasting," *Queen's Quarterly* 68 (Summer 1961): 213–25.

80. See *New Republic,* Jan. 11, 1933, p. 227.

81. For a discussion of some of the differences, see Joseph J. Weed, "Canada's Radio System," *Printers' Ink,* Dec. 22, 1938, pp. 24–26.

82. See Raboy, *Missed Opportunities,* for the most thorough discussion of this history.

83. Colin Sparks, "The Future of Public Service Broadcasting in Britain," *Critical Studies in Mass Communication* 12 (1995): 328–29.

84. Michael Wile, "Blacks' Fave TV Shows Don't Dent Overall Top 10,"

Advertising Age, Apr. 6, 1998, p. 18; Ray Richmond, "TV Sitcoms: The Great Divide," *Variety,* Apr. 13–19, 1998, pp. 1, 40.

85. Richard Collins, "Supper with the Devil — A Case Study in Private/Public Collaboration in Broadcasting: The Genesis of Eurosport," *Media, Culture and Society* 20 (Oct. 1998): 653.

86. Christopher Stern, "Pubcaster Pleased with Tauzin," *Variety,* June 22–28, 1998, p. 24.

87. Ira Yeinowicz, "Public TV Worries about FCC Decision on Sponsors," *Advertising Age,* Dec. 15, 1997, p. 14.

88. Robyn Meredith, "G.M. Sponsors a Maker of Documentaries and Reaches PBS Viewers 15 Seconds at a Time," *New York Times,* Nov. 3, 1997, p. C10.

89. Chuck Ross, "Key PBS Stations Cut Deal with Ad Rep," *Advertising Age,* Mar. 2, 1998, p. 3.

90. Steve McClellen, "Putting Commercial in Noncommercial," *Broadcasting and Cable,* May 11, 1998, p. 38.

91. For a superb examination of the decline of U.S. public broadcasting, see James L. Ledbetter, *Made Possible By . . . : The Death of Public Broadcasting in the United States* (London: Verso, 1997).

92. Patrick M. Reilly, "PBS Will Launch Its Own Music Label with Help of CAA," *Wall Street Journal,* July 30, 1997, p. B2.

93. Adam Sandler, "Pubcaster Humming a New Tune," *Variety,* Dec. 8–14, 1997, p. 36.

94. Constance L. Hays, "A Star Is Licensed: With 'Arthur,' Public TV Stretches Commercial Limits," *New York Times,* Sept. 24, 1997, pp. C1, C4.; Betsy Sharkey, "TV News: That's Showbiz," *Mediaweek,* Sept. 1, 1997, p. 19.

95. Paulette Thomas, "Retailing: Public TV Toy Stores Target the Cerebral," *Wall Street Journal,* Dec. 8, 1997, p. B1.

96. Jeff Jensen, "Single 'Play It Smart' Tag to Brand All CTW Properties," *Advertising Age,* Mar. 2, 1998, p. 8.

97. Stuart Elliott, "Public TV's 'Arthur' Again Cavorts with the Commercial Realm," *New York Times,* Mar. 11, 1998, p. C6.

98. Christopher Stern, "PBS Tries to Keep Eggs in Nest," *Variety,* June 1–7, 1998, pp. 21, 24; Ann Marie Kerwin, "Kellogg Teaming Up with Big Bird," *Advertising Age,* May 25, 1998, p. 8; Lawrie Mifflin, "Joint Venture Would Create New Network," *New York Times,* Apr. 29, 1998, pp. C1, C6.

99. Bill Moyers, "Remarks," Open Society Institute Strategy Meeting on the Gore Commission, New York City, Dec. 8, 1998.

100. David Barsamian, "The Gloomy View from Lake Wobegon," *Nation,* Jan. 5, 1998, p. 10.

101. See James Ledbetter, "Public Television Sells (Out?)," *Nation,* Dec. 1, 1997, pp. 11–14.

102. Gerald O'Dwyer, "US Launch for Scandinavian Channel," *Cable and Satellite Europe,* Mar. 1997, p. 14.

103. Marlene Edmunds, "Dutch B'casters to Place Commercials in Kid Fare," *Variety,* May 12–18, 1997, p. 47.

104. Raymond Snoddy, "Commercial Strains Show in Digital TV Deal," *Financial Times,* Mar. 19, 1997, p. 8.

105. Raymond Snoddy, "Discovery and BBC Explore S America," *Financial Times,* July 11, 1997, p. 25; Rebecca A. Fannin, "BBC to Aim News Channel at U.S.," *Advertising Age,* Dec. 15, 1997, p. 60.

106. Bill Britt, "Teletubbies Are Coming: Brit Hit Sets U.S. Invasion," *Advertising Age,* Jan. 19, 1998, p. 12.

107. Daniel Rooney, "BBC, Mediaset Ink 3-yr. Prod'n Pact," *Variety,* May 4–10, 1998, p. 41.

108. "BBC Launches Commercial Site," *Television Business International,* May 1998, p. 39.

109. Steve Clarke, "Birt's BBC Earthquake," *Television Business International,* Apr. 1997, pp. 38–46.

110. John Gapper, "$125m Gain for BBC Business," *Financial Times,* July 16, 1998, p. 7.

111. John Gapper, "Broadcasting and the Value of Creativity," *Financial Times,* Dec. 1, 1998, p. 13.

112. John Gapper, "BBC Rivals May Lobby on Controls," *Financial Times,* Nov. 24, 1997, p. 6.

113. Andy Stern, "EC Becomes Testy," *Variety,* Nov. 2–8, 1998, p. 33.

114. Maggie Brown, "Public Interest Attack," *Financial Times,* Nov. 25, 1997, p. 28; "Digital Adventure," *Economist,* Mar. 15, 1997, p. 61.

115. Barry Flynn, "Auntie's Brave New World," *Television Business International,* Oct. 1998, p. 66.

116. "The New-Look BBC," *Economist,* Aug. 29, 1998, p. 53.

117. Steve Bowbrick, "The Citizen Birt Days Are Over," *New Media Age,* Oct. 8, 1998, p. 18.

118. Jonathan Lines, "Reading between the Lines," *New Media Age,* Nov. 5, 1998, p. 21.

119. David Hatch, "PBS Sells Ads — on Web," *Electronic Media,* Nov. 8, 1998, p. 43.

120. Anya Sacharow, "Open Sesame: CTW Unveils Ad-Supported Site," *Mediaweek,* Sept. 14, 1998, p. 33.

121. Habermas, "There Are Alternatives," p. 8.

Chapter 6: The New Theology of the First Amendment

1. Floyd Abrams, contribution to special issue "Is First Amendment Absolutism Obsolete?" *Nation,* July 21, 1997, p. 13.

2. See C. Edwin Baker, "Giving the Audience What It Wants," *Ohio State Law Journal* 58, no. 2 (1997): 311–417.

3. For an elaboration of the ACLU position, see Laura W. Murphy, "'We Refuse to Sacrifice the First Amendment in a Desperate Attempt to Adopt Reform Legislation,'" *Progressive* 61 (Dec. 1997): 20–22.

4. See Edward Wolff, *Top Heavy: A Study of the Increasing Inequality of Wealth in America* (New York: Twentieth Century Fund Press, 1995).

5. "What Happens If They Give an Election, and Nobody Comes?" *Sanders Scoop,* Fall 1998, p. 1.

6. See, for example, Charles Lewis, *The Buying of the Congress* (New York: Avon Books, 1998); Ken Silverstein, *Washington on $10 Million a Day* (Monroe, Maine: Common Courage Press, 1998).

7. Dallas Smythe, *Counterclockwise: Perspectives on Communication,* ed. Thomas Guback (Boulder, Colo.: Westview, 1994), p. 107.

8. Sheldon Rampton and John Stauber, "Keeping America Safe from Democracy," *PR Watch* 5 (third quarter 1998): 1–6.

9. Robert Spero, *The Duping of the American Voter* (New York: Lippincott and Crowell, 1980), p. 3.

10. Jeff Mayers and Rick Barrett, "In Your Face," *Wisconsin State Journal,* Oct. 31, 1998, p. 1A.

11. Michael Freeman, "Hot Air Lifts Second Half," *Mediaweek,* Nov. 2, 1998, p. 6.

12. Todd S. Purdum, "TV Political News in California Is Shrinking, Study Confirms," *New York Times,* Jan. 13, 1999, p. A11; Dan Trigoboff, "Political Ads Outnumber Election Stories, Study Finds," *Broadcasting and Cable,* Nov. 2, 1998, p. 26.

13. Ira Teinowitz, "Paid Ads Looming Larger on the Political Landscape," *Advertising Age,* Oct. 5, 1998, p. 28.

14. See, for example, Richard L. Berke, "G.O.P. Begins Ad Campaign Citing Scandal," *New York Times,* Oct. 28, 1998, pp. A1, A21; Francis X. Clines, "Democrats Launch Counterattack Ads," *New York Times,* Oct. 30, 1998, p. A26.

15. Todd S. Purdum, "Race for California Governor Is Not Necessarily the News," *New York Times,* May 6, 1998, p. A1.

16. David M. Rabban, *Free Speech in Its Forgotten Years* (New York: Cambridge University Press, 1997), p. 303.

17. Alexander Meiklejohn, *Free Speech and Its Relation to Self-Government* (New York: Harper and Brothers, 1948), pp. 89, 63.

18. Alexander Meiklejohn, *Political Freedom: The Constitutional Powers of the People* (New York: Harper and Brothers, 1960).

19. See Emerson, *Toward a General Theory of the First Amendment.*

20. Valentine v. Chrestensen, 316 U.S. 52, 54 (1942).

21. Cass R. Sunstein, contribution to special issue "Is First Amendment Absolutism Obsolete?" *Nation,* July 21, 1997, p. 15.

22. Cited in C. Edwin Baker, "Two Misplaced Objections," *Boston Review*, Summer 1998, p. 16.

23. For a superb treatment of this issue see C. Edwin Baker, *Human Liberty and Freedom of Speech* (New York: Oxford University Press, 1989), chap. 9.

24. See, for example, M. T. O'Brien, "Next Battleground: Advertising versus the First Amendment," *Food Product Development*, Dec. 1977, p. 65.

25. Sunstein, "Is the First Amendment Obsolete?" p. 16.

26. Akhil Reed Amar, *The Bill of Rights* (New Haven: Yale University Press, 1998), pp. 21, 23. See Rosenfeld, *American Aurora*; Stanley E. Flink, *Sentinel under Siege* (Boulder, Colo.: Westview Press, 1997).

27. Michael G. Gartner, *Advertising and the First Amendment* (New York: Priority Press, 1989), p. 2.

28. "High Cost of Free Airtime," *Broadcasting and Cable*, Mar. 16, 1998, p. 94.

29. "Hanging Together," *Broadcasting and Cable*, Nov. 9, 1998, p. 90.

30. See Dan Schiller, *Theorizing Communication: A History* (New York: Oxford University Press, 1996).

31. "Are Wisconsin Editors Free to Tell the Truth?" *Capital Times*, Aug. 5, 1922, p. 10.

32. "Here Is Chance to Get $100," *Capital Times*, Aug. 8, 1922.

33. "Merrill's Autocracy Revealed," *Capital Times*, Aug. 26, 1922.

34. "We Will Answer Wausau and Wisconsin Rapids, Too," *Capital Times*, Aug. 23, 1922.

35. See Herbert J. Gans, *Deciding What's News* (New York: Pantheon, 1979).

36. See Jerome A. Barron, "Access to the Press — A New First Amendment Right," *Harvard Law Review* 80 (1967): 1641–78.

37. Miami Herald Publishing Company v. Tornillo, 94 S. Ct. 2831 (1974), pp. 2840, 2841.

38. "'We Paid $3 Billion for These TV Stations. We Will Decide What the News Is,'" *Extra! Update*, June 1998, p. 1.

39. See Frank J. Kahn, ed., *Documents of American Broadcasting*, 3d ed. (Englewood Cliffs, N.J.: Prentice-Hall, 1978), chap. 39.

40. Meiklejohn, *Free Speech*, p. 104.

41. I cover this entire episode and the ACLU's transformation in *Telecommunications, Mass Media, and Democracy*.

42. Steven W. Colford, "Ad Industry Loses Hero in Brennan," *Advertising Age*, July 30, 1990, pp. 1, 44.

43. Morton Mintz, "The ACLU and the Tobacco Companies," *Nieman Reports*, Spring 1998, pp. 66–72.

44. See David Kairys, "Freedom of Speech," in David Kairys, ed., *The Politics of Law: A Progressive Critique* (New York: Pantheon, 1982), pp. 140–71.

45. See Bagdikian, *Media Monopoly*.

46. Angus Mackenzie, *Secrets: The CIA's War at Home* (Berkeley: University of California Press, 1997).

Conclusion

1. See Thomas Ferguson, *Golden Rule* (Chicago: University of Chicago Press, 1995).

2. Joel Rogers, "Turning to the Cities," *In These Times,* Oct. 18, 1998, p. 14.

3. Frances Fox Piven and Richard A. Cloward, *Poor People's Movements: Why They Succeed, How They Fail* (New York: Vintage Books, 1977), p. ix.

4. Quotation taken from Noam Chomsky, *Profit over People: Neoliberalism and the Global Order* (New York: Seven Stories Press, 1999), p. 47.

5. This point is discussed in Josiah Ober, *Mass and Elite in Democratic Athens* (Princeton: Princeton University Press, 1989), pp. 192–93.

6. C. B. Macpherson, *The Rise and Fall of Liberal Democracy* (New York: Oxford University Press, 1977).

7. See Ellen Meiksins Wood and Neal Wood, *A Trumpet of Sedition: Political Theory and the Rise of Capitalism* (New York: New York University Press, 1996), p. 136.

8. For a treatment of this phenomenon in present times, see Richard Sennett, *The Corrosion of Character: The Personal Consequences of Work in the New Capitalism* (New York: W. W. Norton, 1998).

9. Christopher Lasch, *Revolt of the Elites* (New York: W. W. Norton, 1995), p. 22.

10. Goran Therborn, "The Rule of Capital and the Rise of Democracy," *New Left Review* no. 103 (May–June 1977): 3–41.

11. G. E. M. de Ste. Croix, *The Class Struggle in the Ancient Greek World* (Ithaca, N.Y.: Cornell University Press, 1981), esp. chaps. 2, 5, and 7.

12. For the classic statement of this position, see Milton Friedman, *Capitalism and Freedom.*

13. George Seldes, *Witness to a Century* (New York: Ballantine Books, 1987), p. 190.

14. John Stuart Mill, *Considerations on Representative Government* (Oxford: Basil Blackwell, 1948), chaps. 6, 8.

15. Eric Hobsbawm, *The Age of Empire: 1875–1914* (New York: Macmillan, 1989), pp. 87–88.

16. Edward L. Bernays, "The Engineering of Consent," *Annals of the American Academy of Political and Social Science* 250 (Mar. 1947): 113–20; Walter Lippmann, *Public Opinion* (New York: Macmillan, 1922); Harold D. Lasswell, "The Person: Subject and Object of Propaganda," *Annals of the American Academy of Political and Social Science* 179 (May 1935): 187–93.

17. This point is brilliantly presented in Macpherson, *Rise and Fall,* chap. 4. See also Joshua Cohen and Joel Rogers, *On Democracy: Toward a Transformation of American Society* (New York: Penguin Books, 1983); Dahl, *Democracy and Its Critics;* John Bellamy Foster, "Free Market Democracy and Global Hegemony," *Monthly Review,* Sept. 1997, pp. 51–62.

18. Alex Carey, *Taking the Risk Out of Democracy* (Urbana: University of Illinois Press, 1997); see also Stuart Ewen, *PR! A Social History of Spin* (New York: Basic Books, 1996).

19. Philip Lesly, *The People Factor: Managing the Human Climate* (Homewood, Ill.: Dow Jones-Irwin, 1974), pp. 8, 86.

20. Ewen, *PR!* p. 408.

21. Quoted in John Gillott and Manjit Kumar, *Science and the Retreat from Reason* (London: Merlin, 1995), p. 157.

22. Chomsky refers to the classic text on the subject — Michel Crozier, Samuel P. Huntington, and Joji Watanuki, *The Crisis of Democracy* (New York: New York University Press, 1975).

23. Patricia Cayo Sexton, *The War on Labor and the Left* (Boulder, Colo.: Westview, 1991).

24. For a stimulating argument on behalf of socialism, see Ralph Miliband, *Socialism for a Skeptical Age* (London: Verso, 1994).

25. See Alan Dawley, *Struggles for Justice: Social Responsibility and the Liberal State* (Cambridge, Mass.: Belknap Press of Harvard University Press, 1991).

26. Philip Green, *Equality and Democracy* (New York: New Press, 1999), p. 2.

27. Couey and Karliner, "Interview with Noam Chomsky," p. 11.

28. See, for example, Schiller, *Theorizing Communication,* chap. 1.

29. See Steven J. Ross, *Working-Class Hollywood: Silent Film and the Shaping of Class in America* (Princeton: Princeton University Press, 1997).

30. See McChesney, *Telecommunications, Mass Media, and Democracy.*

31. See, for example, Fones-Wolf, *Selling Free Enterprise.*

32. See Godfried, *WCFL: Chicago's Voice of Labor.*

33. Michael Denning, *The Cultural Front* (London: Verso, 1996).

34. See Bob Garfield, "AFL-CIO Spots Labor Vainly against Image," *Advertising Age,* Sept. 1, 1997, p. 37.

35. For the core agenda of the New Party, see John Nichols, "After Fusion: The New Party," *In These Times,* Mar. 22, 1998, pp. 18–19.

36. See Bernie Sanders, *Outsider in the House* (London: Verso, 1997), pp. 231–32.

37. This quote is from an interview conducted by John Nichols with Bernie Sanders in 1997.

38. Elizabeth Lesly, "Self-Censorship Is Still Censorship," *Business Week,* Dec. 16, 1996, p. 78.

39. Habermas, "There Are Alternatives," p. 9.

40. Doug Henwood, post to pen-l@galaxy.csuchico.edu listserve, Aug. 20, 1998.

41. For another version of this same approach, from one of the best U.S. political analysts of our times no less, see Katha Pollitt, "Their Press and Ours," *Nation,* Nov. 10, 1997, p. 9.

42. Rupert Murdoch established the *Weekly Standard* for that reason. The notorious Richard Mellon Scaife has bankrolled a daily newspaper in Pittsburgh

for the same reason. See Iver Peterson, "In a Battle of Newspapers, a Conservative Spends Liberally," *New York Times,* Dec. 8, 1997, pp. C1, C8.

43. Robert Parry, "The Rise of the Right-Wing Media Machine," *Extra!* May–June 1995, p. 9.

44. David Croteau, "Challenging the 'Liberal Media' Claim," *Extra!* July–Aug. 1998, pp. 4–9.

45. See Beth Schulman, "Foundations for a Movement: How the Right Wing Subsidizes Its Press," *Extra!* Mar.–Apr. 1995, pp. 11–12; see also Sally Covington, *Moving a Public Policy Agenda: The Strategic Philanthropy of Conservative Foundations* (Washington, D.C.: National Committee for Responsive Philanthropy, 1997).

46. Janine Jackson, "Film Rejection Highlights PBS Bias," *Extra!* Jan.–Feb. 1998, pp. 6–8.

47. For a critique of progressive foundations, see Michael H. Shuman, "Why Progressive Foundations Give Too Little to Too Many," *Nation,* Jan. 12–19, 1998, pp. 11–16.

48. See Paul Milkman, *PM: A New Deal in Journalism* (New Brunswick, N.J.: Rutgers University Press, 1997).

49. See Norman Solomon, "Press Flails as Lawmakers Make Mess of House," syndicated newspaper column, Nov. 13, 1997; Janine Jackson, "'Fast Track' 1, Democracy 0: Trade Policy Isn't Open for Debate, Say Editorialists," *Extra!* Nov.–Dec. 1997, pp. 9–10.

50. See Keane, *Media and Democracy.*

51. See, for example, Arthur Charity, *Doing Public Journalism* (New York: Guilford Press, 1995).

52. Justin Lewis and Sut Jhally, "The Struggle over Media Literacy," *Journal of Communication* 48 (Winter 1998): 109–20.

53. See Cynthia Peters, "The Politics of Media Literacy," *Z Magazine,* Feb. 1998, pp. 25–30.

54. Ira Teinowitz, "Nader's Commercial Alert Fires First at Telemarketing," *Advertising Age,* Sept. 21, 1998, p. 44.

55. "The Rainbow/PUSH Coalition's Twelve Point Plan to Promote Democratic Access to the Electronic Media and Communications," issued by Rainbow/PUSH Coalition, Chicago, Ill., Mar. 1998.

56. Mary Kuntz, "Is Nothing Sacred?" *Business Week,* May 18, 1998, pp. 130–34.

57. Kate Duncan, "Microbroadcasting," *Z Magazine,* July–Aug. 1998, pp. 40–41; Chris McConnell, "Radio Pirate Walks the Plank," *Broadcasting and Cable,* June 22, 1998, p. 19.

58. Steve Zeltzer, "US Labor Video Production on a Growth Curve," paper presented at Conference on Labor and Media, Seoul, South Korea, 1997.

59. "Remaindered," *New York Times,* Mar. 25, 1998, p. A22.

60. Frank Rose, "There's No Business like Show Business," pp. 86–104.

61. Paige Albiniak, "Tauzin Launches Public Broadcasting Remake," *Broadcasting and Cable,* June 15, 1998, p. 8.

62. Bill McConnell, "FCC Sets the Price for Digital," *Broadcasting and Cable,* Nov. 23, 1998, p. 5.

63. Edward S. Herman, "The Threat from Mergers: Can Antitrust Make a Difference?" *Dollars and Sense,* May–June 1998, p. 10.

64. Alicia Mundy, "DOJ Big Winner in DBS Deal," *Mediaweek,* Dec. 7, 1998, p. 16.

65. Christopher Parkes, "Change of Tack Takes Radio into the US Media Mainstream," *Financial Times,* July 10, 1998, p. 18.

66. Eben Moglen, "Antitrust and American Democracy," *Nation,* Nov. 30, 1998, pp. 11–13.

67. See Robert W. McChesney, Mark Crispin Miller, and John H. Nichols, "Media and Democracy," *Nation,* Oct. 27, 1997.

68. BECTU flyer, London, June 1998.

69. See Elaine Bernard and Sid Shniad, "Fighting Neoliberalism in Canadian Telecommunications," in *Capitalism and the Information Age: The Political Economy of the Global Communication Revolution,* ed. Robert W. McChesney, John Bellamy Foster, and Ellen Meiksins Wood (New York: Monthly Review Press, 1998).

70. All the information in this section not attributed otherwise comes from interviews and research conducted by the author and John H. Nichols in 1997.

71. Goran Sellgren, "Controversy over Kids Ads," *Cable and Satellite Express,* Sept. 11, 1997, p. 6.

72. Greg McIvor, "Jubilant Left Draws Up List of Demands," *Financial Times,* Sept. 22, 1998, p. 2.

73. See Michael Traber and Kaarle Nordenstreng, eds., *Few Voices, Many Worlds: Towards a Media Reform Movement* (London: World Association for Christian Communication, 1992).

INDEX

merger of, 161; owner of, 19; partners of, 148, 164. *See also* @Home; Liberty Media; TCI; Worldnet Service (AT&T)

audience: advertising believability and, 40, 262; fragmentation of, 250; global media and, 104; homogeneity as trend in, 105; hypercommercialism and, 35; newspaper coverage and, 55; possible disappearance of, 58; for public service broadcasting, 246, 247, 249, 251, 254; in supply and demand scenario, 32–34; website promotion and, 171, 174, 177. *See also* Americans; children; consumers

Australia: Internet in, 134; legislation in, 81; media conglomerates in, 89, 91, 96, 104; public broadcasting in, 244, 317–18; television in, 98

Australian Broadcasting Corporation (ABC), 244, 318

Avis Rent a Car, 39

Axel Springer, 88

Aylesworth, Merlin, 207, 208, 215, 221, 235, 237

Azcarraga, Emilio, 113

Baby Bells: competition for, 167; partner of, 162, 163–64. *See also* Bell Atlantic

Bagdikian, Ben, 19, 49

Baker, Dean, 305–6

Baltimore (Md.), local news in, 55

Barlow, John Perry, 120

Barnes & Noble (book retailer), 18, 167, 177, 180

Barnouw, Eric, 211, 231

Barron, Jerome, 274

Bart, Peter, 105

Baskin, Roberta, 58–59

Batman (character), 94

BBC. *See* British Broadcasting Company (BBC)

BBDO Worldwide (ad agency), 85

Beatty, Warren, 32

Beauty and the Beast (play), 45

Beavis and Butt-Head (characters), 37

Beavis and Butt-Head Do America (film), 22

"beeb," website for, 253, 254

Belgium, media conglomerates in, 104

Bell Atlantic: merger of, 160–61; web services of, 181

Bennett, R. B., 236

Benzi, Daren, 64

Berlusconi, Silvio, 89, 253

Bernays, Edward, 287

Bertelsmann (company): domination of, 83, 86–87; headquarters of, 103–4; holdings of, 16–17, 18; Internet interests of, 171, 179–80; joint ventures of, 95

Bertelsmann Online, 180

Bezos, Jeff, 178

Binzel, Peggy, 64

Biondi, Frank, 87

Black, Conrad, 89

Black, Hugo, 267–68, 278

Blackstone Group, 87

Blair, Tony, 99–100

Blancornelas, Jesús, 117

Blockbuster video rental chain, 20, 21

BMW of North America, 39

bol.com (website), 180

Bolton, Chester, 195, 198

Bolton, Frances Payne: broadcasting reform and, 197–99; on NCER, 218–19; role in Payne Fund, 195, 211

Bond, James (character), 39

book publishing industry: global consolidation in, 86, 104; hypercommercialism's impact on, 37–38; independents in, 25–26; oligopolistic character of, 16–17, 18, 37, 92, 95, 96

book retailing: global market for, 80; on Internet, 167, 178, 180; oligopolistic character of, 18–19, 26, 38, 167, 177

books, ads in, 46, 203

Borders (book retailer), 18, 177

Branson, Richard, 33, 43

Brazil: media assets in, 89; media conglomerates in, 95, 107; music production in, 107; protection of culture in, 82; television in, 95, 97; worker protests in, 318

Brennan, William, 278

Brinkley, David, 53

British Broadcasting Company (BBC): attacks on, 233, 236–37, 384n41; commercial broadcasting vs., 249–50, 308; commercialization of, 229–30, 253–54; establishment of, 228–29, 230; funding for, 248; goal of, 242, 247; joint ventures of, 246, 252–53; as model, 204–5, 214–15, 220, 230, 231, 236; NCER overtures to, 212–13; quality of, 68; sale of, 115–16; workers' strike at, 314

British Interactive Broadcasting, 97

British Privy Council, 232

British Sky Broadcasting (BSkyB), 95–97

British Telecommunications, 161, 164

broadcasting: as democratic media, 218, 276–77, 290; as international phenomenon, 229–30; microradio, 302; politics and,

213–18, 229–31, 239–40; public vs. commercial, 246–47, 249–50, 308. *See also* commercial broadcasting; First Amendment; public service broadcasting

Broadcasting and Cable (periodical), on public service recommendation, 157

Broadcom, 147

Broadway theater industry, 45

Broder, David, 52

Bronfman, Edgar, 30. *See also* Seagram

Brown, Les, 174

Brown, Tina, 57

BSkyB. *See* British Sky Broadcasting

Buchanan, Pat, 152

Buckley v. Valeo, 259, 267, 278

Budweiser, 70

Buena Vista, 95

buildings, advertising on, 41

Bulworth (film), 32

Burger, Warren, 274–75

buses, advertising on, 41

Bush, George, 311

business interests: archives of, 235; campaign funds and, 261, 263–65; censorship by, 63, 277; democracy defined by, 286; First Amendment interpreted by, 257–59, 268–79; in Internet, 159–60, 167–68; journalism's emphasis on, 50, 296, 298–99; media and communication's role in, 79; as PBS sponsors, 252; policy making by, 125. *See also* capitalist system; commercial broadcasting; commercial media; global commercial media

cable television systems: advertising and, 149; branding in, 24; channels for children, 45–46, 83–84;

Cato Institute, 62–63

CBC (Canadian Broadcasting Corporation), 247, 248–49, 315

CBS network: advertising on, 41; broadcast and cable interests of, 154; Canadian affiliates of, 231, 235; CEO and directors of, 28–29; as conglomerate, 20; dominance of, 229, 230, 234–35, 276; educational programs of, 71–72, 195–97, 199, 207–9; exposés on, 53, 58–59; global media system of, 88; infomercial on, 38; lobbyists of, 194; news coverage by, 54; radio of, 75–76, 190, 192, 194–97, 199; sports team ownership and, 44; television production of, 21–22, 34

CDNow, 178

celebrities, in television advertising, 42, 70, 109

CEM (Cultural Environment Movement), 302

censorship: by business interests, 63, 277; via funding restraints, 244, 248; laws and regulations vs., 265; legislation on, 131; by national media, 100; overt vs. subtle, 110, 114; power of, 271–72, 274, 297; self-applied, 243. See also First Amendment

Center for Communications and Social Policy (UC, Santa Barbara), 34

Central Intelligence Agency. See CIA

Chancellor Broadcasting, 181

Chanel, 57

Channel One, 47

Channel V music channel, 98

Charren, Peggy, 156, 158

Charters, W. W., 195, 212

Chernin, Peter, 16. See also News Corporation

children: creative programming for, 308–10; global media and, 106; hypercommercialism's impact on, 45–47, 71–72, 83–84, 144; Internet access of, 136; public broadcasting's commercialization and, 252–53; viewing habits of, 81; websites geared toward, 177. See also youth market

Children's Television Workshop (CTW), 72, 252–53, 255

Chile, as neoliberal success, 111–13

Chilton, 95

China: advertising in, 84–85, 115; commercial media in, 101, 114–16; copyright issues and, 102; movies in, 115; television in, 98, 99, 116

ChinaByte, 98

Chiquita Brands International, 58

Chofu cable company, 93

Chomsky, Noam, 279, 288

CIA (Central Intelligence Agency), 50, 59–60, 280

Cincinnati Enquirer, investigation by, 58

Cinecanal pay-TV, 97

Cinemax channel, 92

CIO (Congress of Industrial Organizations), 292. See also AFL-CIO

Cisneros group, 107

Citereseau, 92

Citibank, 86

citizens: antitrust supported by, 313, 315; characterized as mob, 286–87; depoliticization of, 2–3, 5–6, 15, 111–13, 263, 271, 279–80, 281, 285; First Amendment rights and, 266, 271; information needed by, 288; as Internet users, 131–32; in media policy making, 127, 240; organizing of, 118; rare influence of, 66; speech as individuals, 269, 276. *See also* Americans; audience; consumers; public debate; public interest groups

Citizens for Media Education, 67

Clarin, 107

Classic V channel, 93

Claxton, Brooke, 236

Clayton Act, 312

Clinton, Bill: digital technology and, 155–57; Internet commercialization and, 129, 132, 133, 135; media exports and, 102; military budget of, 50–51

Cloward, Richard A., 283

CLT, 88

Club Disney, 95

Clueless (TV show), 41

Cnet, 181

CNNfn channel, 92

CNN International channel, 92, 93, 114

CNN network: control of, 92; establishment of, 182; exposés on, 53; news coverage by, 54; retraction by, 60, 61; website for, 177

CNNSI channel, 92, 174

Coca-Cola, 46, 263

Cohen, Nick, 100

Columbia Broadcasting Service. *See* CBS network

Columbia House record club, 93

Columbia TriStar Television, 41

Columbia University, broadcasts of, 208

Comcast: CEO's salary in, 29; as conglomerate, 20; global media system of, 88; partners of, 148, 162, 164

Comedy Central channel, 92

"Comedy Net" (website), 147

commercial broadcasting: critique of, 239–40, 276; defense of, 208–9; digital technology and, 152–

59; educational programs and, 71–72, 207–13; emergence of, 190–99, 224–25, 229, 231; entrenchment of, 219–24, 231, 247, 277–79; First Amendment and, 276–79; foundations supportive of, 223–24; government subsidies for, 142, 151–52, 307; impact on Canada, 232, 235–37; investments in, 67, 93, 102; joint ventures of, 246; literature on, 8; lobbyists for, 64–66; opposition to, 189–90, 197–99, 201–7, 213, 216, 218, 221, 231, 232–35, 237–38; profitability of, 223, 308; public service and, 155–59, 195–96, 249, 272, 307–8, 310; regulation of, 67–69, 125–26, 275–76, 307–11; U.S. hegemony in, 233–34. *See also* National Association of Broadcasting (NAB); radio broadcasting industry; television industry

commercialism: courts' response to, 268; creativity stifled by, 32, 35–37; as crisis for democracy, 275–76; dominance of, 108; in education, 46–47, 202–3, 296–97, 302; First Amendment and, 260–65, 268–79; history of, 48, 189–90; of journalism, 53, 57–58, 176, 273–74; labor rejected in, 297; public subsidies vs., 241; radio broadcasting industry and, 36, 64, 200–201. *See also* advertising; free market; hypercommercialism

commercial media: as antidemocratic force, 2–3, 184–85, 294–96; antilabor bias of, 297–99; antitrust actions against, 311–15; branding in, 24–25, 36, 48, 72; campaign funds and, 263–65;

CEOs and directors in, 28–30; concentration/conglomeration in, 1, 15–18, 140–41, 292–93; creativity stifled in, 32, 35–37; critique of, 52; cross-promotion in, 22–24; dissatisfaction with, 282, 300, 301; expansion outside media, 43–48, 74, 123, 163–65; externalities of, 144–45; First Amendment and, 269–80; goal of, 41; joint ventures in, 28, 163–64; left and labor space created in, 299–300; literature on, 8–9; lobbyists for, 64–66; political candidates' use of, 69, 157, 194–95, 216, 261–64, 307, 311; profits in, 16, 26, 27, 30; public life absorbed by, 279–80; public service of, 69–70, 127, 307–8; small firms' role in, 140–41; structure of, 304–5; taxation of, 275–76, 309–10; Telecom Act's impact on, 75–76. *See also* commercial broadcasting; concentration/conglomeration; film production industry; global commercial media; hypercommercialism; media reform; newspaper industry; *specific companies*

Committee to Protect Journalists, 117

communication industry. *See* telecommunications industry

Communications Act (1934): context of, 216–17; passage of, 70, 125, 217–18, 222, 229, 239, 277; Radio Act confirmed in, 193–94; superseded, 63

Communist model, 286, 289

Compaq (computers), 167

Competition Commission (EU), 83

computer industry: cultural role of, 145–46; digital television's link to, 146–47, 150–51, 153; expansion outside computers, 163–64; Internet and, 160, 162–63; joint ventures of, 163–64; lobbyists for, 128–29; media's link to, 26. *See also* Internet

concentration/conglomeration: antitrust action against, 311–15; competition in, 138–40; context of, 15, 270–71; debt incurred in, 27–28, 99; defense of, 119–20; explanation for, 30–31; implications of, 29–30, 34–35, 76–77, 160–61, 184–85; increase in, 17–21, 85–87; joint ventures and, 140; media reform and, 304–5; pressure for, 22–24, 74–75, 87–90, 163–64; profitability of, 16–17, 24–25; regulations as encouragement of, 16, 21, 74; superopolies in, 75–76; synergistic choices in, 25–26. *See also* oligopoly; *specific industries*

Condé Nast, 57

Congress of Industrial Organizations. *See* CIO

Consumer Alert, 302

consumers: ads avoided by, 172–73, 238, 277; bundled services for, 163–64; in developing countries, 101, 107; digital technology and, 149–50, 155; training for, 46. *See also* advertising; audience; children; products; youth market

convergence: concept of, 123; of digital technology and Internet, 146–59, 163–65, 170–71

Cooper, William John, 196–98, 206

copyright industries, 102, 133, 179

Corkery, Pam, 316

Corporation for Public Broadcasting (CPB), 248

corporations. *See* business interests;

commercial media; global commercial media; *specific companies*

Court TV channel, 92

Cowles Media, 56

Cox Enterprises, 20, 29, 88

CPB. *See* Corporation for Public Broadcasting

Crandall, Ella Phillips: broadcasting reform and, 197–99; on NCER, 214, 218; role in Payne Fund, 195, 210

Crane, Arthur G., 219

Crawford, Gordon, 27, 28

creativity: hypercommercialism's impact on, 32, 35–37; media reform and, 308–10

Cronkite, Walter, 52

cruise ship line, Disney's, 94

CTW. *See* Children's Television Workshop

Cultural Environment Movement. *See* CEM

cultural exhibits, hypercommercialism's impact on, 48

cultural imperialism: of global media, 101–3; national media vs., 102, 106; protection against, 81–82

culture "jamming," 302

Cumings, Bruce, 9

Cyclone, 181

Daily Blast website, 177

Daily Herald (Merrill, Wis.), commercialism and, 273

Dalai Lama, 115

Daniels, Josephus, 216

Davis, H. O., 213–14

Day-Lewis, Daniel, 42

DDB Needham Worldwide (ad agency), 85

De Forest, Lee, 237

Dell Computer, 167, 168

democracy: antitrust as defense of, 311–15; broadcasting reform and, 202, 203–4, 240; broadcasting's role in, 190, 218, 276–77; capitalism's relation to, 284–87, 289; commercialism as crisis for, 275–76; vs. concentration of power, 30, 260–61; decline of, 2–3, 110; definitions of, 4–6, 243, 284–86; First Amendment and, 260, 269–80; Internet as force for, 2, 119–20, 175–76, 183–84; journalism's link to, 49, 52, 114–15; left's role in, 283–84, 290–91; media reform's implications for, 302–4, 318–19; neoliberalism vs., 111–12; oligopolies' impact on, 17; policy making in, 124–27, 145; public relations vs., 287–88; reclaiming, 285–86; role in public service broadcasting, 226; speech defined in, 265–68, 271–72; tools needed for, 114–15, 240, 255, 269–70, 281, 288, 306–7; viability of, 289–90. *See also* citizens; democratization; left political movement; media/democracy paradox; media reform; public debate; social inequality

Democratic party (Australia), 317–18

democratization: definition of, 5–6; media reform's role in, 282. *See also* left political movement

Deng Xiaoping, 116

Denmark: film production in, 81–82; media conglomerates in, 89; television in, 106

Denning, Michael, 292

Des Moines Register, owner of, 55

Detroit Free Press, profit strategies at, 55

developing countries: consumers in,

GTE/Bell Atlantic, 160–61
Gulf War, news coverage of, 51–52
Guzmán, Jaime, 111

Habermas, Jürgen, 240, 245, 255, 279, 295
Hachette (company), 88
Haiti, Disney sweatshops in, 297
Hal Riney and Partners, 86
Hamilton, Alexander, 6
Hanna-Barbera animation studios, 92
Hannah and Her Sisters (film), 260
Harney, John B., 216–17
HarperCollins book-publishing division, 24, 96, 116
Harvard University, meeting on Internet at, 130
Hasbro (company), 93, 253
hate speech, 269
Hatfield, Henry, 216–17
Havas (company), 88
HBO channel, 92–93, 148
HBO International channel, 92–93
HDTV, 153–55
Headline News channel, 92
Hearst (company), 88
Heineken (company), 39
Hennock, Frieda, 126
Hentoff, Nat, 10
Henwood, Doug, 295
Heritage Media, 97
Heublein's (company), 39
Hicks, Muse, Tate and Furst: as conglomerate, 27, 75; global media system of, 88–89; movie theaters of, 18; sports teams of, 44
Hilfiger, Tommy, 39
history, media's use of, 7, 9–10. *See also* mythology
History channel, 94
Hobsbawm, Eric, 287
Hollinger (company), 88

Hollywood label, 95
Home Improvement (TV show), 23
Homer's Workshop (TV show), 72
Hong Kong, broadcast stations in, 116
horizontal integration: benefits of, 16–17; increase of, 86. *See also* concentration/conglomeration
House Telecommunications Subcommittee, members of, 64, 69, 151
Hughes, Charles Evans, 207
Hundt, Reed, 120–21
Hutchins, Robert M., 207–8, 221, 223
hypercommercialism: context of, 15; defense of, 119–20; dissatisfaction with, 300, 301; evidence of, 34–38; First Amendment and, 257–59; in global media, 79, 108–9; impact on children, 45–47, 71–72, 83–84, 144; role of, 39–42; trends in, 42–48, 76–77, 184–85. *See also* advertising
Hyperion Press, 95

IBM, 179
ICANN (Internet Corporation for Assigned Names and Numbers), 134
IMF (International Monetary Fund), 78, 250
Independent Newspapers Ltd., 98
independents: advertising, 86; global market and, 80; left's and labor's use of, 303; role of, 25–27, 140–41. *See also* alternative media
India: consumers in, 101; foreign ownership in, 99, 100–101; music production in, 107; television in, 98, 99
India Sky Broadcasting, 98

ITV, 254
Ivcher, Baruch, 117
iVillage, 171, 181
Ivory Coast, protection of culture in, 82

Japan: advertising in, 86, 109; cable companies in, 93; Internet in, 134; media conglomerates in, 88, 93, 104; movies shown in, 104; music production in, 107; public service broadcasting in, 240; theme park in, 94
Japan SkyPerfecTV, 98
Jay, John, 6
Jesuit Education Association, 372n42
Jiang Zemin, 115, 116
Johnson, Nicholas, 68
journalism: civic or public type of, 300–301; colleagues' attacks in, 61–62; commercialism of, 53, 57–58, 176, 273–74; conflict-of-interest and, 52; creative programming for, 308–10; decline of, 15, 51–52, 114–15, 144, 274, 307, 316; democracy's link to, 49, 52, 114–15; election campaign coverage by, 264–65; on Internet, 175–77; investigative reporting in, 59–62, 114, 117; left's and labor's use of, 303–4; limitations on, 58–61; neoliberalism's impact on, 113–14; as probusiness/procapitalism, 50, 296, 298–99; profitability of, 51–52, 54–56; as public service, 48–49, 52–53; rightward bias in, 62–63, 244–45, 271; rise of professional, 17, 49, 274, 293; sources for, 49–51, 62–63, 369n9; unions in, 301, 304; watchdog groups for, 301–4. *See*

also media system; newspaper industry
Juicy Juice beverages, 252

Kapor, Mitchell, 131, 150
Keane, John, 114
Keillor, Garrison, 253
Kemp, Jack, 138
Kennard, William, 69, 156
Kent, Arthur, 51–52
Keppel, Frederick P., 206, 208–9, 211
Kinnevik (company), 88
Kirch (company), 83, 88, 97
Kissinger, Henry, 115
Knight-Ridder, 20, 29, 88
Kohlberg, Kravis, Roberts and Co., 18
Kundun (film), 115
Kurtz, Howard, 61

labor interests: broadcasting reform and, 213, 217; campaign contributions of, 261; entertainment and, 203; examples for activism, 314–18; left's relation to, 290; media and, 291–300, 302–4, 305; news coverage of, 50, 55, 297–99; rejected as PBS sponsors, 297; social equality and, 283. *See also* left political movement
Labor party (U.S.), 294, 298
Labour party (New Zealand), 316–17
Lack, Andy, 159
La Follette, Robert M., 272–73
Lasch, Christopher, 285
Lasswell, Harold, 287
Latin America: advertising in, 84–85; censorship in, 100; inequality in, 117, 118; as market, 87, 96; television in, 97, 106
Latin Sky Broadcasting, 97

laws and regulations: in Canada,
231–32; censorship vs., 265; for
commercial broadcasting, 67–69,
125–26, 275–76, 307–11; concentration facilitated by, 16, 21, 74;
First Amendment and, 257–59,
268, 277–78; function of, 63, 67–
68; news coverage of, 65; publicity and, 72–73; on public service
programming, 48–49; for radio,
192. *See also* Communications
Act (1934); Telecommunications
Act (1996)

Lee, Miky, 26

Left party (Sweden), 315–16

left political movement: absence of,
297; concept of, 283, 288–91; examples for activism, 314–18;
goals of, 295–96; heterogeneity
of, 289; labor's relation to, 290;
media and, 291–300, 302–5; reclaiming, 283, 290–91; role of,
282, 288–89. *See also* labor interests

leisure, commercial vs. public, 44.
See also book retailing; entertainment; movies; music; spectator
sports; television

Lenin, V. I., 286

Leonard, John, 31–32

Lesly, Philip, 287

Levey, Mike, 108–9

Levin, Gerald, 30–31, 103. *See also*
Time Warner

Liar, Liar (film), 40

libel, threat of, 58–59

liberalism, use of term, 4–5. *See also*
neoliberalism

Liberty Media, 20, 30, 88, 161, 164.
See also Malone, John

Lifetime channel, 94

Lion King, The (film), 23, 39

Lion King, The (play), 45

Lippmann, Walter, 287

Little House on the Prairie, The (book
series), 24

lobbyists: for broadcasting interests,
64–66, 194–95, 213, 214, 216–17,
239, 308; competition for, 66; for
computer industry, 128–29; for
education, 197–99; for media interests, 64–65, 69, 99–100, 151;
power of, 64–65; for telecommunications industry, 64, 73–74

Looney Tunes (cartoon), 94

L'Oreal, 39

Los Angeles, local news in, 55

Los Angeles Times, profit strategies at,
56

Lott, Trent, 152–53

Lukacs, Georg, 8

MacNeil-Lehrer News Hour (TV
show), 62

Macpherson, C. B., 284

Madison, James, 6, 284

magazine distributors,
hypercommercialism and, 38

magazine production industry: advertising and, 56–57, 173; conglomerates in, 89, 92, 93, 95, 96;
global reach of, 93, 105; profit
strategies of, 56–58

Magaziner, Ira, 79, 132

Magic School Bus, The (TV show), 72

mailing rates, in media reform proposal, 305

MAI (Multilateral Agreement on
Investment), 102, 175–76

Maistre, Joseph de, 287–88

Malone, John: on advertising, 149;
as CEO, 30; on digital offerings,
148; on government intervention, 142; on influence, 62–63;
on Internet, 161–62; on profits,
20. *See also* Liberty Media

music production industry: branding in, 36, 171; distribution system of, 80, 179–80; globalization of, 80, 95, 98, 105, 107; hypercommercialism's impact on, 35–37; independents in, 25–26; Internet as challenge for, 179–80; music development and, 35–37; oligopolistic character of, 18; PBS for-profit label in, 252; radio stations paid by, 43

music retailing: control of, 88, 174; cross-promotion in, 108; on Internet, 174, 178–80; oligopolistic character of, 26

My Best Friend's Wedding (film), 105

mythology: on audience desires, 32–34; as counter to public debate, 257–59; of free market, 136–46, 224, 257, 279; function of, 146; of Internet, 121, 123; in media ideology, 7; "natural" used in, 10, 143, 224

NAB. *See* National Association of Broadcasting (NAB)

Nader, Ralph, 262, 294, 302

NAFTA (North American Free Trade Agreement), 73, 298–99

National Advisory Council on Radio in Education (NACRE): collapse of, 191, 222, 224; educational programs and, 207–13; establishment of, 206–7; legacy of, 224; members of, 207–8; NCER's relations with, 210–12; network relations of, 220–22; role of, 190–91, 208–9; summit on future of, 221–22

National Association of Broadcasting (NAB): BBC attacked by, 215; on broadcast reform, 213, 216–17; on Communications

Act, 217; on coverage levels, 67; lobbyists of, 194; on NCER, 201; power of, 64–65, 69, 156; on public service, 70, 157, 310; tactics of, 72–73, 151–53

National Association of Educational Broadcasters, 372n42

National Association of State Universities, 198

National Broadcasting Company. *See* NBC network

National Catholic Education Association, 372n42

National Committee on Education by Radio (NCER): broadcast reform movement of, 200–206; collapse of, 191, 213–16, 218–19, 224; educational community differences and, 210–13; establishment of, 197–98, 206; on experimental bands, 223; legacy of, 224; NACRE's relations with, 210–12; oppositional forces in, 210; role of, 190–91, 198–99, 217–18

National Conference on Educational Broadcasting, 222

National Congress of Parents and Teachers, 213

National Council of State Superintendents, 372n42

National Education Association (NEA), 196, 198–200, 210

nationalism: in media reform, 231–34; as unprofitable, 103

national media systems: censorship by, 100; consolidation in, 107; protection of, 81–84, 101, 106; WTO rulings against, 81. *See also* public service broadcasting

National Public Radio (NPR), 246, 248, 252

National Telecommunications In-

20; profit strategies in, 55–56, 58; redlining by, 302. *See also* journalism

New Yorker, editor of, 57

New York Post, owner of, 96

New York Times, procapitalism of, 298–99

New York Times Company: CEO and directors of, 29; as conglomerate, 20; global media system of, 88

New Zealand: media conglomerates in, 89; media reform in, 316–17; Natural History Unit in, 97; newspapers in, 98, 316; public service broadcasting in, 241; television in, 98

Nickelodeon network: branding of, 24; cross-promotion of, 37; digital platforms of, 148; editorial coverage on, 43; global reach of, 106; joint ventures of, 252–53; owner of, 20; programs on, 22–23; website for, 170

Nielsen Media Research, 47

Nightline (TV show), 62

Nike, 37, 53, 58–59, 84

Nippon Television, 93

Nixon, Riichard M., 163

N2K, 178

nonprofit groups: corporate sponsors for, 70; for Internet address system, 133; radio broadcasting and, 72–73, 125–26. *See also* media reform; public debate; public interest groups; *specific organizations*

nonprofit/noncommercial media (EU), 84

nonprofit/noncommercial media (U.S.): broadcasting reform and, 204–5, 216–20; clearinghouse for, 219; creation of, 201, 305–6;

decline of, 10, 48; in democratic structure, 5–6, 288; educational programs of, 207–13, 220–23; FRC's impact on, 193; funding for, 275–76; government subsidies for, 142, 307; Internet's origins in, 129; left's and labor's use of, 302–4; microradio, 302; neoliberal attack on, 227; public service and, 158; rationale for, 10, 203, 275; rejection of, 73, 126; status of, 70, 189, 191, 222–25. *See also* public service broadcasting

North American Free Trade Agreement. *See* NAFTA

North American Newspaper Alliance, 369n9

Norway: film production in, 81–82; media firm in, 106

NPR. *See* National Public Radio

N-TV, 93

O'Connell, Maureen, 64

OECD (Organization for Economic Cooperation and Development), 133–34

offline branding, 171

Ogilvie and Mather (firm), 262

Ohlmeyer, Don, 38

oligopoly: definition of, 16; in free market, 138–40; in Internet, 182–83; in media system, 17, 19–21, 28–29, 78–79. *See also* concentration/conglomeration

Oliver, April, 60, 61

Olympics, 41, 53–54, 59

Omnicom Group (ad agency), 85, 86

Online Privacy Alliance, 132

online privacy awareness campaign, 134

Oracle, 135, 148, 164

O'Reilly, Tony, 89, 316
Organization for Economic Cooperation and Development. *See*
OECD
Orwell, George, 110, 242
outdoor advertising, tactics in, 40–
41

Packer, Kerry, 91
Padden, Preston, 177
Pagani, John, 317
Paine, Thomas, 6, 184
Paley, William S., 218
Paramount Pictures, 20, 22, 41
Paramount Television, 23
Parekh, Michael, 168
ParentTime website, 177
Parry, Robert, 296
Parsons, Richard, 164
Patagonic Film, 95
Patten, Chris, 116
Paulist Fathers (religious order),
216–17
Paxson, Bud, 155
Payne Fund: broadcasting reform
and, 197–99, 214; Carnegie
Corporation's relations with,
210–12; on educational pro-
grams, 195–96; funding from,
190, 218–19; publication of, 213,
214
pay-TV, 97–98, 251
PBS. *See* Public Broadcasting Sys-
tem (PBS)
Pearson TV (U.K.), 87–88
People, owner of, 92
People's Daily (China), joint ventures
of, 98, 116
Pepsi-Cola, 38–39, 46, 47, 263
perfumes, 24, 166
Perot, Ross, 73, 259, 262
Perry, Armstrong: BBC and, 212–
13; broadcasting reform and,

200, 203, 204; educational radio
programs and, 195–99; on ex-
perimental bands, 223; NCER
role of, 199–200, 210, 217; on
public attitudes, 214; resignation
of, 219
Peru, politics in, 117
PeterStar (company), 97
Philip Morris (company), 278–79
Phoenix Chinese Channel, 98, 99,
116
Pinochet Ugarte, Augusto, 112
Pittston (Va.), strike in, 298
Piven, Frances Fox, 283
Pixar (firm), 27
Pizza Hut, 109
Plaunt, Alan, 232
PLD Telekom, 97
pluralism: elite foundations of, 287;
restructured public broadcasting
and, 306
PM (newspaper), labor coverage of,
298
Pointcast, 171
Polaroid, 36
policy making. *See* media policy
making
political candidates: airtime for, 69,
157, 194–95, 216, 261–64, 307,
311; campaign funds for, 158,
258–61, 263–64, 265, 267–68,
278, 279; news coverage of, 264–
65; purchase of, 260–62, 279;
"soft money" for, 262, 264–65.
See also elections/campaigns
political involvement: as critical, 11;
decrease in, 2. *See also* citizens;
left political movement
politics: antitrust action and, 312–
13, 315–17; broadcasting and,
213–18, 229–31, 239–40; coverage of, 50–55, 59, 264–65, 281;
of digital technology, 155–59;

First Amendment and, 270–72; global commercial media in, 99–100, 113–14; Internet commercialization and, 129, 183; marginalization of, 110, 111–13, 183–85; media and, 63–64, 118, 246–47, 271, 292, 296–97; public broadcasting and, 227, 241–47, 251, 255; rightward bias of, 62–63, 110–11, 296–97; of Telecom Act, 151–53. *See also* citizens; democracy; lobbyists; neoliberalism; political candidates

PolyGram (corporation), 16, 18

portals (search engines): advertising and, 173; branding and, 171–72; definition of, 165; examples of, 166–68; media firms' interests in, 168–69, 171–72, 181–82; significance of, 123, 161, 165–66

Primestar satellite TV, 65, 92, 93

Prince of Egypt (film), 27

Prisa (company), 88, 90

private property, liberalism and, 4–5

Procter & Gamble: advertising by, 41, 84, 172–73; Internet concerns of, 172–73; joint ventures of, 177; television production by, 41–42

products: branding of, 24–25, 36, 48, 72, 93–94, 101, 171–72, 175; for children, 45–46; controlling price for, 16–17; cross-promotion of, 22–24, 37, 38–39, 54, 108, 149–50; as "democratic," 4; differentiated by race, 250; for digital technology, 154; export market for, 80, 102, 107; global markets for, 39, 85; PBS sales of, 252; taboo colors in, 105. *See also* advertising; consumers; electronic commerce

propaganda, 193

PSAs (public service announcements), 70. *See also* infomercials

publications, mailing of, 305

Public Broadcasting Act (1967), 248

Public Broadcasting System (PBS): commercialization of, 252, 254–55, 297; educational programs of, 72; establishment of, 248; funding for, 252

public debate: absence of, 63, 76, 203–4, 280, 281; on broadcasting, 72–73, 214–15; in democracy, 283–84; on digital technology, 123, 151, 158–59, 313–14; on GATT and NAFTA, 298–99; influence of, 64; on Internet, 122, 128–32, 135, 136–37, 175–76; on media in Canada, 127, 230, 231–37; on media reform, 313–14, 316; mythology to counter, 257–59; role of, 127, 226; on Telecom Act, 131, 151–53

public interest: Internet policy and, 130, 134–36; radio policy and, 193; Telecom Act and, 152–53

public interest groups: media reform and, 302; operation of, 66–67; successes of, 67, 70–71. *See also* nonprofit groups

Publicis (company), 86

public journalism, concept of, 300–301

public relations, concept of, 287–88

public relations industry: labor's use of, 293; media's use of, 65–66, 247; potential of, 113; PSAs by, 70; role of, 49–50; sloganeering of, 289. *See also* media system

public service: in capitalist system, 243–46; commission on, 155–59; conservative move against, 244–46, 272; decline of, 15, 69–70, 77,

251; enforcement of, 48–49, 127, 249, 307–8, 310; journalism as, 48–49, 52–53; media and, 69–70, 127, 155–59, 195–96, 227, 249, 272, 307–10; use of term, 368n2

public service announcements. *See* PSAs

public service broadcasting: argument against, 226–28, 235, 243–46; attacks on, 233, 236–37, 249–50, 384n41; audience for, 246, 247, 249, 251, 254; bands for, 216–18, 222–23; BBC as model for, 204–5, 214–15, 220, 230, 231, 236; censorship of, 243, 244, 297; challenges for, 228, 242, 243–44, 250–51; commercialization of, 246–48, 252–55; competition in, 241–42; decline of, 226–28, 240–42, 247, 255–56; definition of, 226; development of, 228–40, 292; funding for, 240, 244, 248, 251–52, 254, 275–76, 306–7, 309–10; implications of, 255–56; maintaining, 306–7; neoliberalism and, 227–28, 241–47; politics and, 227, 241–47, 251, 255. *See also* nonprofit/noncommercial media (EU and U.S.)

public sphere, commercialism's rule in, 245–46

Publishing and Broadcasting Ltd., 91

Pulitzer, Joseph, 275

Putnam, Robert, 279

QNBC (service), 51

Quayle, Dan, 138

Quello, James, 64–65

Qwest, 162

race: globalization and, 109; Internet access and, 162; prod-

ucts differentiated by, 250; programs specific to, 145

Radio 538, 97

Radio Act (1927), 192–94, 206

radio broadcasting industry: advertising and, 191, 192–94, 202–3, 205, 208–9, 220, 237, 276–77; for children, 45–46; commercialism and, 36, 64, 200–201; congressional hearings about, 72–73, 192; as debate topic, 214–15; declining public service of, 69–70; democratic possibilities in, 190; educational programs and, 195–99, 207–13, 220–22; emergence of, 125, 126, 230–31; First Amendment and, 276; government subsidies for, 142, 307; Internet interests of, 181; labor's investments in, 293–94; lobbyists of, 194–95, 213, 214, 216–18, 239; oligopolistic character of, 18, 69, 75–76, 89, 94, 97, 316; payola in, 43; privatization and, 316; profits for, 76, 125–26, 191–92; reform movement for, 72–73, 125–26, 200–206; regulations for, 192; selections on, 33; Telecom Act's impact on, 75–76. *See also* nonprofit/noncommercial media (EU and U.S.); public service broadcasting

Radio Corporation of America (RCA), 191, 194. *See also* NBC network, radio of

Radio New Zealand, 316

Rainbow/PUSH Coalition, 302

Random House (company), 16–17, 18

rating system, 71

RCA. *See* Radio Corporation of America

Reader's Digest, 88

Reagan, Ronald, 6, 311
Real TV (TV show), 41
Red Lion case, 276
Redstone, Sumner, 22, 87, 141. *See also* Viacom
Reebok, 47, 53
Reed, Ralph, 47
Reed Elsevier (company), 83, 88
Reeves, Richard, 52
Reith, John C. W., 212–13, 215, 221, 229
Republica (music group), 37
Republican party (U.S.), military budget and, 50–51
Reuters, 88
Rhone Cable Vision, 92
Riche, Martha Farnsworth, 105
RJR Nabisco, 278–79
Road Runner, 92, 161, 162, 167, 181
Robinson, Svend, 315
Rockefeller, John D., Jr., 190, 206
Rockefeller Foundation, 223–24
Rocky Mountain Radio Council, 219
Roger and Me (film), 32
Rogers, Joel, 283
Rogers Communication, 88
Rolling Stone (periodical), Internet interests of, 174
Roosevelt, Franklin D., 215–16, 217
Root, Elihu, 207
Roper Starch Worldwide, 105
Rorty, James, 239
RTL$_2$ channel, 95
Rugrats (film), 22–23
Rushkoff, Douglas, 120
Russia, corruption in, 117. *See also* Soviet Union

Sabrina, the Teenage Witch (TV show), 41
Safire, William, 152
Sanders, Bernie, 294

San Jose Mercury News, exposé in, 59–60
Sarnoff, David, 208, 215, 218, 237
satellite systems: as base for expansion, 98–99; digital television's link to, 147–48; effects of, 78, 80; oligopolistic nature of, 92, 96–98; in public service broadcasting debate, 227; sport's role in, 95–96. *See also* digital television (satellite)
SBC Communications, 161, 164, 181
Scaife, Richard Mellon, 392–93n42
Scandinavia: media reform in, 315–16; social democracies in, 286. *See also specific countries*
schools. *See* education
Schorr, Daniel, 61
Scott, Walter Dill, 207
Seagram: amusement parks of, 43; CEO and directors of, 28–30; as conglomerate, 19, 28; distribution system of, 83; global media system of, 86–87; headquarters of, 104; holdings of, 16, 18; Internet and, 179–80. *See also* Universal Studios
Sesame Street (TV show), 252, 255
Sherman Act, 312
Showtime cable network, 20, 148
Showtime Extreme channel, 148
Siepmann, Charles, 239
Simon and Schuster, 20, 21, 37
Simpson, O. J., 54, 55
Simpsons, The (TV show), 38–39
Sinclair, Upton, 273
Sinclair Broadcasting, 76, 154–55
Siti Cable company, 98
60 Minutes (TV show), 53
Sky radio, 97
Sky TV, 97, 98
Smirnoff vodka, 39

videos: of foreign films, 34; full-motion, 159; Internet sales of, 178; on labor, 303; network sales of, 38; rental of, 20, 21
Vietnam War, 59
violence: in ads geared for children, 46; debate on, 124; globalization and, 109; increased in media content, 34, 71, 144; news coverage of, 54, 302
Virgin Records, 33
Visa, 39
Visa USA, 53
VIVA channel, 93
Vox TV network, 97

Wagner, Robert, 216–17
Wagner-Hatfield amendment, 216–17, 221
Al-Waleed (Prince), 99
Wal-Mart, 40
Walt Disney label, 95
Walt Disney Pictures, 95
Warner Brothers (film and television): cross-promotion via, 24, 39; global reach of, 93; local influence on, 106; owner of, 92
Warner Brothers restaurants, 93
Warner Brothers retail stores, 92, 94
Warner Communications, 19–20, 91
Warner Music Group, 92
Washington Post (corporation), 29, 88
Washington Post: exposé in, 61; procapitalism of, 298–99
Watergate investigation, 61
WB network, 21, 92
WEAF radio (New York), 208
Webb, Gary, 59–60, 61
websites: advertising and, 173–75, 180–81; cost of, 170; finding, 176; for media industry, 169–70, 174, 176–82; necessity of, 313;

popular content for, 174; promotion of, 171, 174, 177; for public broadcasting, 253, 254–55; for sports, 174–75, 177; by subscription, 177; user fees for, 171. *See also* electronic commerce; portals (search engines)
WebTV: advertising and, 149; competition for, 141, 166; owner of, 146, 162; technology of, 146–47
Weekly Standard, politics of, 62, 392–93n42
Welch, Jack, 30. *See also* General Electric
WGBH TV (Boston), 252
WHA radio (Madison), 193
White, Byron, 274–75, 276
Wilbur, Ray Lyman, 196–97
Wilbur Committee, 196–97, 206
Willes, Mark, 56
Windows (software), 163
Wisconsin: newspaper oligopoly and, 272–74; U.S. Senate race in, 264–65
WLWL radio (New York), 216
WMAQ radio (Chicago), 207–8
Wolters Kluwer, 83, 88
women, portals targeted at, 171, 181
Wood, Ellen Meiksins, 4
Wooden, Ruth, 70
Workers party (Brazil), 318
World Bank, 78, 112, 117, 250
WorldCom-MCI, 75, 160, 164
World Cup (1998), 177
Worldnet Service (AT&T), 167
World Trade Organization (WTO): effects of, 78; globalization and, 250; Internet and, 102, 134; rulings of, 81–82
World Wide Web, 120, 129, 132, 146–47, 151. *See also* Internet; websites; WebTV
WPP group (ad agency), 85, 86

X-Files (film), 23–24
X-Files (TV show), 23–24

Yahoo!, 166–67, 171, 182
Yankovic, "Weird" Al, 72
Young, Owen D., 206–7, 221
youth market: global media and, 106; hypercommercialism and, 45–47, 71–72, 83–84, 144; Internet and, 136; Japan's advertising for, 109; profitability of, 45–46; websites geared toward, 177. *See also* children
Yudina, Larisa, 117

Zee Cinema channel, 98
Zee TV channel, 98
Zhu Rongii, 116

Robert W. McChesney is Research Associate Professor in the Institute of Communications Research and the Graduate School of Library and Information Science at the University of Illinois at Urbana-Champaign. McChesney is the author or editor of five other books, including *Telecommunications, Mass Media, and Democracy: The Battle for the Control of U.S. Broadcasting, 1928–1935* and, with Edward S. Herman, *The Global Media: The New Missionaries of Corporate Capitalism*. McChesney has written over one hundred journal articles, book chapters, and magazine pieces on media history and media politics. A former magazine publisher, McChesney advises many nonprofit publications and broadcasters and works with several media reform organizations.

The History of Communication

Typeset in 11.3/14 Monotype Garamond

with Officina Bold and Polyoptix Two display

Designed by Rich Hendel

Composed by Jim Proefrock

at the University of Illinois Press

Manufactured by Maple-Vail Book Manufacturing Group